plunderings, until you begin to groan at your hero's Muse being so spectacularly outed. Read the book— it's compelling. Rob Chapman, Sir Rob Chapman, you're a heartbreaker, sir, but what a heroic piece of Cultural Retrieval."

—Julian Cope on the *Head Heritage* website

"Barrett's tragic story has already been the subject of several books, but Rob Chapman's comprehensive biography towers above them all. Exhaustively researched and strongly opinionated, it benefits hugely from the author's access to Syd's correspondence as well as full cooperation from his surviving relatives . . . like all good music biographies, this one sends you back to the songs themselves with renewed appreciation and respect."

—*Sunday Business Post*

"Rob Chapman aims miles beyond another reprisal of the mind-mashed Syd mythography. His account is rich on pretty much all fronts—analysis, social context and revelation."

—*Word Magazine*

"In this, the best account of Barrett's life, Rob Chapman picks out truth from legend while providing insights into Syd's last years and locating him in the great line of English surrealists."

—Paperback Book of the Month, *Choice Magazine*

"[Barrett is] seen as the archetypal rock 'n' roll burnout, a pioneering popster who unlocked the secret of flight, but flew too high and came crashing to earth. Rob Chapman's biography attempts to

crash through the dark lens and catch a glimpse of the ordinary fallen angel behind the zombie mask."
—*Irish Times*

"The most comprehensive and genuine biography of Barrett that's available. It's not only sympathetic to the man himself, but cuts through the myths and half-truths, and details the story of a flawed and erratic genius. . . . It is, quite simply, brilliant. There's really no need for any more biographies of Barrett now, we've seen the flaws, read the myths, and now we've got the human side of the story."
—*What Hi-Fi*

by the same author

non-fiction
SELLING THE SIXTIES: PIRATES AND POP MUSIC RADIO
THE VINYL JUNKYARD

fiction
DUSK MUSIC

A VERY IRREGULAR HEAD
The Life of Syd Barrett

ROB CHAPMAN

DA CAPO PRESS
A Member of the Perseus Books Group

Cataloging-in-Publication data for this book is available from the Library of Congress.

First Da Capo Press edition 2010
Reprinted by arrangement with Faber and Faber Ltd
ISBN-13: 978-0-306-81914-8
Library of Congress Control Number: 2010930948

Published by Da Capo Press
A Member of the Perseus Books Group
www.dacapopress.com

Da Capo Press books are available at special discounts for bulk purchases in the U.S. by corporations, institutions, and other organizations. For more information, please contact the Special Markets Department at the Perseus Books Group, 2300 Chestnut Street, Suite 200, Philadelphia, PA 19103, or call (800) 810-4145, ext. 5000, or e-mail special.markets@perseusbooks.com.

10 9 8 7 6 5 4 3 2 1

Contents

Illustrations

Foreword by Graham Coxon

Syd's magnesium genius, a ballon of magic burst, trampled by a take-take industry and discarded like contrary petulant inconvenience.

Squeezed through the marketing tube . . . no beautiful bubble of the creative can survive it – nor can a free horse after breaking. A spirit harnessed and at once crushed, a talent tethered . . .

I was seventeen and looking through ale-smudged Christmas windows in Colchester, Essex. The air smelled of mince pies and rang with the brassy roundness of the Salvation Army band. I was bewildered and happy – I had heard a song and felt trapped within it.

A boy's innocent voice implored a girl to step into his world, a mouse tap danced on a staircase, an avalanche of bells and clock springs fell from a wardrobe and musky capes flapped and ripped.

By this time I had spent a lot of time in 'Strawberry Fields' but this . . . this was way further out, this was from beyond earth! The brand-new clatter of this sound tickled my virgin spirit, fed it madness and made it hungrier. The voice, the words, the sounds – all reassured and gave strange reference to my own identity. The accent was my own, the childish rhymes came from my own childhood and the music was expressive rather than technical – the rhythms primal. The sound went on forever, it was expansive with no strict structure and at times would float away into chaos leaving your ears jumping to catch it like kite tails and your mind wondering who turned the gravity off. The music was dark and weird, peopled with freaky characters. A cave full of rabid geese pecked at your hair and aloof cats smiled straight through your secrets with milk-green blinking eyes.

I had just discovered Pink Floyd, and Syd Barrett.

Syd was like true poet to my young and plasticine mind, like the best of popstars – riddled with the bricks and paving of an already searching and fidgety youth who soon grew to know something tragic – that Syd was already lost and his hands, retreated, were far beyond reach and were vanishing fast into the ungrabbable depths, his mouth never to scream its last scream.

How I loved Syd, though! He was mischief, the captain of the ship, the blindest leading the blindest into overpowering white-hot foundness and mind-melting vision. His songs told me how it could be and . . . how it could get – the original experience! The creative's Meccano unbolted and here was our beautiful Syd, a constant reminder then and now of the constant struggle and the free dance with the beauty of our language, the madness of bicycle bells, the absurdity of shoes, the blueyness of velvet trousers, the stripes and the paisleys, the discy Telecasters, the mind-pulsing oblivions of sonic assaults and blinding amoebic lights, the nursery rhymes with their laughter and their violence . . .

Take a look at the resulting melee . . . a YouTube chock-full and pretty much all 'professional groups' bowing and singing the Syd word.

'If only I was so gifted, so precious, beautiful, so adored and so (un)forgotten.'

Since I was seventeen I have wished to have been there, to experience the bold and flamboyant optimism of those days. While reading this book, though, I think I just might have been . . . You fancy it?

Acknowledgements

I would like to begin by thanking the members of the Barrett family whose consent and co-operation made my task far less complicated than it might have been. To sister Rosemary for photographic material, artworks, and unique and previously unaired insights into Syd's pre and post fame life, brother Don for the family tree and comments on the Cambridge High School for Boys, and nephew Ian for glimpses of 'Uncle Rog'.

For sensory perceptions beyond the call of duty, thanks to the Cambridge 'band of brothers and sisters', Syd's fellow questers from the County and Perse schools, and the Tech College canteen; namely Andrew Rawlinson, David Gale, Anthony Stern, Nigel and Jenny Lesmoir-Gordon, David Henderson, Seamus and Victoria O'Connell, Bob Klose, Stephen Pyle, Geoff Mottlow and John De Bruyne.

I also spoke to several old school friends who had never been interviewed before. Geoff Leyshon, Terry Mahoney, Chris Rayner, Richard Trim and John Wilson were all able to shed fresh light on the boy they once shared a classroom or a Scout hall with.

For background information and historical documentation on the Cambridge High School for Boys thank you to unofficial school archivist and 'keeper of the keys' Nick Wise.

For additional information regarding Syd's father, Max, I am

ACKNOWLEDGEMENTS

grateful to Jan Moore, secretary of the Cambridge Philharmonic. Thanks to Bryan Biggs of the Bluecoat Arts Centre in Liverpool for sharing his essay on Stuart Sutcliffe, 'A link into something larger', that appeared in the catalogue for the exhibition Stuart Sutcliffe; a retrospective, 2008–9, at the Victoria Gallery & Museum, Liverpool University. Thanks to Moya L. Andrews, Professor of Speech and Hearing Sciences Emerita, at Indiana University, Bloomington and Lizzie MacGregor at the Scottish Poetry Library for helping me crack the enigma code and for locating literature which influenced Syd's songwriting. For other invaluable documentation and memorabilia I am grateful to David Parker, Mark Jones, Jonathan Hemington, Kieran Short and 'Granchester'. And thank you David May for putting invaluable contacts my way and vouching for my general good-eggness.

In a book of this size and scope it is only fair that I should also thank the great unsung, those, too numerous to mention, who either knew Syd directly, or were connected by association, but had no great revelations or anecdotes to impart, only their fond memories and best wishes for my project. Each of these unsung sources provided testimony to the richness of Syd's creative milieu and the impressive cultural resonance and reach of his wider network of friends. They are perhaps best exemplified by Victoria Allen, widow of the artist and illustrator Julian Allen, a contemporary of Syd's at the Tech College, who was responsible in 1994 for the illustrations which put Syd's beloved Ma Rainey and Howlin' Wolf on American postage stamps. How cool and apposite is that?

A very special thank-you to Libby and Neil Chisman for their kind hospitality, food at their table and a view of the sea to die for. Libby grew up as Libby Gausden at 157 Hills Road Cambridge. Thirteen doors down the road lived a boy called Roger. Libby's surviving cache of letters from 1961–5 is undoubtedly the most valuable collection of primary Syd source material in existence.

Libby's decision to return Syd's extensively annotated diaries to their rightful owner in 1971, which he subsequently burnt, remains one of the great haunting 'if only's of this entire project.

For comments on Syd's art life at Camberwell thanks to Stan Willis and Maggi Hambling. For insights into his 'money tryingtoget, smokydark' London pop life thank you Barry Miles, John 'Hoppy' Hopkins, Peter Jenner, Andrew King, Emily Young, Joe Boyd, Keith Rowe, Lawrence Sheaff, Pete Brown, Hester Page, Spike Hawkins, Stash De Rollo, Duggie Fields, Jenny Fabian, Pete Drummond, Kevin Ayers, Hugh Hopper (RIP), Mike Ratledge, Mick Rock, Nick Kent, Chris Welch and Michael Watts.

For archive material on Notting Hill, and for being my psychogeographic tour guide, thank you, Tom Vague. For their observations on Syd's brief time back in Cambridge in the early 1970s and his last attempt at forming a band thanks to Jack Monck and Fred Frith. And for her blessing and support, Jenny Spires. For fond remembrance of the Syd who used to hang out in the Lupus Music office thanks to Cora Barnes.

For insights into Syd's time at Chelsea Cloisters thanks to Ronnie Salmon. For comments on his later life at St Margaret's Square, Cambridge thanks to Radha and the ubiquitous 'anon'. For being uber-fans and for keeping and spreading the faith, thanks to Robyn Hitchcock and Graham Coxon.

For access to the full tape transcripts of his interviews with Messrs Gilmour, Mason, Waters and Wright thank you John Edginton, producer of the Pink Floyd and Syd Barrett TV documentary and DVD. The individual members of the Pink Floyd declined to be interviewed for this book and sadly Rick Wright passed away on 15 September 2008, but David Gilmour provided some invaluable last-minute corrections and amendments at copy-editing stage.

To the Faber and Faber family, especially my editor Lee Brackstone, for letting me be 'on the same label' as T. S. Eliot and

Alan Bennett. 'Now I know how groups feel when they join EMI, and say I'm on the same label as the Beatles,' I said, backstage at the Games For May tribute concert at the Queen Elizabeth Hall in 2007. 'That's how we felt,' said a voice from an adjacent conversation. It was Graham Coxon.

Paul Loasby and Andy Murray, on behalf of the Syd Barrett Estate and the official website www.sydbarrett.com, allowed me unhindered access to Syd's artwork and other illustrative material. Their generosity of spirit and support was vital in the latter stages of this book's development.

Penultimately, to my agent Sarah Such, for acting on my best impulses, for moderating my worst ones, for being a ruthlessly firm but fair taskmaster, and for convincing Faber and Faber in the first place.

Ultimately thank you to my wife Caroline, archivist extra-ordinaire and soulmate. Thank you for indulging my own irregular head, and my pop clouding, and for joining in. Caroline's influence and input threads through this book in ways that it would take a lifetime to explain. One evening in a state of rare contentment I said, 'I know how all the pieces fit.' I'll always treasure her reply. 'Rob,' she said. 'You have your dinner on your face.'

Introduction

I saw Syd Barrett playing live just the once. It was the now infamous Stars at Cambridge Corn Exchange gig in February 1972 when Syd's short-lived music career was in its final stages and the thirty or so people who were there were bearing witness to the wake. Not that it seemed like that to me at the time. I was seventeen and starry-eyed and there he was a few feet in front of me. I wrote a suitably starry-eyed review of the performance for the fan magazine *Terrapin* (we didn't call them fanzines then) not realising at the time that it would constitute the last ever review of a Syd Barrett gig.

Although I didn't know that it was all over for Syd, I had by then already realised that it was all over for the Sixties. I'd pressed my nose up to the sweetshop window of the Underground often enough to realise that there was nothing much going on inside. The goods had gone bad, the sweets gone sour. Whichever analogy you want to use it was pretty clear by 1972 that some sort of dream was over. What I didn't realise for many years was that for Syd Barrett it was pretty much over from the moment it started. That man I saw on *Top of the Pops* three weeks in a row in the summer of 1967 in his tight Hendrix perm and his pop-star clothes had already fallen out of love with the idea of pop stardom.

Most people didn't know half of the story then, and I didn't know any of it. As someone who only entered his teens at the tail end of 1967 pop to me was a magical other world. I'm glad I was twelve during the summer of love. Had I been born ten years earlier I might have been a blues bore, or one of those purists who thought the Beatles sold out the moment they came back from Hamburg. Ten years younger and I'd have been getting all my knowledge of the Sixties as hand-me-downs and received wisdom. As it was, turning twelve at the end of 1966 meant that I moved from *Alice in Wonderland* and *Wind in the Willows* to 'Strawberry Fields' and 'See Emily Play' in what seemed like the twinkling of an eye. English psychedelia was part of my Arcadia, my first musical exotica, and that sense-memory with its multitude of evocations has never left me.

It also means I have first-hand recollections of at least some of what I'm writing about. I remember seeing Pink Floyd perform 'Apples and Oranges' on the hip TV show *Come Here Often*, and the earnest discussions at school the next day as everyone but me decreed that it wasn't as good as 'See Emily Play'. I remember a neighbour of mine going to see the band at the newly opened Caesar's Palace in Bedford (they were billed in the *Beds Courier* as 'Pink Lloyd') and complaining that they just played two long instrumentals and didn't perform the hits. I remember listening to Syd's last-ever session with the band on John Peel's *Top Gear* on New Year's Eve 1967 – in my bedroom through a blizzard of bad medium-wave reception on a tiny tinny transistor radio (which is how most of us experienced the aural splendour of the Sixties.) I scribbled down the session's song titles, none of which were yet on record (and two of which still aren't) and one of which seemed, as far as I could tell, to be called 'Jockvan Blues'. Soon after that radio session Syd's pop life, like my weak PP2 batteries, seemed to go flat and would soon fizzle out altogether.

Comets burn bright before expiring and they exhibit lengthy

trails. The trails of Comet Syd showered all over the early Seventies and the second half of my teens. I grew up twenty miles from Cambridge and know its geography, and its psycho-geography, intimately. A great deal of my misspent youth was misspent there – astral travelling across Parker's Piece, going to free concerts in Grantchester Meadows, wandering in the backs and the shadowed cloisters of the colleges, attempting to gatecrash May Balls, drifting through the maze-like lanes where every second building seemed to be a bookshop belching out its surplus wares onto the pavement. Give or take the odd hideous shopping complex, it is still recognisably the same place it was in the early Seventies. That's the 1670s of course.

Cambridge is a small place, and it was even smaller in the early Seventies. Syd's unfulfilled early promise and dreams abandoned seemed to hover over the city like a spectral presence. You didn't have to go very far to find someone who knew him or had known him. 'Oh, you're into Syd Barrett are you?' someone said to me in a pub one night in 1973. 'See that guy at the bar? He taught Syd at Tech College.' I made a beeline for the bar. Casual conversation ensued, none of which I can remember. I wasn't writing a book then, although in a way I've been writing it in my head for forty years. I phoned his house once, trying to secure an interview for *Terrapin* magazine. His mum, Winifred, answered. 'He's in London doing his music,' she said, in that way that mums do. She was half right. He was back in London, but he wasn't doing his music.

When Nick Kent wrote his legendary tribute, 'The Cracked Ballad of Syd Barrett', for *New Musical Express* in April 1974, it already seemed like a requiem. I can still remember the mixture of joy and puzzlement I experienced as the *NME* popped through my letterbox that Easter morning. Joy at the fact that he was on the front cover, puzzlement as to why. When the founders of *Terrapin*, John Steele and Lawrence Himelfield, wound up the original incarnation of the magazine in 1974, due to what they called 'a lack of Syd', I saw little reason to disagree with them. By then I'd encountered the man, or at least the spectral presence, again. Spurred on by a small ad that appeared in *International Times* in 1973, stating that Syd was now being represented by the Circle Agency, I phoned them up, and asked if it would be possible to interview Syd. Whether they were hoping to shock their client out of his creative lethargy I'll never know, but they gave me a London contact number. The person who answered the phone was unmistakeably Syd. 'You'll have to talk to X,' he said flatly, non-committally. The name of X has been lost in the mists of time, but presuming that he was about to fetch X I sat and waited, and waited. Down the other end of the line I could hear Syd periodically pacing the floor. In the end I realised that no one was coming back to the phone and hung up. The utter surrealism of this brief encounter was magnified by the fact that I was working a student holiday job at the time in a sparsely furnished, newly built factory. I had blagged the free phone-time during my lunch break, claiming that it was a local call. As I cradled the receiver surreptitiously and listened to Syd walking around in his room I was sitting on a dusty concrete factory floor surrounded by a maze of unrouted telephone wires, and gazing out over the cavernous expanse of a huge unoccupied warehouse. The more I think of it the more appropriate and symbolic it seems.

That comet trail was longer than we all thought and illuminated us in all kinds of unlikely ways. By 1978 I was singing with a Bristol punk band, Glaxo Babies. I was word-perfect on most of Syd's songs and whenever Dan our guitarist had to replace a broken string I filled in by serenading the audience with 'Effervescing Elephant'. Dan played like Syd, in that slack-stringed choppy style. He often used to wear a Syd Barrett badge and later joined the Pop Group. The first time one of the Pop

Group spoke to us, it was to say, 'I like Syd Barrett too.' I never met a single punk who didn't like Syd Barrett.

In the early 1980s, by now living in London, I went, one bleak mid-winter's night, to the Crypt, an occasional venue underneath a church in West London, to see a home movie that purported to show Syd's first trip. The blurry footage was projected on to a large white blanket on a bare wall to a sparse but rapt gathering of Syd fans. It seemed like the meeting of some secret society.

Aside from the odd re-issue and rumour, that was it for the next twenty-five years. I wrote about Syd occasionally, mostly for *Mojo* magazine, and thought about him often. Meanwhile the man himself was leading a quiet life back in Cambridge. And then one day in the summer of 2006 I learned that Syd had died. I phoned *Mojo* and asked if I could write the obituary piece. 'Yes please,' said the editor. 'But we go to press in five days. Can you do 5,000 words by Friday?' If it had been anybody else it would have been a chore, but I'd lived and breathed and dreamed Syd's music since that twelve-year-old me first heard 'Arnold Layne'. And so in the hottest week of that long hot summer I sat and wrote 5,000 words about Syd.

Here's another 140,000 to go with them.

ROB CHAPMAN

A VERY IRREGULAR HEAD:
THE LIFE OF SYD BARRETT

Chapter One

Oh Mother, Tell Me More

'It's gone!' sighed the rat, sinking back into his seat again. 'So beautiful and strange and new! Since it was to end too soon I wish I'd never heard it. For it had roused a longing in me that was pain, and nothing seems worth while but just to hear that sound once more and go on listening to it for ever. No! There it is again!' he cried, alert once more. Entranced, he was silent for a long space, spell-bound.

'Now it passes on and I begin to lose it,' he said presently. 'Oh Mole! the beauty of it! The merry bubble and joy, the thin clear happy call of the distant piping! Such music I never dreamed of, and the call of it is stronger even than the music is sweet! Row on, Mole, row! For the music and the call must be for us.'

The Mole, greatly wondering, obeyed. 'I hear nothing myself,' he said, 'but the wind playing in the reeds and rushes and osiers.'

The Rat never answered, if indeed he heard. Rapt, transported, trembling, he was possessed in all his senses by this new divine thing that caught up his helpless soul and swung and dandled it, a powerless but happy infant in a strong sustaining grasp.

THE WIND IN THE WILLOWS KENNETH GRAHAME

'He was a wretched baby – he screamed the whole time,' says Syd Barrett's younger sister Rosemary. 'And then, as soon as he learned to hold a pen and could create and draw, which was at about eighteen months, he was fine. He changed. He turned the corner. My mother always used to say that he just needed that, to get it down on paper. I think a lot of people do, don't they, if that's in their make-up?'

Conceived in the dying days of the Second World War, Syd was born Roger Keith Barrett, on the Epiphany, 6 January 1946. The second youngest of five children, he grew up in a prosperous, loving and secure domestic environment, initially at 60 Glisson Road in Cambridge, and then at 183 Hills Road, a large semi-detached house set slightly off the main thoroughfare that ran east out of the city towards Haverhill. Syd's father, Dr Arthur Max Barrett, had a brilliant academic record as a student and became an eminent pathologist. Arthur, known universally as 'Max', was born in 1909 in Thaxted, Essex, where his father, Arthur Samuel Barrett, conducted a small retail business. Max's grandfather on the maternal side was the Reverend Charles Ashford, who served as Congregational minister at the local church. Max's maternal grandmother, Ellen Garrett, was a cousin of Elizabeth Garrett Anderson, Britain's first female physician.

A Fenland man through and through, Max spent most of his life within rural Essex, Suffolk and Norfolk. He was educated at the progressive Newport Free Grammar School in Saffron Walden, and later at the Cambridge and County High School for Boys, which his three sons would also attend. Max enjoyed the outdoor life of the East Anglian countryside, and was an enthusiastic amateur botanist and ornithologist from his early teens.

In 1927 he was awarded a major scholarship to Pembroke College and began attending the college the following year. At Pembroke he was part of a golden generation of medical students who all went on to become eminent in their respective fields. Max enjoyed an outstanding undergraduate record, achieving a First in the Natural Science Tripos, Parts I and II. In 1931 he won the Freedom entrance scholarship in pathology and commenced his clinical studies at the London Hospital. Here he won several notable prizes including the prestigious Anderson prize in clinical medicine. In 1938 he was appointed university demonstrator in pathology at Cambridge and when the university became responsible for overseeing the pathological services of Addenbrooke's Hospital in 1946 Max was appointed to the newly created consultant post of university morbid

4

anatomist and histologist. He remained in this post for the rest of his life. As a postgraduate teacher of trainee pathologists he was recalled with great affection by his students, many of whom remember his complete disregard for schedules and timetables when teaching his class. In 1961, the year of his death, Max completed a pioneering investigative thesis for his MD degree in arterial hypertrophy. For this he was awarded the Raymond Horton prize for the best dissertation for a doctorate in medicine. Throughout his academic and professional life he had an outstanding record of research publication, writing on subjects as varied as new techniques in the diagnosis of glandular fever, tuberculosis, heart disease, the effects of mustard gas poisoning and malnutrition. Perhaps his most pioneering work, from 1954, was in the area of sudden death in infancy – although contrary to some reports he did not actually coin the expression 'cot death'. To this day there is a Barrett Room at Addenbrooke's Hospital in his honour.

Max had met his future wife, Winifred Flack Heeps, in 1930 while he was an undergraduate. 'Win' and her family had moved from Hackney in London to Cambridge when she was six. 'They met at a mixed Scout and Guide camp, they always laughed that they met on top of a haystack, but I'm not sure how true that is!' says Rosemary Barrett. Although she never worked full time, Win remained actively involved in the Girl Guides throughout her life and for several years also ran a Wolf Cub pack in collaboration with Max. Both Max and Win were practising Quakers at the time and they had a Quaker ceremony when they married in 1935. Their first child, Alan John Barrett, was born on 21 August 1937, and attended the Cambridge and County High School for Boys between 1948 and 1956. He gained good A level passes in advanced chemistry, botany and zoology, and like his father sat the Natural Science Tripos at university before becoming a biochemist. Donald Max Barrett was born on 15

April 1939 and attended the County School between 1950 and 1955. After gaining seven O levels he took an engineering apprenticeship at Vauxhall Motors where he was offered a job in the metallurgical laboratory. Daughter Ruth was born on 8 December 1942 and attended Sawston Village College and the Central School – the Girls' Grammar School – in Cambridge. She became an occupational therapist. Rosemary was born the year after Roger on 10 July 1947, and attended the local secondary modern before training at St George's hospital in Tooting, London, as a nurse. On completing her studies she worked at Addenbrooke's, like her father.

The Barretts enjoyed a rich intellectual life in Cambridge. Max was a member of the Cambridge Philharmonic Society, became its first keeper of the records, and was for more than twenty years its Honorary Secretary. He had a good deep bass voice and was a skilled classical pianist. Don Barrett remembers his father's piano-playing as being the dominant musical sound around the house when he was growing up, and there were, Rosemary remembers, frequent gatherings round the family piano. 'There was always music in the house. My father was a very good pianist and singer and everybody played something. We used to have regular music sessions – we all had recorders, all different sizes – going down to me, I had the little one. And we all learned to play the piano.'

Brother Alan played the saxophone and performed in a skiffle group, and when Roger was seven he and Rosemary won the annual piano prize at the Cambridge Guildhall for their rendition of 'The Blue Danube'. But despite the preponderance of music in the household there was very little other communal activity. 'Although we were all born within ten years, we're all very different, apart from Roger and me, really,' says Rosemary. 'The boys were quite close, but it wasn't a family where we did lots together. We used to go fungi-hunting on a Sunday together which was good – my father was very keen on fungi and mushrooms and things. But generally we didn't do things together.'

Owing to Max's demanding work schedule these Sunday jaunts seem to have been the only real occasions when the Barretts enjoyed outdoor family pursuits together. Max's early love of botany never left him. His opinions on rare fungi were greatly valued by the British Mycological Society and he had his own key to the University Botanical Gardens, just 200 yards from the Barretts' home on the opposite side of Hills Road. He was also a keen amateur watercolour painter and frequently sketched plants and fungi in the Botanical Gardens.

Max spent long hours locked away in his study engrossed in his work. In contrast, Win was a generous and accommodating host, and her involvement with the Guides and other community projects ensured a bustling household that was frequently full of visitors, young and old. The young Roger clearly inherited character traits from both parents. He was a mischievous and boisterous child who displayed much of his mother's sociability and garrulous nature. At the same time he had something of his father's disposition and temperament, particularly in the methodical way he went about his creativity. Max was remembered by one university contemporary as 'extraordinarily mature, quiet, calm and meticulous'. Others recalled a modest, unaffected, and helpful man, initially shy in the company of strangers, but blessed with serene good nature, kindness, and boundless enthusiasm for his subject, characteristics that the young Roger would also display.

The intellectual bias in the family leaned noticeably towards the sciences and medicine. Of the children, Roger alone displayed a lasting propensity for the arts; a talent that his brother Donald believes was clearly inherited from his father.

Although driven by a primal compulsion to draw or paint, the young Roger never sought validation or approval for his endeavours. His artworks, even his earliest childhood daubs, were, it seems, an end in themselves. 'From junior school onwards he had exhibitions of one thing and another,' remembers Rosemary. 'But he never ever wanted anybody to say anything he did was good. It was just never a necessity for him at all. He did it all for himself, for his needs. He never did a commission. My mother's friends used to say, "Oh, would Roger do me a picture of so and so?" He wouldn't. He just didn't understand why anybody would want that. Because to him it wasn't like doing something to show somebody, like you and I would do. For him it was just in his head, he got it out on paper, and then it was finished. He didn't need anybody to say it was good, or admire it. He probably didn't even go back to it. That was how his art was.'

Rosemary does not remember the Barrett household as being a particularly literary one. 'Obviously we were read to and there was books around, of course. *The Little Grey Men* we used to read. I used to read Enid Blyton a lot, and Roger used to read *Alice in Wonderland* and this sort of stuff. We did read, but it wasn't encouraged in any way, there wasn't an emphasis on reading.' Rosemary recalls the young Roger poring over Hilaire Belloc and Lewis Carroll. 'But then in those days all kids had them, didn't they? There was a really quite narrow band of books that everybody read. But the magical ones were the ones that Roger latched on to.'

From 1953 to 1957 like his brothers before him Roger attended the Morley Memorial Junior School in Cambridge, where he was taught by, among others, Roger Waters' mother, Mary. By the time he left junior school his older brothers had both left home to pursue their careers, leaving the young Roger to grow up in a predominantly maternal household, spoiled and cosseted by all who encountered him. 'All my mother's friends were just in love with him – they used to come and see us just to see him, 'cos he was just such a huge character,' remembers Rosemary. Richard Trim, brother of Judy Trim, who would become Roger Waters' first wife, remembers his own mother's frequent visits to the Barrett household. 'She was good friends with Win and she thought he was an amazingly good-looking lad.'

In 1957 Roger passed his eleven-plus examination and following family tradition went to the Cambridgeshire High School for Boys, barely a hundred yards up the road from his home. In the post-war years the school had changed its name from the Cambridge and County High School for Boys but was still known colloquially as 'the County'. It was in every respect a traditional English grammar school, modelled on public school lines with an exclusively male teaching staff that wore mortar boards and gowns. It had a prefect system and a house system, the houses being named after the four main rivers that flowed through Cambridge and Oxford – Cam, Granta, Isis and Cherwell. Roger was placed in Cherwell House.

The school upheld the ideals of the traditional classical curriculum; Latin was compulsory and there was a strictly observed 'two cultures' split between the arts and sciences, with pupils expected to specialise in one discipline or the other in the sixth form. Many members of staff had graduated from the local university; the majority had been public school-educated, and a significant proportion had achieved senior rank in the armed forces. The previous headmaster, Brinley Newton John (father of singer Olivia Newton John), had been a wing commander in the RAF. The heads of geography and modern languages had both been awarded MBEs and both had distinguished war records. Even the school's caretaker, the apparently much-loved Mr Wagstaff, had been a squadron leader in the Second World War. Long service and loyalty were common and during Roger's time at the school it was not untypical for staff members to have worked there for twenty or thirty years. The head of art, G. A. C.

Harden, taught at the County from 1938 to 1971. English teacher W. Gumbrell was there from 1930 to 1965.

Discipline was rigidly enforced with a daily 'dress parade' before morning assembly. Detention classes were held after school and on Saturday mornings and there was regular use of corporal punishment. The school's overriding ethos, as its own promotional literature put it, stressed 'uniformity, obedience, academic achievement, and team spirit'. The County had its own Scout troop (the 7th Cambridgeshire) and, as was common in many other grammar and public schools at the time, a thriving Combined Cadet Force (CCF), with separate sections for army, navy and air force. There was also a strong emphasis on sports, particularly rugby union, cricket and hockey, and a middle-class bias, typical of most grammar schools at the time, against association football.

Anyone seeking evidence of a prodigy in the making would have been severely disappointed by Roger's school record. Apart from his precocious talent for art there is little to indicate that he was anything other than an average scholar. He was mentioned 'in dispatches' in the school magazine, *The Cantabrigian*, as an impressive athlete, and was frequently placed in the first three in the 100-yard and 220-yard sprints on school sports day, but he didn't shine academically, nor did the rules and regulations of school life sit particularly well with his fiercely independent temperament. 'He wasn't very well behaved. Discipline wasn't really his thing,' says Rosemary. 'He got away with it at junior school because he was so adorable. I mean, he was physically very attractive, he'd got wonderfully sparkly eyes and a lovely smile, and he was very funny. He was a clown, so he got away with not doing very much. But then when he went to secondary school, of course, it didn't work quite so well, and so he just didn't bother to do very much.'

The headmaster during Roger's time at the County was

William Eagling, who had gained a double first in classics at St Catharine's College, Cambridge. Eagling was a stickler for discipline, who regularly berated boys in the street if they were seen to be acting in a slovenly or uncouth manner or generally behaving in a way that might otherwise besmirch the reputation of the school. He was also a passionate opponent of the liberalisation of the curriculum, and keen to defend the role of Latin and uphold the demarcation between the arts and sciences. During the 1958 school speech day he felt it incumbent upon himself to warn the attendant gathering of the twin encroaching perils of Labour government and comprehensive education. County scholar and future BBC presenter Nick Barraclough describes Eagling as 'to this day, the scariest man I have ever known'.

'Crippen, we called him,' says another of Roger's grammar school contemporaries, Andrew Rawlinson. 'He was a classicist but he should have been a prison warden. That was his natural talent I think.'

Like his brothers and his father before him, Roger was a keen Scout, and it was here that school friends remember him first taking an interest in the guitar. 'I remember Roger from when he joined our school in September 1957,' says Geoff Leyshon. 'He joined the school Scout group, of which I was a member. I think he was in Mick Taylor's patrol. Mick and I could claim to have taught Roger his first chords on the guitar,' says Leyshon. 'One Saturday morning, we were sorting out equipment prior to summer camp. Mick had brought his guitar along (a Hofner acoustic, I think) and we were having a strum. Roger expressed an interest as any thirteen-year-old would so we showed him how to shape chords. E, A and D, I recollect, good enough for most twelve-bar R & R numbers.'

According to Leyshon it was also during this period that Roger became Syd. 'The "Syd" nickname came from that era,' he maintains, 'bestowed around about 1959, when Roger turned up in a flat cap instead of his Scout beret for a field day at Abington Scout site. Some of our more senior and pretentious members thought this was very working-class and promptly nicknamed him "Syd" as this was felt to be a lower-class name, I suppose, and it stuck.'

Leyshon's recollections pre-date all previous accounts about how 'Roger' became 'Syd'. The most commonly aired theory was that there was a jazz musician in Cambridge, a bass player known as Sid 'the beat' Barrett, who used to play at the Riverside Jazz Club in the early 1960s, which the young Roger used to frequent. This latter account is of course a more attractive and eminently more hip option, but the truth is that the nickname was bestowed upon Roger by his school seniors and not by the denizens of a jazz club. There is no evidence to suggest that Roger was unhappy with the nickname, and he used both his real name and his nickname interchangeably for several years, although it is significant that he was referred to solely as Roger or 'Rog' in the Barrett household. 'He was never Syd at home,' maintains Rosemary. 'He would never have allowed it.' For the sake of clarity, from this point in our story Roger becomes Syd.

'There were 600 boys at the County. Big enough to take some slack,' remembers Andrew Rawlinson. 'On a particular day, I think it was a Thursday, and I've no idea why I did this, but for about two months I would just walk out of school. I don't even know what I did. But with 600 boys you could get away with it. There's always kids going to hospital or aunties dying.'

Two years younger than Rawlinson, Syd also began to take advantage of the school's size and the relative anonymity it afforded, and by the fourth year had started to miss classes regularly. The school punishment book shows that he was caned for truancy on at least two occasions. But whereas Syd drifted through his schooldays with a mixture of indifference and charm it was his future band mate Roger Waters who rebelled most overtly against the system. He attained notoriety for dropping out of the CCF on the grounds that he was a conscientious objector, for which he was given a dishonourable discharge. He did, though, remain an enthusiastic member of the school rifle club, envisaging perhaps some future rooftop scenario, as immortalised in the closing sequence of Lindsay Anderson's 1968 film *If*. Had he wished he might also have continued to take advantage of the CCF's considerable arsenal of wartime weaponry, which included, as one former member recalled, 'racks of 303s, Kalashnikovs, Stens and Brens, and a bazooka that nobody could assemble'.

'Roger [Waters] never really found a subject or a group of masters that he was really into,' says Andrew Rawlinson. 'I was very lucky. I was taught English literature by a guy who himself had been taught by F. R. Leavis, who used the method of "unseens", where you are given a passage and asked, "Where does this come from." I knew how to do that, and I knew that these masters needed me, basically, so I used to muck about and get away with it, and Roger didn't. But they didn't need him.'

Syd was as naturally gifted at painting as Rawlinson was in literature and was allowed the same creative licence in his art classes. 'Syd was a fantastic artist and was the pride and joy of the art teacher, G. A. C. Harden, or "Gach" as he was known,' remembers classmate Chris Rayner. 'Gach used to leave Syd's stuff out on display all the time for everyone to see. He did some superb stuff in oils. Most of us weren't allowed anywhere near the oil paints. You had to be really good before Gach would allow you to work in oils.'

'Of course, there's an extra dimension there with Syd,' observes Rawlinson. 'It's not just because he was good at art, it's because he was so personable. He was an easy boy to like. I was always challenging masters but Syd didn't do that. Why would he bother? Life was working for him on his own terms. If you're a master and you've got somebody like that in your class, you're going to go out of your way for him. But so far as the rest of the school was concerned Syd was happy just to slip through and disappear. He never had the resentment that Roger had.'

Rawlinson and Waters were both A-stream pupils; in fact, most of Syd's friends at the County were. In the streaming system the high flyers received the best education and were treated as an intellectual elite. A-stream pupils generally stayed on for the sixth form and from there were expected to progress to university. There was considerable demarcation between their expectations and life chances and those of pupils from the lower streams, who were more likely to fill mundane administrative and white-collar clerical posts in banking and insurance. These expectations tended to be self-fulfilling, and the County School governors and examiners acknowledged this in the late 1950s, bemoaning the fact that while the A-stream was producing record numbers of Oxbridge entrants, the C stream was, in one of the most academically gifted cities in the country, producing O level results below the national average, i.e. fewer than three O levels per pupil.

'We were privileged, of course, but we were born in the right age and we took our privilege for granted,' says Andrew Rawlinson. 'But at the same time there was a lot of kicking against the system. Mainly I think because society was beginning to provide the ammunition to do that.'

Rawlinson had witnessed an early manifestation of this while waiting for the school coach one Saturday morning to go and play rugby for the first XV. 'There was this boy – I can see him now but I can't remember his name – who had luminescent lime-green socks on. The sort of stuff Elvis was wearing. And, of course, the statement that he made was entirely silent. And we all got it and our system got it too and didn't like it. But it was all getting away from them. There was nothing they could do.'

Rawlinson's own symbolic rebellion paid homage to one of his cultural heroes. 'I was a big Ray Charles fan and this was a time when he was constantly getting busted for possession of drugs. I got my mother to make me a black velvet armband. I used to wear it to school and waited for a master to come up and say, "Someone in your family died, Rawlinson?" I'd say, "No, sir, Ray Charles got busted again." '

In the lower sixth, a year below Rawlinson and Waters, was another bright A-stream pupil who would play an important role in the Syd Barrett story, Paul Charrier. 'I was going through the playground and he was singing "Hit the Road, Jack" when that was a hit,' says Rawlinson of their first encounter in the winter of 1961. ' "My son," I said, "I've got a lot of Ray Charles records and most of them are better than that." He said, "Right, let's go and listen to them." And from there we kind of hit it off immediately. His family was amazingly straight and I don't think they had a clue what was going on with Paul. He was basically independent and had a very strong will.'

Another bright but rebellious A-stream pupil at the County was Seamus O'Connell. Emblazoned on his kitchen wall at home was a quote from Artaud, which read: 'I have a small mind and I mean to use it.' O'Connell took another Artaud quote – 'A vicious society has invented psychiatry in order to defend itself against the investigations of certain superior lucid minds whose intuitive powers were disturbing to it' – and put it on a series of lino-block prints which he sent out to friends as Christmas cards.

'A group of us used to go to Seamus's house,' remembers Rawlinson. 'Seamus lived about five minutes' walk from the school. He had a deeply subversive mother. His mother and father had separated some time before when Seamus was quite little and his mother was devoted to him and supported him.'

Seamus's father was the artist Michael William O'Connell, a descendant of the Irish patriot Daniel O'Connell. His mother,

Ella, was an equally talented embroiderer and printmaker. In 1937 the O'Connells purchased land at Perry Green, near Much Hadham in Hertfordshire, where they built their house, The Chase. During the Second World War the sculptor Henry Moore moved to a nearby farmhouse called Hoglands and then bought the house next to the O'Connells' where he remained for the rest of his life. Soon after the birth of their son in 1943, the O'Connells separated and Ella and Seamus settled in Cambridge. Ella had a keen interest in the occult and other forms of *arcana* and was destined to play a significant part in Syd's spiritual development, as she was responsible for introducing him to tarot and the *I Ching*.

'A lot of these lads will remember my mother with great affection, because she was very progressive, very easy going,' says O'Connell. 'She was quite happy for us to stay up all night, drinking coffee, playing guitars, doing whatever we liked, but as a mother possibly a little bit less than useful because she wasn't directive at all.'

In Cambridge, as in many other places at the time, a new generation of middle-class non-conformists was emerging. The seeds of this aesthetic and cultural rebellion were being sown in the classroom, cloakroom and common-room cabals of the English grammar school system. Syd's generation was the first to benefit from the economic affluence that followed the end of post-war rationing. It was also the first generation to come of age free of the obligation of conscription, compulsory national service in the UK having been abolished at the end of 1960 while Syd was in his fourth year at school. Syd's oldest brother Alan had done national service and Don Barrett had only escaped it because of his engineering apprenticeship.

In his essay, *England Your England*, written at the outset of the Second World War, George Orwell famously wrote: 'Probably the Battle of Waterloo was won on the playing fields of Eton but the opening battles of all subsequent wars have been lost there.' The essay went on to deliver a damning critique of ruling-class stagnation and decay and the moneyed classes' descent into apathy, mediocrity and incompetence. Orwell traced very precisely the trajectory of a regime that had outlived its usefulness and had failed to observe that the world had changed and moved on.

In the late 1950s a curious corollary to this was beginning to take place among middle-class youth in Britain. Deference to the staid values and moribund culture of the older order was slowly but irrevocably being eroded. These middle-class rebels continued to enjoy all the privilege and reap all the rewards that a solid grammar school education could provide but within the security of this environment a groundswell of dissent was beginning to manifest itself.

'We were beginning to pick up on the fact that things were changing and were just at the right age to absorb all of it,' says Andrew Rawlinson. 'Elvis appeared in 1956 when I was thirteen, but Tommy Steele was there at the same time. When you're thirteen you don't really know the difference. At fifteen you more or less do. And when you're seventeen you would never take Tommy Steele seriously. The thing is, it was all one tapestry. As far as I'm concerned Jerry Lee Lewis and Ornette Coleman are in the same neck of the woods.'

Another key element in this cultural rebellion was the literature of the beat generation. Jack Kerouac's novel *On the Road* had been published in 1957 and its be-bop and Benzedrine-fuelled prose was enthusiastically appropriated in the UK by an emerging generation of affluent and questing post-war youth. With its portrayal of life as an endless road of infinite possibilities, *On the Road* exposed them for the first time to ideas and values that lay outside the mainstream of English literature, ideas and values that they were never going to encounter within the school curriculum. Part hip travelogue, part mystic quest, Kerouac's novel offered a spiritual and physical route-map for the new rebellious sensibility, and its central characters, Sal (Kerouac) and Dean Moriarty (Neal Cassady) were readily embraced by a young and receptive readership.

Not that any of this lay within the direct experience of rural backwater boys from East Anglia. You can't drive for more than four hours in England without falling off the map, and somehow a literary portrayal of a journey along the A14 to Stowmarket or traversing the B roads to Wisbech wouldn't have held quite the same allure to a would-be Fenland beatnik in the late 1950s. The beats, though, were part of a wider influx of American iconography that was eagerly appropriated, exoticised and emulated by Syd's generation. Modern jazz, rhythm and blues, and rock 'n' roll provided the musical impulse and offered myriad alternatives to the drabness and conformity of post-war life in Britain. Kerouac and the beat poets provided the primary literary impulse.

Having plunked away on the banjo and ukulele when he was younger, Syd acquired his first guitar, a Hofner Acoustic, when he was fourteen. Chris Rayner, who was in Syd's form during the remove (fourth) and fifth years, remembers him frequently playing guitar in class. 'Whenever it was classed as "Officially Wet" pupils were allowed to stay in their classrooms during break. During those Officially Wet periods Syd and John Gordon used to get out their guitars and strum away, much to the delight of the other pupils.' There were also regular lunchtime jam sessions with Bob Klose, Ivan Carling and others in the school science lab in a basement corridor, which also housed the lunchtime chess club.

Apart from the outdoor life of the Scouts and his enthusiastic endeavours on the running track, learning to play the guitar was one of the few communal activities Syd ever got involved in at school. He wasn't by nature a joiner and was never one for chess club, science club or debating society. Some of his closest friends however were keen team sportsmen. Andrew Rawlinson, Storm Thorgerson and Roger Waters all played regularly for the rugby first XV, as did Bob Klose, who would go on to become the original lead guitarist in Pink Floyd. Storm captained the rugby team and was a talented batsman and leg-spinner for the cricket team. He also represented the school at tennis and badminton and was head of Granta House.

Syd's wider network of friends at this time included David Gale, Anthony Stern, David Henderson and David Gilmour, who all went to the Perse, the Common Entrance private school just up Hills Road. 'The Perse was, I suppose, regarded as half a notch up the social scale from the County,' says Anthony Stern, 'but culturally speaking it was as much in the dark ages as the County was. We were constantly rebelling against the system. We would do things like try to set fire to the school, break into the grounds at night and write meaningless, absurdist slogans on the school walls. Nowadays if a kid did that they would probably end up with an ASBO, whereas we got away with stuff, because we were middle-class – and I noticed that throughout my entire life in Cambridge – you could get away with stuff if you spoke posh. If you told the police where your address was, which in my case was in a salubrious neighbourhood – Barton Road, near Newnham – you could virtually behave like a spoilt brat. The school's head-master, Stanley Stubbs, had one basic motto, which was: "Conform or get out." And while we pretended to conform, we wrote anti-school magazines and published them illegally and stuffed them in people's desks, and generally tried to be a bit subversive.'

The unmistakable whiff of 'Oh well, if you must' pervaded much of the older generation's disapproval of such activities, and middle-class dissent thrived in an atmosphere of benign tolerance. With the confidence that affluence and inheritance bring, many of these well-bred and well-mannered English school boys mediated everything through an arch humour that ranged from cultivated disdain to coruscating satirical wit. Again, Lindsay Anderson's *If* captures the tone perfectly in the languid malice of its dormitory scenes. That same droll tone, which can still be detected in the utterances of Roger Waters et al. to this day, can be traced back to those formative years in the English grammar schools and private schools. It can be detected throughout the County school magazine, *The Cantabrigian*, and was ever present in the activities of the school debating society, where several of Syd's peers, including Andrew Rawlinson, Seamus O'Connell and Roger Waters, cut their intellectual teeth.

At the Perse, as at the County, challenging the system was its own reward, and in such privileged environs much of the rebellion and resistance was essentially symbolic. There was little kicking against the pricks. 'Culture shock for me was being brought up as a potential prototype public schoolboy and then, to his dismay, to find his parents didn't have money to send him to one of these posh public schools,' says Anthony Stern. 'So I ended up with a slight chip on my shoulder, being shovelled off to "The Perse", which in fact turned out to be absolutely brilliant. As soon as I got there I realised that there was F. R. Leavis's grandson, and there was Julian Hough, son of Graham Hough, who's an expert on D. H. Lawrence. There was David Gale, whose father was a biochemist. And we all fitted into this thing, which I later [identified as] "The Cambridge syndrome". In other words, we were the sons and daughters of extremely bright, often dauntingly successful people. There was William Pryor who was the great-great-grandson of Charles Darwin. He was embarrassed about it and proud of it at the same time, but it held him back a lot – because he could never match up to the expectations of his family. And that was the key factor. I didn't match up to my parents' expectations either. So I became a rebel and that sort of deconstructing-society-out-of-necessity was fairly typical of a lot of kids, who either pretended to have intellectual aspirations, or they became a beat character or whatever, or they genuinely were hounded by the intellectual aspirations of their parents. It all added up to the same thing – there was a wonderfully fertile atmosphere of curiosity, I would call it, rather than retaliation against their parents' generation. It was more to do with "What else?", y'know. We ignored our parents rather than fought against them.'

Stern's own father, a Czech Jewish refugee, was a fellow of St John's College and a world authority on Nietzsche. His mother specialised in modern languages and wrote about Proust. It was a characteristic of Syd's generation that most of their parents were either drawn from the intelligentsia or had far left or left-leaning politics. Many were as radicalised, if not more so, than their children. Bob Klose's father, Helmut, fought with the International Brigade in the Spanish Civil War, spent time in a concentration camp, and with his wife Rita had spent the harsh winter of 1947 living as a refugee in a bell tent at Raines Fruit Farm in Madingley. Roger Waters' mother, Mary, was a committed socialist. 'All our parents were filthy reds,' says Richard Trim. 'We were all taken on CND marches as a matter of course. That's how my parents knew Roger Waters' mother.' The Quaker tradition, which shaped Syd's parent's beliefs, was based on anti-doctrinaire principles, shunning credo and iconography, and encouraging the practice of silent prayer and contemplation and communing with God through the concept of 'silent expectancy'. Previous to his time at the County, Storm Thorgerson's mother, Evangeline, had sent him to the progressive Summerhill School. David Gilmour's father Doug was a lecturer in zoology at the university. 'My Dad worked with Helmut Klose and Rado [Bob] was a friend from birth,' remembers Gilmour. 'Helmut was employed at the Downing Street Laboratories after the war as a general assistant, helping my father who ran a research lab there as well as lecturing in zoology. I can remember having outdoor lunches with the whole Klose family on the terrace of our house in Cambridge, which we left when I was about seven, i.e. 1953. Rado's real full name is Radovan – we always called him Rado. He taught me a fair bit of guitar when I was young. He was a bit good. My brother Peter lived with the Kloses for a year when my Dad did a sabbatical in the USA in 1961 and their house, a tiny, very rustic cottage in Haslingfield was my/our second home.'

'There was this cultural atmosphere at Cambridge that really engendered a wonderful level of creativity,' says Anthony Stern. 'I remember, from a very early age, looking at the behaviour of adults, and being aware that they were pretty unusual. You'd see Fred Hoyle and Francis Crick. Francis Crick was constantly going up and down the road outside our house. And you thought, "You mean DNA Crick? Bloody hell!" It's an extraordinary combination of things – bicycling and being eccentric. I could write a whole chapter on the eccentricities of Cambridge dons. They all had their various quirks. And the great thing was, for whatever reason, they expressed their eccentricity. They were middle-class and aspirational, like my parents were, but they weren't conformist, y'know that's the difference. When people say "middle class" generally speaking in British society, it conjured up the image of bank managers and accountants and lawyers, and people who actually want to conform to being middle-class. If anything, middle-class people in Cambridge wanted to be bursting back into eccentricity again.'

It was these factors as much as anything else that helped define the social and cultural ethos of Syd's generation, the lives of whom would blossom and intertwine over the next few years. The Cambridge crowd were, and have largely remained, a close-knit and loyal bunch, several of whom had known each other since junior school, many of whom had grown up within a few hundred yards of each other, and most of whom remain in regular contact with each other to this day, frequently col-laborating on creative projects, offering reciprocal support systems in times of emotional or financial need, and occasionally, as with all extended families, falling out with each other spectacularly and squabbling like errant children.

Syd was the youngest of this group, the precocious kid who could hold his own in senior company. Andrew Rawlinson, Anthony Stern and David Gale were two years above Syd at school, while Storm Thorgerson, Bob Klose and Paul Charrier were a year older. 'He was two years younger than most of us, which is a lot at that age don't forget, but I was impressed by his creativity,' remembers Andrew Rawlinson.

'Was there something in the water?' ponders Anthony Stern. 'How come it happened that in Cambridge, nearly everybody you met was already a sort of proto-eccentric by the age of fourteen? If you weren't doing some mad beat poetry, or jazz or playing the trumpet or something by the age of fifteen you'd better get a move on, 'cos everyone else is doing something wacky.'

'If you're in that scene you just sort of take it for granted,' reflects Andrew Rawlinson. 'There wasn't any planning behind it. It's only later when people start to emerge into social structures which have a resonance behind the immediate Cambridge social group that you begin to think, "Bloody hell, something's really going on here." '

Another prominent figure in this group was Nigel Lesmoir-Gordon. Having been thrown out of the exclusive Oundle school after adopting the mantle and values of the beats a little too enthusiastically ('Jack Kerouac turned my head and Oundle school gave up on me after that,' he says) Lesmoir-Gordon enrolled at Cambridge Tech to take his A levels in 1961. In the same way that the arrival of Aussie beat poet Daevid Allen in Canterbury in late 1960 energised and inspired Robert Wyatt, Kevin Ayers, Hugh Hopper et al., Nigel Lesmoir-Gordon was a key catalyst and enabler in Cambridge: the hip and slightly wayward older-brother figure who introduces his peers to wider bohemian impulses, and galvanises their nascent creative energies into something cohesive and tangible. Like Daevid Allen, Lesmoir-Gordon beat a hipster's path to Paris and met William Burroughs when he was staying at the Beat Hotel. 'The first thing he said to me when I walked into his room was, "Don't sit on my bed in your wet mac," ' he remembers. In Cambridge Lesmoir-Gordon put on poetry readings and 'Happenings', which helped forge crucial counter-cultural connections with the New Departures poetry group and other elements of the growing UK underground. Later, with his wife Jenny, he would again prove to be a galvanising force for all of the Cantabrigians who moved up to London, running what was tantamount to a modern-day salon, and playing host to the great and the good of the beat generation and the musical and literary avant-garde.

Nigel and Jenny first met Syd in 1961 when he was in his final year at school. Nigel's first impressions suggest a creative spirit who was still in the process of finding himself. 'We found him a very attractive and interesting boy but not that remarkable. We weren't magnetised by him. There were so many brilliant people. There was Storm, David Gale, the wonderful artist David Henderson, Andrew Rawlinson – the world's greatest intellect. Paul Charrier – the world's greatest rebel. We were surrounded by brilliance and sparkling power. Syd was just another one of these brilliant beings.'

'When I first knew him Syd lived with his pleasant, slightly distracted auntie-ish Mum and her very eccentric, bicycling husband,' remembers David Gale. 'Cambridge is full of eccentric people on bicycles. You do see people there who clearly need the support of academe, 'cos they look quite frail. In any other town, they'd get stones thrown at them. But in Cambridge – and Oxford I suppose – people know that these are only professors. Syd, at the time I became aware of him as an item in my visual neighbourhood, was a very, very striking young man indeed. He had an extremely sunny disposition. He was extremely good-looking, he was also very muscular and symmetrical and well built, very fit-looking. He was also a man with a mission. A teenager who paints seriously in his bedroom when he doesn't have to is quite unusual.'

Several of Syd's old school friends offer similar testimony to the boy who painted when he didn't have to. Many remember him nipping across the road to his nearby home during the school lunch-break to paint, or getting out of games lessons to do the same. Indeed his ability to depart from the route of the school cross-country run as it passed his house, stop off for an hour or so of sketching, and then rejoin the panting athletes as they headed back on the final leg of the run is still the stuff of legend among those who knew him. Such activity reveals an astonishing degree of devotion to creativity at an age when boys only do things when teachers make them. Most people who bunked off classes or cross-country would go and have a crafty smoke behind the bike sheds. Syd went home and painted.

Precocious and confident around girls, Syd also seemed to be sexually mature and knowing beyond his years. Nick Barraclough, who was at junior school at the same time as Syd and whose sister Alison attended Saturday morning art classes at Homerton with him, remembers the pupils in his class at the age of eleven being asked to paint their impression of a hot summer's day. He recalls that most of the children drew a typically childlike beachscape. Roger, as he still was then, drew a girl lying on a beach in a bikini, with an ice cream dripping over her.

Another school friend Terry Mahoney comments, 'I

remember him as a confident thirteen/fourteen-year-old saying that he lipsticked his penis 'cos the girls liked it. As a completely naive teenager that seemed to me really rude and shocking.' While this was almost certainly teenage bravado and bullshit it does reveal a level of sexual fantasy way beyond that of the average spotty adolescent.

Syd's first serious girlfriend, Libby Gausden, who lived thirteen doors away at 157 Hills Road, also remembers a precocious young teenager whose first words to her when they met in 1961 were, 'They should put you on a Dairy Box,' a reference both to the TV ads for Rowntree's Dairy Box chocolates that were running at the time, featuring a cropped-haired girl dressed in beat chic, and the box itself, which was designed by the French artist and illustrator Raymond Peynet, whose distinctive drawings came to define chocolate-box art and perfumery in the early 1960s.

'It was a double-edged compliment,' maintains Libby. 'What he meant was, they should have people like you on chocolate boxes, not the curly pretties they normally have. I was fifteen. I'd spent a lot of time in Germany and had my hair very short and that was what he liked, very short hair. We met on Jesus Green. There was a huge open-air swimming pool there which we all had membership of and we'd all swim from April to September to get our money's worth. Outside was a kids' playground. I was on the seesaw with somebody when he came up to me. He was very handsome. A bit spotty but lovely looking.'

Libby paints an evocative picture of the Barrett household at that time. 'Max was always in his study. A very serious man. Tall. Very gentle. Not of this world. He was so apart from the house he didn't seem like a dad. My dad was always letting my skirts down or wiping off my black eye make-up, a very visible figure in our house. His father wasn't. He never ate with them. When I went round he'd always say, "Hello, I'm off to my study." I can see him now in his glasses. Syd absolutely adored him and had real respect for him. And he worshipped his mother. Win was extremely mumsy and saw the good in everyone. Everybody was adorable, her own children and other peoples. And she was one of the chief Guides of Cambridgeshire so there would often be a kitchen full of Guides doing their cooking badge. It used to amaze me. I'd never seen a woman who didn't mind mess everywhere.'

School photos of the time reveal Syd as a dark-skinned, dark-eyed boy with naturally curly hair, a bit wild, almost gypsy-looking. 'He had his own style and it was absolutely natural,' says Libby. 'Whatever he did never looked contrived. He wore Ray-Bans before anybody had ever heard of them. People that copied him were buying theirs from Boots for one and ninepence. It's not like there was a group of people exactly like him. Had you asked him, he would have thought that we were all like-minded, but he was different from all of us.'

David Gale also remembers Syd's transformation into junior hipster. 'He was quite precociously taking up the bohemian, beatnik wardrobe of people two or three years older than him. He was a person who, when he walked through town and through the millpond area, where we used to go and hang out – heads would turn. He was, in terms of style, years ahead. He was wearing faded, very tight denims. He had (this is when he wasn't in a school uniform), I remember, grey suede moccasin-like shoes, wrap-around shades and shirt outside trousers, that was quite startling in those days. Only a handful of people could manage to look like that in Cambridge at that time. He was in the vanguard in that respect. And, of course, Syd being so good-looking, had lots of girlfriends. It was kind of obvious to us other chaps that Syd could probably get any girl he wanted.'

Libby Gausden and Syd would go out with each other on and off for the next three and a half years. It was a tempestuous relationship – by Libby's own account they broke up, dated other people and got back together again at least three or four times during this period. In the first year of their relationship though they saw each other virtually every day, and wrote to each other prolifically on the rare occasions when they were apart.

Syd's surviving letters to Libby allow us a valuable glimpse into the everyday commonplace details of his life in the early 1960s. They are frequently gauche and gushing – 'Libby Gausden is Syd's Miss World. She's Miss Universe' – as would be expected in a love-struck boy in his mid teens, and often saucy or smutty (variants on 'Here's some kisses – you know where they're for' are a frequent sign-off). They are also abundant in topical wit ('as that great philosopher Adam Faith said') and self-mockery ('I don't know, fancy being up this late; I think I must be a "young rebel" as Paul [Charrier] says.') The letters cover every aspect of the young Syd's life, from the routine of Scout camp at Saxmundham ('We came third in inspection.') to the mundanity of another Scout trip spent 'in the middle of a lake in the middle of the Norfolk Broads in the middle of nowhere'. 'The whole place is quiet now, except for the strains of Sunday's requests over the water,' he writes before embarking upon more detail about tacking, front winds and valve pumps than a fifteen-year-old girl strictly needs to know. More in keeping with his creative bent are letters from the drama summer school he went to at Winchester, where he attended music-and-movement and improvisation classes and a guest lecture from a visitor from the Royal Shakespeare Company. 'I have the lovely part of a boy who is a witch,' he writes. 'Not the old hag type but just an enchanted person who looks like a human. The whole thing is American and we have to drawl and say things like "hit don't make no matter".'

While on these field trips Syd also expressed some very touching sentiments about loyalty. 'Most people are getting into couples now – all very nice in their own little way,' he observes, 'but how I wish I could show them you, darling, and then they'd see how we really are in love – not just crummy romances for a week or so to occupy the holidays.'

At times in the letters a young man's sexual frustration is palpable. 'Just think: we stayed indoors on Saturday night with your parents in the same room; watching the television! Some achievement – just shows what true love can do. Still, never again.' Another begins 'All this surplus energy spent in writing pukey letters! What a waste.' The pages frequently reek of the unmistakeable pungency of testosterone. 'I adore your lips, especially when they're slightly rough and augmented by lovely cheap Woolworths (or Boots) lip gloss.' At other times Syd is disarmingly irreverent, 'I have more love for your trifficly horrible hair, your lovely little rounded face, your bent eye holes . . . so please don't forget what we said when we parted, because your likely to cos you're a bit stupid quite often.'

In many ways it was a typical early 1960s courtship, with talk of engagement and marriage. Syd cites *Romeo and Juliet* (which he studied for English O level) and frequently showers Libby with romantic epithets, 'My sweet little chiff-chaff/chicory pod/orange blossom', etc. The biro and pencil sketches that accompany many of the letters are exquisite, Syd's use of language equally inventive, and at times arch and knowing beyond his years. He parodies middle-class manners with phrases like 'if you feel extraordinarily pally' while clichés and irony are frequently rendered in inverted commas. When he is being acerbic, it is conveyed with the unmistakeable disdain of a Cambridge grammar school boy. On the train to his summer school at Winchester, for instance, he writes of sharing a compartment with 'a most atrocious American couple with no manners . . . she frequently emitted the most ridiculous cough I have ever heard'. Aside from a penchant for the word 'triffic' and 'your' instead of 'you're' everything is impeccably spelt and punctuated.

'We used to go to the Riverside Jazz Club when we were very

young,' says Libby. 'He took me at fifteen but he'd been going before that. I wasn't allowed to go. I had to lie to go to a jazz club. That was when I first used to notice that adults flocked round him. He did nothing. He didn't play or sing at that time. He was just there in his clothes, looking as he did. I didn't like it 'cos you couldn't dance to it, not like this gorgeous crappy dance music that I used to love. I used to go there because it was interesting. All those Juliette Greco types.'

Apart from evenings at the Riverside, social activity for Syd and his gang at this time revolved around the El Patio coffee bar, the Anchor, Mill and Criterion pubs, and other favoured haunts dotted along the extensive spread of park and meadowland that meanders through Cambridge city centre.

In describing this terrain David Gale paints a picture of those early 1960s summers that is one part idyll to two parts idling. 'The River Cam runs through the backs of the colleges and comes up against a weir at the millpond where the lower river stops, and the upper river, the one that leads to Grantchester, starts. You can hire punts on either river at the Anchor Pub end of the lower river. You could also hire punts fifty yards further on, on the upper river, and take yourself up to Grantchester. Those two punt-hire places were right in the centre of an area of very pleasant meadowland with rivers running either side of it – it was a little tributary of the main river. There was the Anchor Pub and then on the Mill Bridge that actually straddled this waterfall that separates the two rivers, there's another pub – the Mill – very popular with undergraduates. You could take your beer out of this pub, walk a few yards and sit on the bridge, looking in either direction. And adjacent to that was a meadow where groups of young people used to hang out and look at each other. Such was the topography that you could sit on the meadow and see people coming from various directions. People would simply sit there for quite long periods, day after day, in the summer holidays and maybe sometimes after school, just hanging out and chatting.'

Gale's picture evokes a world of teenage boys and girls in the prime of their young lives with their futures spread out ahead of them in a tableau of endless possibilities without worry or woe, languidly checking each other out, working on their cultivated cool gazing like Georges Seurat's bathers and Seine promenaders. Anthony Stern recalls the carefree splendour of those halcyon summers in Cambridge with equal affection.

'Arcadia comes to mind. One of the nicest things to do was to rent a punt from Scudamore's boatyard and punt down the river to Grantchester. In that little hour-and-a-half trip you're confronted by the most beautiful English countryside. Wherever you went, there was this wonderful mixture of culture, painting, music and beautiful scenery. Punting along the Backs, underneath the arches of the various bridges in Cambridge, along by the rear side of the colleges was enchanting, it was up there with Venice, no question about it – especially in terms of the architecture. And when you punted past King's College Chapel – and that's the best way to see King's College Chapel – and King's College itself, it's just like a stage set.'

For Syd this idyllic and indolent way of life was to be shattered in the most devastating manner. On Monday 11 December 1961, two weeks before Christmas in Syd's final year at school, his father died, having been diagnosed with terminal cancer. Max was working up until a week before his death. Syd was a month shy of his sixteenth birthday. The bereavement, although sudden, had been expected and a death notice appeared in the following day's *Daily Telegraph*, specifying 'Cremation private. No flowers please, but donations to Professor Mitchell's Cancer Research Fund, Addenbrooke's Hospital Cambridge if desired.'

'Syd had these huge diaries, eighteen by ten [inches] each page,' remembers Libby. 'It was the only entry page with one line.

"Dear Dad died today." I remember my mother making me write a formal letter of condolence, something I wouldn't have done if my parents hadn't have insisted.'

Syd's heartfelt reply to this letter on 14 December was full of praise for his father. 'It's very difficult to know what to say about poor Dad, Libby,' he wrote. 'He was fair and very, very kind to you always. No doubt, you realised that from the time you saw him. I could write a book about his merits – perhaps I will some time.' Elsewhere in the letter he seems more concerned for his mother's feelings than his own. 'Dear Mum is being very brave, and it is a great help to her having all the family at home, – when Don finishes this week we shall all be with her for several weeks.'

'I think he, probably, more than any of us, was affected by my father dying,' says Rosemary Barrett. 'He was fifteen, sixteen – which is a difficult age. And, although I never knew it, I think that my father and he did understand each other in a weird sort of way. They would never have sat down and talked, but I think that they did understand each other, and I think that meant a lot. When he'd gone it was a difficult time for Roger. What isn't difficult when you're sixteen anyway? And then to have lost the only person that even vaguely understood him, must've been tricky.'

Libby Gausden remembers the period leading up to Max's death as being particularly stressful. 'We used to tiptoe around for quite a long time. He'd been ill for some time and in a lot of pain. He used to scream out in pain. And that affected Syd more than his dad dying. I don't think he could understand why someone had to make these terrible noises, especially someone as gentle as his father. The traumatic time for Syd was the three months or so of suffering beforehand. That definitely distressed him. He'd start the day with "Dad had a good night last night" or "We've got to be quiet. Dad had a terrible night." I think it was a sweet release for him when he died.'

Shortly after Max's death Syd moved from his upstairs

bedroom to the large 'playroom' on the ground floor at Hills Road, which now became his all-purpose bedroom, painting studio and rehearsal room. Here he could entertain friends, and girlfriends, and pursue his creative endeavours without interruption. 'It was rough leaving that little old room,' he wrote to Libby, 'but everything down here is very nice now – I have paint, music and bed all in one room.' As his older siblings had moved out Win began to take in lodgers in order to supplement her widow's pension, mainly students from Homerton Ladies College across the road.

'People who could play had time to sit with him even though he was rubbish,' says Libby. 'It took Syd quite a long time to play guitar, it really did, but people never lost patience with him. He had this personal magnetism that made people want to be with him, whether it was chatting to him, sitting with him or teaching him to play the guitar. But Roger Waters wasn't a good musician either. They used to sit and strum away for hours, all wrong notes.'

Bo Diddley and later Bob Dylan are usually cited as Syd's musical role models during his formative years but others remember some less likely influences. 'Syd was a huge fan of Joe Brown,' recalls Andrew Rawlinson. 'Joe was a very fine guitarist. Still is. And Syd used to try and play some of those solos that Brown played on his early records.' Syd's letters to Libby reveal some equally unlikely favourites, Charlie Drake's 'Tanglefoot' for instance ('quite a laugh') and the Springfields' 'Goodnight Irene' ('great guitar backing').

Early in 1962 Syd and Libby both contracted glandular fever. Known colloquially as 'the kissing disease' – 'as my father was quick to point out' says Libby – it laid up the pair of them for two weeks. The letters that Syd sent to Libby on 6 and 7 February are among his most tender and witty. His letter from the 6th commences, 'It seems at first to be a dream come true doesn't it? – "Libby and Syd are in bed." Instead of that neither of us are experiencing any pleasure – just lying in bed aching all over, and smelling of sweat rather a lot . . . the medicine man has called quite frequently and each time he succeeds in putting something into me, in the form of injections or pills; or else he takes some-thing away from me in the form of blood (gallons and gallons of it!) or throat swabs. He said that I have been working too hard, and apparently I am "run down". That's great – me, run down! Still, if his tests prove positive he suggests that I should have a holiday from school to "regain my strength". Unfortunately Mum insists on me taking "Mock" [exams] so it'll be a battle!'

Syd also mentions that he is reading 'a book about Beats in America, called "On the Road" ' featuring 'a mad big head called Dean Moriarty', which doesn't exactly constitute a major intellectual critique, but it is more in keeping with a sixteen-year-old boy's perception of the beat generation than some of the more fanciful accounts of Syd's early influences might suggest. More insightful and prescient is his assessment of Dean's girlfriend Marylou. 'She puts up with some really rough treat-ment from him, but she's always there, and he's only really testing how nice a girl she is, and when she loves him after it all he feels so proud to be with her that he stays with her. And she smiles gently to herself because she knows him as well as anybody in the world, and she knew he'd really love to be with her, although he acted hard with other girls.' The subtext of that is unmistakeable. 'Please don't be too ill,' the letter ends.

One gets little sense of a genius in the making here, just a regular Cambridge grammar school boy, bedridden and longing for his girlfriend a few doors down the road. 'Mick has just passed by on his way to school, and I can see the road from here,' he writes. 'He shouted Syderneee and waved like mad. He's a good old boy, Mick.'

The letter he writes the following day is wittier and equally revealing about the sixteen-year-old 'Syderneee'. He's obviously laying in bed listening to *Housewives' Choice* on the radio and interweaves details of the show and the host's asinine comments into his letter. ' "Whirling around the kitchen", I should think. Just imagine all the great fat old housewives jumping around the kitchen table! I hope you're listening to the old radio, Lib, otherwise all this will be a lot of rhubarb to you.' He also mentions a 'queer record about Robinson Crusoe and his mate Friday. Makes me sick' and talks favourably about Chubby Checker's new one. 'This is good but isn't the Big Ben Twist the ultimate? (I really rave over that one – Jim Savile type remark.) And it's in fashion. I must be ill.' Again one gets a sense of regular teen enthusiasms here, which present an interesting contrast to the hip young Syd that walked the streets of Cambridge. 'Incidentally something fantastic has happened – we agree about a pop record,' he writes. 'I think "Blue Skies" is the best record out there, along with Brad Newman's one, the name of which I have forgotten.'

The record he refers to, 'Blue Skies', was an instrumental in the Shadows mould by a Dutch group, the Jumping Jewels, who also covered 'The Theme from Exodus', 'Guitar Tango' and 'Ghost Riders in the Sky'. Brad Newman was a Yorkshire-born singer, real name Charles Melvyn Thomas, who had been a stalwart of shows like *6.5 Special* and *Drumbeat* in the 1950s with his trio the Kingpins, before commencing a short and largely unsuccessful solo career. The date, February 1962, would suggest that the New-man record Syd referred to is 'Somebody to Love', a sax and strings arrangement with a disarmingly facile lyric, set to a frantic Twist rhythm, which reached 47 in the chart that month.

'Some nice lady has just come in and given me three oranges,' he writes, breaking off from the pop chat. 'I suppose she thinks I don't get fed enough. Fancy thinking we've not got enough food. We're not tramps.'

In among the mundane domestic detail he finds time to berate Libby for going out with someone else. He draws a picture of a thumb with him under it and labels it 'Little Syd under lib's thumb'. This is next to another sketch labelled 'Great big little Lib (with arms meant to be folded to look sporty)'. The following page contains an ink-pen sketch of a tree and distant hills with 'RB L EG' carved into the bark. On the page after that he has meticulously cut and pasted, from a variety of newspapers, the words, 'As you might guess I've got some spare time!'

Hoping that they might both have recovered by the weekend he ends the letter with disarming bravado. 'We can buy some clothes and stuff – and some guitar strings, and pretend that we've never quarrelled ever. Let's tell everybody that we've been on a little holiday together. Maybe they'll liven up now the most renowned big-head and the most female of the females get back in circulation! That's a morning gone. I love you precious Lib.'

'He continued with his extra art classes at Homerton,' remembers Libby. 'Very early. Nine till eleven every Saturday morning, which meant we didn't meet till eleven which suited me perfectly. Precious time. Stay in bed. Listen to the radio. But he never missed a lesson. I had lunch a while back with Alison Barraclough who also lived in Hills Road and had been at school with me. She said, "I still think about Syd at those Saturday morning art classes." I said, "He adored you, Alison. He thought you were such a lovely girl." She wasn't trendy or anything, just a good artist from a nice family. She said, "Oh I wish I'd known. Nobody dared talk to him." '

Whether out of aloofness or shyness the young Syd could appear distant to those who didn't know him. He often revealed his stylistic snobberies in his letters to Libby. 'There is no girl over about fourteen and they all wear disgusting slacks – all baggy and crumpled, which slope down from a mass of bottom and fat,' he writes from summer school in Winchester. 'And the boys seem to be equally divided between the little, completely thick little rat, and the short haired Grammar School for Boys

(Cambridge) type.' From Scout camp in Saxmundham, Suffolk, he writes, 'I've only seen four girls since leaving Cambridge and they all looked like immature squares – huge horrible pink dresses over a barrow load of petticoats.' East Anglian squares get similar short shrift in another letter while on his sailing trip on the Norfolk Broads. 'You beat every girl I've seen this week, by at least double darling. I've not seen one pair of dark nylons and they've not even heard of chisel points!'

Jealousy occasionally rears its head in the letters. 'I hope so much that you've been faithful to me this weekend,' he writes from summer school in Winchester. From Scout camp he writes, 'to think you've been free all day, Libby, walking amongst the people of Cambridge' and imagines the following piece of dialogue:

'Look – Libby without Syd, where's Syd?'
    'She must have dropped him. I'll see if I can get off with her.'

Elsewhere the possessiveness verges on desperation and anger. 'I don't want to beat up some poor boy when I get back on Saturday so love me Lib. Love me.'

In the same letter under a dense blur of biro scribbles he pens the following oblique message:

spot the daughter – hidden beneath a wealth of confusion under the 'under-standing' eye of her father. Notice the word between the two. Notice the size of the word compared to that of the man. Notice the anger of the whole picture. Notice girl looking out to the distant forms on the horizon. And notice that I'm going to London to get away a bit.

Sometimes in these letters Syd's jealousy is the common or garden type experienced by many a thwarted or insecure adolescent. At other times, his turmoil becomes all-enveloping and hints at something almost metaphysical in its intensity.

I kiss and hold your pretty little body so closely to mine that we seem to fuse, and only then do I lose touch with the rest of the world, and get carried far away – on thinking about it, the first experience of blackness – not just dark but really deep, jet, nothing, and then comes the gentle, warm – so warm sensation – far, far back in the depths of this little heaven.

This is a sixteen-year-old boy talking!

During his final year at the County Syd was a keen and active member of the school dramatic society, taking part in several school productions including *She Stoops to Conquer* (where classmate John Wilson remembers 'we both had a small part in a drunken scene in an inn'), *Oh, What a Lovely War!* and *Lord of the Flies*. On 3 April 1962 he played Mrs Martin in Eugene Ionesco's *La Cantatrice chauve* (*The Bald Prima Donna*). Described by the author as 'An Anti-Play', Ionesco's savage satire on the English comedy of manners was a perfect vehicle for Syd's absurdist sense of humour, and had a lasting influence on his worldview. The idea for the play had first occurred to Ionesco when he was learning English. By adapting the bland logic of his language primer ('there are seven days in the week', 'the floor is down, the ceiling is up') Ionesco transformed this 'found material' into a direct attack on the domestic conformity of the bourgeoisie. The conversation in the play builds on the rhythms of truism and cliché and the characters become interchangeable ciphers, finishing and parroting each other's pointless sentences, until, as Martin Esslin puts it, 'language itself disintegrates into disjointed fragments of words'.

Ionesco required the characters to play it straight and act with deadly seriousness. According to Martin Esslin the actors, during the play's debut production, were requested to take their lead from 'the novels of Jules Verne, whose English people have a peculiar decorum and sang-froid'. The initial stage instruction for Syd's Mrs Martin character is that 'dialogue should be spoken in a drawling monotonous voice, rather sing-song, without light or shade'. Mrs Martin spends half of her time exclaiming senti-ments, such as, 'Oh, good gracious, how very extraordinary and how very amazing.' Syd's character also gets to speak the play's closing lines, a mundane soliloquy to the merits of mayonnaise.

Apart from his beloved art studies the only other subject that Syd showed real interest in at school was English literature. Among the selected texts for his O level were Shakespeare's *Romeo and Juliet*, Joseph Conrad's *Youth* and *Heart of Darkness*, and George Orwell's *Animal Farm*. 'He was also very interested in history,' remembers Rosemary, 'but he wanted to do it on his terms. Sitting down and listening to somebody else was never his thing.'

In the summer of 1962 Syd sat seven O levels. In those days, grades 1 to 6 were passes, grades 7 to 9, fails. In line with the County school's low average for B- or C-streamers Syd passed just three: art (grade 1), English language (grade 2) and English literature (grade 6). He failed history and geography with grade 8 and maths and general science with grade 9. Sitting nine O levels, not seven, was the norm at the County and Rosemary Barrett recalls that her brother simply didn't bother turning up for a couple of exams. 'Although Mother didn't know for ages. He'd started to become chaotic by that time. He'd started dabbling a bit in what you shouldn't, and not doing anything he didn't want to do.' School punishment records show that Syd was caned for 'absence' on 19 July 1962, just a matter of days before he left school, presumably for these missed exams. The brief notes on the school report card evaluating his final year record that he finished seventh out of twenty in his class, that he was 'V. good at art', 'a good runner' and a member of the scout troop but that he was 'rather undisciplined and casual'.

When Max Barrett died the Cambridge Philharmonic Society set up a music prize at the school in his honour. The speech-day programme for 13 November 1962 shows the first recipient to have been an R. J. Lumb. It also shows that the fifth-form special prize for art was won by 'R. K. Barrett'. Syd didn't show up for the ceremony.

'I'm not actually sure of how smart Syd was academically. But when he left school, he went to the Cambridge Technical College to do his Foundation course and became an extremely interesting painter,' says David Gale. 'I saw him painting, and I saw the ones that he'd already done in his room. Some of them were like thick oil paintings with fabric appliquéd on. Very much influenced by emerging American pop art. I always thought his work was a bit like the work of Jim Dine. He was interested in paint and texture. He would seem to be an industrious painter, who played the guitar for pleasure.'

Bob Klose shares this assessment of Syd's creative priorities. 'When I knew him at school he was an accomplished painter and a primitive guitar player,' he says. David Henderson, who took his pre-diploma course at the Tech at the same time as Syd, has a similar view. 'I was much more aware of him as an artist than I was of his music, his art was much more evident, but because it was a Foundation Course there wasn't much room for individual movement in style. It was very much an introduction, more about learning than producing.'

During this period Syd continued to paint diligently, producing work in a variety of styles as he attempted to find his own. However, he found the course rather pedestrian. The real action it seems was in the college refectory. 'The whole social life at the Tech revolved around the canteen,' remembers fellow student John De Bruyne. 'Classes were a maddening interruption to the social life.'

De Bruyne, an old Etonian who forsook his place at the most prestigious school in the country for the bohemian life of the Tech, was initially friendly with David Gilmour who had also enrolled at the college to take (and subsequently fail) his English and French A levels. 'Very middle-class and well behaved,' remembers John De Bruyne. 'We became best mates. I had use of a car, a Vauxhall Victor Estate. David had passed his test first go, and he was always borrowing it to go to gigs. Then I discovered he was borrowing it to see a girl in Linton, who I was going out with too. I thought, "Hang on a minute!" '

De Bruyne's first memory of Syd was of a boy with 'curly hair, tight blue trousers, and posing like anything. He looked like a little angel. He could have been gay by his presentation. Wonderful eyes and up for mischief. There was something special about him, and the thing was he knew it. He would always be holding court at some table.'

Syd and David Gilmour became regular fixtures in the college canteen or basement common-room, the two teenagers enthusiastically trading Chuck Berry licks as they honed their guitar technique. John De Bruyne's assessment of Syd's talents echoes everybody else's at that time. 'My judgement was that he was an artist who did a bit of music.'

Technical colleges in the early 1960s were a fertile environment for experimentation, as influential in their way as art schools. The further education system was full of public school dropouts, ex-grammar school pupils who either hadn't made the grade or couldn't abide the strictures of the sixth form, and council estate kids who had somehow survived the secondary modern school system with their enthusiasm and intelligence undiminished.

In such an informal environment Syd was in his element. 'You'd come into the room and you'd be happy that he was there at the table,' says John De Bruyne. 'All he'd want was a cue from you and then he would just go off on it. We all did Peter Cook impressions, that E. L. Wisty voice and language. And there was a store man in the art school who was a pure E. L. Wisty character. One day Syd came in tremendously excited and said, "I've got an exam today Johnny, and I tried to get some paint." The store man used to hate giving out paint, they were all locked in his cupboard. But Syd needed this paint. Wisty the store man said to him, "I shouldn't tell you this but I'll let you into a secret. It's a fish." Syd said, "What's a fish?" He said, "The still life. It's a fish. And it's grey. You only need grey." And he handed him this pot of grey paint. Syd said, "Well, what about the eyes." And he said, "OK, I'll give you a dash of red." Syd thought this was wonderful. He had phases after that where everything he was doing was grey. He'd just repeat, "It's grey," in this E. L. Wisty voice.'

De Bruyne began socialising with Syd outside of college too, where he was equally up for fun. 'He was on top of a wardrobe once at a party, rolling his own cigarettes with incredible precision. And he said, "Do you think God rolls his own cigarettes?" I said, "No, I don't think he has any need does he?" And then the whole wardrobe came forward really slowly. I said, "Why don't you jump off?" and he said, "I thought I'd go down with the ship." It caused much more damage with him on top than it would have done if he'd just jumped off.'

Other stunts were even more inventive. 'One day we were walking up East Road and there was the army recruiting office,' remembers De Bruyne. 'Syd goes in. I followed. He said, "I want to join the army." So he filled in this form and the chap said, "Oh, you could be an officer." And Syd said, "I want to drive tanks. I want to take the exam. And my friend here wants to take the exam." Before we knew it we are in the back office taking this exam. We got three guineas each. We could have been dragged off, had our hair cut and put in a barracks. And then Syd saw this list where these army recruiting offices were and he said, "John, we could hitch-hike round the country taking exams. We'd have enough for a bed every night." He'd go off on these flights of fantasy. There was a very zany side to him that was quite unusual then. He'd latch on to a fantasy and then live it for a week. He was going to be a professional army exam taker!'

In a similar vein, he was intrigued by a parking-bay sign in the college car park that read 'Staff Cars Only'. Syd urged De Bruyne to use his family connections to find a military staff car, 'preferably German, or even a tank', and drive it into the college car park. Sadly De Bruyne could only manage a Daimler.

By now Syd's social scene had begun to revolve increasingly around an extended network of free and easy households with supportive and tolerant parents. 'Syd's place was very like Seamus's,' remembers Andrew Rawlinson. 'You had a boy and a doting mother and the doting mother simply allowed the boy to bring everybody home. The same was true of Roger Waters and Storm. All these teenage boys just piling in there.'

'I used to go up to his house on Hills Road on Sunday afternoons,' remembers Nigel Lesmoir-Gordon. 'It was very free and easy up at Syd's mum's. Open house. As it was at Storm's place in Earl Street. Storm's mother, Vanji, was so cool. Used to let us all in. You could hang out there as much as you wanted. Smoking dope. Listening to the Rolling Stones' first album over and over again.'

'Syd's place was the place to go for "Sunday joint". That's what we used to call it and take great glee in telling our parents that's where we were going and they'd go, "Oh, how nice," ' says Libby.

'Syd was quite an independent guy,' recalls David Gale. 'He was very well liked but there was something private there, something, possibly because he felt quite entitled, because of the sort of reverence he would get, 'cos of his looks and personality. He didn't seem to join any one particular group, but he used to move between them all. So we all regarded him as our friend. I think you'd find if you spoke to Seamus O'Connell and Andrew Rawlinson, who were at school with him, that they would amplify that as well. This slightly curious question of who did he hang with? I suspect we thought we hung with him, but he was quite independent in a way.'

'He could be very untrusting of people,' says John De Bruyne. 'Very picky about his friends. He didn't not make friends because he was shy. He knew who he wanted to be bothered with. He would just ward off people he didn't like. He used to say to me, "Johnny you do suffer fools." You sometimes had to work quite hard at him.'

This mercurial aspect to Syd's character was something that many others noticed too. 'Syd was soft and malleable, not in a negative sense but because he could adapt,' says Andrew Rawlinson. 'I think he was extremely Protean. He could take on many forms. For him that was freedom. For some people taking on forms is a hollowness. They take on the form because they don't have any original juice. In my view Syd did have original juice but it was multifaceted. He was a painter and musician and he was very, very quick. Life worked for Syd. He could make things. And boom it happened. And he was a very good-looking boy of course. The girls loved him.'

'He loved nature, which was extremely boring for me,' says Libby. 'I'd take something to read or we'd have a picnic by ourselves. The day out would be to go and do something like that in the countryside. We often went to Gog Magog. That was one of his favourites. He thought they were beautiful. One day we drove all the way to Richmond Park and he sat in the park with the deer and the trees. Now I look back and think what a lovely boy to have wanted to do that. Nobody else wanted to do that.'

Syd displayed the same intense focus when he and Libby visited London art galleries together. 'He liked the Tate more than the National Gallery but we did go to both. He liked old masters as well as anything innovative. I just used to go, and think, "Yeah that's all right," but he'd stand and look at the paintings for ages. I'd think it was a bit of a drag. Oh goodness! Let's go to the cafeteria where we can go and smoke and sit with all the interesting people. He was far happier looking at the paintings. He would sit for hours looking at one painting. The coffee was just something you did afterwards. Art galleries at that time were full of poseurs but he wasn't. With him it wasn't put on.'

Another trip to London with John De Bruyne was equally revealing about Syd's character. 'I was talking to him about why I'd left Eton and he said, "I want to see it." So we got in my Vauxhall and drove up there. I went to my old house and he was fascinated by it. He said, "This is heaven on earth. Why didn't you stay?" I took him down to the art school. The guy running it was Wilfrid Blunt, the brother of the disgraced Anthony Blunt. In fact, the term I left I won the drawing prize, and it was given to me by Anthony Blunt. I was told by my friend, "Don't have tea with him." I must have been so unappetising. No pass was made at me. There was something monk-like about Syd and Eton appealed to him enormously. He said, "You have your own room? And you can come into this art school and walk into Windsor. Why would you leave all this and go to Tech?" He thought the dress was a hoot too.'

Syd would soon move up to London permanently to take up a place at Camberwell Art College. His formal interview, to his utter dismay, took place on 26 November 1963, the very day that the Beatles played at the Regal Cinema in Cambridge. 'I went to see the Beatles on his tickets,' remembers Libby. 'I took my sister, because he had his Camberwell interview, which was dreadful for him. Then he got tickets for somebody else, could have been the Beatles again, and I took somebody I really liked. I took a chap who was cavalry twills, quite a handsome boy, I'd always quite liked him. Syd came to meet me outside and because I'd taken my sister the first time he assumed I'd take her again. He was furious.'

In the period between his final year at school and moving to London in September 1964 Syd made his first tentative steps towards performing in public. In 1962 he briefly joined the band of a County School contemporary, Geoff Mottlow, called Geoff Mott and the Mottoes. The band featured Mottlow on vocals, Syd on rhythm guitar, one of Syd's early 'tutors', Nobby Clarke, on lead guitar, Clive Welham on drums and Tony Sainty on bass.

They often rehearsed at Syd's house, and performed a repertoire of rock 'n' roll and Shadows covers. Welham and Sainty, along with Syd's old school friend John Gordon, would subsequently go on to form Jokers Wild with David Gilmour. From the summer of 1963 through to early 1965 Syd was also an occasional member of the equally occasional Those Without, playing bass and later lead guitar alongside Steve Pyle on drums and Alan Sizer and 'Smudge' on guitars. Those Without played a selection of R & B cover versions by Jimmy Reed, Bo Diddley, Chuck Berry, the Animals and the Rolling Stones.

It is debatable, despite what some previous accounts have claimed, whether Syd had written any songs at this stage. If he had no one had heard them. He certainly hadn't performed any in public. His 'original juice' as Andrew Rawlinson called it was still most clearly evident in his painting.

In September 1964 the painter man moved to London.

Chapter Two

Watching Buttercups Cup the Light

On either side of them, as they glided onwards, the rich meadow-grass seemed that morning of a freshness and a greenness unsurpassable. Never had they noticed the roses so vivid, the willow herb so riotous, the meadow-sweet so odorous and pervading.

THE WIND IN THE WILLOWS KENNETH GRAHAME

'Roger, as he was then, was by far the most glamorous person at Camberwell,' remembers painter and sculptress Maggi Hambling, a contemporary of Syd on his Dip AD course at art school. 'I wouldn't even say the most glamorous boy, he was the most glamorous person in the year, boy or girl. I remember the dark curly hair and the intensity of his eyes when he looked at you. He had this ability to really concentrate on you. If you went up to him to say something – even if it was just, "Do you want a cup of tea" – he absolutely gave you his utmost undivided concentration. He was glamour on legs.'

The Diploma in Art and Design at Camberwell, which Syd commenced in September 1964, gave him a new and exciting conceptual framework to operate within, an environment in which he could explore new techniques and hone his craft skills. After the rather pedestrian apprenticeship provided by his two-year pre-diploma course in Cambridge he really began to thrive in the creative atmosphere of the art school.

Syd had originally wanted to get into Chelsea but had been rejected. 'He was devastated when he didn't get into Chelsea,' confirms Libby Gausden. 'He got turned down at St Martins as well. The two big ones.' This turned out to be a blessing.

'Apart from the Royal College, the Slade and the Royal Academy, Camberwell was the top art school,' says Maggi Hambling. 'It was really terrific to get in there. The first year was run by Dick Lee. The painter Adrian Berg nicknamed him Baden Powell, because he was just like a Scout master. As regards work, after that first year of having to do certain things on certain days, life drawing, art history, all these things, it was freer. I made experimental forays into everything that was going on, pop art, op art, abstract expressionism. American abstract expressionism was the big thing and that's actually the thing that I remember Roger's work being closest to.' Hambling also remembers Adrian Berg setting his students the challenge of drawing in reverse perspective, which she says, 'was totally engrossing and totally impossible to do'.

Jazz saxophonist Stan Willis, another contemporary of Syd's at Camberwell, remembers the college as being one of the few where figurative painting was still encouraged. 'At the Royal College of Art – which would have been one of the top two schools to apply to – I found that every student there was producing large hard-edged abstract paintings, apart from a friend of mine who seemed to be treated as a figure of fun. I also got the impression that in all London Dip AD schools, apart from Camberwell, figurative art was not taken seriously. Camberwell had the excellent painter Robert Medley as principal and several other impressive figurative painters on the staff. I remember Roger producing slightly romantic "painterly" figure paintings.'

Syd's old Cambridge friend David Henderson was also now thriving in the creative fervour of the art school, having gained a place at Corsham Art College in Bath. 'For me when I got there it was, "Ah, here we are. This makes sense", whereas everything else prior to that had been not terribly to the point. People thought at a more theoretical level at art school than in other academic disciplines or subject areas.' Henderson, like many of the Cambridge crowd, used to go and stay with Syd when in London. 'I didn't notice anything significant in Syd's work until he was at Camberwell. Then it did become very painterly, very Soutine-ish. Very thick broad paint, very adept. Syd's work had that kind of panache.'

Estonian-born Chaim Soutine (1894–1943) had moved to Paris to study in his teens and was the only French-based expressionist of note. There was an extreme physicality to his canvases utilising what Robert Hughes called 'thick squidgy excited paint'. Although Syd's painting lacked the overt macabre violence of Soutine's more extreme works, there is, in the visual evidence that exists from the time, an undeniable influence in the way he used thick broad brushstrokes.

'Syd was also influenced by Nicolas de Staël who was also a very big influence on Stu Sutcliffe,' maintains Barry Miles. The Russian-born aristocrat de Staël (1914–55) was also influenced by Soutine, and like Soutine worked with thick broad luscious layers of paint, often applied 'impasto', with a palette knife rather than a brush. In his later work in particular de Staël blurred the boundaries between figurative painting and abstraction with blocks of colour that merely suggested their subject matter – beachscapes, reclining nudes, still life studies, etc. – rather than formally represent it. De Staël's paintings, as Denys Sutton of the Whitechapel Gallery put it in 1956, were 'views that exist in the haze of half life which occurs when reality and dreams intermingle'. Unlike Soutine de Staël was a synthetist, more concerned with beauty and harmony than chaos, but again, the influence on Syd's work, and more pertinently on his perception, is undeniable.

Writing about Stu Sutcliffe's art Peter Davies calls the former Beatles bass player 'the sophisticated pasticheur, but it was done so well that he subconsciously developed existing ideas for his own ends'. There was something of the sophisticated pasticheur in Syd too. Like many young artists he was confronting the essential paradox that all young artists face: the more you assimilate of other people's ideas, the sooner you transcend your influences and find your own identity.

'He did these very painterly thick abstract paintings as well as delicate little watercolours and collages,' remembers Maggi Hambling. 'He had a feel for the paint and a feel for colour which is unusual because in art school in my experience – and I was told this by the painter who taught me at Ipswich art school – the boys tend to be good at drawing and the girls good at colour and then the boys pick up on the colour but the girls often don't pick up on the drawing. And when I taught at art schools I found this to be absolutely true, the male side being structure and the female side being colour and emotions. Roger had a very well-developed sense of colour. He was way ahead of the other boys in his use of the paint and colour.'

This feminised side of Syd's personality was evident in other aspects of his creative life too. Photos of him performing with his early bands show an androgynous-looking young man holding his guitar high in the classical or folk-protest style, a million miles from the gunslinger posture adopted by more phallocentric rock and rollers. He would retain this guitar stance throughout his career. These unconsciously adopted, sometimes overtly feminised, traits, like wearing make-up, would also become an integral part of his rock and roll id. 'He used to read *She* magazine at fifteen and *She* at the time was quite innovative,' remembers Libby. 'It was quite risqué for its time. His older sister Ruth must have got it and he got fashion tips and things from that.'

Even his occasional Tech college band, Those Without, had taken their name from a novel by a feminist icon, Françoise Sagan. Sagan, the daughter of a French industrialist, had been born Françoise Quoirez but changed her surname in her teens to that of a character in Proust's *Remembrance of Things Past*. After dropping out of the Sorbonne she wrote her first novel, *Bonjour Tristesse (Hello Sadness)*, which was published in 1954 when she was just eighteen. *Bonjour Tristesse* was made into a Hollywood film (which she hated) and the novel later had a huge influence on the doom-laden ambience and imagery of Paul Simon's 'The Sound of Silence'. Sagan quickly became a spokesperson for disillusioned and rootless youth, as iconic in her way as James Dean or Marlon Brando. She was the embodiment of Left Bank radical chic, hanging out with Sartre, Godard, Hemingway and Henry Miller. She also had her own Parisian posse, La Bande Sagan, with Juliette Greco. Scorned and hated in equal measure by the older generation, she was dubbed Franchise Sagan by *Time* magazine, and the French nationalist politician Jean-Marie Le Pen would later call for the guillotine to be reintroduced just for her. *Those Without Shadows* was Sagan's third novel, published in 1957. Drummer Steve Pyle adapted it for the band name after casually glancing up at the bookshelves of the band's manager – an appropriately literary moniker for a Cambridge-based outfit that indicated just how well even the most run-of-the-mill local beat combo selected its iconography. The feminised band name provided an interesting counterpoint to the machismo of the blues and R&B material that they were performing. Syd would take a similar approach when re-naming the next band he joined.

Syd spent his first year in London lodging in a large house in Stanhope Gardens, Highgate, owned by Mike Leonard, a part-time lecturer at Hornsey College of Art and Regent Street Polytechnic, where Roger Waters was a student. Waters was already a lodger at Stanhope Gardens, having moved to the capital in 1962 to study architecture. At the Regent Street Polytechnic Waters met fellow students Nick Mason and Rick Wright, and, along with Keith Noble, Noble's sister Sheilagh and

Clive Metcalfe, formed a group called Sigma 6, named after Alexander Trocchi's manifesto – Trocchi called it a tactical blue-print – for 'the spontaneous university'. Sigma 6 played a mixture of R&B, blues and pop covers, which included John Lee Hooker's 'Crawling King Snake' and the Searchers' 'Sweets for My Sweet'.

Sigma 6 went through various line-up changes during 1963 and 1964 – Rick Wright's girlfriend and future wife Juliette Gale was the band's singer for a while, belting out passable versions of 'Summertime' and 'Careless Love' – and playing mostly for fun at college functions and private parties. During this period they were also known as the Megadeaths, the Screaming Abdabs and the Abdabs.

Former County school friend Bob Klose joined the band on lead guitar when he, like Syd, moved up to London in September 1964, lodged in Mike Leonard's Highgate house, and enrolled on the architecture course at Regent Street Poly. 'I'd met up with Roger Waters on an Aldermaston march, and had decided to go to college,' says Klose. 'We formulated the idea for the band there and then.' Klose was by far the most accomplished musician in the group and added a degree of competence and a few sophisticated jazz licks to their repertoire. They also acquired a singer called Chris Dennis, a stalwart of the Cambridge music scene who was now with the RAF at Northolt in Middlesex. Dennis's specialities were novelty introductions to the band's blues numbers and a penchant for making Hitler moustaches with his harmonica. His inclusion in the group, and the band's tolerance of his quirks, gives clear indication of just how seriously they were taking their own musical ambitions at this juncture. Eventually it became obvious that Dennis and his 'hilarious' Führer routines had to go. The band members were spared the embarrassment of sacking him when he announced that he was being posted to Bahrain with the RAF.

Syd's induction into the band in the autumn of 1964 did not lead to a sudden transformation in outlook, ambition and repertoire. He was still little more than a rudimentary guitarist and they continued to play R&B covers by the likes of Bo Diddley, Chuck Berry and the Rolling Stones, along with jazz standards like 'How High the Moon', which was performed as an interlude number. What Syd did give them was a new name.

Although occasionally working as the Tea Set (a sly nod to the old jazzers' term for pot-smoking and a campaign slogan of the time, 'Join the tea set', advertising Britain's favourite beverage) Syd had found references to two North Carolina bluesmen, Pink Anderson and Floyd Council, on a record sleeve. Both artists were obscure, even to blues scholars, and there is no evidence that Syd had actually heard recordings by either of them. But his choice of iconography was never less than immaculate and his ultimate bequest to the band, the naming of them, was one of his earliest lyrical masterstrokes.

However oblique or obvious his thought processes may have been, Syd's naming of Pink Floyd was inspired by a creative impulse that springs as much from painting as literature and has its precedents in cubism, surrealism and pop art. The sophisticated word for it is juxtaposition, but really it's just the simple joy of putting things next to each other. Syd merely adapted the collaging of image and textures and applied it to text. It was as effortless as that

Although Syd's relationship with Libby Gausden was more off than on by this point, he still wrote to her regularly throughout 1964 and 1965. 'Did you see the Stones yesterday darling?' he writes in December 1964. 'I thought they were a drag, but I liked Mick's trousers.' Another letter from the same month is equally waspish. ' "Little Red Rooster" is top of the hit parade today and that's marvellous. It just shows how impressive an American tour is to English people.' He also mentions having seen Joyce Grenfell on TV and enthusiastically recites her classic schoolteacher sketch for Libby's benefit. In the same letter he mentions that 'yesterday we did a recording of eight numbers and they're all good enough for an LP'. He gives no further details of the recording but it is most likely that the tape consisted of cover versions recorded for demo purposes, one of the numerous audition tapes the band submitted, unsuccessfully, to music publishers around this time.

'We entered various band contests that were proliferating at the time and didn't do terribly well,' remembers Bob Klose. During 1965 the group failed numerous auditions, including one for the ATV pop programme *Ready Steady Go*, and another to get work as a support act at the club Beat City. They also entered *Melody Maker*'s annual beat contest without success. With the beat group explosion in full swing, several of the music weeklies and most of the offshore pirate radio stations held regular band contests, and although intensely competitive there had arguably never been a better time to make some sort of mark on the scene. Pink Floyd were, by their own admission, part-timers among pros and semi-pros, and simply not up to it. In his auto-biography, Nick Mason remembers being particularly blown away when the Floyd supported a band called the Tridents, featuring Jeff Beck just before he replaced Eric Clapton in the Yardbirds. The gig obviously made a big impression on Syd too, as he writes in a letter to new girlfriend Jenny Spires that the Floyd had just played with 'the best group in the world except for the Stones and Beatles. They are called the Tridents and the lead guitarist looks a bit like Mick Jagger and the drummer is very pretty.' The letter is illustrated with one of Syd's trademark biro drawings of the group. Under Beck (who is drawn incorrectly playing left-handed) Syd writes 'not very good but you get the idea, very thin and pretty with his head down all the time'.

At some point during 1965 Syd made his first tentative foray into writing songs, although just how many, and specifically which ones, has long been a matter for conjecture. In his seminal but factually flawed *NME* profile, 'The Cracked Ballad of Syd Barrett', published in April 1974, Nick Kent suggests that 'he'd come up with a nonsense song called "Effervescing Elephant" when he was maybe sixteen' and had set James Joyce's poem 'Golden Hair' to music. In fact there isn't a shred of evidence to substantiate either of these claims. Despite this, and despite Kent's own wary proviso 'maybe', they have been repeated verbatim, and on occasions considerably embellished, in numerous Barrett biographies for many years.

Drawing upon his own childhood reading, and released on the Barrett album in 1970, 'Effervescing Elephant' was a perfectly executed, metrically precise pastiche of the verse form and macabre twists contained in Hilaire Belloc's 'Cautionary Tales for Children'. The song is full of subtle rhythms and an instinctive feel for pace and scansion. Here, on the other hand is a poem that Syd wrote for Libby Gausden in November 1961, a few weeks before his sixteenth birthday.

> One day I'll hold you close to me
> I'll hug your body close to mine
> We'll love and love and realize
> That, if before we told some lies
> Or kissed some Frogs (whom I despise)
> Or laughed at us, or pushed us down
> Then all these things will leave our minds
> We shall forgive. We will be one
> We'll love like no one has before
> We'll need each other more and more
> You will be mine. I will be yours
> That day is not so far away.

Interestingly enough the poem is metrically identical to 'Effervescing Elephant', indicating that the Belloc influence was already there by the time he was sixteen, and that 'whom I despise' is a nice touch, and typically Syd, but both the vocabulary and the lapses in grammar are more in keeping with the capabilities of a boy in his mid-teens than the mastery of rhyme and nuance that he later reveals in 'Effervescing Elephant'.

The claims for 'Golden Hair' can be similarly dismissed. Syd's plaintive arrangement of the poem indicates a highly developed melodic sensibility, which is completely at odds with the basic musical abilities he displayed in his mid- to late teens. Peter Jenner remembers Syd playing him 'Golden Hair' for the first time during his earliest solo sessions in 1968. Jenner thought, and assumed for many years, that it was an original Syd composition, created during his last days with Pink Floyd. There is no reason, and certainly no first-hand testimony to suggest otherwise.

These simple unsubstantiated assertions, that Syd was writing impeccably crafted and cleverly arranged pop songs when he was sixteen, suggest some Chatterton-esque child prodigy, and all the attendant iconography of doomed youth that goes with it, none of which is borne out by the evidence. In fact, Syd was a relatively late developer as a songwriter. His early efforts were simply the works of a pasticheur, and not a particularly sophisticated one at that.

Biographer Tim Willis compounds this notion of gifted youth in his book *Madcap* where he makes the contentious and utterly misleading assertion that 'Sydologists will be astounded to learn that by '64, Barrett had already written "Let's Roll Another One" as well as two songs called "Butterfly" and "Remember Me".'

This mistake is based on Willis's misreading of Syd's letters to Libby Gausden. He incorrectly attributes a sequence of letters, including one where Syd mentions the above compositions, to December 1964 when the correspondence is in fact from December 1965. This can be verified by Syd's repeated references in the letters to Ichikawa's film of the 1964 Tokyo Olympics, which was released in the UK in September 1965. He also mentions that he is listening to the pirate station Radio London, which did not begin broadcasting until Christmas Eve 1964. The clincher though is Syd's statement 'I still haven't been to the Big L Discotheque.' Radio London's discotheque nights commenced on Friday, 3 December 1965, at 122–4 Charing Cross Road (the site of a former Lyons teahouse which had closed in April 1965.

In the same letter that mentions 'Let's Roll Another One', 'Butterfly' and 'Remember Me', Syd confesses to Libby that he has very little faith in his musical and vocal abilities, and states, 'Emo says why don't I give up 'cos it sounds horrible and I would, but I can't get Fred to join because he's got a group (p'raps you knew!) so I still have to sing.' 'Emo' was Cambridge friend Ian Moore. 'Fred' was a nickname for none other than David Gilmour, whose own group Jokers Wild was making a living of sorts performing Four Seasons and Beach Boys covers at this time. Willis and subsequent writers have made significant capital out of the notion that Syd wanted David Gilmour to join or replace him in the band in December 1964, when the sentiment was expressed in late 1965. In fact restoring Syd's confession to its correct date, late 1965, makes his apparent lack of confidence in his musical skills even more striking. Just over a year later he would be in the pop charts.

While 'Butterfly' and 'Remember Me' have both disappeared without trace, an adapted version of 'Let's Roll Another One' eventually re-emerged as 'Candy and a Currant Bun', the B-side of the first Pink Floyd single 'Arnold Layne'. In its original form it was a brazenly unambiguous and unsubtle paean to the joys of dope-smoking. Taking its riff from Howlin' Wolf's 'Smokestack Lightning' it boasted lines like: 'I'm high | don't try to spoil my fun | don't cry | we'll have another one.' It also included a wry lyrical nod to Syd's schooldays. In 1962 the County school's tuck shop, on the advice of the school's dental officer, had banned the sale of sweets and ordered that only nuts and currant buns could be sold.

Another song referred to in Syd's letters to Libby, 'Walk With Me Sydney', was a Roger Waters composition that took its title from Hank Ballard and the Midnighters' 'Work With Me Henry'. 'Walk With Me Sydney' was a novelty number, which Waters had written for Syd and Juliette Gale to sing. With its gauche and gimmicky lyrics it wouldn't have been out of place in the average university revue of the time. Its inclusion in the band's repertoire in 1965 speaks volumes about their lack of scope and ambition.

Although considerably more witty, Syd's own pastiches were no more sophisticated or ambitious in outlook. 'I have written a song about Bob Dylan. Yeah yeah. Soul. God, etc.,' he writes to Jenny Spires in 1965. 'It starts off "I got the Bob Dylan blues and the Bob Dylan shoes and my hair an' my clothes in a mess but you know I just couldn't care less". In fact a bit satirical and humorous. Ho! Ha! Hee! Tee!'

From its nuances and reference points 'Bob Dylan Blues' is evidently Syd's response to the first wave of Dylan worship that accompanied the singer's visit to England in 1964. 'He took me to see Dylan for my birthday present,' remembers Libby Gausden. 'We arrived at the South Bank and he said, "Look, it's the me and you from every town." We all looked exactly the same.'

Aside from the sheer childish glee of rhyming 'I'm a poet' with 'Don't you know it', 'Bob Dylan Blues' is an arch and knowing little number, which sends up the Dylan phenomenon and the trappings of fame. The song's lyrics allude to several Dylan titles including 'Blowin' in the Wind', 'Girl of the North Country', 'Down the Highway', 'Masters of War', 'Bob Dylan's Blues', 'A Hard Rain's Gonna Fall', and 'Bob Dylan's Dream', all of which appear on *The Freewheelin' Bob Dylan* album which was released in the UK in the spring of 1964.

Living in Highgate and having to make the long trek to Camberwell every day meant that Syd wasn't a regular attender at art college. In one letter to Libby he complains about having to get up before everybody else in the house to get to college. ('I got up earlier than all the others as usual and got out by eight. Guffaw! Guffaw! Eight!') In another he mentions, in arch and infantilised tones, that he is thinking of transferring to Hornsey. 'When I went to Camberwell this morning they said run away because they said I went to Hornsey, but Hornsey said I didn't yet, but I have got an interview tomorrow or Wednesday, so I only hope they accept me, otherwise I believe plumbing is a very steady job.'

'Syd was actually a bit detached from the college,' confirms Stan Willis. 'He lived across the river with his band and wasn't about in the evenings. But in the daytime he fitted in easily, was well liked and didn't seem to have any ego to throw around. If he hadn't become famous I would still remember him as the most charming character of the year.'

During his first year at Camberwell Syd was still getting much of his cultural input in his home town. 'He went back to Cambridge quite a lot,' remembers Maggi Hambling. 'And because of the music he wasn't exactly a daily attender so I don't think any of us got to know him terribly well. He was just this dark angel who would appear and produce an attractive painting and then disappear again.'

Many of the Cambridge crowd continued to return to their home city regularly to enjoy the rich cultural life on offer. There were three art cinemas showing the best of the European new wave and at the Cambridge Union building behind the Round Church Nigel Lesmoir-Gordon, William Pryor and Andrew Rawlinson were putting on regular Happenings. These events, although basically exercises in emulation and homage, drew upon an impressively avant-garde legacy of cut-ups, concrete poetry, action painting, hard bop-jazz and musique concrete for their influences and source material.

'We were copying what we'd read,' says Rawlinson. 'I'd never been to a Happening. I've only ever put one on. Nigel and William were the aspiring poets. Cage and Rauschenberg were the influences. I remember going to the Rauschenberg exhibition in London. Those big screens he used to do of JFK and the astronauts. Fantastic stuff. The painted bed and the goat with the tyre round its stomach. We'd never seen anything like that.'

In the 1940s Robert Rauschenberg had studied at Black Mountain College in North Carolina under the Bauhaus émigré Josef Albers. Here he befriended pianist and composer John Cage. The two men were united by a desire to break down the barriers between art and life and this shared philosophy would subsequently have a massive influence on performance art, modern dance and many of the mixed media experiments of the early 1960s. Like most of his contemporaries Syd visited the major Rauschenberg exhibition that took place at the Whitechapel Gallery in London during February and March 1964, where he would have seen many of the exhibits that Rawlinson refers to above: the Kennedy canvas (*Retroactive 1*, 1964), the painted bed (*Bed*, 1955) and the Duchampian goat with the tyre round its stomach (*Monogram*, 1955–9). Rauschenberg's silkscreen assemblages, which juxtaposed strikingly iconic found images (dead presidents, coke bottles, the space race, etc.) with abstract expressionistic drips and smears, began to influence Syd's art directly around this time.

During this same period Andrew Rawlinson performed a concrete poetry Happening called 'Rose Machine Buddha' with Bob Cobbing, which was broadcast on the BBC Third Programme. Cobbing is another integral figure in the development of the English counter-culture. He was the poetry underground before there was a poetry underground and was doing cut-ups at least three years before Brion Gysin and William Burroughs adopted and adapted the technique. In 1963 he started a publishing outlet called Writers Forum, doing monographs of poetry in runs of 1,000, mostly by British beat poets, who couldn't get their work published through mainstream outlets. Writers Forum also facilitated regular meeting places whereby cultural renegades could get together and read and discuss their work in an atmosphere which Jeff Nuttall described in *Bomb Culture* as 'that odd mixture of middle-class liberalism and flat out mad', terminology that might equally be applied to the British counter-culture per se.

When Cobbing took over the running of Better Books, the independent bookshop in London's Charing Cross Road started by Tony Godwin in 1948 which had done so much to promote the Angry Young Men generation of playwrights and novelists, he engendered a similar collaborative atmosphere. Old beats, new beats, dead beats, performance artists, prophets, and pissheads alike gathered in the alternative bookshop's proto-Arts Lab atmosphere to put on readings, art installations, and mixed media Happenings.

Cobbing's own experiments with sound poetry and audio-concrete played with visual puns, palindromes, anagrams, phonetics and typography. Syd assimilated all of this eagerly. Another conceptual framework. Another vocabulary. Another set of possibilities to be assembled, disassembled, rearranged.

'Syd was open to everything at that time,' states Andrew Rawlinson, 'but his natural genius was popular. I don't mean, "I'm going to be popular." I just think he could pick up on the best quality of popular culture. He would always prefer the Beatles to John Cage. His natural direction was that which is immediate, in the best sense of the word. He worked in the immediate context, but was hugely transformative of it because that's how he was. My thing was, "There's something right over there that I like the look of. Think I'll go over there and have a look." Whereas stuff came to Syd. I don't think he went looking particularly. But, of course, there was a lot about so he didn't miss much!'

Another of Rawlinson's participatory ventures at this time was based on a idea borrowed from painter Jasper Johns who had painted over a map of the USA sent to him by Robert Rauschenberg in 1960. 'I did one where I took a map of the world and traced out all the countries,' explains Rawlinson. 'Then I sent the shape of the United States to someone and Canada to someone else and Brazil to someone else and said decorate these any way you want and then send them back to me, and I stuck them back on the map. I sent Syd Russia and he painted it blue and sent it back.'

In a similar spirit of reciprocity he sent Syd a Marvel comics collage. What Syd sent back, largely unprompted, was twelve sides of A4 artwork pasted and mounted on brown card. Entitled *Fart Enjoy*, the work documents Syd's artistic development at this time in all its uneven glory. His debt to Rauschenberg is clearly evident in both the brushwork and the method of collage. Hugely influential in this respect were a pair of near-identical Rauschenberg artworks from 1957 called *Factum I* and *Factum II*, a combine painting in oil, ink, pencil, crayon, paper, fabric, newspaper, printed reproductions and painted paper on canvas; these had a tangible effect both on Syd's technique and on his choice of found material. Much of Rauschenberg's work was witty and personalised and he thought nothing of utilising strikingly bad visual puns. His 1956 work *Gloria*, for instance, includes a newspaper headline 'Gloria weds third time' alongside a photo of Gloria Vanderbilt reproduced three times. Much of *Fart Enjoy* has the same playfulness about it, from the crude wordplay of the booklet's title to the porn-mag photo of a topless woman encrypted with toilet-wall graffiti daubs. Accompanying the photo is a Cobbing-style concrete poem playing with the typographic possibilities of the words 'Boys', 'Fuck' and 'Girl.'

Typed across the top of another page of Rauschenbergian smears, another Cobbing-influenced text reads:

Topical . . . Typical . . . Mr Heath . . . Mr Wilson
   Typical . . . Topical . . . Tip Up . . . Political . . . Joke Grimace

Aside from the obvious nod to Bob Cobbing this is probably the nearest that Syd ever came to making anything that remotely resembled a political statement, assuming one discounts the Aldermaston march that he went on with Libby – 'but had to give up at Slough because of blisters,' she remembers.

Also evident throughout *Fart Enjoy* is the delicate feminised sense of coloration that Maggi Hambling noticed at Camberwell. This is complemented by a series of distinctive and original cartoon figures that suggest Syd could easily have made a living as an illustrator of children's books.

The other main component of *Fart Enjoy* is cut-ups. These are directly utilised on seven of the booklet's twelve pages. They range from extracts lifted from R. D. Laing's *The Divided Self* to more subtle word montages which play with vocabulary drawn variously from the Bible, art history books, teen pop magazines and fashion magazines. Another page collages words and images from a promotional pamphlet for the recently built Post Office Tower, while another cuts up a wild flower guide, a botany text book and Beatrix Potter's *The Tale of Mr Jeremy Fisher*.

Children's literature is also utilised in two pages of cut-up nursery rhymes. One reads:

      Sprat Locket Patch Lift The Latch.
      Johnny Shall Have A New Bonnet
The other reads:
      Hark! Jack Was Diddlty Dumpty
        All Jolly
      To Market To Buy A Plum Cake

The former is accompanied by a drawing of a three-headed creature (turkey, pig and cockerel?) which mimics the style of Edward Lear's animal grotesques. The letters ABC are stencilled across it – a reference to Cobbing's recently published 'ABC In Sound'. The latter is accompanied by a drawing of a rouge-cheeked boy wearing green cap, shorts, sandals and a blue T-shirt.

These cut-ups are composites of eight rhymes: 'Hark! Hark! The Dogs Do Bark', 'Little Jack Horner', 'Diddlty Diddlty Dumpty', 'We're All Jolly Boys', 'To Market to Market to Buy a Plum Cake', 'Lucy Locket Lost her Pocket', 'Cross Patch Draw the Latch' and 'Johnny Shall Have a New Bonnet'. Syd took these rhymes from   Kate Greenaway's illustrated *Mother Goose* anthology, where they comprise eight of the first twelve rhymes in the book.

The first edition of Greenaway's pocket book was published in 1881 and contained fifty-four pages of colour chromolithograph illustrations and rhymes. It ran into numerous reprints. Many households of Syd's generation would have had one of the many *Mother Goose* anthologies that had been in circulation since folklorists began collecting nursery rhymes during the Victorian era. These rhymes, frequently dark and macabre in tone, and the lavish illustrations that accompanied them, burned their way into many a young child's imagination. Nursery rhymes in general, and the *Mother Goose* rhymes in particular, were integral to Syd's development as a songwriter. His use of them in the *Fart Enjoy* booklet gives us the first indication of the centrality of childhood motifs to his work, and they would become a common thematic thread in his lyrics for Pink Floyd. The way they are utilised in *Fart Enjoy* suggests that Syd, transforming whatever materials he had at his disposal and working, as Andrew Rawlinson put it, 'in the immediate context', was now beginning to develop a highly inventive approach to language to match the sophisticated touch and technique of his painting.

There was nothing rigorous or methodical about it. Syd simply used whatever was available, in this instance a pocket book of nursery rhymes, and deconstructed it.

Shortly after Syd sent his artwork to Andrew Rawlinson, Pink Floyd entered the studio again. Recorded in down time at Regent Sound studios where an engineer friend of Rick Wright's worked, five tracks were put down on demo tape – 'Lucy Leave', 'I'm a King Bee', 'Double O Bo', 'Butterfly' and 'Remember Me' – only the first two of which have survived on acetate. 'Double O Bo' was a John Barry/James Bond pastiche set to a Bo Diddley beat, in the same gimmicky vein as the Who's 'Bucket T'. Like 'Butterfly' and 'Remember Me', it has long since disappeared.

Of the two tracks that have survived, 'I'm a King Bee' is a somewhat pedestrian version of the old Slim Harpo track covered by the Rolling Stones on their debut album. The recording is most notable for Syd's convincingly droll pastiche of Mick Jagger's pseudo-classless vowels. 'Lucy Leave', also known as 'Lucy Lea in Blue Tights', is a stranger beast altogether. Musically it is as derivative as everything else the band was playing at this time, taking its cue from Pretty Things tracks like 'Midnight to Six' and 'Buzz the Jerk'. Bob Klose plays a passable solo, but the rest of the musicianship is mediocre and Syd is an unconvincing lead vocalist, delivering his lyrics in a forced and strangulated manner.

Syd presumably shared this assessment of his own abilities, as a letter he wrote to Jenny Spires in the summer of 1965 telling her about the session echoes the insecurities he revealed in his letters to Libby Gausden around the same time. 'We recorded five numbers more or less straight off, but only the guitars and drums,' he begins brightly. 'We're going to add all the singing and piano next Wednesday. The tracks sound terrific so far, especially "King Bee". When I sing I have to stand in the middle of the studio with earphones on, and everyone else watches from the other room, and I can't see them at all, but they can all see me.

Also I can only just hear what I'm singing.'

Enclosed with the letter is a biro sketch of the band and the studio layout. Accompanying the drawing of himself singing is a black box denoting the studio room and the caption 'everyone is in here larfing'.

Despite his own misgivings, the lyrics to 'Lucy Leave' reveal Syd's unique songwriting talents for the first time. Commencing with a frenetically delivered 'Leave', that isn't so much sung as howled, the song is an unsettling and disjointed ditty, far removed from the machismo and surliness that characterised most British R&B of the time. The song's sentiments leap randomly from line to line, conveying rejection ('Leave when I ask you to leave, Lucy'), dream-like disengagement ('Please fall away from me, Lucy'), misery ('Seeing as I'm so broken up about you, Lucy'), blues parody ('Mean treating me and done me harm, Lucy') and English poesy ('Been in love with you and your charms, Lucy'). When he expresses confinement and claustrophobia ('You got my heart, you got my heart, oh no, you tear me apart, you just won't let me go, you hold on so tight, so tight I just can't breathe') he does so in a way that verges on despair. The whole thing feels slightly out of sync with the norm. No English R&B song of the time would have included the word 'charms'. No English pop song of the time would have utilised the faintly hallucinatory refrain, 'Please fall away from me'. But then again, by the summer of 1965 something more than faintly hallucinatory had entered and refreshed Syd's repertoire.

When Dr Albert Hoffman wibbled home from work on his bicycle one day in April 1943 having synthesised and accidentally ingested a potent new hallucinogen, which he classified as lysergic acid diethylamide-25, he inadvertently set into motion a chain of events that would have a seismic effect on the development of pop culture in the mid-1960s. Aldous Huxley had given mind-altering drugs intellectual, theological and philosophical credence. His mescaline co-pilot Dr Humphrey Osmond had synthesised the words 'psyche' and 'delirium' and given the world the term psychedelic. In the 1950s the CIA and military intelligence had attempted to use LSD as a truth serum and chemical agent of interrogation and mind control through a programme called project MKULTRA, and the American medical establishment had utilised it for psychiatric and therapeutic treatment on everyone from prisoners, schizophrenics and war veterans to stressed businessmen and student volunteers at Menlo Park Laboratory and UCLA. By 1963 behavioural psychologist Timothy Leary had been ostracised by the scientific establishment and had left his job at Harvard to set up his orbiting space-station on earth at Millbrook in New York State. In 1964 original Menlo Park acid-test volunteer Ken Kesey and his gang of Merry Pranksters painted an old school bus in day-glo colours and set off with original beat Neal Cassady in tow to turn on America. By 1965 enough pure liquid LSD – and its formula – had leaked out of the Sandoz laboratory in Basel to trip out the entire planet. The genie was literally out of the bottle.

'This extraordinary man, John Esam, used to come round to 101 Cromwell Road,' remembers Nigel Lesmoir-Gordon. 'I'd never heard of lysergic acid. He said you should try this substance. So John was our link into LSD. He was a friend of Michael Hollingshead who was getting the LSD from Timothy Leary who was getting it from the Sandoz Laboratory and the acid that came through 101 was the business, the absolute best.'

LSD soon found its way to Cambridge. Indeed, pretty soon the stuff was being discreetly synthesised in the university's research laboratories. Most of the Cambridge crowd were enthusiastic dope-smokers; indeed, many of the places they hung out were determined by whose host, or parents, had the most benign or blind-eyed attitude towards joint-rolling. Acid brought something else entirely to the party. With acid you lay all your psychological chips on the table. All barriers were down, all floodgates open. Acid disintegrated will and ego, warped perception, blurred the boundaries between fantasy and reality, synthesised the senses, divided the self into microcosmic particles, located the universe in a grain of sand. Even psilocybin, Michael Hollingshead had told an initially sceptical Timothy Leary, was a house cat compared to the roaring lion of lysergic acid.

'I think because we were not ready for it we were very disorganised,' says poet Spike Hawkins. 'All these things were new to everybody. Everything was happening at such a rapid pace. The multicoloured cake of the universe just went thwwwwp, zow, slap!'

'We were softened up by cannabis, of course,' admits David Gale, 'but even a few spliffs is nothing compared to the holocaust of acid. People were taking LSD in what these days are regarded as so-called "heroic doses". It was considered common to take 500 micrograms – which is a double dose in some people's current estimation. And there was no "mucking about" with that dosage – it just came in like a tsunami, erased all resistance to just tinsel and moved through you – and the idea of putting up a fight was ridiculous.'

'I would spend hours crumpling and uncrumpling tissues and seeing the birth and death of the universe. Or cut an orange in half and see eternity,' says Nigel Lesmoir-Gordon. 'Amphetamines and pot and heroin didn't come anywhere, compared to that, they were just not in the same league. I thought that my pot-smoking and experiences of alternative states would prepare me for LSD, it did not.'

'I thought, my god, I can think and fly in five dimensions,' says Spike Hawkins. 'I was writing in the sky with my finger. I looked up at the stars. Remember those very old maps of the star system with faces painted on them? Suddenly the sky looked like that. There were five people with me. An assortment of actors and writers. I said, "In two minutes a giant eagle is going to fly out of that clock." Everyone tried to find a watch. And yeah, a giant eagle did fly out of the clock!'

'The best quote I know on the subject comes from Jerry Garcia,' says Andrew Rawlinson. 'He said, "What I got from my first trip was that my little personal fiction was just that. It was a fiction." It was Aldous Huxley made real. All the stuff that Huxley wrote about in *The Doors of Perception* was confirmed by LSD.'

Even though there had been considerable cultural accord between the 1950s and 1960s generations of pharmaceutical voyagers, the arrival of drugs like LSD caused a massive schism between the beats and the coming hippie generation. While Allen Ginsberg was a proselytiser for acid, Jack Kerouac famously dismissed hallucinogens after one psilocybin trip with the words, 'Walking on water wasn't built in a day.' Burroughs too railed against psychedelic drug-users and their accompanying theology, which he referred to witheringly as 'all that west coast Vedantist horseshit'. 'I saw Burroughs at a party in London and he said, "You people have got to stop taking this LSD," ' remembers Nigel Lesmoir-Gordon. 'He was still pumping himself up with heroin. He wasn't on the acid scene at all and didn't get it.'

Acid was embraced enthusiastically by almost all of the Cambridge crowd and it wove its way into the common fabric. 'It became absolutely essential to get it and to take it,' said David Gale. 'Syd took acid at that time in Cambridge, and had a perfectly OK time.'

'LSD was obviously a key turning point for Syd,' maintains Anthony Stern, who had been one of the original Cambridge acid pioneers, having taken the drug for the first time in 1963. 'The discovery of the brilliance of his own subconscious, I'm sure that's what it was. He discovered how absolutely fascinating the inside, the interior world really was – the colours, the movements, the things spiralling – the constant breaking up and fractal imagery all happening at the same time.'

'Alan Watts wrote a book about taking LSD called *The Joyous Cosmology*,' says Andrew Rawlinson. 'We'd all read it and I said to them all, "What do you reckon?", and Nick Sedgwick, who was a big mate of Roger Waters, said, "Well, actually, I think listening to everybody else talking about their trips is quite as interesting as reading Alan Watts," and Nick was a fan of Watts. And I think that was one of the things about that period for us, it was discovery with a small group, and an interesting group. If you look at Storm's group you haven't just got grammar school boys. You've also got Emo [Ian Moore] and Pip [Pip Carter]. They were Cambridge lads. The educational system did not favour their particular talents. As far as we were concerned they pulled their weight completely.'

Ian 'Emo' Moore and Pip Carter both came from rough and ready – in Emo's case violent and abusive – working-class house-holds. Both were quick-witted no-bullshit merchants, and fully paid-up hedonists who were an essential part of the Cambridge group dynamic. Court jesters and ego deflators in unison.

'I remember being in Storm's room with five or six other people, either coming down off a trip or very stoned, I can't remember, but I noticed the pattern,' observed Rawlinson. 'Someone like Nick Sedgwick would say something and some-body else would pick it up and embellish it. The tickover rate would go up and it would go up through Dave Gale, who is a very fast-thinking fast-speaking funny man. It would be lifting up and then suddenly at the end Emo would come in and the whole room would explode with laughter. What I always noticed was Emo needed the build-up. The group dynamic was very powerful. We needed somebody to start things off. We needed an embellisher. We needed somebody to take it a bit surreal and we needed a final witticism. I'm sure all groups of friends have dynamics that are similar. We had a good one and it was at a time when we were discovering things and society was changing.

Which is why in the memory of the Cambridge group it's very strong. You're the right age. You're absorbing a huge amount and the group itself is absorbing as a group. And it works.'

Syd had a natural affinity with Emo and Pip and loved them for their quick and savage wit. Where he fitted into the group dynamic was another matter entirely. 'Syd wasn't really a group man,' concedes Andrew Rawlinson. 'That's not to say he was against it. It's just that there are people for whom participating in the group is in itself a kind of buzz, and he wasn't like that. Plus when he was with women he got something that he wasn't going to get from a load of blokes, much as he was friends with them.'

Another friend who wished to remain anonymous confirmed this. 'I went round to his house one day and he said, "Listen to this," and he played a tape and it was Syd and his girlfriend fucking. He said, "It was her idea." Well, if you're doing your music and your painting and you've got women like that you've got a pretty full bag before you start.'

'He reminded me metaphorically of David Hume, the philosopher,' says Andrew Rawlinson. 'Hume said, "When I've had enough of philosophy I go and play a bit of billiards." And I think Syd was like that. When he wanted a bit of company he would join in but then he would go back to his own place. Most of us at that time were exploring in the company of others but Syd didn't have to do that.'

'He struck me as someone who was very sensitive,' notes Maggi Hambling. 'Wild, but very sensitive. He was actually a terribly nice person. A generous, kind person. If you'd run out of money for a cup of tea or anything he'd give it to you if he'd got it. But he was sort of like on his own. When he came in he'd go straight to his painting and do it. He wasn't naturally a jolly social person. He was much more in a world of his own. He was very easy to talk to if you went up to him but he wouldn't go out of his way to be outgoing.'

What is noticeable about this is just how similar it is to descriptions of Max Barrett, remembered by his peers as sensitive, kind, generous, modest, undidactic, unaffected. Like father like son.

It is debatable to what extent Syd's initial acid use seeped into his creativity. Nothing overtly detectable appeared in his painting, there were no Dalíesque dreamscapes, no soft watches. Nor was there a sudden outpouring of songs about space travel, but then Syd was rarely that literal in his motives or his assimilation. It has often been suggested that LSD was the catalyst that transformed Pink Floyd from run of the mill R & B combo to full-tilt sonic explorers. But Syd's band mates were, and largely remained, drug-free, preferring alcohol to the mind-scrambling possibilities of LSD. In fact, the real catalyst for the band's forays into lengthy improvisation was Mike Leonard.

All of Pink Floyd rented rooms in Mike Leonard's house at one time or another; they were even briefly known as Leonard's Lodgers. As well as being their landlord Leonard had a cool jazz record collection, and a fine array of exotic instruments for the group to experiment with. He also had a Siamese kitten called Tunji, named after the Coltrane tune, who, according to Syd's letters to Libby, delighted in sitting on his lap when it wanted to cough up its fur balls. Most importantly it was Leonard who introduced the group to the idea of light shows and mixed media performance.

'He was absolutely seminal,' says Bob Klose. 'He was an architect but not in a suited and bow-tied way. He had a little Farfisa organ and played a bit in the first version of Pink Floyd, but at Hornsey he was doing his light and sound workshop. We used to go up there just for the rehearsal space and on one occasion we were in the space where the light show would go and everyone started noodling away while the lights were flashing. That was a very embryonic version of what eventually became the Pink Floyd sound. That's where the original impulse came from. That sort of lodged in everyone's subconscious.'

Anthony Stern agrees that Mike Leonard's influence was absolutely fundamental, particularly on Syd. 'One of the big changes in Syd's life was when he stopped thinking Bo Diddley was God and started to deconstruct himself a bit, and became much more abstract. And that's all to do with the light show, I think. The light shows with music. I think that was a very important part of Syd's progression. In terms of what to do with your music and how to make it more painterly, or how to make the paintings more musical, that is the key to it. And Mike Leonard, to my mind, is the absolute key. He probably feels pissed off that he wasn't recognised for the contribution he made to Pink Floyd early on. When he was at Hornsey he had this laboratory where they were dreaming up all kinds of wonderful stuff with light shows and light boxes. Now that seems to me a very key point. The history of light boxes is a very interesting subject, and that's where Mike Leonard was coming from. He didn't invent it as such, but he had this sort of light-box workshop thing going on at his house.'

Although constantly underplayed in the Pink Floyd story it was ultimately Mike Leonard's light show, rather than Syd's acid use or any overt musical leanings, that enabled the band's music to develop and deconstruct in the way that it did. It would take time for the technology to become an integral part of Pink Floyd's live act, and just as long for the abstract possibilities to filter through into Syd's thinking and playing. There was no eureka moment, no sudden blinding flash of inspiration, just a gradual evolution. During 1965 the band continued to perform their standard R & B repertoire whenever and wherever they could get a gig. Stan Willis remembers them playing at Camberwell 'as "The Tea Set" or "Rodger's Lodgers" [sic] or one of the other names they were considering', with Leonard's slides projecting moving images over the band, 'the first time I had seen that. But I don't remember them playing much else than blues.'

The one aspect of Anthony Stern's assessment that Bob Klose disagrees with is the jettisoning of the Bo Diddley influence. 'I don't think Syd would ever have thought Bo Diddley was not wonderful. And in a way you can say it's not a discontinuity at all. Bo Diddley was a terrific rhythm player. He was hardly Barney Kessel.'

Between 29 May and 25 June 1964, shortly before he left for London, Syd had participated in a joint exhibition of paintings with Anthony Stern at the Lion and Lamb in Milton, a village near Cambridge. The local newspaper review of Syd's contribution said, 'His prints, monotypes, and drawings are slight, but necessary student exercises, but in two still lives, a landscape and two convincing portraits he is already showing himself a sensitive handler of oil paint who wisely limits his palette to gain richness and density.'

The second half of that review was both prescient and perceptive. As the *Fart Enjoy* booklet and his early song pastiches show, 'limiting his palette to gain richness and density' was something that Syd readily adapted to his wordplay. Instead of doing what most aspiring writers do, utilising a wide and intricate vocabulary in order to impress, Syd used cut-ups, found objects, nursery rhymes, restricting his emotional and verbal palette and submitting it to the dictates of form. Eventually he began applying this approach to his guitar playing too. In short, he stopped worrying about technique.

'You only ever really need enough to play what your musical vision is and I don't think he ever pursued the athletic physical thing particularly assiduously,' notes Bob Klose. 'But you need to get all that in fairly early. I was influenced by people like Django Reinhardt, and developed a fairly reasonable technique fairly young, and a lot of people didn't do that. But I think Syd made a virtue of necessity. He wasn't interested in playing sequences of notes like a be-bop guitar player, but then all sorts of things grow out of what you can't do as well as those you can. I think if he'd had a fantastic virtuoso technique, he'd have been a lot less interesting. He realised his musical vision and his limitations pushed him in certain directions. Your creativity then takes you into something new and unexpected.'

Klose left the band in the summer of 1965, partly due to parental and college pressure to concentrate on his studies, but also partly due to a realisation that his sophisticated approach and mastery of technique was not what the band required. Klose has always been philosophical about his departure from Pink Floyd. 'It needed me to leave,' he says. Without him less became more.

In contrast to the self-imposed limitations of his musical search Syd's mind expansion continued apace. Limiting his palette to gain richness and density was something that could hardly be applied to his psychedelic explorations. And among his wider circle of friends there were those who were positively evangelical about the experience.

'It brought to me an understanding that all is not as it seems,' says Nigel Lesmoir-Gordon. 'There are other realities and a consciousness that is eternal. A sense of the infinite, and that you could leave yourself behind and become at one with this infinite mystery. And, of course, that infinity sense was love. If you could avoid the bad trip, seeing the devils and the horrible lizardy things everywhere, if you could avoid the hell, which is why we used the Tibetan *Book of the Dead*, to take us through the hellish places, if you could get to let go of this "Nigel ego" you could become one with eternity and know that you were this pure consciousness. The poet George Andrews, who lived at 101 for a while, used to write a lot of acid poems, and he wrote this wonderful line: "I am the wind that blows through me." '

The wind was beginning to blow through everybody that first

English acid summer of 1965 when the drug was new and not even illegal yet. Most of the original acid initiates adhered to Leary's notion of 'Set and Setting', creating the right ambience and environment in order to enhance the experience. Phone off the hook, pleasant music, appropriate accessories, avoidance of anything or anybody that might cause bad vibes and trigger a bad trip.

'There were a lot of people around the Floyd who were into that,' says artist Duggie Fields, who was living at 101 Cromwell Road during this period. 'It's an intellectual perception of drug-taking. Not a raver's perception.'

'That's not to say that we weren't also irresponsible,' admits Jenny Lesmoir-Gordon. 'I think we were.' 'Yeah, but in the beginning you wouldn't think of going out on it, would you?' says Nigel. 'I think quite early on we did, actually,' maintains Jenny. 'I do remember going to the West London air terminal, which has now gone, which was opposite 101 Cromwell Road. But that was in the early hours of the morning and the place was deserted,' concedes Nigel. 'There was this posh restaurant in Knightsbridge we used to go to,' says Jenny. 'One night our friend Chris Case wanted a glass of milk for himself and one for me. He asked for "a glass of two milks". I thought, they'll know that we're tripping!'

These exchanges illustrate the myriad route-maps that acid was charting. Some were using the drug as religious sacrament or transcendental experience. Others enjoyed a pleasantly diverting away day, turning parks and playgrounds into pure astral theatre, but still ensuring they were home on time for supper. For everyone who subscribed to the principles of Set and Setting there were others who gleefully tore up dreary old Leary's rule book, stepped metaphorically on to the Merry Prankster's bus, went about their hedonistic business and had a good time. Syd clearly had a foot in both camps.

'There was this so-called legendary occasion, in my parents' back garden,' says David Gale, referring to the time his parents went to Australia for six months during 1965, leaving him to look after the house. 'Syd, Paul Charrier and one or two others took acid. Syd found a matchbox, a plum and an orange, and studied them for hours and hours. He sat in my parents' garden looking at these objects very intensely for a very, very long time. Who knows what he saw? Maybe he was looking at them as an art student and seeing extraordinary, visual qualities in them. Paul Charrier, a very lively young man, just seized these objects and jumped up and down on them 'cos he thought it was unwholesome that Syd should be so centred on these objects on this lovely summer's day, in a garden full of people rioting around. And at that point Syd just snapped out of it. Paul and Syd went upstairs to my parents' bathroom and just turned the shower on each other. They played like children, soaking each other and shouting and throwing wet clothes out the window and stuff like that.'

Back in London the Lesmoir-Gordons' flat at 101 Cromwell Road was fast becoming a modern-day salon, that David Gale called 'the white-hot centre of the London scene'. Through their connection with John Dunbar and his girlfriend Marianne Faithfull, Nigel and Jenny's wider circle now included the Rolling Stones, Donovan and gallery-owner Robert Fraser, as well as the major figures in the beat movement. Nigel and Jenny were the archetypal beautiful people, playing host to the swinging London in-set. 'And because they were holding open house at 101 Cromwell Road, some quite remarkable, international figures passed through – Burroughs and Ginsberg among them,' says Gale. 'It was actually quite intimidating at times, because there were people there who were SO cool, that you'd feel just like you were some teenager from the Fens.'

Donovan name-checks Cromwell Road in his song 'Sunny South Kensington' and the legendary Wholly Communion Poetry Reading at the Royal Albert Hall was partly mapped out there. The event, organised at ten days' notice, took place on 11 June 1965, attracting between six and seven thousand people. The organisers had been praying for 450 so that they might break even. The Wholly Communion has been recognised as the first major occasion on which the gathering alternative tribe recognised its strength and its numbers. As poet Adrian Mitchell said at the time, 'It wasn't the beginning of anything, it was public proof that something had been accelerating for years.' Michael Horovitz was equally aware of the event's significance, stating that this was the moment when 'the Esperanto of the subconscious sown by dada & the surrealists & the beats bore fruit'.

'The important thing about the Albert Hall reading was that it was the first time we all recognised each other as a constituency, as a community,' says Barry Miles, another of the event's co-organisers. 'Before that we had all been doing our separate little things, spread out all over the place. The King's Road Set was down there and the Hampstead lot were up there. There was no real centre. We'd never had the cafe culture that Paris has or the really well-established downtown art scene that New York has. There had never been anywhere for people to meet except to wander around Soho, and that had always been a drinking and pub scene. And these were young people, a much younger generation that Adrian Mitchell talked about, who saw each other for the first time at the Albert Hall and recognised that all these things had been going on for years.'

As an omen perhaps of what was to come, the event itself was chaotic. Allen Ginsberg was colossally pissed and egos and reputations clashed as old guard and new guard squabbled over billing. 'When we did the Albert Hall poetry thing with Ginsberg we were united, as it were, with our inspirers,' says Pete Brown. 'But it was also a fulcrum for loonies and dodgy drugs and God knows what as well.'

The audience at the Wholly Communion was every bit as

interesting as the performers on stage. Warhol star Kate Heliczer and her friends wore granny dresses, painted their faces and handed out flowers. Both gesture and wardrobe would soon become commonplace. A good proportion of the audience was tripping too. Jenny Lesmoir-Gordon remembers that summer's influx of acid coinciding with the Albert Hall reading. There were, though, those who still had major reservations about some of the more messianic claims being made on behalf of the drug by its advocates. 'I think we all had a very literate education,' says Duggie Fields. 'Everyone read a lot of books. Everyone saw a lot of movies. It was a very creative period. And drugs weren't just for fun. They were the catalyst to change the world for some people. I'm not saying I went along with that, but I would certainly have considered that a possibility. Whereas now you know it wasn't a possibility. When I first moved in to Cromwell Road I was smoking dope and half the people in that flat didn't. It was divided into [whispers] "They're taking drugs, shocking" and the other half who were drinking – until they all got tripped out one weekend by the people downstairs from Cambridge who were real acid proselytisers. And suddenly their lives changed. Acid was going to change the world. And I thought, "Hmmm, this is a little dubious." Not sure I could go for that.'

Pete Brown was another of those who had reservations about Leary's mission to turn on the world. Having been on the scene since the 1950s he was well equipped to trace the drug culture's evolution from the nihilism and sensory obliteration of the Ban the Bomb period through to the current fanciful aesthetics of acid enlightenment. 'There was a lot of anger at what was happening politically. Everyone hated The Bomb, everyone was afraid to die. I suppose that made people live faster. It made people look at drugs and it made people look at forms of spirituality as a possible escape-route from the horror that was building up. We all came out of that CND liberal ethos and all took different routes. My main schism with the rest of them was that I began to see it as being very, very destructive. Not just to me – which it was, but to everybody else. I got very angry with it because it was a diversion and people were getting damaged. And also in hindsight of course it looks very much like it was pushed to the underground as a kind of semi-conspiracy thing. I mean, I am a paranoid conspiracy freak, I have to say that. But then most of it's come true, hasn't it? Most of it's been sussed since then. Acid was made very appealing, with a nice PR campaign, and people got destroyed by it. It blunted the teeth of the so-called "underground", quite honestly. I don't think that political awareness or even, for that matter, artistic awareness, is aided by continual drug use. I'm not saying that you shouldn't have the odd joint and relax, or have the odd pint down the pub. But you can't build a revolution on it. You can't even build one in your mind. I was very suspicious of Leary and all those people. They had dodgy connections. I wouldn't have trusted them with a bag of peas. I didn't buy those people. I think they did more damage than good.'

This schism continued to develop throughout the 1960s. Some, like Brown, began to see the drug culture as politically divisive and culturally destructive. The dominant stance on the traditional left was that drugs were just another diversionary exercise in bourgeois hedonism. Even among acid-takers there was a split between those who were swallowing god drops and hearing a thousand monks chanting in their heads and those who just wanted to go gallivanting in the park, get in touch with their inner child and play on the swings. Matters weren't helped at all by the fact that when on a trip both tendencies could manifest themselves within microseconds. Even Huxley got the giggles the first time he took mescaline, famously recording that once he and Humphry Osmond left the sanctuary of their own set and setting they exploded in gales of laughter when they saw a large blue automobile in the street. To them its bloated shape symbolised the folly of twentieth-century aspiration and greed.

Back in London for the new college year, Syd moved out of Mike Leonard's place in Highgate and down to the West End, the first of a series of central London addresses he would occupy over the next couple of years. Seamus O'Connell's mother, Ella, had uprooted from Cambridge in 1963 and was renting rooms at 12 Tottenham Street, just off Tottenham Court Road, close to Goodge Street tube station.

'She had a bit of money from the sale of our house in Cambridge,' remembers Seamus. 'What she should have done was buy a small house somewhere like Shepherd's Bush or Kentish Town, like her friends did. But she was a ludicrous snob and refused to live north of the Marylebone Road so actually ended up in what was a slum tenement with a very basic kind of greasy-spoon-type restaurant underneath. But it was W1 and she knew the Heal family who owned the department store so that was all right. She was indifferent to the fact that she was living in a slum with a dangerous paraffin heater and a filthy lavatory outside and everything just a mess. It was a good place to live when you were young, but not for someone of my mother's age to end up at.'

Seamus, having flunked out during his final year at the County school, had gone to live with her. 'I made a big mess of my A levels and went off the rails somewhat,' he says. 'I was just out of it really, not in a Sixties way. Just had a bad adolescence.'

Seamus went to the City of Westminster College to retake his A levels. He remembers the house initially being populated by 'bohemian types, the typical kind of people who would be attracted by low-rent places in the centre of town'. While Ella and Seamus occupied rooms on the first floor, Syd had a room on the second. He was soon joined by Cambridge compatriot David Gale who had just finished his degree at St John's and was taking a year out from academic studies before commencing a course at the Royal College Film School in 1966 along with Storm Thorgerson. In the meantime he took a job at Better Books in Charing Cross Road, thus forging another crucial link between the Cambridge crowd and the London alternative scene. 'A real low-rent place,' he says of Tottenham Street. He remembers Ella O'Connell as 'a strange eccentric palm-reading character'.

'She was a very eccentric woman,' agrees Seamus. 'She stood out as being different from a lot of other parents. I can't think of anyone else who would have been doing palm-reading. She was very intuitive and sometimes it clicked into something more than just reading the hand. But she was very cautious with it. She wasn't irresponsible, telling people their numbers of children or marriages or anything like that. But she would talk about people's emotional make-up and balance. Tarot-reading was the same. It wasn't a party trick. It was just something she did if people asked.'

It was Ella who introduced Syd to a wealth of esoterica, including palm-reading, astrological star-charts, tarot and the *I Ching*. 'The *I Ching* was very, very popular, and used by most people I knew,' says David Gale. 'I don't know if Syd was a heavy user or a more considered user who nevertheless made a lot of what he found in it, but I did have friends who used it every day, and I knew one or two people who used it every few hours. It went hand in hand with some subscription to the meaning-fulness of coincidence and by extension, what the universe was actually like. And Syd was as gung-ho for all that as anybody else.'

By now Syd's receptors were well and truly open and he was gung-ho for pretty much everything. This is not to imply that he simply become a passive adherent to the psychic onslaught of acid and all the philosophical trappings that went with it. Throughout this period he retained his sense of mischief and sardonic wit.

'Syd was still very sunny and humorous,' says David Gale. 'And his humour could be quite satirical and it wasn't completely innocent. It was very much teasing the emerging values of the Sixties. At the same time, he wished to participate, as we all did, in this extraordinary cultural party that was going on. We were in the right city at the right time, and Syd was always a very good laugh and so staying in Tottenham Street was a huge adventure. Just going out every day and walking through London was a laugh. That's when we'd play games like "Celebrity Spotter" and win points for who saw what celebrity. I saw Petula Clark in a white open-topped car, driving through the street. Syd would award points for this, and then he'd tell me who he saw, Hank Marvin for instance, and I would award him points.'

As 1965 drew to a close Syd was still extremely focused on his art, writing to Libby Gausden in December that he was looking forward to the college break so he could paint at home during the holidays. 'I'm doing some nice pottery this weekend – I'm gonna make some clay pipes,' he writes cheerfully.

His letters to Libby during this period still predominantly reflect his carefree attitude to life. He enthuses about being within walking distance of the British Museum and makes frequent jokey references to being 'close to the heart of beatland'.

Closer than he thought, as it turned out.

Chapter Three

Flicker Flicker Flicker Blam Pow!

As if in a dream he found himself, somehow, seated in the driver's seat: as if in a dream, he pulled the lever and swung the car round the yard and out through the archway, and as if in a dream, all sense of right and wrong, all fear of obvious consequences, seemed temporarily suspended . . . He chanted as he flew, and the car responded with sonorous drone, the miles were eaten up under him as he sped he knew not whither, fulfilling his instincts, living his hour, reckless of what might come to him.

THE WIND IN THE WILLOWS KENNETH GRAHAME

At the beginning of 1966 the English underground was still an amorphous collection of creative tendencies and unrealised possibilities. Ideologically, the counter-culture continued to be informed, on the one hand by various flavourings of old and new left politics that had grown out of the CND movement, and on the other by a distinctly apolitical or anti-political strand of radicalism based on an increasing disenchantment with parliamentary democracy and its attendant institutions. Musically the underground was still marching to the tune of CND. Jazz (in both its trad and modernist guises) and folk (revered for its 'authenticity' and the militancy of its protest wing) remained the music of choice for those who had walked to Aldermaston.

Pop music came late to the party – and in 1966 it was still referred to as pop music; the demarcation between pop groups and rock bands had not yet emerged. The Beatles were referred to as a pop group, and pop singles were the dominant currency. It is important to remember this when analysing the evolution of the English counter-culture. The underground was not spawned by the rock culture of the late 1960s – if anything the opposite is true. The term 'underground' was not even associated with music until 1967. Before then the term, in Britain at least, was chiefly applied to the film-makers who were influenced by the New York underground cinema of the early 1960s, and to the New Departure and Liverpool poets who had shed their beat influences or met them head on at the Wholly Communion poetry festival.

Much of this activity was going on completely outside the mainstream of British cultural life. What little attention it received tended to be either dismissive on the part of the arts establishment – what Michael Horovitz called 'the stock-in-trade clichés and categories of literary urban sniping' – or sensationalist on the part of the tabloid press. More often than not the counter-culture was simply mocked, covered merely for its novelty value. This patronising tone pervaded even the most quasi-liberal arts coverage in the quality press. In the face of such universal dismissal or indifference the underground thrived, as undergrounds usually do.

Meanwhile the UK music industry went obliviously about its business, and its drinking, in London's Soho. The old money and the trust-fund libertarianism that had floated Mary Quant's first boutique and Britain's first offshore pirate radio station, Radio Caroline, were in Chelsea, but by 1966 the counter-culture was gravitating towards W11, that geographic sprawl, rich in socio-political resonance that encompassed Notting Hill Gate, Ladbroke Grove and Westbourne Park.

In her book *Borderlands/La Frontera*, the feminist poet and fiction writer Gloria E. Anzaldúa memorably depicted the US–Mexico border as a place 'where the Third World grates against the First and bleeds'. The same could be said of London's W11 in the 1950s and early 1960s. W11, then as now, masked great diversities in circumstance, aspiration and wealth. The fragmented urban geography of the area reflected its social history. An inharmonious mix of grand Victorian mansion blocks and half-completed stucco terraces, the result of successive generations of speculation and bankruptcy, sat side by side with rat-infested tenements and dereliction. Inequality was always highly visible in the urban landscape of W11, and became more pronounced the further north you ventured. This remained the case even when London began to swing in the 1960s. At the Notting Hill end of Portobello Road tourists flocked to the antique stalls and shops. At the Goldhawk Road end the poor sifted through second-hand clothes on old wooden barrows and rag-and-bone merchants still plied their trade on horse and cart. It was at this end, the Ladbroke Grove end, where the cultural action would be in the latter half of the decade. This is where the English underground took root, and this, owing to a mixture of happenstance and cultural convergence, is where Pink Floyd would find themselves by the autumn of 1966.

At the beginning of the year they were mainly performing their repertoire of R & B and blues covers at private functions and parties. According to Nick Mason the group had no more than five or six original compositions in its set at this time; these presumably would have been 'Let's Roll Another One', 'Lucy Leave', 'Butterfly', 'Remember Me' and 'Walk With Me Sydney'. By the end of 1966 Pink Floyd would be the underground's house band. At the beginning of the year they were occasionally billed as 'The Pink Floyd Sound'. By the end of the year they would have one.

W11 was as far removed from the ambience and architecture of Cambridge as it was possible to get, a perfect example of what the Chicago School of Urban Sociologists called 'a zone of transition'. Dickens had called the area 'a plague spot, scarcely equalled for insalubrity by any other in London'. *The Times* had called the area 'a social dustbin' and 'a square mile of squalor'. The *Kensington Post* dubbed it 'Rotting Hill'. The black underground paper *Hustler* called it 'a transit area for vagrants, gypsies, and casual workers'.

This was where many of the *Empire Windrush* migrants headed from 1948 onwards, in many cases exchanging one shanty-town for another. This was where the mass murderer John Reginald Christie lived and carried out his crimes during the same period, promising back-street abortions to the desperate and dispossessed, knowing that most of them would not be traceable or even missed in this square mile of flotsam and flux. This was where Peter Rachman did most of his business, a slum landlord so notorious for his ruthless and exploitative methods that he gave his name to an -ism. Rachmanism continued to thrive long after the man himself died in 1962. This was where the Fascist leader Oswald Mosley enjoyed his last hurrah, exploiting the racial tensions that existed in the area and which spilled over into full-scale racially motivated riots during the summer of 1958.

W11 has always been characterised by division, dislocation and displacement. Its grid-lines and boundaries have been shaped historically by the transport routes that have been carved through it. In 1801 the Paddington branch of the Grand Union (at that time the Grand Junction) Canal was opened. In 1864 the western extension of the Metropolitan Railway opened, cutting another swathe through Ladbroke Grove and Westbourne Park. Exactly one hundred years later work began on the Westway, the controversial extension of the M40 route out of London, which displaced residents and turned the area into a huge building site for much of the decade.

In *Borderlands/La Frontera* Gloria Anzaldúa describes the particular hybrid psychology that develops among those who inhabit territories that are subdivided by such arbitrarily imposed intersections. She defines the borderland as 'a vague and undetermined place created by the emotional residue of an unnatural boundary. It is in a constant state of transition. The prohibited and forbidden are its inhabitants.' Anzaldúa traces the cultural diversity specific to the Tex/Mex region she was familiar with. But in her evocation of annexation, alienation and unrest she could just as easily have been talking about the economic refugees and cultural renegades who gravitated towards W11.

Even the most liberal of inhabitants or cultural commentators admits that there was not much racial integration in the area during the early 1960s. What little interaction there was appeared to be confined to dope-scoring and visits to the numerous shebeens (illicit bars) that thrived after dark. It was here that Stephen Ward and Christine Keeler used to come to score, and where Keeler's fractious relationship with dealer Lucky Gordon would bring unwelcome police attention to the area. In his auto-biography, *Give the Anarchist a Cigarette*, Mick Farren writes of the subtle behavioural codes that had to be learned in order for the visitor to be adopted, or at least tolerated, in cafes like the Rio where dope could be scored. Even here things were demarcated along racial lines: white dealers sold hash, black dealers dealt in grass. The terminology people used to define the area also denoted their ethnic background. The white population tended to refer to 'The Gate'. Afro-Caribbeans spoke of 'The Grove'.

It was partly as a way of counteracting this divide and galvanising the disparate strands of social activism and cultural energy in the area that the Notting Hill Free School was set up. The Free School is crucial to any account of the Pink Floyd story. This brief and uneasy liaison between pragmatically politicised housing activists and hippie utopians was a key convergence point for counter-cultural energy in the mid-1960s, and some of the movement's most important and influential initiatives were spawned in its wake. The underground's first newspaper,

International Times, the appropriation of the Chalk Farm Roundhouse as a venue, the UFO club and the Notting Hill carnival all owe their existence to Free School thinking.

W11 had a history of philanthropic activity, motivated by slum housing and government indifference stretching back to the nineteenth century. This mixture of *noblesse oblige* and autonomous community action was part of the political fabric of the area long before the Free School was talked of. The most recent antecedents for the Free School were to be found in Alexander Trocchi's *The Invisible Insurrection of a Million Minds* and *Sigma, a Tactical Blueprint* which called for a rejection of conventional politics and, according to Jeff Nuttall in his book *Bomb Culture*, 'a kind of cultural jam session: out of which will evolve the prototype of our spontaneous university'. The roots (and routes) of the Free School could also be traced to the free university movement in the USA, and the initiatives of Joseph Berke and the radical psychiatry movement that was centred on Kingsley Hall in London. Indeed, one of the early participants in the activities of the Free School was pioneering psychoanalyst R. D. Laing. Jeff Nuttall was also an early participant, as were black activist and former Rachman henchman Michael De Freitas (later Michael X), Beatles manager Brian Epstein and poet Michael Horovitz.

The inaugural public meeting of the Free School on 8 March 1966 was attended by Warhol actress and Wholly Communion participant Kate Heliczer, who had also brought to England the first demo tapes of the Velvet Underground, jazz writer Ron Atkins, Alan Beckett of *The New Left Review*, and ufologist and ley-line expert John Michell. Also in attendance were four people who would play an integral part in the Pink Floyd story: John Hopkins, Peter Jenner, Andrew King and Joe Boyd.

John 'Hoppy' Hopkins had left Cambridge University with a third-class degree in 1958. In order to avoid national service he took a job with the atomic energy authority at Harwell, near Oxford. 'There I was with a questionable science degree, dodging the draft, and enjoying all the benefits of student life without having to be a student.' Poet Mike Horovitz put him in touch with what he calls 'grassroots avant-garde culture, the new left review people, people into film, poets and musicians'.

Hoppy's 'anti-career' simultaneously mirrored and informed the wider development of the English underground. He was the counter-culture's enabler, the man who talked schemes into existence and got things done. 'He was the catalyst and the energiser. He was unbelievably active,' says Barry Miles, who would also play no small part in the future scheme of things. 'It was ridiculous the things he had a hand in, in getting going. I was absolutely in awe of Hoppy.'

Hopkins had moved to London at the end of 1960 to become a photographer, 'working both for the straight press, like the *Sunday Times*, the *Observer* and *Melody Maker*, and with one foot in the alternative camp, including a lot of work for *Peace News*. By 1964 I was organising photo-coverage of the Aldermaston march for CND.' He also worked for the Labour Party in the run-up to their 1964 election victory, and describes Harold Wilson's subsequent u-turn from anti-nuclear weapons to pro-nuclear deterrent as a seminal moment. 'The biggest political lesson I've ever learned. It left me with a disillusion with conventional politics which has lasted to this day.'

Hoppy's Westbourne Grove flat soon became a drop-in centre and crash-pad for kindred spirits. Everyone who would eventually play a part in the English counter-culture seemed to pass within Hoppy's orbit. Barry Miles was one of those who used to stay at Hoppy's when in London, eventually moving up to the city from Cirencester in 1962. Miles initially worked at Better Books, which was in effect a drop-in centre itself for writers, poets, artists and other like-minded souls.

Peter Jenner was the son of a vicar. His grandfather was a Labour MP. 'Very left-wing family,' he says, describing his background and social milieu as 'that middle-class group of people, as it were children of the Bloomsbury Set, children of the Spanish Civil War, the Popular Front and the ISP. We'd all gone to posh universities with grants, for free. I was anti-hanging, pro-CND, went on all the early Aldermaston marches, and the anti-Suez demo where Nye Bevan spoke. Big jazz fan. Got into smoking dope at Cambridge.'

Hoppy describes W11 at that time as being littered with bomb sites, boarded-up shop-fronts that were just facades for waste ground that children played on, 'and land clearance for building future motorways including the Westway. Whether you were politicised or not, sooner or later you came into contact with the problems that bad housing caused. Does the name Rachman mean anything to you?'

Peter Jenner remembers the area as being characterised by 'big old dilapidated houses with ten rooms and maybe ten families and two bathrooms. Mainly immigrants who didn't know how to protect themselves. A lot of the more decent accommodation was for whites only. The gap was being filled by Rachman and people like that, these horrible landlords were buying up old houses for three, four, five thousand pounds and letting rooms for six pounds a week when people were only earning ten pounds a week and if you didn't pay they sent round people who broke your legs or threw you out on the streets. We had an awareness of all that. We'd all been bought up in post-war austerity and we were questioning what was going on. In a way what was carried over into the Fifties was a good version of the Thirties, i.e. no unemployment, but it was still a bit drab and dreary. By the Sixties we were saying, come on, there's more to life than this.'

Joe Boyd had grown up in New Jersey, immersed in music. As a young, Princeton-educated promoter he had organised gigs for

Sleepy John Estes, Jesse Fuller, Sonny Terry and Brownie McGhee, Skip James, Muddy Waters and the Reverend Gary Davis. He'd seen the American folk and jug band scene evolve and go electric and the folk record labels, Elektra and Vanguard, follow likewise. He had also been involved with the Newport folk and jazz festivals, where he had witnessed that watershed moment on the night of 25 July 1965 when Bob Dylan outraged the folk movement by inserting a jack plug into an electric guitar and kick-starting the second half of the Sixties.

Boyd had previously visited England in 1964 and 1965, managing the Blues and Gospel Caravan, and touring Europe with Coleman Hawkins and Roland Kirk. It was on the former tour that he first met John Hopkins when Hoppy was still a freelance photographer. By September 1965 Boyd was running the London office for Jac Holzman's Elektra label and ideally positioned to witness the gathering momentum of the English counter-culture.

The first meeting of the Free School was held in the basement of a house in Powis Terrace. 'The house belonged to John Michell. He had some sort of partnership with Michael De Freitas,' says Hoppy. 'Michael and John made the basement of this run-down terraced house available. Most of the activity of the Free School was not actually at the basement, but in informal classes elsewhere. There were lots of different groups of people doing different things. Some of it was to do with the political side of being a housing activist. Other stuff was to do with arts and crafts and photography. That was the crucible out of which the carnival was re-invented. The carnival had existed in some form before the free school, but it had gone dormant.'

'The Free School was to do with the fact that the education system was very old-fashioned and teaching us in a locked-door way,' says Peter Jenner. 'I was a sociologist and economist and at the LSE I was getting involved in social work and psychology.

The more I, and a lot of others, got involved, the links between the subjects were becoming more interesting than the subjects. In social terms there were a lot more West Indians around and there was an interesting cultural mix for me to live in, and a lot more interesting music around. In that sense the Free School was like a Workers' Education[al] Association idea but in a more progressive way.'

In Courtney Tulloch's *The Grove* newsletter of 23 May 1966 Hoppy defined the Free School's ongoing mission as 'a way in which people could get together to discuss questions which were vital to their everyday life. For instance how can one find out more about the school system, facilities for young children, legal matters, housing groups, consumer associations, sports groups, nursery groups, etc. How can people make their own entertainment? How can one try one's hand at dramatics, or music, or painting?'

'The only way it would have differed from any other kind of community project was that it was supposed to be a two-way thing,' says Barry Miles. 'Everybody who had a skill that they could teach was encouraged to go to the Free School and make themselves available. The idea was you would learn from the people who were coming to you. This is why Michael X was interested. He taught basic English. He knew a lot of people in the area who were basically illiterate but were too proud to ever have gone to an evening class. He thought this would be a good two-way movement, a situation where people were passing on their life skills to the person who was teaching them in a way they wouldn't have done if it was being run by the council.'

One early convert to the Free School was Emily Young, the free-spirited daughter of the distinguished writer and politician Wayland Young (Lord Kennet). Young hung out at the Free School with her school friend Anjelica Huston (daughter of the film-maker John Huston) and was destined to play a pivotal role in the Pink Floyd story as the inspiration for Syd Barrett's wayward muse in his song 'See Emily Play'. 'I was quite a serious girl, quite grumpy really. I was very bright but quite frustrated intellectually at school, so I didn't go to school. I used to hang out with all these mad people and bohos at the Free School instead, and loved it. I was so hungry for interesting things. My resources were very good in my family life. There were a lot of books and amazing people coming through the house, upper-class, faintly bohemian, academic intellectual people, so I was well informed about the possibilities in life. Then John Hopkins, this ex-physicist, came to the morning assembly in school and said, "We've got this thing going. Everyone's welcome to come. It's a local resource. We're here for the community. We do all these classes in music and dancing, and what's going on in science and what's going on in the arts. Come along. Join in." So I went. I was that hungry and curious. I was a kid. I was fourteen–fifteen years old during that eighteen months, however long it was. Everyone else was much older. I don't know what they thought of me. I used to pretend I'd gone to bed and then creep out of the house and go off and have this much more interesting life. Most nights I was down there. Then in the morning I'd creep in and say I'd been staying with a school friend over night, then pretend I was going to school and then go back to the Free School and sleep.'

'A lot of people were turned off by the basement in Powis Terrace because all the walls were covered with psychedelic paintings,' remembers Barry Miles. 'And you'd have Michael De Freitas lurking around with his silver-top cane. Most people still regarded him as a pretty shifty character. Up until a few weeks before the Free School that room had still been a gambling club and he'd run a brothel in another part of the same building.'

'It was pretty grungy. It wasn't a nice place,' admits Emily Young. 'Earth floors, filthy stairs. You'd go down there and have interesting conversations and interesting drugs. I'd be sitting there, ears flapping, eyes wide, you know, with that adolescent self-consciousness. I didn't say much, but I loved it. There were conversations about what was going on in cosmology. Plate tectonics, that was really new. Geologists were very resistant to it but it was making sense. And the age of the universe, they were just starting to tie those things in, nuclear decay times and half-lifes, and dating the age of the earth. Nowadays people think the Sixties was very modern and progressive. In fact there were all kinds of assumptions about the state of the universe that were wrong. And all this was taking place in a Dickensian slum. It was cold so we'd go and find old railway sleepers. There were lots of demolitions and we'd find lots of wood there. There was a cold-water tap at the back. And that's how you'd make tea. Put the kettle over the fire. But on these huge swathes of demolition where everything was being ripped out for the motorway we'd go and have happenings. People playing saxophones and huge bonfires and drinking and dancing and poets doing their mad stuff. There were paupers, street people with absolutely no money. God knows how they lived. Really quite extreme some of them. Then there were these Americans coming over with their acid. They were wonderful, visionary, clean, healthy people talking about the way forward and the golden future and all the dreams of the hippy world and global consciousness.'

The Free School, for all its subsequent failings, can be seen as a microcosm of the wider questioning of society that was going on at the time, just one of many crucial convergence points for the radical ideas, philosophies and initiatives that were being articulated in the 1960s. It is important to place the early blossoming of Pink Floyd in this context. In the early autumn of 1966 their presence at the Free School was no more significant than many other factors. Emily Young acknowledges this when recalling the benefit gigs they played. 'The Free School was going to do a fund-raising dance on a Saturday night at the old Church hall in All Saints Road. That's where the Pink Floyd Sound was brought in to be a soundtrack. From my point of view that wasn't the reason I was there. I was there because of all this other stuff that was going on which was much more to do with sociology and life philosophy. You know? How do you find a way through life?'

'My impression was that many people were open to lots of different influences,' says Hoppy. 'There was a great deal of crossover. Musicians of one sort listening to what musicians of another sort were doing; black soul music, white rock and pop music, classical and serious avant-garde stuff, the Cornelius Cardew end of things. There were American jazz musicians visiting like Ornette Coleman and Steve Lacy. There was also the British jazz of course and there was AMM. Their music was so far out it was on the border between music and noise and street sound. Of all the music and groups and ideas from that era, the ones that have stayed closest to the original concept are AMM, who are still around today. They have a very strong ideological basis for what they do. Try talking to Eddie Prévost or Keith Rowe about what they do. They'll whack you over the head with their critical understanding. They're tough people.'

He's not wrong. AMM are a crucial component in the evolution of the English underground. The rigour and longevity of their intellectual quest remains unparalleled, and the nature of their artistic development offers a revealing counterpoint to that of Pink Floyd, indicating how the avant-garde wing of the English rock scene might have evolved in a parallel universe if it hadn't been co-opted and commercialised so swiftly.

AMM's musical performances placed great emphasis on spontaneity, improvisation, collectivity and the strategic importance of silence. 'For me, AMM wasn't really about playing music,' says founder member Lawrence Sheaff. 'It was an examination of, a revelling in, a fathoming of, the nature of sound and silence itself and the relationship between the two. AMM, its performances and its discussions, helped bring the "where does it all come from" into sharper focus for me.'

Resisting commodification and complacency at every turn AMM adopted a strenuously analytical approach to their music, involving regular discussion sessions and performances that critiqued the very nature of music itself. Keith Rowe's deconstructionist approach to the guitar in particular would have considerable impact on Syd Barrett. Rowe liberated the guitar from functionality and conventional tuning, often laying it flat, in 'table top position' as he called it, and manipulating the sound in the same way that John Cage had done with the prepared piano.

'Steel rulers and ball bearings were the first thing I used, and coins, very English coins from the period with the serrated edge,' says the AMM guitarist. 'Knives over the pickup was quite a breakthrough for me too, because it perfectly matched this kind of "Duchampian" thing, and cubism too, which had already interested me in the sense that an object could have lots of different utilisations.'

As Rowe's nod to Duchamp and cubism indicates, AMM's theorising about practice and process was predominantly informed by painting. The members of AMM had all been to art school and it was the intellectual rigour of that environment which initially guided the group's strategy.

'The American painters had centre stage: Pollock, Rothko, Rauschenberg, Kline, Newman, Kelly, Stella, Oldenburg, Warhol, Lichtenstein, Johns. They covered everything,' remembers Lawrence Sheaff. 'But it didn't tell us where it all comes from. On this the world of art was mute. Still is. I guess I wanted to know where it all comes from. All the surface possibilities had been laid out. In painting, in music, what was left? Only subdivisions of the subdivisions. If you got that picture, where to go from there?

97

"In" was where to go. "In" not "out". For me AMM was a way to go "in": to cut beneath the surface of things. For me, a great, silent whisper of a question was hanging behind every perform-ance, "Where does it all come from?" '

Keith Rowe's own search, although equally philosophical, was more informed by pragmatic responses to material problems. 'It was a straightforward contradiction between my day life and my night life,' he explains. 'When I was studying at art school during the day, the artistic agenda was, who are you, what do you have to say, and was about developing your language. In the evenings we'd play jazz where I was just imitating Americans. Well, that's just a basic contradiction – what I was doing on the canvas was contrary to what I was doing on the guitar. On the guitar I was not finding my own language. I was basically hijacking someone else's language like Jim Hall or Wes Montgomery and emulating what they did. In the world of painting you don't have per-mission to paint other people's painting. You only have permission to do your own work, whereas in the world of jazz you could do someone else's work. You could just rip off Coltrane, and play just like Coltrane – and that was fine. There was nothing wrong in doing that. I just didn't like that relation-ship. I wanted to develop my own language. So I took this instrument and looked at it more like an art project of what can I do with this, rather than coming with a whole load of baggage about what it is you do with it. And I think I very simply just applied the agenda of painting to the guitar. But what does that actually mean in practice? For the Americans to develop an American school of painting, they somehow had to ditch or lose European easel painting techniques. They had to make a break with the past. What did that possibly mean if you were a jazz guitar player? For me, symbolically, it was Pollock laying the canvas on the floor, which immediately abandons European easel technique. I could see that by laying the canvas down, it became inappropriate to apply easel techniques. I thought if I did that with a guitar, then I would just lose all those techniques, because they would be physically impossible to do. So if it meant laying it on the table, I would lay it on the table.'

AMM's modus operandi, and in particular Keith Rowe's ideas about how to break with tradition and transcend technique, provided the context in which Syd Barrett was able to validate his own instinctive approach to music-making, and gave him the confidence to press ahead with his own style of experimentation. It was Rowe's attempt to apply art-school thinking to the mechanics of guitar playing which finally liberated Syd from his own shackles of tradition and technique. He had been incorporating radical and untutored slide techniques into his playing for some time – David Gale maintains that in a spirit of 'Hey, listen to this!' he saw Syd running a Zippo lighter up and down his guitar as early as 1963 – now he had added conceptual justification for what he was doing.

AMM played several significant gigs with Pink Floyd between March 1966 and February 1967 including the Spontaneous Underground events at the Marquee club that took place between March and June 1966, gigs at All Saints Hall in Notting Hill, and the *International Times* launch party at the Roundhouse in October of that year. Syd also attended the recording session for AMM's debut album in June 1966.

'It wasn't "underground" at that point,' says Keith Rowe. 'At the time it just felt like we were doing the things which were interesting for us to do. It just happened to become something called "the underground" afterwards, but at the time I don't think I was aware of it in that way. John Hopkins probably was aware of it. But I think we were just fighting for a new piece of territory, like everyone else.'

'I first heard the Pink Floyd at the Spontaneous Underground in the spring of 1966 at the Marquee club on a Sunday afternoon,'

99

says Hoppy. 'They were a series of Sunday afternoon gigs put on by Steve Stollman, the brother of Bernard Stollman who started up the ESP label in New York.' Hoppy describes his first encounter with Pink Floyd as 'like walking into a wall of sound, not unmusical, but certainly something like I'd never heard before. They had quite a lot of amplification for those days, all improvising over a theme, and some of the improvisations seemed to be pretty wild, but it all seemed coherent if you stood back and listened to it. They may well have played some more conventional rock 'n' roll numbers but what I remember is their wall of sound.'

The now legendary Spontaneous Underground gigs were essentially a series of invitation-only events organised by Steve Stollman as a way of galvanising the creative energies that had become apparent at the previous year's Wholly Communion poetry reading. A mimeographed flyer for the first one read:

Spontaneous Underground at the Marquee this Sunday January 30th organised by Steve Stollman of ESP Disk with the aid of everybody. Among those taking part will be Donovan/Mose Allison/Graham Bond/Pop/Mime/Kinetic Sculpture/Discotheque/Boutique. THIS TRIP begins at 4.30 and goes on. Liquor licence applied for: Costume, masque, ethnic, space, Edwardian, Victorian and hipness generally . . . face and body makeup – certainly. This is a spontaneous party, any profit to be held in trust by Louis Diamond, Solicitor, that such spontaneities may continue. Invitation only, donation at door 6/6.

The iconography and hip argot of the flyer was a thinly codified calling card to initiates, those few hundred people who constituted the counter-culture at that time. Stollman's flyers for the Marquee events were works of art in themselves, stream of consciousness signifiers and cut-up poetry for the in-crowd. Only the first of these events was actually called Spontaneous Underground. The others were simply, and unambiguously, known as the Trip. The flyer for the second event, held on 27 February, read:

In memoriam. King Charles. Marquee de Sade. Superman. Supergirl. Ulysses.
Charlie Chaplin. All tripping lightly looning Phoenician moon mad sailors –
in character as IN characters – characterised in costume at the Marquee this
Sunday at 5 o'clock

The third event two weeks later was the first to feature the
Pink Floyd Sound, although in keeping with the anti-star ethos
of the Underground the flyer mentioned no bands at all.

TRIP bring furniture toy prop paper rug pant balloon jumble costume mask
robot candle incense ladder wheel light self all others march 13th 5pm

One Trip event was advertised with cut-ups of Alexander
Trocchi's *Sigma*. Another arrived on thick card advertising
forthcoming ESP disk releases by the New York Art Quartet, Ran
Blake, the Giuseppi Logan Quartet, the Albert Ayler Trio, Sun Ra,
and Pharoah Sanders. The card had a very faint two-coloured
Roneo overlay with the virtually indecipherable details of the gig.

'It was an entirely conceptual idea,' says Barry Miles. 'Cut up a
bunch of stuff. Tip it in an envelope, send it off and you know
that something is happening. On one of them I don't think it
even said where it was or anything. They just arrived in the post
and that meant there was one on.'

Aside from Donovan, Mose Allison and Graham Bond, other
participants in those early Trip gigs were Soft Machine, members
of what would become Spontaneous Musical Ensemble and
poets Johnny Byrne and Spike Hawkins, who were billed as the
Poison Bellows and took to the stage with a wind-up gramo-
phone in an old pram and proceeded to shock or annoy the
audience out of their stoned reverie with deliberately bad
conjuring tricks and Dadaist polemic.

'They were quite unorganised. It was quite random,'
remembers Jenny Lesmoir-Gordon. 'We painted our faces and
took acid whenever we went there.'

'It was a very social thing, and it was a very small world,' says

Peter Jenner, who also attended the Marquee events. 'There was an awareness that something was going on in America and we didn't quite know what it was. We knew more about New York than we did about LA and San Francisco. We read about hippies and the few who came over from America found us. We knew the people who managed the Fugs and that's how I first got to know the Floyd.'

Inspired by the set-up at ESP Peter Jenner decided to launch his own record label. 'The four of us, Ron Atkins, Felix Mendelsohn, myself and Hoppy, were going to have this label called DNA. It was going to be an avant-garde label. Delia Derbyshire and all those people, the Radiophonic Workshop, were just up the road. We could see what was happening in music. It was all going in a similar direction, avant-garde folk, avant-garde jazz, avant-garde classical, avant-garde pop. It was all about crossing over boundaries, which was also what the London Free School was all about. It was all the same general, I won't say, philosophy, that would be too grand, but the same general mindset, certainly; the same way of thinking, or the same way of getting stoned, at any rate.'

DNA's first, and, as it transpired, only release was AMM's *AMMMusic*. Recorded at Sound Technique Studios in June 1966 and produced by Hoppy, Peter Jenner, Ron Atkins and Alan Beckett, the album was a boundary-crossing amalgam of noise, which although alluding to classical, jazz and avant-garde influences defied easy categorisation.

AMMMusic featured Cornelius Cardew, whom Hoppy had known in Oxford, playing piano and cello, Lou Gare on tenor sax and violin, Eddie Prévost on percussion, Keith Rowe on electric guitar and Lawrence Sheaff on cello, accordion and clarinet. Cardew, Rowe and Sheaff also manipulated transistor radios, adding a textural layer of audio-concrete to the sound.

It says much about the sheer Utopian spirit of the time that an album like *AMMMusic* could ever be considered a viable venture, let alone launched as the showcase debut LP on a new record label. 'The producers of our first album were all connected with the Pink Floyd,' noted Eddie Prévost. 'I suspect they thought it just possible that AMM might be marketable in the heady days of the Sixties.'

'In fairness to them [Jenner and King], I don't suppose they knew at the time that the Pink Floyd would become as big as they did,' says Keith Rowe. 'I don't think they were thinking commercially at all. I think they actually, genuinely, appreciated it, and understood the music as something they knew about, and felt deserved a wider audience.'

At this particular juncture artistic boundaries remained fluid and undefined; everything was still up for grabs. 'I've often mischievously said that I think a whole load of us could've been in the Rolling Stones, or it was very possible for some of us to be in the Pink Floyd or one of your best mates to be in the Beatles. It was still like that at that point,' says Rowe. 'It wasn't ossified. It wasn't set in stone already – it was flexible. People were moving round and it was just one huge scene. The divisions had not been set up.'

Unfortunately for DNA little of the label's energy and AMM's idealism translated into record sales. 'We'd made this one record with AMM,' recalls Peter Jenner. 'Great record, very seminal, seriously avant-garde, but I'd started adding up and I'd worked out that [with] the deal we had, we got 2 per cent of retail, out of which we, the label, had to pay for recording costs and pay ourselves. I came to the conclusion that we were going to have to sell a hell of a lot of records just to pay the recording costs, let alone pay ourselves any money and build a label, so I realised we had to have a pop band because pop bands sold a lot of records. It was as simple as that and I was as naive as that. I saw the Floyd and thought, hey, that looks fun. They're definitely avant-garde.

Why were they avant-garde? Because I couldn't work out who was making the noise. You couldn't distinguish between the guitar and the keyboards. There was lots of sustained reverb and Binson Echorec going like mad. These walls of sound – well, more like little fences of sound . . . but it was enough to get me confused. However, I wasn't impressed with the material they were playing.'

At the Marquee Trip gigs the band were still playing the R&B and blues repertoire that had sustained them through the previous couple of years; the Kingsmen's 'Louie Louie', Elmore James's 'Dust My Broom', Bo Diddley's 'You Can't Judge a Book by the Cover', etc., but by now it had become noticeable that their crude extemporisations had developed into something altogether more innovative.

'Instead of having wailing Eric Clapton [and] Pete Green guitar solos, they were having these free-form jams,' says Jenner. 'I thought that was the interesting part. But I thought they needed to play their own material and when I met them I discovered they did have their own material: Syd had songs. But I guess it was easier then to play familiar songs on stage. I could see why they did it. The blues boom was big so if you played "Dust My Broom" everyone knew where they were and you didn't have to get to grips with all this weird shit. It was a pretty sensible way to get through your gigs and get booked again. And Syd wasn't this great wailing player, he was a very inventive musician, but he wasn't a practise-five-hours-a-day type. He was an inspirational guitar player rather than a technical one.'

Somewhere between Bob Klose leaving the band in the summer of 1965 and the first real flowering of the English underground in the spring of 1966, Pink Floyd had, almost imperceptibly and largely outside of the public gaze, made their major conceptual breakthrough. The reasons for this were three-fold: the light show, the Binson Echorec and the influence of AMM.

Anthony Stern remains convinced that the light show was the chief catalyst for the band's change of direction. 'The reason their music changed into what it became is because that was the way to go with the light show, the mixture of light and music, painting with light and sound, and sound that becomes music. Which comes originally from the psychedelic experience, 'cos when you take acid, you may well have an experience where a sound heard will produce a flurry of images. It's almost like you've had two hearts, two sensory systems in our brains are wired across to each other, someone had patched them through together so that when you see something, you hear something, when you hear something you see something.'

A second key factor was the introduction of the Binson Echorec. The Echorec was essentially the fifth member of Pink Floyd at this stage of their development. Introduced in the late 1950s the device was a pre-pedal echo unit powered by valves and driven by tape-heads. Used, with restraint, on some of the Shadows' early recordings it enabled tape delay, echo, reverb and vari-speed. Used by Pink Floyd it greatly enhanced Syd's ringing Telecaster tones and Rick Wright's unorthodox phrasing and ethereal tone.

'If you just have a jazz guitar and an amplifier there's not that much you can do. You just have that sound and that's it folks,' says Bob Klose of his role in the band. 'But once you have some echo units and so on you can start to get into repeat and that sort of pushes you in a certain direction. It's not a negative thing, it's a creative thing. You've got this other dimension you can use. And there was a kind of movement of music at that time that just wanted to deal with sound and not to think so much about traditional musicological harmonic logic. You didn't need to have an orthodox technique at all.'

As Bob Klose indicates, Syd was now firmly aligned to a movement in music which eschewed convention and orthodoxy. Inspired by AMM, Syd's musical thinking had finally caught up with his art-school thinking and he increasingly began to approach the guitar in terms of texture rather than technique. He stopped worrying about his competence and began to fly. The band still wasn't confident enough at this stage to drop the cover versions altogether, in fact they would continue to include R & B standards in the set right up to the end of 1966, but Syd and Rick Wright in particular were beginning to construct their sound pictures from a whole new sonic palette.

When Peter Jenner approached the band with a view to putting them on his record label, the university term was just coming to an end. Roger Waters told Jenner to come back in September and everyone went off on their holidays. Waters and Mason in particular still had one foot provisionally planted in the academic camp and readily assumed that they would be continuing their architectural studies in the autumn.

'That summer we went to Greece with Roger Waters and Rick Wright, and I gave them their first and only acid trip on the island of Patmos, where St John had the Revelation,' says Nigel Lesmoir-Gordon. 'They both had such an appalling time I don't think they ever took it again. Roger had a really bad time on it and I was trying to help him. I had this Bible and I thought I was this black leopard. I just lay on the ground with this Bible, a long sleek cat. And there was Roger on the bed going "Argh!" Rick's back got sunburnt. I remember the pink of his back being the colour of the wall and he just disappeared and merged into the wall. The sea looked like scales and I remember a boat came chugging in puffing black smoke. I thought, "The dragon's coming. Oh, God help us." '

David Gale remained wary of the more Utopian claims being made by acid users but he recognised both the drug's ubiquity and its role as a catalyst during 1966. 'There was an enormous, almost like an occult, revival sweeping through, in as much as hitherto abandoned outposts of interest in Eastern mysticism suddenly became mainstream. Kids convinced themselves that some kind of eclectic amalgam of bits and pieces of largely Eastern mystical or occult stuff could be assembled into some kind of guidance system. It was very cool to be thought of as spiritual. And accordingly, if that's what you pressingly want to be, then your LSD experiences tend to confirm that. It may be possible to have a completely secular LSD experience – but not then – because one was surrounded by a belief in coincidence and synchronicity and the value of it, the significance of it. The density of it was actually overwhelming – it was everywhere.'

For some of the Cambridge crowd the soul-searching would lead to religious conversion in the form of Radha Soami Satsang Beas, referred to by its followers as Sant Mat, literally 'Path of the Saints'. Sant Mat, a branch cut from the same tree as Sikhism, was led by a guru called Maharaj Charan Singh Ji, known by devotees, the satsangis, as 'the Master'. The Cambridge exodus to Sant Mat began innocuously enough early in 1966 when Paul Charrier, who until then had been a fully paid-up hedonist, chanced upon a book about the movement.

'That's an interesting story in itself,' says Andrew Rawlinson, 'because all the books were privately published. You couldn't buy them in bookshops. But there was one satsangi, Joseph Leeming, who was a professional writer. He used to go to publishers and say, "What do you need?" and they'd say, "We need a book on boating for boys," or "stamp collecting in Ethiopia," and he'd say, "I'll have it for you in three months." He went to them at one point and said, "How would you like a book on yoga and the Bible?" and they said, "Yeah, that might sell." So here was a book by an established publisher that you could buy in any bookshop. A friend of ours bought it and [was reading] it. Paul picked it up and said "What's this?" They said, "You don't want to read that, Paul. You can't do it without a master." Paul read it and thought, "This is it." The address of the master was in the back so Paul borrowed £200 off his girlfriend Bridget and flew to Delhi. He had no idea where Beas was. It's a tiny village. Population of 500. So he rolls up out of the blue in an air force great coat with a toothbrush and his big wild hair and I would say he was the first Western youngster ever to do that.'

Rawlinson maintains that the whole subsequent hippie trail from Western Europe to mystical East began with those initial impulsive footsteps taken by Paul Charrier. 'People of our age started to appear out of the hills a bit later but he'd actually gone there with an address. And he was totally bowled over. There was an ashram with self-contained buildings next to the river. India is chaotic. It's like being in a cross-current of waves all the time and he gets to this place and it's ordered and clean. No one is trying to get any money off you and you're fed for nothing and for big meetings they were providing one million chapattis a day free. Paul sent some ecstatic letters back. He got initiated by a maharaji and came back a changed man. He said, "My aim is to work in the same office as my parents." His parents worked for the local council!'

Charrier's conversion had a massive impact on his Cambridge friends, as Andrew Rawlinson acknowledges. 'He went out in March '66 and came back in April and by coincidence the Master came to London in July. More or less all of us went to see him because of Paul.'

Over the next two years several of Syd's friends converted to Sant Mat: Andrew Rawlinson and his girlfriend Lucy Prior, Paul Charrier and his girlfriend Bridget, Nigel and Jenny Lesmoir-Gordon, William Pryor and 'Ponji' Robinson among them.

'What you had in no time at all was satsangis who were young,' notes Rawlinson. 'All the people who had been before were over fifty. They would all have come through theosophy and Rosicrucianism and tarot. They were old-time esotericists, whereas we were LSD hipsters.'

'We were very spiritually influenced by LSD,' agrees Nigel Lesmoir-Gordon, 'because we suddenly saw that there was maybe eternal life. It's not a physical universe. It's a consciousness universe and the human body is just a result of consciousness. Consciousness comes first. Other people became more interested in the mind and a lot of people ended the 1960s going to shrinks to find out more about their psychological make-up. Some people got seriously into their spiritual side, some people got seriously into psychiatry and some people just carried on drinking alcohol.'

David Gale was one of those who got into radical psychiatry and remained sceptical about Sant Mat and the satsangis. 'A lot of people of Syd's acquaintance were drawn quite hysterically, with massive enthusiasm, into it. And the Master, the Maharaj Charan Singh Ji – he of the audible life-stream – was successful in recruiting some of the best minds of my generation, including Andrew Rawlinson, probably the cleverest person in that whole group, and countless others. One by one, starting with Paul Charrier, they went to India, got initiated [and] saw the white light explode before them. [They] came back home, cut their hair off, threw away their hippie clothes, got suits, got a job, became vegetarians, stopped drinking, smoking and taking drugs, married women of the same persuasion as them, only had sex for procreative purposes, were advised to be 'ordinary' and to keep their heads down. Every morning when they got up they would meditate for two hours in an attempt to leave this earthly level of consciousness and get on to higher levels. It was slightly crazed. There was something hysterical about it. But a lot of hedonistic young men and women plumped for a lifestyle of utter asceticism and drew strength from denial. It may be that some of them on LSD went to the edge of the abyss and looked down, and backed off in horror and settled for something very strict. It may be there was guilt there. Or it may be that they weren't that radical when the chips were down. But what happened was [that] this perfectly healthy riotous group of promiscuous, drug-taking, largely cheerful young men and women were split right down the middle. Half of them went to India, half of us stayed home.'

'It went right down the middle, fifty–fifty,' agrees Andrew Rawlinson, 'if you count the Cambridge scene and all its London extensions. Half of us went into it and half of us didn't. Syd would have gone into it. He asked the Master and the Master said, "I will not take an emotional request." At that time it was very unusual for the Master to turn anybody down, but he did turn Syd down. Syd told me that he told him that his request to be initiated was emotional and not based on genuine spiritual research. But, of course, it's typical of Syd that he would have done that because he didn't look over his shoulder – that was the thing about Syd. He just thought, "I'm going to give this a go." '

Jenny Lesmoir-Gordon, who was yet to convert, gives a slightly different account of Syd's rejection. 'Syd asked if he could have initiation and the Master said, "Not yet, go and finish your studies." Syd was really disappointed because Paul Charrier was already following this path. I remember Syd coming round to Cromwell Road and saying, "I'm not going to smoke any more. I'm going to be a vegetarian and I'm going to follow this path." I said, "Oh no, you can't give up smoking dope, come and have a joint." But he was very upset that the Master had turned him down.'

While some of his friends thought that Syd was merely dabbling, Andrew Rawlinson has no doubt about his sincerity. 'I have a volume which Syd bought, which was one of the books produced by Maharaj Charan Singh Ji which is on the nature of love and Syd had underlined several sentences. So he clearly was influenced. He was interested in it before I was actually, despite the fact that I was two years older. Syd was in there right at the beginning.'

'Syd was more than mildly interested,' agrees David Gale. 'He went along for an audience with the Master when he took over a suite of rooms in the Russell Hotel. And the Master said Syd wasn't ready for the spiritual life. Now Storm thinks this was very disappointing for Syd because he'd been told he wasn't spiritually mature, or had no spiritual potential. Or was on the road to becoming fucked up big time. Quite what the Master saw, nobody will ever know. So Syd couldn't go to India and do that stuff. But he did take it a lot more seriously than Storm and me, who remain to this day the sceptics of that crew. And whether it depressed him and made him react in some way is debatable. I couldn't say, but the moment when he was turned off the spiritual is certainly significant. Whether that made him determined to prove himself in other quarters – I don't know.'

During the summer of 1966 Syd moved out of Tottenham Street and with his new girlfriend, fashion model Lindsay Corner, took up residence in the top-floor flat at 2 Earlham Street, just off Shaftesbury Avenue. The house was part of a block of run-down buildings, since demolished and rebuilt, next to the Marquis of Granby pub, conveniently close to the Indica Bookshop and the old vegetable market in Covent Garden. David Gale and Seamus O'Connell lived downstairs, along with artist John Whitely, who would later design the marbling effect on the second Pink Floyd LP *A Saucerful of Secrets*. The building was rented from the Church of England by light-show operator and Sant Mat convert Peter Wynne Wilson and his girlfriend and fellow satsangi, Susie Gawler-Wright. Both came from extremely privileged backgrounds, Wynne Wilson's uncle was the Bishop of Bath and Wells. Also living at Earlham Street at the time were 'Ponji' Robinson and Jean-Simone Kaminsky, an absconder from the French Foreign Legion who ran a nice sideline in 'adult literature' from the house until one of his printing presses caught fire and the tenants had to dispose of the hardcore evidence hastily before the police were alerted.

It was here, in the top-floor flat at Earlham Street, surrounded by Indian prints, beads and bells that Syd to all intents and purposes shrugged off his Sant Mat rejection and wrote most of the songs that would make up the bulk of the first Pink Floyd album. Peter Jenner had asked the rest of the band to contribute songs as well but initially it was Syd who seized the initiative. Drawing upon all the experiences he had absorbed and assimilated in his late teens, and working, as Andrew Rawlinson observed, 'quick, in the immediate context and with original juice', he found the lyrics pouring out of him. Songs about scarecrows and transvestites, songs about bicycles and Siamese cats, songs about gnomes and getting stoned, songs about the *I Ching* and sci-fi, songs about Cambridge and childhood.

While Syd wrote, Nick Mason toured America by Greyhound bus. In New York he read a review in the *East Village Other* of up-and-coming London bands which mentioned the 'Pink Floyd Sound'. In fact, it was Barry Miles, in his capacity as the *East Village Other*'s London correspondent, who had penned the review, the first the band had received outside of the student press. As Mason stated in his autobiography, he had fully assumed that in September he would be back on the academic treadmill. Peter Jenner and Andrew King had other ideas.

'We decided in the spring of 1966 that we'd quite like to manage them,' says King, 'but we didn't talk about it seriously with them until the start of the next academic year in September 1966 when they played the gigs at the All Saints Church Hall. We said to them we'd like to be your managers, and they said, "Well, no one else wants to be, so you might as well be." '

By the autumn of 1966 the initial energy and focus of the Notting Hill Free School had dissipated somewhat, and the physical spaces set aside for a broad range of cultural activity had now become little more than rehearsal rooms for local musicians. More importantly the venture was running low on funds.

'Andrew King and myself were both vicar's sons,' says Peter Jenner, 'and we knew that when you want to raise money for the parish you have to have a social. So in a very old-fashioned way we said, "Let's put on a social." Like in the *Just William* books, like a whist drive. We thought, "You can't have a whist drive. That's not cool. Let's have a band. That would be cool." And the only band we knew was the band I was starting to get involved with.'

The first Free School benefit ran on Friday, 30 September. Nine further benefit gigs would be held throughout October, November and December. These gigs would do more than any others to cement Pink Floyd's growing reputation. A surviving set list from the second of these gigs on 14 October reveals that Syd's intense bout of creativity during the summer had borne fruit. The band performed seven of the tracks that would appear on their debut album: 'The Gnome', 'Interstellar Overdrive', 'Take Up Thy Stethoscope and Walk', 'Snowing [aka 'Flaming'], 'Matilda Mother', 'Pow R. Toc H.', and 'Astronomy Domine', as well as Barrett compositions 'Let's Roll Another One' (aka 'Candy and a Currant Bun'), 'Lucy Leave' and 'Stoned Alone'. They also performed the instrumental 'Flapdoodle Dealing', and three Bo Diddley compositions, 'Gimme A Break', 'I Can Tell' and 'Piggy Bank Surfers'.

Artist Duggie Fields had first heard the Floyd when he was living at 101 Cromwell Road, where the band sometimes rehearsed. Raised on Mose Allison, James Brown and the Motown and Stax Revues, he wasn't initially impressed. 'I used to put on whatever I had that had a better rhythm, hoping they might get it, but they never did.' However, he was captivated by what he saw in a live environment. 'They were totally new. There was a sound you hadn't heard anywhere else. It was free-form experimental pop,' he says. 'And they were pop,' he emphasises.

'Either at the first benefit or the second one, someone came from Millbrook, Leary's estate in upper New York State, with a projector and some slides,' says Hoppy. 'The happy coincidence was the light show and the band combined.'

Inspired by Joel and Tony Brown, the two visitors from Timothy Leary's League of Spiritual Discovery in New York who had rigged up their light show at the Free School benefits, Jenner and King now had a go.

'Hoppy was a bit of a magnet and he'd brought in these people who were draft dodgers and they'd done this light show,' says Jenner. 'We thought, that's great, we want to have lights like that. We just got some oil paint and put them in a projector between two slides. Subsequently they got more sophisticated. You got a hairdryer to blow them and make them move faster, or to cool them down. That was more sophistication! Me and Andrew just got home domestic sealed spotlights and mounted them on bits of wood on the wall and then we got some gels and stapled them to the bits of wood and that was your lights, just close spots. And, of course, they didn't throw very far and weren't very strong, so we had to have them very close to the band. And when you did that you got these incredible shadows and colours moving within the shadows. It was just an accident but it enhanced the mystery of the band. Who were these people? Whoo! You can't really see their faces. They didn't come on and say, "Hi." It was all very moody.'

King remembers 'this absurd system put together with domestic lights which I operated by flicking the on–off switch very fast. None of us knew anything about theatrical lighting. We could have wasted a lot of time and resources and money if we'd had any contact with the world of theatrical lighting. It was a complete Heath Robinson job.'

'It took off like a house on fire,' says Hoppy. 'By the third or fourth benefit there were queues round the block. We'd stumbled on some sort of cultural nexus which obviously had a lot of energy in it. Joe Boyd looked at me and said, "Look, why don't we try and find a premises in the West End and run it as a club?"

'A lot of the people we ended up doing business with for years afterwards were coming down to those gigs. That was a big focal point,' agrees Andrew King. 'Then the whole thing morphed into UFO.'

One day in December 1966 Boyd and Hopkins set off on a reconnaissance mission around central London in Hoppy's purple Mini, scouting for, as Boyd put it, 'derelict cinemas and nightclubs fallen on hard times'. They eventually found what was to become the epicentre of psychedelia at the Blarney Club, an Irish ballroom underneath the Berkeley and Continentale cinemas at 31 Tottenham Court Road. It had a genial owner, Mr Gannon, and as Hoppy noted 'a basement dance floor with a beautiful polished sprung floor'.

'You couldn't have bought what happened in a way. It was so sudden,' says Peter Jenner. 'Within four weeks they had to move it to the Blarney Club in Tottenham Court Road. Within weeks we'd sold out the Roundhouse, which was a venue no one knew and which was a complete shit pit. It all went off at an incredible speed. We started doing gigs with the Floyd in September. By December we had the centre-page spread in the Christmas edition of the *Melody Maker*, saying this was the most important band of the year. All the record companies wanted to sign us. All the publishers wanted to sign us. All the agents wanted to sign us.'

'By the early winter of '66 it was all starting to take off,' agrees King. 'But it didn't surprise me. It was the first time I'd ever been involved in group management so I assumed that what was happening was normal. Y'know. You manage a band. You end up in the papers and then all these curious geezers come round and offer you funny deals. And then you get rich and famous and have sex with thousands of flower children.'

This was the high point for the English underground, the moment when Ken Kesey's 'century flower' came into full bloom.

'The summer of love was '66 in Britain, rather than '67,' maintains Barry Miles. 'Most of the things we think of as the Underground were happening by 1966. That was the time that people first started to hang out and smoke dope and dress in nice ways and parade around the King's Road. Hung on You and Granny Takes a Trip [King's Road boutiques] were late '66, although even at the Albert Hall reading Kate Heliczer and all her friends had face paint on and were wearing granny dresses and psychedelic clothing. But it seems to me that '66 was the great year. Indica had started in late '65. That was another centre where everyone met. The newly emerging rock 'n' roll aristocrats who used to go to the Scotch of St James, which was virtually next door – they were starting to come in and mix up with the artists who had been doing happenings since the early 1960s. And Better Books, instead of folding like we thought it would, carried on with Bob Cobbing as manager. Hoppy and I did a test run for *International Times* for the Aldermaston march in April, and by late '66 *International Times* was up and running. By then, boy, everyone was around.'

International Times was launched with an all-night rave at the Roundhouse in Chalk Farm in north London on 15 October 1966. The building had been constructed in 1847 as a turning shed for steam engines but had not served its original function for nearly a century. Latterly it had been used as a bonded store by Gilbey's, the gin distillers, and as the base for playwright Arnold Wesker's theatre group, Project 43. When the *IT* founders commandeered the Roundhouse for their launch party it was in a filthy state, a dark dank circular shell of a building with a leaky conical roof. Undaunted, the flyer for the launch night was promising:

Pop/Op/Costume/Masque/Fantasy-loon/Blowout Drag Ball. All night rave to launch International Times with the Soft Machine, Pink Floyd, steel bands, strips, trips, happenings, movies. Bring your own poison and flowers & gas filled balloons & submarines & rocket ships & candy & striped boxes & ladders & paint & flutes & feet & ladders & locomotives & madness & autumn & blow lamps.

The organisers draped the filthy soot-covered building in psychedelic finery and handed out placebo acid on the door. An estimated 2,500 people turned up. Soft Machine played to the occasional accompaniment of an amplified motorcycle. Performance artist Yoko Ono got up on stage halfway through their set and invited the audience to 'touch the person next to you'. Three weeks later she would meet John Lennon for the first time at the Indica gallery. Bob Cobbing and the newly formed London Film-Makers' Co-operative projected Kenneth Anger's *Scorpio Rising* and William Burroughs' *Towers Open Fire* on to the wall. The toilets flooded and the huge sculpted jelly laid on for the guests was reduced to squidgy mess when Syd and Pip Carter took away the wooden supports that were holding up its makeshift mould and used them for Pink Floyd's light show.

The band ran their entire equipment and Jenner and King's hand-built light unit through a single thirteen-amp lead, thus ensuring that the sound tripped out – appropriately enough – at regular intervals. The power blew completely during 'Interstellar Overdrive', bringing the night's proceedings to an inglorious end. But the underground had felt its strength and found its momentum. The second edition of *IT* unsurprisingly gave its own opening night a glowing review, stating that 'The Pink Floyd, psychedelic pop group, did weird things to the feel of the event with their scary feedback sounds, slide projections playing on their skin.'

Despite being embraced by the underground the band weren't so well received within the wider musical community. Here they were seen as outsiders, gimmick-ridden arrivistes who had ponced around at private parties instead of paying their dues in the correct manner by schlepping up and down the dual carriageways of Britain in a battered Transit van.

'They didn't play the blues properly. That upset people for a start,' says Peter Jenner. 'So what the fuck was this all about? It was all about a light show. That's what they thought.'

The first live review to appear in the mainstream music press seemed to confirm this perception of the band. The *NME* in December 1966 reported 'the slides were excellent, colourful, frightening grotesque, beautiful, and the group's trips into outer-space sounds promised very interesting things to come. Unfortunately all fell a bit flat in the cold reality of All Saints Hall.' Presciently the review added, 'Psychedelic versions of "Louie Louie" won't come off but if they can incorporate their electronic prowess with some lyrical and melodic songs – getting away from R & B things – they could well score in the near future.'

'There was some resentment towards them because they weren't rock musicians,' says Chris Welch of *Melody Maker*. 'They'd all come from an educated background – architects, Cambridge, and all that – and there was a perception of them as elitist metropolitan kind of people, certainly among other musicians. When they were playing at the Marquee the support bands thought they were a bit snooty. They appealed to people who liked music as an adventure, as an ongoing experiment, that's what they brought that was new and fresh. They weren't yet another blues band playing in the style of the Yardbirds.'

When Pink Floyd returned to the Marquee club in December for the first time since Steve Stollman's private parties, they played before the regular Marquee crowd and found themselves disliked by support acts, punters and proprietor John Gee alike. At UFO, however, the band were in their element.

A club is just bricks and mortars. A venue. A name. A location. A licensing deal. What makes a club is the creative energy that is unleashed there. The Cavern in Liverpool was just a dank cellar where you could get soup and a bun, but it gave birth to the Mersey sound. CBGB was a piss-pit on New York's less than salubrious Bowery. The acronym stood, unironically, for Country, Bluegrass and Blues, but the thirty or so musicians who gathered there during the mid-1970s were responsible for punk rock. During the day Manchester's Haçienda looked just like what it had once been, a yacht salesroom. At night it witnessed acid-house frenzy.

And so it was at UFO. You walked downstairs on faded and frayed beer-stained carpet tacked crudely to the concrete steps into a low-ceilinged ballroom with standard Gaelic pub decor, shamrocks and suchlike, on the walls. The small nondescript stage, which normally hosted ceilidhs, show bands and floor singers, had makeshift curtains draped unceremoniously across the front. However, between 23 December 1966 and its enforced closure at the end of September 1967 it hosted the revolution. The bouncers on the door sold, or gave away, acid. The best of the era's light show exponents – Mark Boyle and Joan Hills, Jack Bracelin, Jo Gannon, Peter Wynne Wilson, Dermot Harvey, etc. – projected and perfected their art, experimenting on the hoof with oils and inks until their colours ran dry or their equipment overheated.

This was Syd's creative zenith. Immersed in liquid projections and riding the crest of that final pure wave of Sandoz acid before the supply lines were shut down, Syd dissolved his ego in dappled shades of lime and limpid green, turquoise, violet and indigo. Hunched over his guitar he threw spontaneous improvised shapes and patterns on his Telecaster to match the improvised shapes and patterns that were being projected on to him. Shimmering blobs and bubbles and multilayered constellations of colours washed over him as he choreographed his own sonic abstractions which seemed to synchronise with the pulsating stimuli that emerged from the slides and celluloid wheels of the light shows. Visuals and sounds merged in one amorphous amoebic squall. Each enhanced and intensified the other.

'Synchronising, that's a very important part of it,' says Anthony Stern. 'It was like the early days of the silent screen, where you have the screen and you have musicians or the pianist down to the left- or right-hand side. I think that's how they conceived of it. They didn't want to be up there and in your face.'

The light show allowed Syd and his fellow band members to indulge in a minimalist kinetic ballet where the merest gesture and genuflection could be transformed into an infinitesimal array of projected possibilities. Equally importantly, it allowed them to sidestep the conventions and trappings of stagecraft completely.

'The whole thing was a form of pop art,' maintains Pete Brown, who witnessed the synergy of sound and light at UFO many times. 'Mark Boyle was a terrific light-show guy; when he was down at the UFO, he did some beautiful things. It was very inventive. People responded to it, and the band played as part of that whole kind of space. They became creatures that existed in a visual environment. It was exciting to watch. Syd wasn't just a rock star in the spotlight.'

Keith Rowe draws parallels between the disengaging possibilities of the table-top guitar and the ego-free environment of the light show. 'If you think of laying the guitar down, it's almost the equivalent of that light show. You're actually putting it one step away from yourself. The attention's not on you so much. When the guitar's on the table, the attention's on the table. When people are looking, they're not looking at you any more, they're looking at that. And so it's this distance thing. I wasn't at the centre of it. It had all those things, which Syd was feeling too. I can understand that act of "reclusement" with Syd. In a sense it's already beginning there isn't it? There's a sign there of not wanting that gaze.'

Meanwhile the benevolent Mr Gannon averted his gaze too, turning a blind eye when 'art-house' movies were projected on to its walls, stating, 'I've seen far worse than that in the navy.' An occasional crate of whisky found its way to the police station just up the road so that the constabulary might also turn a blind eye to the licensing violations going on inside (a situation, it should be remembered, that also applied to the Blarney Club's regular Irish clientele who were known to enjoy the occasional lock-in).

Almost everyone who was there agrees that this was the golden era, the paradise moment before the trappings of fame and career began to assert themselves, before the Sunday newspapers came sniffing for sensationalism and sin, before the gangsters who ran clubland came asking for protection money and before the councils, constabulary and judiciary began applying their draconian measures.

On Saturday, 31 December 1966, an all-night rave – Psychedelicamania – took place at the Roundhouse, featuring the Who, the Move and Pink Floyd. The event ran from 10 p.m. till dawn. The publicity posters promised 'Central Heating and Improved Entrance Facilities'. The UK underground's growing East Coast connections and avant-garde credentials were confirmed by mentions of 'Psychedelic Psounds from the Mothers of Invention, the Fugs, Brain Police, Radiophonic Workshop, etc.' Tickets were available from radical bookshops, such as Indica Books, Housmans and Better Books, and boutiques, including Biba and I Was Lord Kitchener's Valet, and Hampstead Record Centre – an indication of how tightly bound and self-supportive the underground still was at this stage. 'Come and Watch the Pretty Lights' cajoled the flyers, with the customary knowing nod to the lysergic faithful.

Mark Boyle, who had been working with light shows since 1963, was a purist in such matters and prided himself on creating new effects every week at UFO. He was dismissive of bandwagon-jumpers with their crudely assembled kits and badly executed visuals. 'To get the real quality you had to have these things going Pow!! Right across the screen in three colours, lightning effects, turbulence.'

As the Roundhouse ravers, freak dancing the night away, saw in 1967, the whole scene was about to go POW.

Chapter Four

Distorted View – See Through Baby Blue

A capricious little breeze, dancing up from the surface of the water, tossed the aspens, shook the dewy roses, and blew lightly and caressingly in their faces; and with its soft touch came instant oblivion.
THE WIND IN THE WILLOWS KENNETH GRAHAME

On 11 and 12 January 1967 Pink Floyd went into the Sound Techniques studios in Chelsea and recorded two tracks, 'Interstellar Overdrive' and 'Nick's Boogie'. The sessions, produced by Joe Boyd, were paid for by film-maker Peter Whitehead who wanted some contemporary soundtrack music for his film, *Tonite Let's All Make Love in London*. In the end only a brief segment of the Floyd's contribution was used in the film, and the complete footage of the thirty-minute performance only resurfaced on a commercial VHS release in 1994. As an audio and visual document the footage is seminal, being the earliest complete live performance by Pink Floyd in existence. In it Syd Barrett can be seen seated and hunched over his guitar, gouging out shards of dischordancy. He is wearing a red-and-black-hooped T-shirt and an ill-advised and thankfully short-lived pencil moustache. His hair, curly and unkempt, is not particularly long by East Coast beat and West Coast hippie standards, but it is about the same length as that worn by most English groups at the time including the Beatles, the Rolling Stones and the Who. Nick Mason, neatly coiffured and wearing a luminous purple turtleneck, looks stiff and self-conscious as he plays his Premier kit, with sticks on 'Interstellar Overdrive' and mallets on 'Nick's Boogie'. Roger Waters, wearing tinted shades and a malevolent pout, actively plays to the cameras whenever he is in close-up. His is the most physically imposing presence throughout. In contrast Rick Wright is mostly dwarfed by his Farfisa Combo Compact organ and the Binson Echorec unit that sits on top of it.

'Interstellar Overdrive' was a zeitgeist moment in the development of English pop music, the moment when pop liberated itself from its blues roots. With an opening theme, a lengthy passage of group improvisation, a minor key variation on the theme and a conclusion that restates the introductory theme, it is closer in structure to jazz than pop, but, if anything, the interplay between Syd Barrett's atonal abstractions and Rick Wright's Morse stabs and eerie vibrato squalls were closer in spirit to the European avant-garde than anything else. 'It's a magnificent piece of contemporary music. It stands up against *The Rite of Spring*. I'm not being hysterical about that,' says Anthony Stern, who was assistant director on Peter Whitehead's *Tonite Let's All Make Love in London*.

Any one of a number of R & B combos could have annihilated Pink Floyd musically during this period. Many contained an abundance of gifted and technically proficient musicians steeped in the legacy and tradition of the blues and jazz. Pink Floyd carried no such baggage. Suddenly, their lack of conventional musical skills, the very factor that had previously counted against them and had consigned them to failed auditions and occasional gigs at private functions, became a prime asset in the newly exploratory sound-world of psychedelia. 'That sudden switch from Bo Diddley to John Cage – it's a much more abstract style of music,' says Anthony Stern of 'Interstellar Overdrive'. 'And that was really the most exciting part about Syd's growth, 'cos I think he really was a forerunner of all kinds of stuff. That ability to capture a real rhythmic pulse in 'Interstellar Overdrive', having that drive which comes from rock music – you can say the one thing he kept from Bo Diddley is that relentless pulse. And then there's the fragmentation of the melody line in the most beautiful jazzy kind of way, but you'd never say "Interstellar Overdrive" was a piece of jazz. It's just this wonderful, hybrid thing where rock 'n' roll just lets go of itself and lets its hair down.'

'Interstellar Overdrive' may have been partly inspired by 'The New Thing' in jazz but unlike most modern jazz pieces (or indeed the club acts of most R & B groups) it contains no solos. The band simply didn't have the chops to venture into extravagant extemporisation with any degree of conviction. Indeed there are moments in Peter Whitehead's footage, as there were many times at UFO, where Syd and Rick's sonic voyaging simply runs out of impetus and begins to strain both credulity and patience. But 'Interstellar Overdrive' isn't about proficiency and technique. Instead, what Pink Floyd do with the resources available to them is create something entirely new out of ensemble playing. Like the Velvet Underground's 'European Son' or 'Sister Ray', 'Interstellar Overdrive' functions as a kind of anti-music. Individually the members of Pink Floyd have none of the abrasive presence or musical pedigree of the Velvets, but collectively they lock into exactly the same kind of primal empathy. It was this very lack of proficiency that gave Pink Floyd's extended pieces their unique edge. That careful counterbalancing of Syd and Rick's abstractions, enhanced by the Binson Echorec, and underpinned by Nick and Roger's basic and uncomplicated rhythm section brought into play a whole new dynamic previously unheard in English pop music.

Peter Jenner has always claimed that Syd Barrett's descending opening theme to 'Interstellar Overdrive' was based on Jenner's tone-deaf rendition of Love's version of Bacharach and David's

'My Little Red Book', which they covered on their debut album released on Elektra in the early summer of 1966. A conflicting school of thought, one championed by Roger Waters among others, is that the theme is Syd's pastiche of 'Old Ned', Ron Goodwin's opening theme to Galton and Simpson's *Steptoe and Son*, which was firmly established by 1966 as the most successful comedy show of the era. It never seems to have occurred to anyone that both theories are equally plausible, and that by working in the immediate context with the tools available at his disposal Syd, as he had done with the words 'Pink' and 'Floyd', simply forged a hybrid out of these disparate sources and created something entirely new in the process.

One thing the Whitehead footage does confirm is the extent to which Syd had absorbed and adapted the techniques he had seen used by Keith Rowe and AMM. Three minutes into 'Nick's Boogie' he lays his guitar in his lap and begins to play 'table-top' style. 'When the guitar is against your stomach it becomes very much an expression of what you're about, who you are, your thoughts. It's about you,' says Keith Rowe. 'When you lay the guitar on the table, there's a kind of a distancing. It tends to reflect issues rather than express you. Environment is reflected rather than you expressing something about the environment.'

This is precisely what Syd was doing in the midst of the light shows at the Free School and UFO, acting as an ego-free conduit for musical exploration, distancing and decentring himself, reflecting as much as expressing. Early in 1967 he took a bunch of small circular polished metal discs, of the kind that were beginning to appear on girls' belts and op-art mini dresses, and glued them to his Fender Esquire, making the instrument literally reflective (and refractive.) Throughout the Whitehead footage he can be seen constantly challenging the gestural lexicon of the rock guitar, whether by radically detuning his instrument or adopting unconventional and untutored slide techniques.

'Syd was an incredible performer,' says Peter Brown, who saw Pink Floyd play several times during this period. 'Miles had invited me down to Powis Square. "You've gotta hear this band." I didn't think that much of them actually, but I liked Syd. And then because I was kind of *persona grata* at UFO I used to go down there a lot – partly chasing girls, but partly because it was a kind of a loose community at the time, and we all had certain aims in common. Syd was incredibly charismatic, and within his limitations he could do things on guitar that were very, very interesting. Some of them were textural things and others were definitely kind of linear improvisational type things. I mean, when he was on, when he was happening, he was really happening, y'know?'

'I have to admit that he never struck me as special as everyone now thinks he was,' says Barry Miles. 'But to me he was the most sympathetic one out of the Pink Floyd. He was the one that was most in tune with what was going on at the UFO club and avant-garde music in general. He was very interested in electronic music, like Luciano Berio, who was very important at that time with his recordings of speeded-up and slowed-down collages of tape. Syd was very interested in this sort of thing, which is why he was so interested in AMM. And he certainly knew a lot about art. He was fascinated by the subject. He genuinely cared about what was going on in America. He would talk about De Kooning and Rothko and all the stuff that was being shown at the Whitechapel Gallery. I was never a close friend of Syd's, but the few conversations we had were usually on that kind of level, because we had the same art school background and the same influences.'

Syd's fascination with the Dutch abstract expressionist Willem De Kooning reveals another line of contact. Chaim Soutine's 'thick squidgy excited paint', as Robert Hughes put it, had a big influence on De Kooning, the originator of what became known as action painting, and influenced Syd further on down the line.

Indeed Robert Hughes' description of De Kooning as 'a creature of Protean vitality who subsumes the history of art in his own person, becomes a touchstone of the culture, and so transcends all questions of originality' echoes Andrew Rawlinson's early assessment of Syd, and like so many comments on his influences might just as easily have been applied to Syd himself.

Co-manager Andrew King agrees that, for all his apparent spontaneity and improvisation, it was clear that Syd had thought things through conceptually. 'Someone once said to Picasso, "I could do that in five minutes", and Picasso replied, "Well, it took me seventy years and five minutes." Syd's guitar explorations were like that. They didn't come out of nowhere.'

'I think that's a quote from Whistler, actually,' says Anthony Stern. 'I think Whistler was sued by somebody for fraud, because he'd painted in a very abstract kind of way. And someone said, "You could do that in twenty minutes." And he replied in the same spirit, "I've been doing this for a lifetime. So, it's twenty minutes plus a lifetime." But yes, Syd definitely did put in the hours and he put in the persistence.'

Andrew Rawlinson also draws a comparison with the modus operandi of the twentieth century's greatest artist. 'Just as Picasso is said to have said, "I don't seek, I find", I think it's true of Syd. And I think Syd is quite Picasso-like. I mean in his method of working. I'm not comparing him with Picasso, but we all know Picasso would try anything. And whatever you want to say about him as a self-promoter and making himself out to be the genius artist, which is probably all true, it's clearly the case that he thought, "Oh, I think I'll have a go at that. Why not?" And he did it all his life. Syd was the same. It's just that Syd's creative life didn't last very long.'

In January 1967 a German film crew from Bavarian Rundfunk came to London and made a one-hour documentary entitled *Die Jungen Nachtwandler* (*The Young Nightcrawler*) directed by

Edmund Wolf, who also provided the commentary. Much of the footage was shot at UFO. As with Peter Whitehead's film, it captures the raw innovation of Pink Floyd's music in their early days. Wolf's footage allows us to hear approximately four and a half minutes of an astounding live version of 'Interstellar Overdrive', which is immeasurably more free-form and abstract than the version that would eventually appear on the Floyd's debut album.

Of course, as with any truly exploratory music, the Floyd's sonic journeys could be notoriously variable in quality. By its very definition, genuine experimentation does not always have a tangible outcome. Even Coltrane had his off nights, flailing away in the outer reaches of the cosmos, and there were certainly nights at UFO when the individual components weren't gelling and when chemically induced voyaging among audience and performers alike gave way to uninspired noodling and musical cul-de-sacs.

'There was very little finesse in the early days,' concedes Barry Miles. 'Syd was never a brilliant guitar virtuoso. He was much better at exploring ideas. There were often, particularly at the UFO club where they'd play for hours, long periods where it would get really boring to be quite honest. I'm sure that sounds sacrilegious but you'd be thinking "Jesus, God, please" as Syd went up and down the keys with his bloody lighter or marbles or steel ball bearings. And Roger was barely competent on bass. Nick would be the only person who would keep it going some nights. The leapers at the front were often dancing to him because the rest would be way off the beat.'

Nick Mason's role in the architecture of things is often underplayed. Like Mo Tucker in the Velvet Underground he leaned more towards primitivism than proficiency, but his contribution was essential. Pink Floyd simply would not have worked with an Elvin Jones, a Mitch Mitchell or a Ginger Baker.

A tyro like Keith Moon would have unbalanced them irrevocably. Mason's very lack of combustibility, coupled with that uncomplicated repertoire of mallet touches and simple rhythms, was an essential chemical ingredient. Syd Barrett is normally credited with bringing the Bo Diddley influence to Pink Floyd's music, but it is noticeably Nick Mason in the Peter Whitehead footage who introduces 'Nick's Boogie' with that tell-tale Bo Diddley shuffle beat.

It was once unkindly said of Ringo Starr that not only was he not the best drummer in the world but he probably wasn't even the best drummer in the Beatles. Hearing David Gilmour's perfectly functional contribution to some of Syd Barrett's later solo tracks, the same might be said of Nick Mason. But in the same way that Ringo's languid technique came into its own during the Beatles' psychedelic phase (on 'Rain', 'Tomorrow Never Knows' and 'Strawberry Fields Forever', for instance) Nick Mason had exactly the right aesthetic temperament for what was required in Pink Floyd.

More audio evidence of the Floyd's raw power can be heard on the thirty-minute Granada TV documentary *Underground: Scene Special* which, like Whitehead's and Wolf's footage, was filmed in January 1967. In the programme the staff of *IT* can be seen working on issue number seven. 'Arrest the Home Secretary' reads the front-page headline. Under the wary eye of the local constabulary and to the general bemusement of passers-by, Hoppy and placard-carrying friends embark upon a Happening around the Eros statue in Piccadilly Circus. 'Pot Is Fun' reads Hoppy's banner. 'Legagise It' [*sic!*] reads another. Bus passengers stare out of their rain-spattered windows with impeccably English bemusement. Jeff Nuttall and the People Show are filmed performing one of their provocative theatre pieces, and Miles is interviewed at Indica talking optimistically about what he describes as 'an embryonic scene'. Paul McCartney adds stoned gravitas to proceedings with his plea for common sense and tolerance. Pink Floyd are filmed in an untypically well-lit UFO, performing a full-tilt version of 'Interstellar Overdrive', while a smattering of freaky dancers gallivant about the dance floor with varying degrees of self-consciousness. Early in the programme, as Hoppy and friends perform their Eros Happening, a brief snippet of an early version of the Floyd's 'Matilda Mother' can be heard. The lyrics are mostly inaudible but they appear to be completely different from the ones eventually recorded for the band's debut album. In one of the few intelligible snippets Syd sneers sardonically 'Oh what a drag | caught in a bag', while on the recorded version he implores 'Oh mother | tell me more'. Musically it is considerably less refined than the polished studio effort that would appear on *The Piper at the Gates of Dawn* LP. It sounds more like a prototype for the Stooges or the MC5 than a template for English psychedelia, and provides a salutary reminder that the band had been performing mutated versions of 'Louie Louie' only a couple of months earlier.

Although their musical activity still lay completely outside the mainstream of English pop taste, Pink Floyd and their R&B mutations were in the vanguard of a peculiar development during the latter half of 1966 and the early part of 1967. Something odd and unforeseen was going on, the evolution of which is clearly evident in the music of the period. Mod beat went a bit blurred at the edges. Jerky dexedrine-driven riffs got slacker. The increased use of reverb, echo, distortion and compression on recordings only added to this sense of auditory disorientation. Simultaneously, it seems, arrangements became more ornate, decorative, pastoral. Groups began embroidering their songs with plain chant, piccolos, harpsichords, zithers or sitars.

On 'My Minds Eye', the Small Faces Christmas hit of 1966, the band shed their R&B reference points in favour of descant singing and the *Hosanna in excelsis* refrain from a sixteenth-century French children's carol. When Southend-based R & B band the Paramounts, who had scored a minor hit with their version of Leiber and Stoller's 'Poison Ivy' in 1964, were relaunched as Procol Harum, they unveiled their brand of Bach-influenced 'baroque and roll' with 'A Whiter Shade of Pale'. The Pretty Things, Eric Burdon and the Animals and Zoot Money's Big Roll Band made similarly rapid transformations from rhythm-and-blues stalwarts to psychedelic voyagers. Hendrix sniffed the air and caught the mood immediately when he arrived in England. His first single was a cover of the revenge blues ballad 'Hey Joe'. His second was called 'Purple Haze'.

Presiding over this entire cultural shift, of course, were the Beatles. The 'four stately kings of EMI', as the Monkees would dub them on 'Alternate Title', had already fanfared the future with the *Revolver* album, an album that Syd Barrett played constantly during the summer of 1966. Although no one knew it at the time, they were about to write the next chapter in pop history.

Meanwhile on 29 January 1967 Pink Floyd returned to Sound Techniques studio with Joe Boyd producing, and recorded 'Arnold Layne' and 'Candy and a Currant Bun', the two tracks that would become their debut single. It was Boyd's intention that the tracks should be recorded and presented to potential record companies as finished items rather than hawked around as demos. Boyd had initially used his connections to secure the band an audition with a distinctly unimpressed Jac Holzman at Elektra who offered the band a derisory deal. Polydor Records came up with a marginally better offer and it was envisaged that the single would be released on the label's new subsidiary, Track Records, which would also sign the Who, Cream and Jimi Hendrix, but Polydor was effectively gazumped at the eleventh hour when agent Bryan Morrison secured the Floyd a better deal with EMI. This had immediate ramifications for Joe Boyd, as it was EMI policy to use in-house producers only, so the band were forced to dispense with his services. Despite being so comprehensively shafted, Boyd's legacy was a quirky little pop song about a clothes fetishist that would propel Pink Floyd into the pop charts.

'Arnold Layne' contained many of the trademark elements of Syd Barrett's writing style: subject matter drawn from his immediate context (there was an actual clothes-line thief in Cambridge at the time); concise and economical form (the song consists of just three four-line verses of fifteen to eighteen words); ellipsis of syntax and narrative ('doors bang | chain gang'); an instinctive sense of phrasing; a clever balancing of regular and irregular metre, assonance, imperfect and internal rhyme (Layne/strange; Wall/tall; caught/sort) and subtle rhythmic shifts and elongations of syllables and vowels which, although 'Arnold Layne' contains no drug references, replicated the disorientation of an acid trip (straaange/hobby; taaaall/mirror.)

'Arnold Layne' doesn't celebrate or sensationalise its subject matter: indeed, lurking beneath the freak-show facade lies a curiously old-fashioned morality tale whose tone ranges from the gently admonishing ('Oh Arnold Layne | it's not the same') to the anguished pay-off 'Why can't you see', where Syd's constricted larynx sounds just like it did on 'Lucy Leave'.

'Arnold Layne' was in the vanguard of a peculiarly English type of character vignette that would become synonymous with psych-pop but it was by no means the first. The Who's 'Happy Jack', a paean to retarded innocence and simmering cruelty, and Cat Stevens' 'Matthew and Son', a story of a beleaguered and down-trodden office clerk, were both in the charts the week 'Arnold Layne' was recorded. And in among the mod anthems and soul covers on the Who's *A Quick One* LP, released in December 1966, were curios like John Entwistle's 'Boris the Spider' and Keith Moon's 'Cobwebs and Strange', while Pete Townshend had signposted the lyrical territory for gender crisis and dysfunction several months earlier with the Who's previous single, 'I'm A Boy'.

If 'Arnold Layne' was somewhat understated, its B-side, 'Candy and a Currant Bun', bristles with untamed energy. From Rick Wright's opening drone and Syd's initial over-amplified chord to the wild Echorec loop at the end, the song perfectly captures the band in transition from raw R&B to full-tilt psychedelia. Essentially a minimally adapted version of the Floyd's live staple 'Let's Roll Another One', there is still a trace element of the original's 'Smokestack Lightning' riff in the melody, but the reworked lyric drips with innuendo and suggestiveness ('I'd like to see you | lick that') and manages to sound more subversive, more sensuous and paradoxically enough, more drug-tinged than the original's unabashed tribute to the joys of pot-smoking. Syd's singing alternates between arch (he slips a cleverly disguised 'fock' into the chorus and makes it sound like 'walk') and eerie. No other pop song of the time would have contained an ego-disintegrating refrain like 'Ooh, you know, I'm feeling frail', while a hastily added middle eight, 'Don't try another cat tonight | Don't go a lot on that', previously absent from 'Let's Roll Another One', undercuts the playfulness of the song with jealousy and menace.

Three weeks after Pink Floyd recorded their debut single, the Beatles released the double-A-sided single 'Penny Lane/ Strawberry Fields Forever'. The band's publicist Derek Taylor once famously said that when the Beatles took acid they discovered their inner Scouser, and here was the evidence. Both tracks referred to the psychogeography of favoured Liverpool childhood haunts. Each represented different, and defining, facets of the LSD experience as mediated through England's two most famous songwriters at the height of their creative powers. McCartney's 'Penny Lane' represented psychedelia's yin, with its clarity, its exuberance, its piccolo trumpet fanfare, its surrealism of the commonplace (bankers and barbers, poppies in trays, firemen rushing in from the pouring rain) and that tell-tale reality-blurring reference to the nurse who thinks she's in a play and is anyway. Lennon's 'Strawberry Fields Forever', with its dirge like tempo, its hazy drawl, its stream-of-consciousness lyric taken to the brink of inarticulacy, its introversion, its pitch shifts, woozy Mellotron, sawing cellos, false ending and hallucinatory coda, was psychedelia's yang.

'I always say to people that "Arnold Layne", "Strawberry Fields" and "Penny Lane" were the three breakthrough British rock songs, where you could actually write about British subjects in a semi-social, poetic, historical kind of way,' says Pete Brown. 'That was great for me. That really helped me an awful lot to see where I was going and what I could do, and I just started writing it all for Cream. It was very good to see those things being successful and prominent, and that people liked them, 'cos I could see that there was something for me in it, too. It was the way I was going at the time and it really enforced that I was doing the right thing and opened it up for people like me big time. You could look at English subjects, you didn't have to be transatlantic.'

Within weeks of the release of 'Penny Lane/Strawberry Fields Forever' and 'Arnold Layne' every former mod on the block seemed to be writing songs about toy shops, teddy bears, toffee apples, magicians, mad men, mythical beasts, penny-farthings, children's playgrounds, weather vanes, fairground rides and rainbows. Inspired by the Beatles and Syd Barrett, everyone threw off the shackles of R&B and got in touch with their inner infant. Steve Winwood, who up to the end of 1966 had been the best teenage Ray Charles imitator in the business, left the Spencer Davis Group and formed Traffic, who collectively retreated to the country to pen songs about paper suns and Berkshire poppies. Winwood's old band, not to be outdone, recorded the cello-drenched 'Time Seller'. Fellow Brum-beat boys the Move, who possessed a threatening and thuggish beauty all of their own, became UFO regulars with a pop art–Happening stage act that involved smashing up TV sets and burning effigies of Harold Wilson. Their first two singles, 'Night of Fear' and 'I Can Hear the Grass Grow' (released in January and April 1967 respectively), crackled with pill-induced paranoia and bad-trip imagery.

It wasn't all down to LSD. The Move's songwriter, Roy Wood, maintains that he never went near the stuff and, as the more astute chroniclers observed, plenty of compliant pop musicians merely donned paisley and chiffon and pretended in the name of the cause, overlaying their routine 'Route 66' riffs with suitably lavender-scented lyrics and prettified vocal delivery. Record companies, still giddy from the profits of the mid-1960s Beat Boom continued to hand out generous recording budgets, allowing arrangers to embroider tracks with string sections, brass bands, sitars and Mellotrons, while producers doused everything in echo and phasing. For a brief moment that collusion of warped whimsy and auditory disorientation became the dominant sound of English pop.

During this period the members of Pink Floyd finally gave up their academic studies in order to devote themselves to music. Nick Mason, by his own admission, was not shaping up to be a convincing architect and had spent his final months at Regent Street Polytechnic getting other people to write his essays for him. Mason was offered a timely sabbatical from college and never went back. Rick Wright, too, had long since ceased to attend music college. Roger Waters had a day job gaining work experience at the prestigious design consultancy firm of Fitzroy Robinson and Partners but gave up a potentially lucrative career as an architect to devote himself to the band. Syd had also pretty much dropped out of college by 1967 and like Nick Mason had been offered a sabbatical, as Maggi Hambling recalls. 'Robert

Medley, who was the very inspired head of painting at Camberwell, believed that, when the person left, they left with the present of their personality – this gift from the art school of your personality, not personality as we think of it, but as a painter or sculptor. Roger told me he'd been to see Robert Medley and said to him that he was doing two gigs a week and earning £200 a week and would it be all right for him to have a sabbatical and have a year off and then come back in a year's time. He seemed quite sensible about it. He said, "You never know. It's all fashion, and you never know how long this success will last." Robert, being a very civilised humane human being, said, "Of course," and he never came back.'

Several of Syd's contemporaries were surprised to see him give up his art for the music business. 'He was such a nice guy that I felt really sorry when he got mixed up with rock music,' says Stan Willis. Syd's close friend Anna Murray agreed. 'He was very carried away by the music and he liked performing, but at the time I thought he'd be better off as a painter,' she told John Cavanagh. 'His temperament suited it better. I was really surprised when he took off into the music so hugely. I felt he was swept up and it wasn't necessarily his intention or his driving force. It wasn't apparent to me that it was the most important thing in his life at all.'

'I remember Juliette Gale telling me what a wrench it was for Syd to go back on his idea of being a painter. It wasn't an easy decision for him to take at all,' confirms Bob Klose.

Pink Floyd officially turned professional on 1 February. Later that month they signed on the dotted line with EMI for an advance of £5,000. Publicity photos from the day show the band members grinning and high-kicking in the street outside EMI's Manchester Square headquarters.

The band signed to EMI during a period when the tabloid press was at the height of a scaremongering campaign to inform its readership of the drug peril afflicting Britain's youth. The very week that Pink Floyd joined EMI, the *News of the World* was in the middle of a three-part exposé called 'Pop Stars and Drugs' which implicated almost every leading pop star in the land, including the Beatles, the Rolling Stones, Jimi Hendrix, the Moody Blues, the Move, Cream and Donovan (among other gems, the *News of the World* called for Donovan's 'Sunshine Superman' to be banned and for pop stars to be dope-tested like race horses or athletes). The series provided the moral catalyst, and indeed the direct tip-off, that led to the arrest, on 12 February, of Mick Jagger and Keith Richard at Richards' Sussex home. The subsequent conviction, overturned on appeal, prompted William Rees-Mogg's famous *Times* editorial, 'Who Breaks a Butterfly on a Wheel'. Pink Floyd themselves were implicated in the concluding week of the *News of the World* features, and were directly linked with the psychedelic drug scene.

This, then, was the climate in which the underground's house band signed to one of the biggest and most strait-laced record labels in the world. EMI immediately felt compelled to put out a press release disassociating the group from 'psychedelic pop' and drug use. 'The Pink Floyd are not trying to create hallucinatory effects on their audience,' it read. This prompted John Hopkins to write in issue ten of *International Times* in March 1967: 'Actually, I think I prefer it when the Floyd give me hallucinations.'

This wasn't the first time that EMI had been embroiled in such controversy. In January 1967 mod group the Game had caused seven minutes of an episode of BBC's *Juke Box Jury* to be pulled after a heated discussion about their Parlophone single, 'The Addicted Man', boiled over. The single was hastily withdrawn even though it conveyed an anti-drug message. Another EMI signing, the Shots, had changed their name to the Smoke – suitably ambiguous – in the summer of 1966 and penned a song called 'My Friend Jack' ('eats sugar lumps'). Mindful of the

1 & 2 Pink Floyd with Bob Klose at Highgate, early 1965. From left in 2: Bob Klose,
Syd Barrett, Roger Waters, Nick Mason and Rick Wright

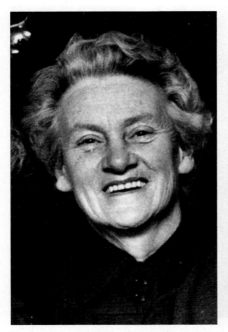

3 Syd's mother, Win
4 Libby Gausden with Syd in 1961
5 Vanji Thorgerson with her son Storm

6 Ella O'Connell in her Tottenham Street flat

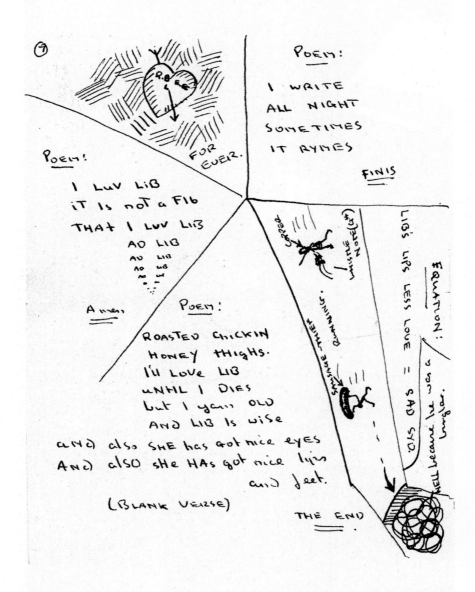

7 Letter to Libby Gausden from Syd, dated 1962

8 Nigel and Jenny Lesmoir-Gordon outside Galloway and Porter bookshop, Sidney Street, Cambridge 1964

9 Syd performing at Hornsey College of Art, 18 November 1966
10 Pink Floyd at the UFO Club, December 1966/January 1967

11 Pink Floyd around the time of their *Look of the Week* appearance, July 1967
12 At the Saville Theatre, London, October 1967

13 Syd with his mirrored Fender Esquire guitar, *c.*1967

controversy that had greeted the Game's single, EMI made them change the lyrics of the chorus, 'Oh, what beautiful things he sees'. The band complied with the equally drug-soaked 'He's been travelling everywhere', which seemed to satisfy the censorious record company, who presumably thought it was a travelogue. Had they possessed a keener ear for vernacular and nuance they would have realised that lots of people were singing about going on journeys during 1967.

Peter Jenner defends EMI's stance and public utterances regarding the signing of their new charges. 'They had to distance themselves. They absolutely had to. They couldn't possibly have said, "Oh yes, they're a drug band and we support them and we're giving them money." Sir Joseph Lockwood was a crafty old sod. He knew we were playing on that psychedelic thing and the drug culture. And the *News of the World* had exposed us. When I first saw that I was still working at the LSE. I thought, "What shit are we going to get?" I still don't know how EMI dealt with it. To this day I'm surprised how little trouble we got. I have no recollection of us being pursued or photographers camping outside. It just came and went. It was a non-story. They didn't quite get what was going down and how rampant the whole psychedelic drug thing was, and the theology of it.'

One person who did get the theology of it was Syd. He was no more of a proselytiser than his beer-supping band mates but he was living the lifestyle to the full. 'Syd and I moved from Tottenham Street down to Earlham Street,' says David Gale. 'I had a room that was under an advertisement for Cadet cigarettes and looked out across to the Cambridge Theatre over the road. Syd had a room upstairs and there was a guy there – who'd better remain nameless even to this day, insofar as he was responsible for stealing a very large block of opium from the Botanical Museum in Kew Gardens. This is a typical lurid hippie aside, but Syd was partaking, like everybody else, of whatever people came up with, y'know? If somebody came in with a bunch of opium, you'd take it. Probably heroin retained its scary profile, but even that was dabbled in. It was kick out the jams, no holds barred. And Syd was right in there, and clearly got swept up in a way that outstripped him.'

Nigel Lesmoir-Gordon had detected the shape of things to come in the way that Roger Waters had reacted to his maiden acid voyage a year earlier. 'Roger wouldn't have wanted to go with it. He wouldn't have wanted to let go of being Roger Waters. Major ego. He wanted fame and fortune. Syd was more transcendental.'

'I remember Syd being really excited one night at UFO because Paul McCartney was there,' remembers Jenny Lesmoir-Gordon. 'But he wasn't as driven as Roger to be a famous and enriched person,' adds Nigel. 'He wanted to be on stage and do his music and communicate his stuff but I don't think he craved fame.'

Another resident of 101 Cromwell Road, Hester Page, also noticed the differences at close quarters. 'Syd was delightful to be with. Very sensitive. Quietly spoken. Didn't show off. There was no side to him at all. He was just a very sweet guy so people liked being around him. Whereas someone like Roger was much more of a showman. A bigger ego. Had more presence about him and he was more aware of the world they were entering into.'

Anthony Stern qualifies this assessment somewhat. 'I think a natural modesty was characteristic of the whole Cambridge gang, actually. None of us had massive egos. I think it was slightly frowned upon. It was a bit vulgar, a bit cheap to beat your chest and want to be like a pop star. But there was a social divide in music. The working-class lads – and that counted for most pop stars and pop musicians – had this burning desire to make something of themselves to get away from their backgrounds. They had a sense of ego, which I don't think Pink Floyd ever had, perhaps because they come from middle-class, very secure backgrounds.

But you did see that with all the other bands that were going on in London at the time, who weren't perhaps from that privileged background. There was a much greater urgency to make it. The Floyd just wanted to get on and do what they wanted to do best. The word "ambition" has a slightly different meaning in their careers than in other people's careers. I used to work with Tony Secunda, who was managing the Move. He had an office underneath the flat where I was living with Peter Whitehead, and he would say to me things like "I've got this band called the Move. They're *so* much better than the Floyd." And I said, "Tony, you just don't get it do you?" The Move hadn't got an ounce of that psychic spirituality that the Floyd had. So there was this big divide. It was basically the Floyd versus the Rolling Stones' mentalities. One was an inward-looking, very English, slightly middle- and upper-middle-class, airy-fairy, Arcadian view of music and the other was a driving ambition to be big in America.'

Whatever the merit of these observations one thing is indisputable. Fame changed everything. Even though 'Arnold Layne' was only a minor hit, reaching number 20 in the charts, it kick-started a process that propelled the band out of the security bubble of the London underground and into the mainstream.

On the day of its release, Saturday, 11 March, 'Arnold Layne' was played on *Juke Box Jury*, the long-running BBC1 light entertainment show where new records were judged 'Hit' or 'Miss' by a panel of guest celebrities. Hosted by old Etonian and stalwart of the Light Programme David Jacobs, the reviewing panel that evening comprised disc jockeys Pete Murray and Jimmy Savile, the 'reigning' Miss World Reita Faria and actress Judy Geeson. Murray denounced Pink Floyd as 'a con' and psychedelia as a 'one-month wonder'. 'No wonder Pete Murray thought it was a hype,' says Peter Jenner, 'because suddenly it was everywhere.' Despite Murray's withering assessment, BBC radio did play 'Arnold Layne', as did most of the offshore pirate stations. However, the most mainstream and popular offshore station, Radio London, in a fit of moral pique banned the record completely.

The gigs changed too. The Floyd left the sanctuary of the counter-culture and ventured out into Top Rank territory where their live set was often met with indifference or downright hostility. The Birdcage Dancehall, Portsmouth, the Top Spot, Ross-on-Wye or the California Ballroom, Dunstable, were not UFO or the Roundhouse. The Birdcage in Portsmouth was a mod stronghold and the audience greeted 'Interstellar Overdrive' accordingly. At the California Ballroom punters poured beer on the stage from the balcony and hurled pint pots and coins at the band. Elsewhere audiences waited for the feedback and cater-wauling to stop and the resident DJ to come back on and play some hit-parade music so they could resume dancing and fighting and copping off and all the other things audiences do when they remain singularly unimpressed with light shows, lengthy improvisations and songs about currant buns and transvestites.

A few weeks after signing with EMI Pink Floyd entered Abbey Road studios and began recording their debut album. Commencing on 21 February with 'Matilda Mother' and concluding on 21 May with 'Bike', the tracks that were recorded fell into two distinct styles; the lengthy improvisations featured in the band's live act, 'Astronomy Domine', 'Interstellar Overdrive', 'Pow R. Toc H.', and 'Take Up Thy Stethoscope and Walk', and the shorter songs that Syd had penned, mostly at Earlham Street during the summer and autumn of 1966, 'Lucifer Sam', 'Matilda Mother', 'Flaming', 'The Gnome', 'Chapter 24', 'The Scarecrow' and 'Bike'.

If acid had put the Beatles in touch with their inner Scouser, it put Syd Barrett in touch with his inner Cantabrigian. Regression and rebirth was a well-trodden path among acid initiates. Back in 1943, Albert Hoffman on his initial LSD trip had experienced profound reminders of his childhood, likening the oneness with nature he experienced to the mystical visions he had while walking in the woods as a young boy. More recently John Lennon had mixed images of ego-death and karmic renewal on 'Tomorrow Never Knows' and 'She Said She Said', ending the former with the mantric 'of the beginning | of the beginning' and interjecting the poignant 'when I was a boy | everything was right' into the latter. For Syd childhood now chimed with equal resonance. Barely out of his teens, for him acid was the magic ingredient that enabled him to dissolve the fortress walls of adulthood and skip gleefully back to infancy. From this vantage point he could invoke and reflect upon a world of certainty, a time before anxiety, before the expectations of ambition and the imposition of status, a time when tea was on the table and his father was in his study.

'You've gotta look at Cambridge really; you've gotta look at Lewis Carroll and Edward Lear, more than the lifestyle thing,' says Pete Brown of Syd's influences. 'Maybe it's inspired by people like Rimbaud and Verlaine and people like that, but I think the English fringe thing is more to do with it, always has been. Language, lateral thinking, looking at the weirdness of British existence, looking at rural or semi-rural peculiarities.'

No account of Syd Barrett's creative blossoming can take place without examining these earliest and most enduring influences. The lives and works of Edward Lear (1812–88), Charles Dodgson, aka Lewis Carroll (1832–98), Kenneth Grahame (1859–1932) and Hilaire Belloc (1870–1953) form a thematic framework within which Syd's initial flowering as a songwriter can be contextualised and understood. The songs that were overtly influenced by Belloc, Grahame et al. only constitute a very small body of his oeuvre but these are the songs for which he is best known and on which his reputation as a songwriter largely rests.

'That English Robin and Puck and Goodfellow thing. The slightly whimsical faery quality that he had,' notes Emily Young. 'It's from the English folk tradition, but not the English working-man one. You're not quite sure if he will appear or disappear. More of the Irish and Celtic and less of the Germanic. Something of "the trees have secrets". I think he was absolutely in touch with that.'

As Emily Young suggests, Syd was very precise in his absorption of childhood literature. There is nothing of the Germanic or Norse tradition, no Hans Christian Andersen, no Aesop, no Brothers Grimm and, despite what some have suggested, little or no Tolkien either. He draws very directly upon Belloc, Grahame, Lear and Carroll, and little else but the merest hint of C. S. Lewis and the found material he plundered from a few nursery rhyme pocket-books.

Lear's *A Book of Nonsense*, Carroll's *Alice's Adventures in Wonderland* and *Alice Through the Looking-Glass*, Grahame's *The Wind in the Willows* and Belloc's *Cautionary Tales* are among the best-loved works in English children's literature. The characters and settings they spawned, the Owl and the Pussycat, the Mad Hatter's tea-party, Toad of Toad Hall and the rest were, until the advent of Harry Potter, the bedrock and stimulus of children's imaginations for the best part of a century.

Like Syd Barrett, all four authors suffered the loss of a parent at an early age. Edward Lear, the youngest of twenty children, was rejected by his mother and given to an older sister to bring up when he was four. From an early age he suffered from what he called 'the morbids', an all-enveloping depression that dogged him periodically throughout his life. His work, he once said, 'was a "universal panacea for the ills of life" – it left no time for brooding or recrimination and kept the morbids at bay'.

Kenneth Grahame's mother died of scarlet fever in 1864 when he was five. As his father, a chronic alcoholic, was incapable of looking after his children, Kenneth, along with his three brothers and sisters, was uprooted from his childhood in Scotland and sent to Cookham Dean in Berkshire, where he was brought up by his paternal grandmother. During the last twenty years of his life

Grahame senior neither saw nor provided for his children.

Hilaire Belloc's father, Louis, died aged forty-two in 1872, when the child was just two years old. The infant Hilaire was the designated chief mourner at the funeral, walking behind the coffin, holding his mother's hand. Charles Dodgson's mother died in 1851 during his first year at Oxford University, when he was eighteen. His mother's unmarried sister, Lucy, subsequently looked after the Dodgson family and remained with them for the rest of her life.

These absences had an undeniable impact on each author's creative life. Certain themes recur throughout their work directly as a result of these early traumatic losses. Disembodied identity, a dream-like sense of the self in limbo without place or purpose, rootlessness, restlessness, rejection, detachment, escapism, retreat into imaginary worlds, the past recounted in reverie, the lost grandeur of classicism and antiquity, faded or unreachable Arcadia, protracted childhood and the potency of myth — all crop up time and time again and in many guises, as they do through Syd Barrett's songs.

There are other connections, too. Hilaire Belloc's childhood in France was characterised by a total absence of men in his family. He was an indulged, precocious, combative, gifted and belligerent child in a chaotic maternal household, cosseted and protected by a widowed mother and two widowed grand-mothers. In 1871, the year after Hilaire was born, the family had to flee their home when Paris was besieged by the Prussian invasion. The family home was subsequently occupied and sacked by the Prussian army. Hilaire subsequently grew up, as A. N. Wilson put it in his biography of Belloc, 'with an in-built domestic mythology of Paradise Lost ... of bittersweet memories of a France which had vanished forever'. Belloc's mother, Bessie, later wrote a biography entitled *I Too Have Lived In Arcadia*. To ward off grief and disruption the young Hilaire immersed himself in literature, read prodigiously from an early age and was writing metrically precise poetry by the age of seven.

Kenneth Grahame also spent his childhood living in a world of his own imagination. When he wasn't exploring his large Berkshire home with its numerous nooks and crannies, its womb-like cupboards and corners, its winding staircase and its dusty vaulted attic, he was roaming the surrounding countryside, projecting on to its fir-tree woods, meadows and willow-bordered river an anthropomorphic vision of a fantasy world populated by creatures of his own creation. He regarded the house's unkempt wild orchard as elf-haunted, and its duck pond as the source of the Nile.

Something else that Lear, Dodgson, Grahame and Belloc's best-remembered works have in common is that they were all part of a satirical backlash against the conventions of their genre. Nineteenth-century children's literature was puritanical and doctrinaire in tone, with an evangelical emphasis on morality and an overriding duty to instruct. For countless generations the appeal of the Alice stories, *The Wind in the Willows*, the nonsense verse and *Cautionary Tales* lay in their subversive connotations. The best-loved of these works were essentially rebellious texts, loved equally by adults and children alike. Children were captivated by an inventive cast of the mischievous, the macabre, the nonsensical and the grotesque, and by the explicit rejection, or complete absence, of adult authority. Adults recognised their richly parodic nature and the way they mocked the social order and the moral certainties of the adult universe.

In the 1960s *Alice's Adventures in Wonderland* and *Alice Through the Looking-Glass* would be eagerly reclaimed by the acid generation. Alice's shifting identity, the logic twists of the narrative and the dreamscape of bizarre characters were fruitful thematic territory for any imaginative child who had grown up in the shadow of the bomb and had come of age in the era of

146

psychedelic drugs. In America the love generation appropriated Walt Disney's largely forgotten *Fantasia* for much the same reason. In the case of Alice, though, the appropriation began much earlier, and is embedded deep in the psyche of English nostalgia. Although it was well received in his lifetime, interest in Carroll's work declined rapidly after his death in 1898. It was the horrors of the Great War of 1914–1918 that restored Alice to the English literary consciousness. While European avant-garde sensibilities turned to Dada, futurism, and nihilism, the English cultivated a fondness for the lost world of Edwardiana and Victoriana. When English pop music adopted the same iconography in the mid-1960s, it was merely tapping in to a potent strain of nostalgia that has been there since Passchendaele, the Somme and Flanders destroyed the faith, trust and patriotism (and limbs) of an entire generation of youth.

Edward Lear created a fascinating nonsensical cosmogony of human, animal and plant life, populated by such creatures as the Jumblies, the Quangle Wangle, the Pelican Chorus, the Akond of Swat and, perhaps most famously, the Dong with the Luminous Nose. He wrote nonsense botany, nonsense recipes, nonsense limericks and nonsense songs and constructed an entire nonsense alphabet.

John Lennon was clearly the pop world's most obvious descendant of Lear. The characters that populate his books *John Lennon in His Own Write* (1964) and *A Spaniard in the Works* (1965), such as Eric Hearble, Treasure Ivan, the Wumberlog and Mr Boris Morris, as well as the language that describes them and the sketches that accompany them, are highly reminiscent of Lear. Although the influence was never as overt in Syd's work (his influences rarely were), he exhibited the same sense of playful absurdity.

Syd's letters to Libby crackle with the same kind of offbeat wit and invention that characterised much of Lear's own correspondence. Often Syd is undeniably juvenile – e.g. a drawing of a limbless man sunbathing is accompanied with the caption 'Don't disturb him, he's quite armless' – but then so is much of Edward Lear's work. Documenting his travels through the Scottish Highlands with his friend Phipps Hornby in 1841 Lear drew a series of bizarre illustrations depicting the two men cramming huge game birds into their knee-high boots ('P & L being hurried insert the remains of their lunch in their boots') and Lear being comically poked in the eye by a brush-wielding child ('L – on ascending the cabin stairs – nearly loses his eye by the abrupt and injudicious promission of a new broom in the hands of a misguided infant'). Syd sent Libby illustrations depicting, among other things, a stick man carrying a huge sausage above his head ('sausage thief running') being pursued by another stick man ('copper – whistle note (G#)'). Another drawing, captioned 'A retch [*sic*] goes to school with his paints in a box while all sleep and are not bothered', is pure modern-day Lear in its lyrical inventiveness.

Syd even walked like a Lear illustration. As biographer Vivian Noakes noted, many of Lear's drawings were suffused with 'a sense of movement – the arms are flung spontaneously back like bird's in flight and the legs stride out or stand poised expectantly on tip-toe as if they are going to be spun round like a child's top'.

Like Lear, Syd would populate his lyrics with imagery drawn from botany, zoology and nature. Lear and Carroll influenced the clarity of his lyrics too, and, of course, a key chapter in Kenneth Grahame's *Wind in the Willows*, 'The Piper at the Gates of Dawn', where Rat and Mole embark upon a mystic odyssey downriver and encounter the great god Pan, provided the title of the first Pink Floyd LP. Interestingly enough, Grahame only wrote the 'Piper' and 'Wayfarers All' chapters in the book almost as an afterthought, in order to give the book its mystic dimension. Coincidentally Syd only named Pink Floyd's debut

LP at the last minute. The album's working title right up until July 1967 was *Projection*.

Of course, Grahame's influence ran far deeper than the mere naming of an LP. Syd's notion of transcendentalism and pantheism, the symbolism of the wild wood and his vision of protracted childhood and lost Arcadia were all informed by the author of *The Wind in the Willows*.

Several of Syd's most famous songs are pastiches of things that were already pastiches themselves. Belloc took the morally improving literature of the nineteenth century as the model for his mockery in *Cautionary Tales*. Carroll drew on familiar rhymes and traditional fairy tales as the basis for his own mimicry. In *Alice's Adventures in Wonderland* he directly parodies Isaac Watts' 'How Doth the Little Busy Bee' and Robert Southey's 'You Are Old, Father William', while the Mock Turtle sings a parody of Mary Howitt's 'Will you walk into my parlour said the spider to the fly'. The opening stanza from 'Jabberwocky' ('Twas brillig and the slithy toves . . .) was lifted from a parody of Anglo-Saxon verse that Carroll had written ten years earlier, complete with portmanteau words and 'learned' footnotes of the kind that would be found in an authentic academic text.

Belloc, of course, had the most explicit influence of all. Syd's song 'Effervescing Elephant' was a masterful Belloc pastiche and in its original form 'Matilda Mother', the first track that the Pink Floyd recorded for the *Piper* album, lifted its lyrics verbatim from Belloc's 'Jim Who Ran Away from his Nurse and Was Eaten by a Lion', 'Henry King Who Chewed Bits of String, and Was Early Cut Off in Dreadful Agonies', and 'Matilda Who Told Lies and was Burned to Death'.

'Matilda Mother' is pivotal when considering Syd's vision of childhood. Any notion of fey whimsy is constantly undercut by unsettling images which constantly rock the song out of its kindergarten complacency. In Syd's child-world, security always comes with conditions attached, certainty is always juxtaposed with poignancy. The gestation of the song was simple enough. Like 'Let's Roll Another One' the lyrics of 'Matilda Mother' were hastily amended at the last minute. Syd simply replaced Hilaire Belloc's words with his own and submitted them to the same metrical beat as the *Cautionary Tales*, even here though he still retained an element of mimicry. For the song's opening line he minimally adapted the children's poem 'When Good King Arthur Ruled the Land' to read 'There was a king who ruled the land'. What is original about the song is not the verses, which are largely drawn from the common stock of fairy-tale imagery, but the sudden urgent interjection of the chorus where Syd steps out of his myth-world to plead, 'Why d'yer have to leave me there, hanging in my infant air | waiting', and then attempts, not wholly successfully, to resolve this air of restlessness with the reassuring and placatory, 'You only have to read the lines of scribbly black and everything shines'. The song's opening verse is sung by Rick Wright, and Syd comes in for the chorus with that unnervingly strangulated plea. Wright sings the second chorus, the ambiguous 'Wondering and dreaming | the words had different meaning', which leaves the listener pondering whether Syd means that the words had different meaning when he was a child, or different meaning when transformed by the sensory bombardment of LSD. What takes the song entirely out of its realm is Syd's astonishing denouement in the final verse. 'For all the time spent in that room' shocks the listener out of reverie and transports us to somewhere more sinister and unsettling. The next line, 'The doll's house darkness | old perfume' is without precedent in English pop song. We are invited, *Alice in Wonderland*-style, to peer in through tiny windows, to see beyond the props and into the shadow world. It evokes the synaesthesia of scent memory and maternal warmth, the stale lingering perfume of lily-of-the-valley and maiden aunts.

Cambridge compatriot Matthew Scurfield recalls that both he and Syd owned a Pollock's toy theatre, the lavishly embellished and beautifully lit wooden model theatres that were in vogue during the nineteenth century and allowed imaginative children to stage their own miniature productions at home. Many eminent Victorian artists had them, including John Everett Millais and Dante Gabriel Rossetti. Robert Louis Stevenson was also a fan and eulogised them in print. By the 1930s they had fallen out of favour. Benjamin Pollock was one of the last manufacturers of these curios and his name has become synonymous with the brand. In the era of Triang, Airfix and Scalextric, it speaks volumes about Syd's imagination that he owned and treasured one of these arcane toys. The tableau of possibilities presented by the Pollock's theatre had an enduring influence on his outlook and his writing. The tranquil and dispassionate gaze and a sense of peering in from a disengaged vantage point would recur time and time again in his lyrics.

The week after recording 'Matilda Mother' Pink Floyd returned to the studio to record a condensed and reined-in version of 'Interstellar Overdrive', which, although completely innovative in terms of what anyone else was doing at the time, lacked the drive and the sheer inventive onslaught of its live counterpart. During the same session the band recorded 'Chapter 24', which took its words almost unchanged from the Fu hexagram of the *I Ching*. As he had done with Belloc for 'Matilda Mother', Syd drew upon what was close to hand, this time his copy of the Richard Wilhelm translation of the ancient Chinese oracle, which Barry Miles remembers him purchasing from the Indica Bookshop. Syd's audibly stoned delivery of the adapted text has a certain wasted charm, but his stilted singing style and a tendency to roll his 'r's self-consciously reveal a man who is still not entirely at ease with his vocal capabilities.

The song's real strength lies in its arrangement, which for the first time allowed Pink Floyd to take full advantage of the generous facilities of Abbey Road studios. 'Chapter 24' is embellished with harmonium, bells and Mellotron, and also gives the first real indication of Syd's strength as a melodist. Sometimes the found nature of his material, the parodying element in his writing and the simple nursery-rhyme bounce of his lyrics could detract from the marvellous tunes he wrote. 'Chapter 24' contains a palpable folk influence and cadences and inflections which could only have been drawn from the English hymn tradition.

'Flaming', recorded in one take on Thursday, 16 March, was originally called 'Snowing' and had been a feature of the band's live set since the previous summer. The change of title can be interpreted in two ways. 'Flaming' was acid-users' slang for the visual after-glow effect experienced while hallucinating. It was also part of the title of the opening track on AMM's debut album, 'Later During a Flaming Riviera Sunset', and the opening effects sequence on the Pink Floyd track directly refers to a segment of the AMM piece. Either way, 'Flaming' is an exuberant piece of nursery-psych, sending us whirling through Syd's acid wonderland in two minutes and forty-two seconds. The lyric, like that of 'Matilda Mother', is pitched ambivalently between childhood innocence and drug-heightened sensations, mixing fantasia ('sitting on a unicorn'), a painterly eye ('watching buttercups cup the light') and acid visions ('streaming through the starlit skies') while utilising English colloquialisms ('yippee', 'no fear') that had never previously appeared in English pop song. The song's 'Hey ho, here we go' refrain was adapted from the traditional work song 'Donkey Riding', which itself is based on the Scottish shanty 'Hieland Laddie', recorded by Pete Seeger among others, and contained in the Pete Seeger *Songbook*, one of Syd's earliest guitar-tuition guides. The donkey referred to in the title is actually a donkey engine, a device for lifting cargo from ships, but because of the animal's biblical associations the song was sung widely in schools by children of Syd's generation.

Easily the weakest of Syd Barrett's fantasy songs is 'The Gnome'. It has a twee and lazy lyric, which is rendered in Syd's most self-conscious and stilted style, replete with rolled 'r's. From the opening 'I want to tell you a story' – which evokes Max Bygraves as much as furry-booted trolls – to the relief of the final 'hooray', 'The Gnome' gives ready ammunition to all those surly mods who stood around at gigs waiting for the band to stop and the resident DJ to start spinning Motown again. The song was partly inspired by one of Syd's favourite childhood stories, Denys Watkins-Pitchford's *The Little Grey Men*, which tells the tale of three gnomes, Dodder, Sneezewort and Baldmoney, who search for their long-lost brother, Cloudberry. It certainly brought out Syd's most fey and impressionable tendencies. The only section that doesn't evoke an embarrassed wince is the wide-eyed wonder of 'look at the sky | look at the river | isn't it good' which evokes those warm summer evenings spent with Libby, gazing silently out of car windows at the Cambridgeshire countryside. Syd's hushed semi-spoken delivery connects the song for one brief welcoming moment to the pantheism of *The Wind in the Willows*, but it is only brief respite: all too soon we are being 'twee'ed to death by those wine-drinking tunic-wearing elfin folk.

On Monday, 20 March, a day after attempting six takes of 'The Gnome', the band returned to the studio to work on the Roger Waters composition 'Take Up Thy Stethoscope and Walk'. Lyrically it's risible, and recognisably from the same hand that penned the gimmicky 'Walk with Me, Sydney' three years earlier. The song's vamping by numbers is pure university revue fodder from a man who hasn't yet found his voice. For this reason alone 'Stethoscope' rarely warrants a mention in critiques of the early Pink Floyd. In fact, the song contains some of the most breathtaking musical interplay on the entire *Piper* album, and some of the most riveting and intense soloing that Syd ever committed to vinyl.

Waters' forgettable lyrics are, in fact, mere bookends. After thirty-three seconds they give way to a mutated 4/4 jam between what Fred Frith called 'charmingly inept blues clichés on the bagpipe stop of the Farfisa organ and a non-stop barrage of clipped rhythmic noises from Mr Barrett, clearly on a totally different plane of existence from his fellow musicians'. At two minutes and fifteen seconds Syd releases a pained yelp and the whole thing hurtles headlong into a breakneck crescendo: the tempo is the fastest the Floyd ever attempted on record. 'Take Up Thy Stethoscope and Walk' is the sound of a discarded R&B template splintering into a thousand sonic shards.

As if to illustrate the sheer breadth and scope of Syd's creativity, the same day that the Floyd worked on 'Take Up Thy Stethoscope and Walk' they also recorded 'The Scarecrow' in a single take. 'The Scarecrow' bears all the hallmarks of Syd's 'toy theatre' aesthetic. The dispassionate gaze is rendered in a pastorale. 'The Scarecrow' can best be described as a frieze, formal and illustrative in construction, and adhering to principles that the poet Charles Baudelaire applied to his depictions of Parisian dandies a century earlier: 'I want to show the moderns moving about on friezes,' Baudelaire said, 'stripped to their essentials, to place them in paintings arranged in harmonies of colour, in harmonies of lines, line and colour fitted to each other.' 'The Scarecrow' is one of Syd's most painterly songs, a picture-book evocation of rural life. But this is not Kenneth Grahame or even A. A Milne territory, where a precisely mapped-out narrative is based on those enchanted places of a child's youth. 'The Scarecrow' is essentially a landscape of the mind, disengaged and uninvolved, where the imagery remains unencumbered by human intrusion.

Although not overtly analogous, the inert, passive, all-seeing scarecrow is a perfect vehicle for Syd's own neutrality, and even though the song's finale is notionally uplifting – the scarecrow is both resigned and carefree – there is a sense of foreboding in the denouement. It's apparent in the prescient 'his head did no thinking | his arms didn't move', and even more so in the ambivalent and understated 'the black and green scarecrow is sadder than me'. What does Syd mean here? Does he mean even sadder than me, or sad in contrast to my happiness? If it's the former then the song hints at some underlying and, so far, unarticulated unease that will soon surface both in Syd's psyche and his behaviour.

Like 'Chapter 24', the melody of 'The Scarecrow' is infused with a folk sensibility, while the cadences again reveal an instinctive awareness of the English hymnal. The marrying of words to music is flawless, and the lyric, with its clever rhythmic shifts and clipped internal rhymes ('everywhere | he didn't care'; 'around | on the ground'; 'not unkind | he doesn't mind') is among the best that Syd ever wrote.

The song's instrumental outro adds sympathetic pastoral touches, although given the strength of the melody it would probably have worked just as well sung a cappella. The wood blocks which simulate the clip-clop of horses' hooves at the beginning of the track are in truth mildly intrusive and burden the song with a heavy-handed literalism that it doesn't warrant or need, detracting as they do from the wind-blown frailty of the lyric and the song's disarmingly subtle waltz-time tempo.

The next three tracks that were recorded were 'Astronomy Domine', 'Interstellar Overdrive' and 'Pow R. Toc H.', all with lengthy instrumental sections. Worked on extensively between 21 March and 12 April – fourteen takes alone were attempted of 'Astronomy Domine' – these three tracks formed the bedrock of the band's live set and did much to cement their reputation as the high priests of psychedelia. But for all their space-rock credentials, what is noticeable about all three tracks is just how rooted they are in the commonplace. 'Interstellar Overdrive', as Roger Waters once said, suggests space exploration in name only, and although its opening riff probably launched a thousand trips down at UFO, it was, as we now know, based on Syd's uncanny ability to transform any material that came to hand into something entirely new. The structure and tonal palette of 'Interstellar Overdrive' may align it to jazz and the European avant-garde but it began life as a TV theme tune and a Bacharach and David song. The track's cosmic connotations might have been sidestepped completely had they called it 'Steptoe' or 'The Red Book Variations'. After all, 'Pow R. Toc H.', with equally appropriate acid route-map tones, attracts little of the cosmic baggage of 'Interstellar Overdrive' simply by having a title that was derived from army signalling terminology and a fellowship organisation for soldiers founded during the First World War. Although ostensibly a group composition in temperament, 'Pow R. Toc H.' is indisputably Roger Waters' brainchild. And although Rick Wright, as so often, drives the melodic content with his tinkling interludes of cocktail jazz it is Waters' eerie vocalisations that give the track its brooding and menacing momentum. In fact 'Pow R. Toc H.' is utterly bereft of psychedelic leitmotifs, being closer in spirit to the exotica of Martin Denny and Les Baxter than it is to acid rock.

On 'Astronomy Domine', Syd the imagist poet comes to the fore for the first time and the meaning of the lyrics is almost wholly subservient to the shapes they make. The song is built on layers of internal rhyme, onomatopoeia and alliteration (one of the few occasions that Syd resorted to the device) as Syd revels in wordplay for its own sake. The imagery conveys a strong sense of synaesthesia (a condition which some have suggested that Syd experienced), as if designed to replicate the sensations of a light show, with colours colliding, congealing and bursting into a thousand fragments. The whole thing seems to have been conceived during sensory bombardment from one of Mike Leonard's light machines. But even in the midst of this bombardment other elements of the track are reassuringly grounded in Syd's childhood. The descending 'whoo-ooo' chorus is pure comic-book spooky, and while the line 'Neptune Titan | Stars can frighten' was never going to challenge George Ligeti or Richard Strauss for pride of place in Stanley Kubrick's *2001*, it encapsulates Syd's fairy-tale take on the cosmos perfectly. Even more rooted in childhood is the telling reference to Dan Dare, Frank Hampson's legendary cartoon creation for the *Eagle* comic which ran from 1950. The rugged action hero Dan, with his arch-enemy the Mekon, Digby his faithful batman and his personal spaceship, *Anastasia*, was staple reading for any middle-class school boy in the 1950s. It featured beautifully drawn panels which paid meticulous attention to detail, and the strip's golden years, 1956 to 1959, coincided exactly with Syd's early teens.

Although the adventures of Dan Dare are notionally set in outer space, the storylines and much of the terminology are rooted in the familiar English military argot of the Second World War. Planes are 'crates', the space-fleet controller Sir Hubert is RAF to the core and one of the most damning insults that can be heaped upon the Mekons is that they are humourless. It seems entirely appropriate, then, that Syd should bring Dan Dare into his repertoire. Even in the midst of his free-association versifying, his muse remains reassuringly unmistakeably English. Syd may have been one of psychedelia's progenitors but he was never a card-carrying literalist for the cause. He would never have written anything as self-consciously à la mode as 'Lucy in the Sky with Diamonds' with its tangerine trees and newspaper taxis – although it is probably fair to say that, when stoned ennui set in, he was more than capable of emulating Lennon's 'I'm Only Sleeping'.

'Lucifer Sam' is the odd track out on the *Piper* album. Neither lengthy instrumental nor three-minute fairy tale, its taut style is a throwback to the Floyd's earlier raw R & B. 'Lucifer Sam' has a compact form and driving riff that would have made it a prime candidate for a single (or at least a perfectly serviceable B-side) if there hadn't already been stronger contenders. It's a character song like 'Arnold Layne' rather than a still-life study like 'The Scarecrow', and by Syd's oblique standards it is specific and direct. Jenny Spires appears thinly disguised as Jennifer Gentle and although the whole thing whiffs of stoned paranoia ('that cat's something I can't explain' – it's just a cat, Syd, there really is nothing to explain) and menacing undertones it also possesses a nimble and playful wit.

Syd made remarkable progress both as a singer and interpreter during the *Piper* sessions and 'Lucifer Sam' was one of his best vocal outings to date. Syd's singing was often wilfully artless and uninvolved. Here he sounds impassioned. 'Lucifer Sam' has none of the strangulated delivery of 'Lucy Leave', the archness of 'Candy and a Currant Bun' or the self-conscious tweeness of 'The Gnome' or 'Chapter 24'. The way he slurs the enunciation of 'Lucifer' and 'Jennifer' and exaggerates the hard 't' at the end of 'cat' shows a singer growing in confidence. This new-found confidence is particularly noticeable in the complex phrasing of the final verse where the mysterious nocturnal actions of Sam are very precisely aligned to assonance and internal rhymes (ground/found/around) which deliberately mimics the sound of a miaowing cat. 'Lucifer Sam' was worked on extensively between Wednesday, 12 April, and Tuesday, 18 April. The track was augmented with a distinctive bowed bass, maracas and organ; Syd attempted several vocal takes until he got his phrasing just right.

After these intensive sessions there was no more studio activity until 21 May. While they were recording their debut album Pink Floyd continued to gig extensively. Although they still played predominantly in and around London their appearances at UFO became less frequent. As their popularity grew, fuelled by the success of 'Arnold Layne', they found themselves playing provincial theatres, often to indifferent or hostile audiences. When they weren't touring the Top Rank and Starlight Ballrooms, the band did find time to play two epoch-making underground gigs. In the early hours of Sunday, 30 April, hot on the heels of a gig at the Tabernacle Club in Stockport on the 28th and a day trip to Zaandam in Holland for a TV appearance, the band played the legendary 14 Hour Technicolor Dream at Alexandra Palace. The bill read like a who's who of the underground and featured among others the Move, Soft Machine, the Pretty Things, the Crazy World of Arthur Brown, Tomorrow, John's Children, the Social Deviants, the Purple Gang, Syn and the Flies. Bands played simultaneously on two stages erected at either end of the huge hall, which created a cacophony of noise for the 10,000 who attended the event. Less discerning trippers chose to stand equidistant between the two stages, all the better to fully absorb the maelstrom.

Syd was at this time in his psychedelic pomp. He played delicate glissandi and as the dawn crept in he held his mirrored guitar up to the rising sun and reflected shards of light back onto the appreciative audience. Daevid Allen of Soft Machine credits this performance as the inspiration for his own glissando guitar technique. 'The rest of the band looked a bit sheepish, I thought, but there was this incredible Wagnerian music coming off them,' he remembers. 'It sounded like the music of the spheres.'

The event had been planned as a way of raising money for *International Times* and the newly formed Arts Lab in Covent Garden but little of the money found its way back into underground coffers. John Lennon and John Dunbar were peaking on acid at Lennon's Weybridge Mansion when they saw a report of the event on the BBC evening news and decided to go down and check it out. In the iconic footage shot by Peter Whitehead they can be seen wandering about in a dazed state, Lennon, in granny glasses and afghan coat, licks his lips as come-down dehydration sets in.

Reviews of the 14 Hour Technicolor Dream were decidedly mixed. The *Sunday Mirror* saw it as 'the last struggle of a doomed tribe trying to save itself' and the more sceptical elements within the underground press viewed it as a 'rip-off waiting to happen'. The perennially good-natured Hoppy shook hands with everyone as they left, like the vicar at some alternative village fete. Meanwhile some of the stragglers enacted an impromptu happening, constructing a giant joint out of stage back-drops, which a bunch of aggrieved mods then proceeded to trample to bits. The symbolism was not lost on those who witnessed it.

In stark contrast to the chaotic nature of the Alexandra Palace event Pink Floyd played one of their most creatively fulfilling concerts at the Queen Elizabeth Hall on Friday, 12 May. Called 'Games for May – Space Age Relaxation for the Climax of Spring', the multimedia event showcased the first quadraphonic sound system ever used in Britain. Nick Mason in his autobiography remembers Games for May as one of the most significant events the band ever performed. *International Times* hailed it as 'a genuine twentieth-century music chamber concert.' Games for May featured Peter Wynne Wilson's elaborate light show, electronic tape installations especially recorded by Roger, Rick and Syd, and the by now common sight of a cast of beautiful people handing out flowers to the audience. According to the concert programme the band performed 'Matilda Mother', 'Flaming', 'The Scarecrow', 'Games for May', 'Bicycle' (*sic*), 'Arnold Layne', 'Candy and a Currant Bun', 'Pow R. Toc H.', 'Interstellar Overdrive' and 'Lucifer Sam'. The set was greeted by an enraptured audience in what was one of the key events of the summer of love.

A slightly adapted and retitled version of the song that Syd wrote especially for the event became Pink Floyd's next single. Recorded a week after the Festival Hall concert, 'See Emily Play' was the high point of English psychedelia, Pink Floyd's perfect pop moment. As economical as a haiku, as enigmatic as a Zen koan, 'See Emily Play' distilled all of Syd's dreamy evocation, mystery, and wistfulness into three two-line verses. No other pop song of the period conveyed such crystalline clarity. No other pop song of the period said so much by saying so little.

There is still some conjecture as to whom the Emily of the title referred. Libby Gausden maintains that Emily was going to be the name of their first child when she and Syd talked about getting married. The most obvious candidate though is Emily Young, the earnest, questing and rebellious Free School teenager who, like the Emily of the song, wore a long black gown that touched the ground and as she sat imbibing all the knowledge, hash and collective lunacy going on around her in the autumn and winter of 1966.

'They'd written this song about Emily and, I thought, that's probably me,' she says. 'There weren't any other Emilys. Now there's a billion. I decided that it was about me but I didn't know, really and truly. I tucked it away in my heart and didn't think about it again as anything I would claim. It was just something that went on in my head and it spoke to my own little creative spirit.'

As with the debate over 'Interstellar Overdrive' and Steptoe and Son/My Little Red Book, it is just as likely that 'Emily' was derived from both sources, beginning life as Libby and Syd's dream-child, then made flesh in the hinterlands of Notting Hill four years later. The song's opening verse is a perfect cameo of an adolescent flower child trying on personae, searching for identity, and like all adolescents, sometimes trying a little too hard. The depiction causes Emily Young little consternation.

'The thing about "Emily tries but misunderstands" – I'm not

really sure what that was about. Maybe I was in the wrong place at the wrong time and everyone could see it. I was so young to be hanging out with all these people in their twenties and thirties and forties and fifties. I was like a child. I was like a sponge. You have to borrow someone else's dreams till tomorrow at that age. Me and Anjelica were fifteen-year-old schoolgirls and very innocent and ignorant really, but very pleased to be getting these experiences. I had this incredible hunger so to "try and misunderstand". I don't know, maybe I was trying to be clever and sophisticated. Maybe it's a good thing to try and misunderstand. Maybe I was trying to do the wrong thing and misunderstood and was actually doing the right thing.'

The song's second verse 'Soon after dark Emily cries | Gazing through trees in sorrow | Hardly a sound till tomorrow' would not have looked out of place etched into a nineteenth-century woodcut, or accompanying an illustration in one of Syd's beloved fairy-tale books. It's not simply Carrollesque. It sounds as though it could have come from the pen of Charles Dodgson himself.

Whether he knew it or not, Syd had written an anthem for all the questers, all the Emilys. 'Float on a river forever and ever? Absolutely! I'm going to float on a river forever and ever. That's the human condition. That's what everybody does,' says Emily Young, who having followed her own true path these past forty years is now a world-renowned sculptress.

The final track recorded for *Piper at the Gates of Dawn* and the closing track on the album, 'Bike', was Syd's supreme homage to gleeful unrepentant infantilism. Written well before Pink Floyd hit the big time, 'Bike' was legendary among Syd's circle of friends possibly as early as the summer of 1965 as they first witnessed the blossoming of his eccentric songwriting gifts. 'I remember Syd playing things in Roger's back garden,' says Andrew Rawlinson. 'I think I remember him playing "I've got a bike" but don't rely on that memory because there's too many people who say, "Ah, I remember the time Syd composed a tune while I was sitting there . . ." I don't know if that's true but I do remember him singing it on his own.'

The song's most likely inspiration was A. A. Milne's 'The Engineer' from *Now We Are Six*. The poem's jerky scansion and pay-off line ('It's a good sort of brake | But it hasn't worked yet') are replicated perfectly in Syd's song.

The disarming simplicity of 'Bike' has often overshadowed what a cleverly constructed and complex little ditty it is. As in all the best nursery rhymes the certainty of Syd's list of 'I've gots' – the bike, the cloak, the mouse, the gingerbread men, the room – is constantly qualified and undermined both within the verses, where each qualifier is rendered with immaculate middle-class politeness ('I'd give it to you if I could | But I borrowed it'; 'If you think it could look good | Then I guess it should'; 'Take a couple if you wish | They're on the dish') and by the refrain 'You're the kind of girl that fits in with my world' which like the dynamics and denouement of 'Matilda Mother' takes us into another perceptual realm entirely. The first half of that ambiguous refrain, with its simultaneous hints at commitment, convenience and selfishness, is undermined by the subtle disavowal implicit in the rejoinder 'I'll give you anything | Everything, if you want things', where a jaded sense of 'Oh well, if *things* are what you want . . .' is palpable. 'Bike', like so many of Syd's songs, is full of these hidden layers of distancing and disengagement. Nothing is ever fully embraced. The song is constantly destabilising and sabotaging its own certainties.

A looped coda of sound effects brings 'Bike' to an unnerving hallucinatory conclusion. As with the horses' hooves on 'The Scarecrow', the collage of goose-squawks and clock chimes in 'Bike' (enthusiastically plundered from the same series of EMI sound effects EPs that the Beatles used on *Sgt Pepper's Lonely*

Hearts Club Band) lends the song a degree of literalism that it doesn't really need. Where the clip-clops in 'The Scarecrow' detract from its charming waltz time, the clanging melange of tape effects in 'Bike' somewhat overshadows the 'psychedelic music hall' mood of the final verse, which slows to half speed to great effect and burdens Syd's kindergarten whimsy with an implied madness that isn't apparent in the song itself.

'OK. He writes a song about a bike,' notes Pete Brown. 'If you compare that to something like "My White Bicycle" by Tomorrow, it's a completely different idea. One of them is clearly set in the English countryside and it's a kind of modest thing. The other is like a kind of tribal, but also much more commercial, idea of a song. It's much more deliberately "rocky" and commercial and produced.'

The recording of 'Bike' brought to an end a fruitful period that had seen Pink Floyd move from underground cult to fully-fledged pop stars. By July 'See Emily Play' was in the Top 10. The band had made prestigious TV and concert appearances and received critical approval in the mainstream press. Behind the scenes, though, the cracks were beginning to show.

In an astute recollection of the 14 Hour Technicolor Dream contained in his biography, *Give the Anarchist a Cigarette*, Mick Farren noted the wind of change that was blowing through the cavernous Alexandra Palace as the underground found itself for the first time in the full glare of mainstream news reportage. Farren suspected, with good reason, that the counter-culture wasn't ideologically equipped to deal with the transformation. With an air of foreboding he pointed to the palpable air of exploitation and naivety that hung over the Alexandra Palace event. Farren's most telling observations lay in what he detected in the minor details. Since his band, the Social Deviants, had opened the event, he had plenty of time to observe the pageantry unfolding behind the scenes.

'My first surprise was how the denizens of backstage — considering that they were looked up to as the prime motivators — were actually more conservative than the punters outside. Considerably more drinking was going on backstage, and although a few world-class druggers were among those assembled, I quickly realised two things. Most bands, even though they might have their flamboyant extremists, also had members who, despite their long hair and floral shirts, still clung to a decidedly brown-ale consciousness and would probably never change. Too many didn't believe a word of all this counter-culture malarkey, and were only embracing the trend as another avenue to rock-business success.'

In such incidentals the future was being forged. Gestural politics and notional support for 'the cause' were slowly giving ways to careers. Sincere creative impulses were essentially at the beck and call of fashion and trend. The shrewder and more hard-nosed participants were wising up and cashing in. Pharmaceutical enlightenment and obliteration were an active hindrance to the dictates of commerce. For all the counter-culture's claims of building a new psychedelic Jerusalem the only real blurring of boundaries between performers and audiences was in the minds of those who were too fried on acid to notice that, stripped of its day-glo finery, it was business as usual.

'It's interesting isn't it?' says David Gale, as he ponders Farren's observations. 'It puts the artists in the role of making consumables, and the kids as consumers. So it shifts that idea that we were all equal celebrants at this great cultural party.'

As Syd was about to find out.

Chapter Five

His Head Did No Thinking:
His Arms Didn't Move

'Glorious stirring sight!' murmured Toad, never offering to move. 'The poetry of motion! The real way to travel! The only way to travel! Here today – in next week tomorrow! Villages skipped, towns and cities jumped – always somebody else's horizon!

THE WIND IN THE WILLOWS KENNETH GRAHAME

In April 1967 AMM played a gig at the Commonwealth Institute in London. It was to be oboist Lawrence Sheaff's last. In a unit as volatile and self-analytical as AMM there were bound to be what Eddie Prévost called 'tensions and uncertainties about the line and direction we were taking'. In particular, the task of prioritising collectivism and collaboration in a cultural climate where individualism and ego were paramount was a factor that constantly threatened to undermine the band's idealism. Lawrence Sheaff felt this tension as keenly as his fellow band members, and found himself increasingly questioning not just his method of musical exploration but the very nature of the quest itself.

'AMM, in a natural way, opened me to inner experience,' he says. 'This allowed me to connect to Maharishi's Transcendental Meditation. I began the regular practice of TM in 1966 while I was still a member of AMM. By 1967, a year later, the experiential and philosophical frameworks that had been operating in AMM began to make me feel a little uncomfortable. I felt at odds with them. I wondered if the group would shift direction. It didn't. I think the ethos of the group sensed my discomfort and that ethos in turn felt discomfort with me. When that discomfort came to the surface it seemed to be to do with personalities. But it wasn't really. They were my brothers. Still are. The feeling-at-odds wasn't a superficial thing: it was on a deep level. The strict egalitarian nature of AMM's structure meant that one's individual ego had to always be expanding to encompass the whole group. I think this posed a continuing challenge to the members, all of whom were strong personalities. But in performance, whenever that unity was fully actualised as a living flow, it was invincible. Nothing could deny the authority of that wall of sound. When I saw individual members beginning to lay some claim to certain territories of sound, it signalled on a deeper level that it might be time to move on.'

Anti-individualism had always fuelled what Eddie Prévost called AMM's 'desire to break away from an emulative way of playing', but when personal tensions surfaced in the band they centred on Lawrence's relationship with the rest of the unit. Prévost recalls, in the sleeve notes to the CD reissue of AMM's debut album, 'a somewhat painful discussion – which typically English hated getting to the point'. Things came to a head at the Commonwealth Institute gig where, according to Prévost, 'Lawrence sat crouching immobile and silent over his cello. I don't think he ever played again. In effect he had been banished.'

Lawrence Sheaff doesn't dispute his former band mate's version of events; indeed he never did play again. He didn't even resume painting until 1995. The one detail that was inaccurate in Prévost's account was the nature of Sheaff's dismissal. He hadn't been banished. He effectively banished himself. Four decades on he remains resolutely unapologetic for taking the path that he did.

'In retrospect, I see the "territories of sound" phenomenon as a natural thing,' he says. 'Specialisation enhances clarity of expression. Thus, even in aspiring to absolute freedom in relation to expression, values of order always become, and inevitably so, a concomitant factor. There can be no freedom without order: likewise, there can be no order without freedom. Life is a balancing act between these two: mastering that balancing act is called wisdom. At the time, however, I read this hint of an encroaching order as restrictive. So, after a while I very reluctantly left the group. Even if it were perhaps for the wrong reasons, and even though I never played music again, it was absolutely the right thing for me to do.'

It is important to relay this story in detail because it parallels what happened to Syd Barrett in 1967. AMM were the conscience of the underground, the band that rose above rhetoric and actually meant it. Syd Barrett meant it too and, although his artistic quest propelled him into a more popular arena, he was for an all-too-brief period just as idealist and just as driven by the very impulses that guided AMM. The moment those instincts encountered the full force of the music industry, Syd began to play up. 'Always accustomed from a boy to go my own way uncontrolled, I cannot help fearing that I should run rusty and sulky by reason of retinues and routines,' said Edward Lear a hundred years earlier, and there was something of this in Syd too. This unwillingness to conform to expectation manifested itself in the three Rs of anti-stardom: reluctance, recalcitrance and refusal, until finally Syd too was effectively banished, or banished himself, from his own band. The crucial difference between Syd's disengagement and Lawrence Sheaff's was that Sheaff's was sudden and clear-headed and driven by purity of intent. Syd's was messy, painful, prolonged and debilitating. Sheaff found peace of mind in transcendental meditation. Syd would find no such peace of mind.

Signing to one of the biggest record companies in the world and being afforded the opportunity to record at Abbey Road studios proved to be both advantageous and problematic for Syd Barrett. On the plus side Pink Floyd got to record with state-of-the-art equipment secure in the knowledge that their records would be efficiently promoted and distributed.

Until the Beatles broke the mould with the recording of *Sgt Pepper*, EMI's strict working practices and procedures had always been adhered to. Recording sessions ran from 10 a.m. to 1 p.m., 2 p.m. until 5 p.m. and 7 p.m. until 10 p.m. and were observed meticulously to comply with Musicians' Union payment rules. Production staff wore white lab coats and, observing the principles of scientific management and union agreements, there was rigid demarcation between the roles of recording artists and technical staff. Although they were not the first EMI artists to be allowed to break the 10 p.m. deadline, the Beatles made late-night sessions the norm while recording *Sgt Pepper*. Pink Floyd commenced work on their debut LP just as the Beatles were putting the finishing touches to their landmark album, and immediately followed suit. The recording of 'Matilda Mother' ran from 11 p.m. to 6 a.m., and was to be the first of several all-night sessions.

As well as taking full advantage of the loosening up of recording schedules, Pink Floyd benefited considerably from EMI's five-star facilities. Abbey Road had its own on-site maintenance department and engineers were able to re-jig the studio on request to facilitate new ideas. The band members were given access to a wide range of miscellaneous instrument-ation, as well as material from EMI's substantial library of sound effects, which they were encouraged to embellish and augment to their hearts' content, For someone of Syd's impulsive temperament, though, adhering to the disciplined procedures of Abbey Road proved to be a mixed blessing. His relationship with

Norman Smith, the record producer assigned to the band, proved to be particularly fractious.

Although he had worked with the Beatles, Smith came from a jazz background and was always open and honest about his lack of empathy with Pink Floyd's music. He was equally upfront about viewing the band primarily as a commercial rather than an artistic proposition.

Smith's pivotal role in the recording of *The Piper at the Gates of Dawn* would prove to be a major source of antagonism. For a producer he was very 'hands on'. It was Smith, for example, who played the drum-roll which introduced the closing theme on 'Interstellar Overdrive' when Nick Mason proved incapable. He also proved to be a skilful embellisher, often fleshing out the band's basic ideas with suggestions for vocal and instrumental arrangements. It was Smith's idea to append the wordless choral coda to 'Matilda Mother', and he also had a hand in the instrumental outros on 'The Scarecrow' and 'Chapter 24'. He encouraged the band to use sound effects on 'The Scarecrow', 'Bike' and 'Flaming', and can even be heard singing backing vocals on some tracks.

Smith's approach to recording the band's lengthy instrumentals and improvisations and his crudely and hastily executed stereo mix of the album were more contentious. The tracks which have improvisation at their core, 'Interstellar Overdrive', 'Astronomy Domine', 'Take Up Thy Stethoscope and Walk', and 'Pow R. Toc H.', all have a compacted and reined quality on record which conveys little of the impact and intensity of their live counterparts.

'It was good for the band,' maintains Peter Jenner, defending Norman Smith's mode of operation. 'I suspect the slightly intimidating lab-coat aspect of EMI made them more professional. I think that what Norman did was give them discipline and an awareness of what you could do in the studio.

Joe Boyd would have given them freedom, but he wouldn't have given them the musical help, and I don't think he would have made such a big record. I think there would have been a danger of them getting lost in self-indulgence a lot earlier on. If it had all been 'Interstellar Overdrive' – which it could well have done if we'd had our own way – it would have been a darling of the in-set but it wouldn't have been a big hit.'

Barry Miles takes the opposite view. 'Really Joe should have produced it. There's no question at all. Everybody hated that album when it came out. All the UFO people, who admittedly were a bunch of snobs when you get right down to it, they all thought it was terrible that Norman Smith had just turned them into some sort of commercial pap. And we all felt the same. It was a mistake. A big, big mistake. But this was what record companies did then. They said, "Oh, we've got to make this into something commercial." '

'To get the same sound for "See Emily Play" they had to go back to Sound Techniques where they did "Arnold Layne", notes Miles. 'Now "Arnold Layne" *did* sound like the Floyd. That's exactly what they sounded like. There's a certain sonic quality there that is not on the album. I don't know if it was miking technique or what, because Sound Techniques was a piece of shit too, but Joe Boyd got a very good mix there. Good acoustics. Good live sound.'

From its opening moment when Syd slid a plastic ruler up and down the frets of his guitar, 'See Emily Play' sounded like a hit. This time round the pirate station Radio London didn't have a fit of moral panic, and they played the record on constant rotation. 'See Emily Play' was released on 16 June, entered the charts on 1 July at number 28 and spent five weeks in the Top Ten. Pink Floyd were now fully fledged pop stars. 'See Emily Play' was in the charts at the same time as Cream's 'Strange Brew', Traffic's 'Paper Sun', Procol Harum's 'A Whiter Shade of Pale' and the

Beatles' 'All You Need Is Love', one of the great psychedelic moments from the summer of love. Poignantly, though, 'Emily' represents the last occasion when Syd Barrett's creative impulses were in harmony with the demands of the marketplace. When the band was asked to play *Top of the Pops* his recalcitrance came to the fore. 'That's when he started to get difficult,' remembers Andrew King. 'We did three *Top of the Pops*. First one was fine. Second one was very difficult. Third one was awful. We couldn't find him. We had to go and look for him.' Norman Smith remembered things differently and maintained that there was trouble from the band's very first appearance on the programme.

Faced with the prospect of appearing on *Top of the Pops* with the likes of Topol, Vikki Carr and Engelbert Humperdinck (who were all in the Top 10 at the same time), Syd made his stand, absolving himself of all obligation to the demands of light entertainment television.

'There was that whole time when pop was seen as a shallow medium and the thing to do was make albums and express yourself,' notes Robyn Hitchcock. 'Maybe he was no different from the rest of them. "I don't want to be on *Top of the Pops*, man. That's not where it's at. Dylan wouldn't be singing 'Sad Eyed Lady' on *Top of the Pops*." '

Norman Smith recalled that by the time the band appeared for a third time on *Top of the Pops* Syd had taken to letting his guitar dangle low, dropping his head and not even pretending to look like he was miming. The posture would become an increasingly familiar one as the year wore on and the allure of stardom wore off.

The Piper at the Gates of Dawn LP was released on 5 August 1967, the same week as *Absolutely Free*, the second album by the Mothers of Invention and *5,000 Spirits or the Layers of the Onion* by the Incredible String Band. It was universally well received by the critics and spent seven weeks in the Top 10 albums chart reaching a high of number 6.

From being a sweet and charming boy, and possibly the least ambitious of the Cambridge crowd, Syd was now the most famous of the lot. Even friends like Nigel Lesmoir-Gordon, who hadn't thought Syd exceptional four or five years earlier, marvelled at the transformation. 'He was very much that *Wind in the Willows* character, a faery-land dweller. You really felt here was a poet, in the purist sense, in the Coleridge tradition.'

What had been unique about Pink Floyd up to this point was the way they took radical experimentation out of the rarefied confines of the underground and into the mainstream. Syd's creative instincts were after all, both populist and avant-garde. He was a full-on sonic explorer and sound-painter who could also write three-minute pop hits. In that respect he was a one-off. But even in the everything-up-for-grabs context of the times this was a problematic combination, and the band was ill equipped to deal with it. 'I don't know how conscious they were of wanting to take it anywhere,' says Duggie Fields. 'They were just doing it and then suddenly they got this huge response. The response really was from nowhere. Shockingly suddenly they were *the* underground band. Then suddenly they were on *Top of the Pops*, which I don't think they were prepared for. And the repetition that was necessary they weren't prepared for either. Syd certainly wasn't.'

'I think Roger Waters might have thought that it's all very well to be knock-kneed with excitement at the prospect of success, but that's actually not good enough. The thing is to work hard,' says David Gale. 'I remember Nick Mason saying Syd really didn't realise what being a pop star means. That you do actually have to get up in the morning and that they've scripted you lots of interviews and you've got to talk to money people all the time. You've gotta do studio work, you've gotta sign photographs – and this goes on and on and on. And then in the evening you get to play. And Nick Mason thought that Syd was quite shocked by that, and that this was a side of the coin he hadn't foreseen.'

The fact that Syd wrote so fast and worked so intuitively was in many ways his undoing. Instincts that worked in his favour as a source of creativity became problematic when subjected to the machinations of the music industry.

'He was the most facilely gifted person,' emphasises Andrew Rawlinson. 'I'm not using facile in a pejorative way. I just mean for him it was, "Let's see if we can make this work. Ooh, blimey, it does!" I think that was normal for him. I don't think he had to work at it. That's one of the differences between Roger and Syd. Roger had to pick up the reins because Syd had let them drop and he applied himself to it and learned how to do it and turned out to be an outstanding lyricist. Musically, though, he's nothing special and I don't think he would claim to be, whereas Syd was. Syd came up with all that feedback stuff and was influenced by avant-garde musicians. He just absorbed things because his antennae were up.'

Increasingly, however, as the year went on it became abundantly clear that Syd's antennae were no longer up, or at least no longer finely attuned to the idea of commercial success. As a result he began to recoil from the taxing and unseemly business of being a pop star. The great irony, perhaps the greatest irony of all in this whole story, is that during the second half of 1967 Syd blossomed into the most beautiful-looking creature. Once he ditched the pencil moustache and the Hendrix perm that Eric Clapton, Jack Bruce and several others briefly adopted, he reverted to the hip instincts of 'Syd the beat'. He grew his hair long and shaggy and he took on the look and bohemian aspect of a nineteenth-century Romantic poet. Like Brian Jones and Jimi Hendrix he draped himself in scarves and shawls, silk and velvet, and wildly clashing colours. It was a slightly dandified look, androgynous but never camp. Unlike Hendrix or *Sgt Pepper*-period Beatles Syd never went for the military jackets or overt Victoriana. No beads, no bells, no kaftans. Like everything else he had done up to that point, his dress sense was executed with style and panache. 'It was only Syd who could really pull it off. The others always looked slightly uncomfortable,' says Barry Miles.

This was the period when feminised Syd really came to the fore. 'That's why women liked him,' says Hester Page. 'Women like feminine-type men. They're pretty, they're gentle, they're more sensitive and they're not playing that big macho game which most women find really boring. Syd didn't do any of that.'

'He was androgynous,' agrees Anthony Stern. 'I don't think Syd would ever have been called "gay", although I don't know, maybe he was interested in the "Arnold Layne" syndrome of dressing up in women's clothes from time to time. I think he probably did at some time, I think there were rumours.'

'Men dressed up in frilly shirts and had a very feminine way of presenting themselves,' says Hester Page. 'Syd was into decking himself up because that's what the girls did. So [he'd] put on a bit of eye-liner at the same time as we all were, [and] we used to draw eyelashes on him, and draw roses on our cheeks – so if he's witnessing all that just before he's about to go and play a gig, he'd grab a pencil and put some on. It wasn't being gay or anything like that. It was to do with the time. It was a decorative time.'

'It's not just what he wore, it was the way he wore things,' says Anthony Stern. 'And he had this extraordinary "lolloping" way of walking, as if he were some character out of *Peter Rabbit*. He was almost like a fairy-tale, dancing joker kind of character in a pantomime, imitating some animalistic way of being; he would bounce along in the most extraordinary way. And that's what you most were struck by, his energy and lightness of touch and his self-mocking sense of humour. No sort of pomposity there – didn't even know what the word meant.'

'I used to go to Portobello Road every Saturday, because we all used to dress in the stage clothes that were on sale up at the far end, velvet cloaks and fancy dresses and amazing fabrics,' remembers Hester Page. 'Syd used to give me money to buy him stuff to wear on stage. He liked little – sort of – boleros to go over his shirts or something sequinned or an old-fashioned frilly shirt. He loved all that stuff and had a great sense of style. He used to go through the sack that I brought back with half a dozen things in it, take whatever he liked and then Lindsay and I would share the rest. Then we'd go and see Syd play in all his finery.'

During this period the Floyd continued to play provincial ballrooms, and found themselves performing at such unlikely functions as the Gwent Constabulary Dance in Abergavenny, the Rolls-Royce Ball at the Derby Locarno, the Stowmarket Annual Carnival and Clifton Hall, Rotherham – a run-down former Rifle Volunteers Drill Hall.

'When they were out of town I remember Roger told me that it was hellish for them because their music was so misunderstood,' says Chris Welch. 'They'd had a couple of pop hits and people expected that all the time. People expected the new pop sensation and Pink Floyd were doing twenty-minute versions of "Interstellar Overdrive". When they were playing Notting Hill or the Roundhouse it was fine. Out of town it was bottles and cans being thrown.'

This was not entirely true. The Tabernacle Club in Stockport, where the Floyd played two days before the 14 Hour Technicolor Dream event, was a hip venue that played host to all of the top underground groups of the late 1960s, including the Jimi Hendrix Experience, Cream, Family and Led Zeppelin. There was the Moulin Rouge in Southport, where the band played on 3 May, which despite boasting a 'Teen Room' where you could 'wine, dine, dance, and have a gay time' attracted an appreciative art school crowd. However, it was a different story at the Benn Memorial Hall in Rugby on 22 April, where the review in the local *Rugby Advertiser* noted 'the 45-minute stint was about all the average onlooker could take'. At the Wellington Club in East

Dereham in Suffolk, on 29 July, Nick Mason recalls pint pots being thrown at the stage. It wasn't down to narrow-minded provincialism. The band didn't necessarily fare any better when they played the London suburbs. At the Blue Opera Club at the Feathers pub in Ealing, two days after the Rugby gig, Roger Waters was cut on the forehead by a penny thrown from the hostile crowd who then, according to Waters, proceeded to vent their aggression on the lone hippie in the audience and gave him a sound beating.

It's perhaps hard to understand now just how obliged bands were to go out on the road to play these unrewarding and often unlucrative gigs. No one questioned it. It's just how things were done back then. There's probably no better way to illustrate the point than by mentioning that on the weekend of the legendary, and legend-making, Monterey Pop Festival, manager Robert Stigwood had Cream playing at former boxer Billy Walker's Uppercut Club in East London. The Beatles were the lone exception in getting off the treadmill of touring.

'You'd have your date sheet, a piece of A4, and you'd have six months on it,' says Peter Jenner. 'You'd look at that and if it wasn't full and there were a few gaps you worried because that's how you made your living. You didn't make money from records. The royalties were tiny.'

All of this pressure began to take its toll on Syd. On 28 July, the day before the East Dereham gig where pint pots rained down on the stage, Pink Floyd had been booked to record a session for the BBC Light Programme's *Saturday Club*, to be aired the following week. Syd walked out shortly after the band arrived at the BBC's Playhouse Theatre. In his Barrett sessionography, *Random Precision*, David Parker quotes producer Bernie Andrews as saying: 'I still have a copy of the letter sent to Peter Jenner from Patrick Newman the "Light Entertainment Booking Manager" asking for an explanation as to why a member of the group left the studio . . . without completing the recording of the first number.' The letter was dated 3 August and received an apologetic reply from Peter Jenner on the 14th, citing a 'nervous collapse'.

'I was working for *MM*, so I would hear all the news and gossip and other musicians talking about Syd; so it was pretty common knowledge throughout London that Syd was causing problems. The word was out,' says Chris Welch. 'The under-ground scene was very small and very gossipy so you knew exactly what was going on. The word spread pretty quickly.'

It was during this period that stories about Syd's increasing unreliability and erratic behaviour began to flourish. David Gilmour remembers being invited to Sound Techniques studio on 21 May to attend the 'See Emily Play' recording sessions, and being greeted by blank stares and indifference from Syd. Joe Boyd recalls a similarly fraught encounter at UFO. Boyd hadn't seen Syd for a few weeks and was shocked at his appearance as he squeezed past him in the crowded entrance to the Blarney Club dressing rooms. He noted that where previously Syd had always possessed a twinkle in his eye and a bounce in his step he now seemed vacant and detached. Boyd's account has been elevated to universal truth over the years, supposedly capturing the defining moment when Syd's lights went out. The generally agreed date for this encounter is 2 June. If this is the case then Syd's decline must have been sudden and cataclysmic, for only two weeks earlier he could be seen clear-eyed and amused on BBC television as he endured a bizarre grilling from musicologist Hans Keller on the arts programme *The Look of the Week*. And just days before that he had played what many consider to be Pink Floyd's finest gig at the Games for May concert. A week later, he was at his creative zenith recording 'Bike' and 'See Emily Play'. Joe Boyd's story makes more sense if we assume that the actual date of the encounter was the Floyd's next, and what turned out to be their last UFO appearance on 28 July. This was by common consent a lost weekend for Syd.

The day after the *Saturday Club* debacle and Pink Floyd's final UFO performance (where, according to *Melody Maker*, Roger Waters kept things together and 'gave the group a powerful depth') the band was pelted with beer mugs by farm boys in East Dereham and then travelled back to London for the International Love-In at Alexandra Palace. The event was supposed to be a reprise of the legendary 14 Hour Technicolor Dream three months earlier. In fact it merely compounded a growing suspicion that the game was pretty much up for the underground. Syd, apparently tripping his brains out, was barely capable of performing. After another lacklustre gig at Torquay Town Hall on Monday, 31 July, the band cancelled all live performances for the following month, including prestigious appearances at the Festival of the Flower Children at Woburn Abbey and the Seventh National Blues and Jazz Festival at Windsor, the forerunner to the Reading Festival. Under the headline 'Pink Floyd flake out', the *Melody Maker* of 19 August reported that Syd was suffering from 'nervous exhaustion'.

Many would argue that Syd Barrett was in permanent decline from this moment on, but what becomes apparent when examining his uneven trajectory during the second half of 1967 is just how selective Syd's recalcitrance could be. He certainly didn't act up when the Floyd recorded two further BBC sessions for John Peel's *Top Gear* in September and December 1967; in fact he turned in some of his best work. But then Peel wasn't perceived to be part of the establishment. He had always been a massive supporter of the band, playing rough acetates (and noticeably different mixes) of their debut album weeks before it was released on his *Perfumed Garden* show on Radio London. Those early Peel sessions had a sympathetic producer in Bernie Andrews, whose temperament and approach were far removed from the BBC house style – so far removed, in fact, that they eventually got him sacked. *Saturday Club* however was a different kettle of light entertainment altogether.

In the days before Radio 1 *Saturday Club* was the BBC's flagship pop show. It had started on the Light Programme in the 1950s as *Skiffle Club* and had retained that programme's chummy 'youth club of the airwaves' ambience. Presented by Brian Matthew, who introduced himself as 'your old mate', the show had a typically BBC 'one size fits all' approach to pop. As with *Juke Box Jury* everybody and everything, product and performers alike, were equal under the auspices of commerce. This approach was a hangover from the late 1950s and early 1960s when *Saturday Club* drew its guests from trad jazz bands, balladeers and derivative English rock 'n' rollers. As an approach to programme-making, it still held sway during the beat group era, when the Troggs and the Swinging Blue Jeans of this world were expected to perform alongside singers such as Helen Shapiro or Susan Maughan who hailed from the previous era. By 1967 that 'one size fits all' approach was no longer tenable and guest line-ups became increasingly incongruous and anachronistic in their diversity. On 8 July, three weeks before Pink Floyd's non-appearance, the guests were ex-Yardbird Jeff Beck, Pinkerton's Assorted Colours and Kenny Ball and his Jazzmen. The following week's main guest was balladeer Matt Monro. The week before the Floyd session the guests were the Shadows and Tom Jones. Given that the BBC's policy for recording sessions was far more regimented than EMI's, and that the Floyd would have been allowed to play no part in the mixing process, is it any wonder that Syd walked?

In the late summer of 1967 Syd and Lindsay Corner moved out of Earlham Street and into 101 Cromwell Road. Many of the stories regarding Syd's unhinged behaviour emanate from this infamous address. Cromwell Road had changed somewhat since the high point of 1965–6 when Donovan mentioned it in song and David Gale remembered it as a salon for the hip crowd. Now darker forces were at work. 'There were still some culturally powerful, influential people moving through but there were also some quite damaged people,' remembers Gale. 'People who couldn't stop talking, people who couldn't stop shooting heroin, people who rolled over on their babies and smothered them 'cos they were on smack.'

'A major burn-out joint,' says former resident Mick Rock. 'Definitely acid overload there.'

'I never went to see him at Cromwell Road and I don't know who they all were, but I think they were acid crazies,' says Peter Jenner. 'They probably thought of him as some sort of guru guide. They were really pleased and proud of him, and what would be best would be to give him more acid so he could expand his mind. There was all this weird shit going down but I don't see these people as malicious. It was damaging but it wasn't malicious.'

Long-time Cromwell Road resident Nigel Lesmoir-Gordon strongly refutes any suggestion of malicious intent. 'I've heard it said that people at Cromwell Road used to spike his food. Absolute nonsense. We would never have dreamt of such a thing.'

'The extent to which Syd picked up, or was intoxicated by, the irrationality of those around him is, I think, important,' reasons David Gale. 'It's important to an explosive and highly experimental culture at that time. Whether these were noble experiments is neither here nor there. The times were feverish and Syd was a creature of those times. He subscribed up to the hilt almost, apart from a certain amount of satirical attitude. All that ferment – he really wanted to be part of it. You have to remember that the systematic and wilful suspension of rationality was widespread.'

Jenny Lesmoir-Gordon is equally non-judgemental about the sheer no-holds-barred irrationality of those times. 'I don't think anyone's to blame. A lot of the people at Cromwell Road were very sweet and caring people. I think we were all in the same boat. We're all struggling souls. I just think he was too sensitive.'

'I don't see Syd as a drug casualty,' agrees Duggie Fields. 'That's the thing. He had other friends who definitely were. I would say they were a catalyst in his downfall but they were not the cause of it.'

'I knew a woman called Carol Mason,' recalls Pete Brown. 'Her real name was Carol Masonovitch. She was a Liverpool person, a friend of Brian Patten's. And she was around Earlham Street when Syd lived there. I remember going up there with her once, only once, as far as I can remember. It was a sort of semi-grotty, semi-psychedelic hippie pad. I remember him kinda holding court in it a little bit. He was surrounded by sycophants. There were some friends there, but a lot of hangers-on too. I don't remember him being particularly out of it.'

'He'd come up from Cambridge as a country boy almost,' says Hester Page. 'Played with a group of friends that he liked. Then someone gives them a gig, playing to a small crowd. I felt that was always Syd. He was not into the big time. He didn't have ambition in that way. He was too private. And, yes, he took lots of drugs and lots of acid like everybody else did at that time. But no more or no less than anybody else. We basically all lived on it for two or three years. But I think that he felt he was being swept in to another world because of the popularity of his music and managers coming in to the situation. And he went along with it because he was easy-going, but I think that must have started disturbing him more than the drugs ever did. You know, when you feel your life's going in a direction you don't particularly want it to go in but your friends are going that way – so you go along with it for a while, but I think he just got more and more wound up about it and started to retreat into himself.'

David Gale also attributes many of Syd's problems to the unwanted attention that came with fame. 'I can remember groupies coming to the door of Egerton Court, which was the next place we all lived in South Kensington, where I lived with Syd and Storm and others. And Syd lived next door to my room with Lindsay Corner. But groupies would come to the door bearing frilly shirts that they had sewn together for Syd. And I realised it was this kind of industry of cock-sucking nubile girls, making gorgeous shirts out of unusual fabrics for rock stars. There'd be these girls coming into Syd's room, he'd try on all these shirts with massive frills, ballooned cuffs and things and I got a brief glimpse there of the kind of attention paid to rock stars.'

'He was getting the acclaim from the beginning,' agrees Duggie Fields. 'Syd was the charismatic one, the good-looking one. Syd was also the charming one. Sitting in a group at home, Syd could be the centre of attention, just like that. He was witty. He was talkative. But he did start retreating even before the band became successful. He would be the one closed off in his room with people knocking on his door. So Syd retreated, over-whelmed by people wanting his attention. That was before any pop fame, before any real performing fame. He was already the one drawing in the attention and at the same time pushing himself away from it.'

'He had many facets to his personality, a very strong gothic presence,' says poet Spike Hawkins, who first got to know Syd during this period. 'There was this incredible energy that flowed from Syd. Although to look at him you would think he was about to pass out. Women were attracted to him by his distance. That's what I meant by his gothic presence. One couldn't reach the centre of it. There were many women who wanted to bed him. He gave the impression of being extremely silent and deep. He was deep but he was far from being silent. I found with Syd that he was trying to get out of a room. He was screaming at the top of his voice to get to the outside world. It's an odd metaphor but he was rotating inside. Inside he was a dynamo of energy.'

Photographer Mick Rock had known Syd since 1965 and similarly remembers a quiet undemonstrative spirit, not given to excess or eccentricity while on acid. 'It was really quite a light relationship. Maybe I didn't impose any identity on him – I simply liked him and got on with him. I took an acid trip with him once and I have taken acid with a number of different people in those years, and there were certainly some pretty fucking weird people out there. But Syd was not that strange on a trip – at least, not compared with some of the people I'd known. On that trip we sat around and played music, got a little higher, played Go, probably read the *Psychedelic Review*. And maybe just drew and painted.'

'I found with Syd that he was incredibly shy over certain dimensions of his character,' says Spike Hawkins. 'He would hush all of a sudden when we moved into some areas. "Oh, I don't want to talk about that, man," and he would withdraw. Or we'd go to a party and it would be, "Oh, there's that impossible man over there," and he would hide in the shade. That's why he liked the light show. It coveted him. It protected him.'

'Syd was expected to be a spokesman for his generation,' says Peter Jenner. 'I think that was part of the problem and one of the things he found quite difficult to cope with. Spokesman? Me? Why? What? Didn't compute. I don't think he was at all political. He was much more buttercup sandwiches and pixies. More cosmic. More mystic. But he wasn't missionary about any of that stuff. He didn't fully sign up.'

The one aspect of Peter Jenner's statement that can be questioned is the extent to which Syd was, in his manager's words, 'buttercup sandwiches'. Donovan was buttercup sandwiches and went on being buttercup sandwiches long after everyone else had stopped. What is noticeable about Syd's output is that the fairy-tale imagery he is best known for constitutes only a small part and a relatively short-lived aspect of his work.

Syd was arguably only 'buttercup sandwiches' during that brief, fruitful flourish in 1966–7 when he was writing songs like 'Matilda Mother', 'Flaming' and 'The Gnome'. Pink Floyd rarely performed any of these songs on stage, and after the summer of 1967 they didn't perform them at all, favouring lengthy instrumentals. The songs that Syd did write in the second half of 1967 got darker, more sardonic, more abstract. Once the Floyd had finished recording their debut album there was a complete sea-change in his songwriting style. There would be no more trite ditties about gnomes. No more recitations of the *I-Ching*. No more buttercup sandwiches. The extraordinary series of songs that Syd wrote and recorded with Pink Floyd during the latter half of 1967, 'Scream Thy Last Scream (Old Woman with a Casket)', 'Vegetable Man', 'Jugband Blues' and 'Apples and Oranges', are not like anything he, or indeed anyone, had ever written before. They mark the end of his juvenilia and the beginning of a new stage of experimentation in his writing.

Unfortunately, by now any genuine critical appreciation of Syd's lyrical gifts had taken a back seat to speculation about his mental state. His fragile psyche rather than his muse became the dominant concern as evaluation of Syd the songwriter took a back seat to speculation about Syd the casualty, as if somehow his increasingly complex and convoluted imagery was merely a symptom of mental decay. Such crude and deterministic criteria do Syd the songwriter – and for that matter Syd the casualty – few favours. This is not to make light of Syd's subsequent problems, which were indisputably severe and lasted a lifetime, but to reduce his post-*Piper* output to a mere 'effect' of psychological imbalance does scant justice to the extraordinary sequence of songs he wrote in the late summer and autumn of 1967.

Aside from the crudely speculative nature of much of what has subsequently been written about this period of Syd's life, almost all of it basks in the retrospective glow of hindsight. Had John Lennon gone AWoL in 1967, 'Strawberry Fields Forever', 'I Am the Walrus' and 'What's the New Mary Jane' would have been similarly regarded as the dribbling testimony of a babbling lunatic. Had Bob Dylan died after penning the speed-driven prose of his novel *Tarantula* he would have been assigned a similar legacy.

Strip Syd's post-*Piper* songs of their daunting subtext and they still stand up as the work of a gifted and innovative lyricist, who was genuinely foraging into new and exploratory territory previously uncharted in pop songs.

The first of these songs, 'Scream Thy Last Scream (Old Woman with a Casket)', was recorded on 8 August, a week after Syd had been deemed incapable of live performance (although not, it would appear, incapable of fulfilling an obligation to a studio booking at Abbey Road.) 'Scream Thy Last Scream' is a dark and disturbing nursery rhyme that treads a fine line between linearity and abstraction. As with the *Fart Enjoy* booklet Syd takes elements of the *Mother Goose* rhymes and other traditional fairy tales – 'A Tisket, a Tasket', 'There Was an Old Woman Who Lived in a Shoe', *Little Red Riding Hood* – and reconfigures them in an altogether more eerie landscape. Despite remaining unreleased for over forty years, and clearly in need of further work, the whole thing hangs together with an inner coherence all of its own, propelled beautifully by its own unsettled and unsettling momentum, skipping effortlessly in and out of waltz time to emphasis the warped lilt of the lyric.

Nick Mason sings lead vocal, enunciating the lyric in a clipped accent over layers of speeded-up backing voices, provided by Syd. Syd's only vocal contribution in 'real time' is an audibly wasted 'She'll be scrubbing bubbles on all fours' and a seemingly sarcastic 'Oh, sock it to me' during the instrumental break. There is nothing wasted about his guitar-playing, though, which is deft and incisive throughout, as are Rick Wright's cluster chords and wah-wah effects on the Farfisa. The whole thing fades into a hazy swell of children's playground voices and the ringing of a school bell. Only two takes of the song were ever completed.

'I thought it was a really great song, quite absolutely from nowhere,' Andrew King told David Parker. 'It's a genre all of its own. I was thinking . . . supposing Syd writes a whole load of songs as strong and as extraordinary as this. It would have changed everything.'

To accompany 'Scream Thy Last Scream', poet Spike Hawkins devised an equally strange promotional film. 'I saw this overcoat hanging up and I thought, "That's a sinister thing. It's dark. I can't see the arms." This wonderful poet called Ted Milton lent me the overcoat, and it was rigged up – do you know those isolated little alleyways at the back of Tottenham Court Road and New Oxford Street? We had the overcoat move and filmed it and it still looked sinister in these dark Victorian alleys where anything could happen. Then we had an office set up with two telephones, typewriter, girl sitting there doing her nails and suddenly she sees this overcoat, face on. Then the Floyd roared in and rescued this girl. Unfortunately we didn't have sound but the Floyd were going to use it for a single they were going to bring out called "Scream scream scream" [*sic*]. I thought it was bloody great. The film as it was made was paced by the song, but even as a black-and-white silent film it was spectacular.'

If the imagery of 'Scream Thy Last Scream' skirted the very edges of coherence and comprehensibility, 'Vegetable Man', recorded two months later, was an altogether more sharp-edged affair. Often misleadingly interpreted as an autobiographical account of Syd's descent into madness, the song's aura of hollow-headed vacancy has generally been emphasised at the expense of its sheer sardonic onslaught on the superficiality of fame. 'Vegetable Man' is worthy of Bob Dylan at his most contemptuous – the Dylan of 'Positively 4th Street' and 'Can You Please Crawl Out Your Window' – full of self-parody ('In my Paisley shirt | I look a jerk') and dripping in contempt for the whole process of stardom ('It's what you see | It must be me') and the vagaries of fashion ('So I change my gear | And I find my knees | And cover them up with the latest cuts'). Written as a spontaneous response to Peter Jenner's request for new material, specifically a follow-up single to 'See Emily Play', it is essentially a song about having to write a song in two minutes, and a significant portion of its ire is directed at that very practice. Penned at Jenner's flat moments before they set off for a recording session, 'Vegetable Man' was written in the time it takes to sing it. That's a painter's conceptual response as much as it is a songwriter's emotive response. The fact that the lyric is based on what Syd was wearing and thinking at the time is almost secondary to the circumstances of its creation.

'Vegetable Man' may be an uncomfortably direct portrait of a man losing his sense of self and his self-worth, but it is no mere exercise in debilitation. It is self-referential only in as much as it is about process as much as end-product. Its delivery is assured and its lyric is carefully weighted and almost wholly parodic in nature. Syd sounds uncannily like Soft Machine's Daevid Allen, as he sings the 'ha-ha-ha-has' that lead into the middle eight. That middle eight, 'I've been looking all over the place | For a place for me | But it ain't anywhere', could be read as the testimonial of a drowning man adrift in an ocean of despair if it wasn't for the fact that Syd sounds more wistful and resigned than anything else.

Musically, 'Vegetable Man' reverts to Pink Floyd's earlier R & B style, with traditional blues progressions and a parody of the Batman theme at the end. At the conclusion of one of the takes the band can be heard collapsing with laughter, which somewhat refutes the supposed tortuous circumstances of its creation. 'Vegetable Man' would have made a great single.

The song that was eventually chosen to be the next single, 'Apples and Oranges', was recorded on 26 and 27 October, immediately prior to the band's first American tour. Although not an obvious candidate for a single, it's a terrific song, catchy, carefree and throwaway in the best sense of the word.

The irregular metre of the lyrics is underpinned by 'Taxman'-style rhythm guitar stabs on the offbeat and tonal coloration provided by innovative use of effects pedals. The ringing trebly tone of Syd's wah-wah playing, understated but bristling with menace on 'Scream Thy Last Scream', is applied with great delicacy here. Fred Frith, writing in *NME* in 1973, called 'Apples and Oranges' 'my favourite wah-wah playing of all time – incredibly incisive and articulate'. Frith observes the way that 'he makes the pedal hang always on the edge of feedback, which eventually breaks through as the final sound of the song' and notes that 'overall, the guitar acts as a fixed entity in an excellent construction, giving coherence to all the various departures. Considered in detail it's great the way the lines which underpin the first part of each verse are made up of tiny units, each contributing to something which becomes greater in concept than any of them.' Frith concludes by saying, 'The playing not only reveals an acute perception of sound, but explores a little exploited region and menacingly undermines the apparent harmless and half sense lyric.'

'It reads just fine BUT it's in the context of articles written specifically and only about guitar-playing. So that's what I'm talking about,' says Frith when presented with his words half a lifetime later. 'In fact, I'm much more interested in the song itself, of which the guitar-playing is an important part, but only a part. It wasn't really his playing that was the centre of my interest, though he was obviously great at it. I was interested in the songs, and the arrangements of the songs, the sound of them. Syd was first and foremost a songwriter, and in his own way he was every bit as revolutionary as the Beatles. – And it WAS pop music,' he adds in an echo of what Duggie Fields said when he first encountered the band.

The stop-start lyric of 'Apples and Oranges', like the wah-wah work that Fred Frith so greatly admired, is delivered with a dexterity that seems to pivot permanently on the edge of collapse but never quite descends into chaos. The song itself is full of neat verbal twists. The opening staccato salvo ('Got a flip-top pack of cigarettes in her pocket | Feeling good at the top | Shopping at shops') would have looked great stencilled or speech-ballooned on to a Richard Hamilton canvas. This tongue-twister suddenly melts into the elongated acid-vowel distortion of 'sheeees walking'. A similar derailing device occurs in the second verse's 'She's on time again | and then', as Syd once again displays an effortless capacity to expand and contract, truncate and time-stretch, seemingly at will, in a way that enhances and never detracts from the momentum of the song.

The middle eight ('I love she | She loves me | See you | See you') is almost contemptuously facile in its simplicity. Although supposedly written about Lindsay Corner, it is equally evocative of Syd's earlier 'I love Lib | Ad Lib ad Lib' billet-doux to Libby Gausden. As the wah-wah pedal finally spills over into feedback at the end, Syd launches into a spot of music-hall scat (doo-doo-loo-doo-doo-doo-doo-doo-doo-loo-doo-doo-doo-doo-doodla-dah!'). You half expect to hear Pete Townshend shouting 'I saw yer' as he does at the end of 'Happy Jack'.

The song most closely associated with Syd's malaise is 'Jugband Blues'. Because it was eventually included as the closing track on Pink Floyd's second album, *A Saucerful of Secrets*, released after Syd had left the band, it is often seen as Syd's valediction, his farewell to the Floyd, to fame – some would say to sanity itself. But although there is an undeniable air of detachment to the song, it is no mere portrait of mental disintegration.

'Jugband Blues' was written and recorded during the same period that produced 'Vegetable Man' and it is out of a similar mould, sharing much of that song's sardonic humour. In 'Vegetable Man' the sarcasm is directed at the pop process and at Syd himself. In 'Jugband Blues' it is aimed directly at those within Syd's immediate orbit. With almost disdainful mock-politeness Syd puts particular emphasis on the phrases 'awfully considerate' and 'most obliged', as he thanks everyone for 'making it clear that I'm not here'. Most interpretations of 'Jugband Blues' as an essay in schizophrenia seem to hinge on that line, and the subsequent 'and I'm wondering who could be writing this song'. It is never entirely clear though who or what Syd is waving goodbye too. Himself? His career? Or simply the persona of 'Syd' the pop star? Before we've had time to make up our minds the scathing contempt of the opening verse gives way to the disarming simplicity of the second. 'I don't care if the sun don't shine | And I don't care if nothing is mine.' This is carefree unburdened Syd. The Syd of 'The Scarecrow'. The Syd of 'Whoopee | you can't see me'. The next line, 'I don't care if I'm nervous with you', suggests the coquettish Syd of 'Ooh, you know I'm feeling frail' rather than a fragmented and turmoil-ridden soul. Indeed, once you discard the cultivated sarcasm of the opening lines and the Carrollesque quality of the closing couplet 'And what exactly is a dream | And what exactly is a joke?', the remainder of the song is remarkably robust. A Salvation Army Band interlude in the middle section injects a playful element into proceedings, but this unfortunately was merely the catalyst for another run-in between Syd and producer Norman Smith. When Smith enquired as to what Syd wanted the band to play, he replied 'I don't care. Let them do what they like.' Once again Syd's wilfully anarchic approach was in direct conflict with the regimented working methods of an unsympathetic producer. When the Beatles approached George Martin with similar whims and ill-thought-out ideas for 'Penny Lane' and the end of 'A Day in the Life', Martin went away and scored a distinctive piccolo-trumpet figure for the former and presented the orchestra with helpful structural parameters for the later which they fashioned into one of the most iconic song-endings of the 1960s. When Norman Smith was presented with a similar creative quandary, he complained about studio costs, session fees and Syd's irresponsible and directionless approach.

By now Syd's every last utterance was being interpreted as symptomatic of a deeper malaise. Even Peter Jenner subscribes to the view that Syd was fast becoming a lost cause. 'I think they should be released,' he says of 'Scream Thy Last Scream' and 'Vegetable Man'. 'I think the Floyd and his family should OK them. They are a self-description of what he was feeling. On "Vegetable Man" the description of the person in there is him, what he was wearing, what he was becoming. I was with him in the room when he was writing it. He was in one corner and I was in the other, and then he read it out and it was a description of him and what was going on in his head. "Scream Your Last Scream" was very disturbing but a powerful, powerful song. And "Jugband Blues". They are three amazing songs. If you put them up against "Bike" and "Scarecrow", you think, "Well, OK, those are all right, but these are powerful disturbing art." I wouldn't want anyone to have to go as mad and disturbed as Syd did to get that, but if you are going to go that disturbed give me something like that. That's great art. "Jugband Blues" is an extraordinary song. "I don't know if I'm here", you know. I think every psychiatrist should be made to listen to those songs. I think they should be part of the curriculum of every medical college along with those Van Gogh paintings like *The Crows*.'

Several other tracks were worked on at Abbey Road during August and September 1967. The instrumental 'Reaction in G' was devised as a defiant riposte to all those indifferent and uncaring live audiences who just wanted to hear the hits. Although it became a regular fixture in the band's live act, often opening the set, a satisfactory recorded version was never completed. Also abandoned was 'In the Beechwoods', a song inspired by the wooded area in Fulborne Road, Cambridge, where Syd's Scout troop used to have regular camps. The four-and-a-half-minute backing track minus vocals which has appeared on numerous bootlegs reveals a punchy and atmospheric tune, propelled by Syd's 'Taxman'-style rhythm guitar and Rick Wright's trademark ethereal keyboard, heavy on the treated wah-wah.

The day after 'Scream Thy Last Scream' was recorded Pink Floyd began work on Roger Waters' 'Set the Controls for the Heart of the Sun'. This track was effectively the blueprint for how the Floyd's sound would develop over the next couple of years, and was Waters' first substantial composition of note. It immediately became a staple of the band's live act and gave the first real indication that the creative momentum within the Floyd was shifting away from Syd. During this period the band also recorded two Rick Wright compositions, 'Remember a Day' and 'Paintbox'. Wright was still Syd's closest kindred spirit in the band at this point and both songs are affectionate pastiches of Syd's wistful writing style. 'Remember a Day' would eventually turn up on the *Saucerful of Secrets* album with Syd playing beautifully delicate slide guitar. 'Paintbox' ended up on the B-side of 'Apples and Oranges'.

Perhaps the most interesting of the Floyd's abandoned recording sessions was a proposed mixed media collaboration with the artist John Latham. 'He's a very important man. Very influential,' stresses Andrew King. 'He lived in Portland Road then, round the corner from everybody in Holland Park. He was very influential on Roger and Syd.'

Latham's creative life drew upon a wide range of media, including painting, sculpture, film, environmental installations, performance and conceptual art. He participated in many of the key underground events of the 1960s including the Wholly Communion Poetry Reading and the basement happenings at Better Books with Jeff Nuttall and Bruce Lacy. Latham had been an original faculty member of the Anti-University, the forerunner to the Notting Hill Free School, and in September 1966 took part in a series of events for the Destruction in Arts Symposium held at the Free School Adventure Playground with Gustav Metzger, Yoko Ono and her then husband Anthony Cox, and Pete Townshend. *Speak*, Latham's ten-minute 1962 animated op-art film made up of stroboscopic coloured discs, dots and concentric rings, was frequently projected during the Floyd's performances at the Free School and UFO. The Floyd also collaborated with Latham on the Music in Colour show at the Commonwealth Institute in January 1967, the same venue where Lawrence Sheaff made his final definitive gesture of silence with AMM.

Pink Floyd were asked to provide soundtrack music for the *Speak* film, but the session was aborted and nothing further came of the association. For Syd, this abandoned venture was a salutary reminder of how far he had drifted from the intellectual rigour and exploratory ethos of his art apprenticeship. Both men had trodden parallel paths up to this point. One of Latham's tutors at Chelsea School of Art, where he studied between 1947 and 1950, was Robert Medley, later head of art at Camberwell. Latham, like Syd, utilised both figuration and abstraction in his painting, and had a similar disregard for being bound by genre or the requirements of the marketplace. Both men embraced immediacy, and in their respective endeavours attempted to get beyond what Latham called the 'event-surface'. Here, unfortunately, the similarities end. In the art world radical gestures are the norm, the *enfant terrible* and the agent provocateur are actively encouraged and indulged. The pop scene had no such tradition of dissent. What was commonplace in the art world was treated as aberration in pop music.

194

'The rock world is very conservative and very conventional,' says Anthony Stern. 'Musicians have to funnel themselves through the bottleneck of normality that the A & R men from record companies represent. It's always the people in record companies who act as a kind of tiny little orifice through which the creativity has to fit, so it can be chopped up into convenient little sausages which can be marketed. That's the dilemma of the rock world, whereas with an artist you don't have that situation. You might have an agent or a representative, or a gallery that represents you, but in the music business, you've got to fit through this little gap, so that you can be marketed.'

John Latham eventually added his own soundtrack to *Speak*, placing a contact mike on the floor to pick up the rhythmic beat of a motor-driven circular saw as it gouged its way through a series of books. When Syd later presented the engineers at EMI with a cassette full of similar machine-noise recorded from the back of a friend's motorbike, he was met with bemusement. His suggestion that a saxophonist, two female singers and a banjo player be added to Pink Floyd's line-up was similarly greeted as the behaviour of a mad man.

Latham, like Syd, was versed in the tradition of cut-up and collage. The two men shared a legacy: Kurt Schwitters, Hugo Ball, Tristan Tzara, Robert Rauschenberg. In the literary world both men were drawn to James Joyce and Bob Cobbing. But while Latham moved in the same circles as many of his influences, befriending Alexander Trocchi and William Burroughs as he sought collaborators and kindred spirits for his textual and contextual experiments with process and form, Syd was having his dark nursery rhymes rejected by his producer, record company and band mates for being too weird. While Latham questioned the dominance of space over time in art-making, and forged a fresh language out of collage and text, Syd was asked to come up with a follow-up to 'See Emily Play'. And when he did his endeavours were considered not good enough or not suitable for the singles market.

Latham's most notorious artwork, remembered by Andrew King as having a seminal impact on Syd, was entitled *Still and Chew/Art and Culture in 1966–67*. In August 1966, while lecturing at St Martin's School of Art, where Syd had failed to gain entry two years earlier, Latham borrowed a copy of *Art and Culture*, Clement Greenberg's 1961 collection of essays, from the college library. Working with sculpture student Barry Flanagan and a small group of specially invited guests Latham ripped out several of the book's pages, chewed them and placed them in a vial. These were then distilled in sulphuric acid until the solution turned to sugar. When the college library sent Latham an 'overdue' notice in May 1967 he returned the vial full of fermented solution and labelled it 'the essence of Greenberg'. He was immediately sacked from his post.

Still and Chew, John A. Walker maintains, was John Latham's 'sardonic gesture of defiance against a pedagogy and a critic'. Such gestures recurred throughout Latham's career. In 1961 he had produced a work called 'The Life and Death of Great Uncle' for critic Lawrence Alloway's short-lived *Gazette* magazine. Believing that the artist should not have to explain his work, his contribution to *Gazette* was itself a protest against elaboration, and consisted of typed repetition of the words 'the same', first in lower then upper case. These gradually mutate into 'the sime' and then 'the seme' before ending in a spray of dots generated by the full stop key of the typewriter. Next to this typographic mantra is, what John A. Walker calls 'a jocular meta-text' purporting to 'explain' the piece, but which merely adds another layer of parody by satirising explanation itself.

Syd was also exploring sardonic gestures of defiance at this time, both in the satirical lyrics of 'Vegetable Man' and 'Jugband Blues', and in a legendary recording session where he attempted to teach the band a new song called 'Have You Got It Yet?' which he kept changing every time they played it. Even Syd's increasing and well-documented tendency to play one note throughout a live set around this time can be seen as purposeful, rather than, has been so often suggested, the consequence of drug-fuelled incapacity. Had such behaviour merely been a result of the latter, it is unlikely that Syd would have been capable of taking to the stage at all, and had he made it that far any attempt to play would have resulted in incompetence and embarrassment. To play one note constantly hints at some sort of striving for purity, the paring down of things to their essence. Such gestures, intentional to the point of bloody-mindedness on Syd's part, echo the rapid-fire purity of Latham's series of one-second paintings which he executed with a spray gun. When Latham pursued such gestures he was seen to be challenging the boundaries of conceptual art. When Syd did it, he was seen to be sabotaging the career prospects and commercial viability of his band.

Central to Latham's working practices was a process he called the 'least-event', the utilisation of spray paint being merely one of many ways in which he attempted to capture the 'zero moment' on canvas. Latham drew upon Rauschenberg's black-on-black and white-on-white canvases and John Cage's '4' 33' to give credence and validation to his methodology. He even evoked Leonardo da Vinci when he discovered an entry in Leonardo's notebooks that read, 'Among the great things which are found among us the existence of Nothing is the greatest.' Syd was now cut adrift from any comparable aesthetic. He was deemed merely irresponsible.

According to Chrissie Iles, John Latham's 'unprimed canvases and spray-gun or action-based mark-making raised funda-mental questions about the end of painting and the dissolution of the body. Figures emerging out of void-like surfaces evoked the ethereal body prints of Yves Klein, dispersing the image into a dematerialized state that questioned the very basis of representation.' Syd had explored the same anti-gestural possibilities with his guitar within the amoeba blobs and hypnotic pulses of the light show. 'It's quite a revelation to have people operating something like a light show while you're playing as a direct stimulus to what you're playing,' he told CBC radio in 1967. 'It's rather like audience reaction except it's on a higher level.' Exiled from these impulses and the kinetic energy of UFO Syd was thrust into the unforgiving glare of the music industry's spotlight, where he visibly wilted.

While John Latham continued to explore the parameters of art and life, Syd Barrett was sent to America to play the *Pat Boone Show*.

Pink Floyd's aborted American tour of November 1967 is seen by many, including Peter Jenner and Andrew King, and his fellow band members, as Syd's tipping point, the moment everyone realised that something was seriously wrong and that drastic remedies had to be sought. 'We were fighting a losing battle from the word go,' says Andrew King. 'Everything that could go wrong went wrong. From the very first gig, which was the old Fillmore West in San Francisco, Syd was starting to do nothing on stage. He was blowing a referee's whistle at one gig.'

Nick Mason is completely unambiguous in his assessment of the American tour, claiming in his autobiography that 'Syd went mad' and that 'he detuned his guitar on stage at Venice LA and just stood there rattling the strings'. In fact, as Peter Whitehead's studio footage from late 1966 confirms, Syd had been radically detuning his guitar during performance for some time. A year earlier such AMM-inspired experimentation was tolerated, encouraged even. Now it was seen as a symptom of madness. Pink Floyd were trying to 'break America' and Syd was fucking up.

Despite this apparent handicap, several live gigs were received favourably. The *Los Angeles Free Press*, for instance, spoke in glowing terms of the band's performance in Santa Monica, describing 'a hurricane of sound bringing total sensual involvement of audience and performers'. The real problems arose when the band made their TV appearances. On 6 November they mimed 'See Emily Play' on CBS's *Pat Boone Show*. The following night they mimed 'Apples and Oranges' on the legendary ABC show *Dick Clark's Bandstand*. Time and myth have conspired to transform these performances into celluloid testimonials to 'Syd the casualty'. He is variously said to have stood open-mouthed, eyes rolling back in his head, arms limp by his side during both performances, refusing to mime and meeting his hosts' attempts at an interview with a catatonic stare. No footage has yet come to light to confirm the Pat Boone incident but the 'Apples and Oranges' section of the *Dick Clark's Bandstand* appearance has turned up on the internet in recent years and refutes all suggestions that Syd was either unhinged or incapable. On the contrary, the visual evidence reveals a clear-eyed Syd staring directly at the camera as he lip-synchs a significant portion of the song, including the tongue-twisting opening verse. At the end he answers Dick Clark's banal questions with customary Cambridge politeness. During the performance he looks no more embarrassed to be miming than the rest of the band. Rather than speculate over Syd's state of mind on that American tour, perhaps the real question that should be posed is this: what the fuck were Pink Floyd doing on the *Pat Boone Show* in the first place?

'We were inexperienced,' admits Andrew King. 'There were very few shows that you could go on. We should probably have never even gone to America. We did pack up and come home in the end after playing the Cheetah Club in New York.'

In refusing to kow-tow to the strictures of network television, Syd was simply ahead of the game. Within a couple of years Led Zeppelin would show that you didn't have to make concessions of any kind to these mainstream outlets. In the meantime the

Box Tops and Lemon Pipers and Electric Prunes of this world continued to file on to *Where the Action Is* or the *Merv Griffin Show*, to be introduced with corny references to their name, mime their latest single and then be subject to patronising interviews from their host. Even Cream at the height of their fame were reduced to miming 'Anyone for Tennis' on American pop shows while prancing about inanely with tennis rackets. The Who mimed half an hour of 'Tommy' on the German show *Beat Club*. Syd sensibly took one look at all this shit and opted out.

'He wasn't enjoying himself on that tour but then none of us were,' Andrew King rationalises. 'Its not like he was going behind our backs and going ha-ha-ha, I'm sabotaging the tour.'

Shortly after he returned from the American tour Syd met up with old girlfriend Libby Gausden. 'I'd just got engaged and Syd came in to where I was working,' she remembers. 'He was still very funny then. I can see him now, standing there, laughing himself sick. Telling me how everyone was saving and buying houses and he was spending every single penny he'd earned. He'd bought an expensive American car and was having it shipped over here. He was smiling and laughing about it, thin as a rake in green corduroy trousers. My boss said, "What's that, a blade of grass?" I told him who it was. He said, "I hope you're not thinking of giving up your fiancé for that." '

It was becoming increasingly obvious by now that Syd could no longer reconcile his creative energies with the requirements of the music business. Duggie Fields lays the blame for his disenchantment squarely at the feet of the industry. 'I saw one of their tour schedules and I thought, that's the maddest thing I've ever read. The way they'd be performing around England, they'd be going up here then coming down here then going over there then going back up there day after day in crappy transport, staying in crappy places, playing to people who didn't have any clue what they were trying to do. Then they must have had the conflict between performing the same thing the way they did before or performing it differently. Throw drugs into that and you've got a big cause for stress, if nothing else.'

And yet no sooner had Pink Floyd returned from their aborted visit to America than they were off on the road again. Given the supposed concern about Syd's deteriorating mental state, this strategy was baffling, to say the least. What do you do if your lead guitarist is becoming erratic/unstable/unhinged? Simple. You send him off round the UK on a package tour with six other groups. Two shows a night for sixteen nights.

Commencing at the Royal Albert Hall on 14 November and concluding at the Glasgow Playhouse on 5 December, the Hendrix–Move–Pink Floyd–Nice–Amen Corner–Eire Apparent –Outer Limits show that trawled the Winter Gardens, Theatre Royals and Guildhalls of Great Britain was to be the last of the great 1960s package tours. As with the BBC's one-size-fits-all approach to pop programming, the package tours were an idea that had had their day. Earlier in 1967 the Jimi Hendrix Experience had set off on a similar jaunt around the Gaumonts and Granadas with Engelbert Humperdinck, Cat Stevens and the Walker Brothers. It seems incongruous in hindsight, but it was part of the prevailing 'it's all showbiz' ethos of the time. Just as the Hendrix–Floyd–Move tour was commencing, the Who were just winding up a similar UK tour with Marmalade, the Tremeloes and the Herd.

'It was an amazing bill,' says Andrew King. 'Seven groups in two hours. Some nights we had eight minutes. Some groups had even less. Jimi only had thirty minutes. Did a few numbers, then did the one where he sets fire to the guitar. One night we came off stage and the promoter said, "You went thirty seconds over. Do that again and you're off the tour." '

By the end of 1967 the sheer physical toll was beginning to tell on Syd. Photos from the late summer through to the American trip reveal a tousle-haired youth with the beauty of a Romantic poet. A group photo from the Hendrix package tour shows a frazzled-looking Syd with a penetrating and unsettling stare. And by now more disturbing evidence of Syd's decline was beginning to surface too. 'Egerton Court was the flat where we first started to hear thumping noises coming from downstairs,' says David Gale. 'It transpired that Syd would tickle Lindsay to the point of her desperation. She'd be screaming at him to stop and he wouldn't. And he would bang her head on the floor. And Syd started to beat Lindsay Corner up.'

Some people dispute this assessment, including Lindsay herself in a rare public pronouncement on her time with Syd. Others, though, including Aubrey 'Po' Powell, Storm Thorgerson and Ian Moore are adamant that Syd's behaviour towards Lindsay became abusive and intolerable. 'This angelic boy became this thousand-yard stare, sullen, black bags under the eyes, pale, listless, not talking, moody, impossible to work with, violent man,' says David Gale sadly.

An accumulation of several factors seems to have brought about this unsavoury situation whereby the previously sweet, charming and twinkle-eyed Syd was now by all accounts turning into a deeply unpleasant and anti-social human being. In addition to the intolerable pressures of pop stardom and a tendency to self-medicate with powerful hallucinogens, another crucial factor to take into account was the laissez-faire and non-judgemental ethos that prevailed at the time. Syd may or may not have been frying his brain, but in the main friends and onlookers alike were too damned cool to do anything about it.

'In a way it all seemed quite romantic. It was all part of the mystique,' says Chris Welch. 'It seemed to upset the band more than it did the public. You expected an underground band like Floyd to be acting in an eccentric and crazy way. That was the whole vibe of the psychedelic scene in 1967. I don't think people understood the depth of the problem in terms of psychiatric illness. Everyone was freaking out, so Syd was freaking out and so much the better, that was my perception of it at the time.'

'And we didn't know it wasn't poetic genius,' rationalises Nigel Lesmoir-Gordon. 'We thought, "This is just another crazy way of living." '

'A number of us – those who didn't get tied up in Indian-ness – were very interested in R. D. Laing,' says David Gale. 'Tremendous reverence was paid to the thinking of Laing and his colleagues – Joe Burke, David Cooper and so forth. And they – inadvertently I think – heroised the idea of madness. And hippies made of it what they wanted. The ones that read books made Laing's *Divided Self* and so forth into what they wanted to hear.'

It was through his own connections with Laing and Cooper that Gale attempted to get help for Syd. 'I rang up R. D. Laing and said, "I want to talk to you about Syd Barrett, because myself and his friends think he's in deep trouble and would benefit from seeing you." So Laing said, "Well, y'know, no therapy can ever take place unless the patient wants it to." He said, "You've got to make him want to come and see me." And I said, "Well, can we make an appointment, and then in the interim", I said, "we'll get to work on him. And then if we can't, and he won't come, we'll cancel the appointment." So he said, "Sure. Why don't you come next Wednesday at three o'clock?" So we hired a cab which pulled up outside Egerton Court, and we said – I think we hadn't done it well – "Oh, Syd, we've arranged for you to go and see R. D. Laing." We didn't really build it up, maybe we should've done, but we thought we would get rebuffed. And he point-blank refused – would not go. And that was that.'

And yet – and it is the most monumental 'and yet' of all – throughout all this turbulence and turmoil Syd, against all odds, continued to function as a creative being. Every piece of visual or audio evidence that survives from this period refutes the received wisdom that Syd was turning into the 'Vegetable Man' and that his meltdown was instantaneous and incapacitating.

It is worth looking in detail at this evidence, as all of it casts doubt on the notion that Syd was no longer able to function. From the recording of 'Scream Thy Last Scream' on 7 August 1967 to footage shot in December 1967 for a feature on Mike Leonard's light show, which was shown on the *Tomorrow's World* TV programme in January 1968 – the very period when Syd was supposedly in irreversible freefall – there is substantial material to counteract the myths, namely the four compositions that have already been considered ('Scream Thy Last Scream', 'Vegetable Man', 'Jugband Blues' and 'Apples and Oranges') and the band's performance on *Dick Clark's Bandstand* on 6 November. To these can be added widely circulated bootleg recordings of live performances at the Starclub Club in Copenhagen on 13 September and the Hippy-Happy Fair in Rotterdam on 13 November, the two BBC sessions for John Peel's *Top Gear* recorded on 25 September and 20 December and a promotional film for 'Jugband Blues' shot in December.

The recording of the Copenhagen gig captures a punchier, less polished outfit than that heard on the *Piper at the Gates of Dawn* album. Versions of 'Reaction in G', 'Arnold Layne' and 'Matilda Mother' are driven by pulverising R & B riffs and the Floyd sound as unrestrained as they do in the early UFO footage. Syd sounds competent and compos mentis throughout. His playing, particularly on 'Reaction in G' and 'Astronomy Domine', is exemplary.

The Rotterdam concert on 13 November took place one day after the Floyd had aborted their American tour with a gig at the Cheetah Club in New York. One therefore might expect to hear a substandard performance from a burned-out Syd. In fact, the band's energy levels are frantic and brutalising. One is struck, not only by the searing intensity of it all, but by the realisation that the band went out and did this 137 times during 1967. As much as anything else it's worth considering how anyone could achieve that kind of intensity every night without burning out. If anything, it is Waters and Mason who sound uninspired. The Rotterdam version of 'Pow R. Toc H.' cruelly exposes the short-comings of the Floyd's rhythm section, while Waters delivers some spectacularly out-of-tune vocals on 'Set the Controls for the Heart of the Sun'. Rick Wright is the musical force behind most numbers, laying down subtle textures over which Syd thrashes wildly. During the lengthy middle section of 'Interstellar Overdrive', now unrecognisable from the Morse blips and clicks of early versions, Syd sends out shards of machine-metal noise into the night, but on 'Scream Thy Last Scream' (announced by Waters as 'Old Woman with a Casket') he plays the nifty changes with great delicacy. This, remember, is a man who was supposedly ga-ga on American TV a few days earlier.

The first of the band's Radio 1 sessions was recorded on 25 September 1967 and aired on the very first *Top Gear* programme on 1 October, the second day of broadcasting from the BBC's new pop service. The band, probably out of obligation, play a selection of the shorter poppier tracks from the *Piper* album – 'Flaming', 'The Scarecrow', 'Matilda Mother' and 'The Gnome' – which remain largely faithful to the recorded versions (although Syd gets the words wrong on 'Flaming'). 'The Scarecrow' and 'The Gnome' are both taken at a languid pace, giving them a lighter, airier feel than the augmented album versions. On 'The Scarecrow' the instrumental outro is less busy, the song's rurality more pronounced. On 'The Gnome' Syd's vocals are less forced than they are on the album, his enunciation less awestruck when he sings 'Look at the sky, look at the river'. Both performances give credence to those who contend that the subtlety of these songs was swamped by over-production on the LP versions.

The Floyd's second *Top Gear* session was recorded on 20 December and aired on New Year's Eve on a show co-presented by John Peel and Tommy Vance. By the end of 1967 Syd's fellow band members were apparently tearing their hair out in frustration at his erratic behaviour and were already manoeuvring to have him replaced – which makes it all the more curious to report that the second *Top Gear* session is magnificent.

Responding to the mixed reception the band were receiving in the media John Peel introduces the first number with the words, 'It's nice to have the Pink Floyd on the programme this week 'cos they get a lot of knocking in the musical press which is quite undeserved. I think they're one of the best groups in the country.'

Syd's guitar playing on 'Vegetable Man' is all tonal coloration, with leitmotif pedal work that permanently hovers on the brink of feedback. The band camp it up on the 'Vegetable Man – where are you?' refrain and vamp like crazy on the 'Batman' outro. Everyone sounds like they are having a ball. 'Scream Thy Last Scream' similarly has impressive tone and texture from Syd and his playing in the higher register evokes the best nights at UFO. 'The incredible sound of the Pink Floyd along with Ray Barrett,' gushes a splendidly clueless Tommy Vance at the end of the track, momentarily confusing Syd with the Australian-born TV actor of that name.

The *Top Gear* version of 'Jugband Blues' is slower than the one that eventually appeared as Syd's curtain-call on the *Saucerful of Secrets* LP. Rick Wright plays churchy organ, and the band sing harmonies on the closing section, adding warmth to Syd's plaintive eulogy. Stripped of its Sally Army band section, Syd's astonishing abstract sound palette comes to the fore, while the appearance of a kazoo – that universal signifier of derision utilised by everyone from Bela Bartok to Frank Zappa – blows a raspberry in the face of this supposed anthem to schizophrenia.

This version of 'Jugband Blues', rather than the album version, was used on a short promo film shot for the Central Office of Information in London shortly after the end of the Hendrix package tour. Although never officially released, it is freely available on the internet: it shows Roger Waters pretending to play the euphonium and Syd looking stiff and uninvolved as he mimes to what was still being mooted as the band's next single. The moment the song ends he turns his back on the camera.

Syd looks far more relaxed in a five-minute item filmed in December 1967 and transmitted on the BBC's popular science programme *Tomorrow's World* on 17 January 1968. The item featured a display of Mike Leonard's latest light projector, or more precisely 'a piece of apparatus for designing light machines . . . part of a circuit controlled by relays based on the logic system of a computer'. The light effects are shown being tried out on the Christmas edition of *Top of the Pops* while the Tremeloes perform their number 1 hit 'Silence is Golden'. The piece then cuts to Pink Floyd who play a languid bluesy version of 'Green Onions'. Syd, in candy-striped shirt, is seated with his right foot resting on his Binson Echorec. He demonstrates some nifty slide work, while deftly manipulating the wah-wah pedal to the brink of feedback. At one point he glances lazily up at the camera. There is no catatonic stare. He looks entirely relaxed.

Only on the 'Jugband Blues' promo film does Syd look un-engaged and a tad frazzled. In the rest of the material considered here (some dozen or so items, if we include the post-*Piper* recording sessions) he is still clearly capable of inspired performance. Should any previously unseen evidence come to light that shows Syd acting like a babbling maniac then clearly a little reassessment will be in order. In the meantime, on the evidence available, it would appear that the stories about Syd's supposed intransigence and incapacity during his final months with the Floyd have been somewhat exaggerated, and that the circumstances of his departure from the band have as much to do with pragmatism and hard-nosed commercial decisions as anything else.

'To me the problems became obvious on the Hendrix tour and when Andrew came back from America,' says Peter Jenner. 'I never got the full story but it got to be too much. It became clear that there was a problem. Then it got to be an ongoing struggle to try and see if we could keep the band together and make it work. And the answer was, we couldn't. I kept on trying to find excuses and reasons and how we could understand it. We had to do this and the band had to do that and everything would be all right. But it just went on getting worse and in the end it was unarguable. They had to get someone in to cover for him.'

'When I left 101 I went to live in Earlham Street above Seamus in the top room. And that's where I first met Dave Gilmour,' says Hester Page. 'I came home one day and there's this beautiful guy sitting on the end of my bed. I said, "Ooh, hello, who are you?" He said, "I've come up to see the manager of Pink Floyd because they want to replace Syd." That was the first time that I digested that Syd was not going to be around.'

'Hester's memory is faulty,' maintains David Gilmour. 'I could well have met Hester there; I went there several times, but my invitation to join Pink Floyd was initially by a phone call from Nigel Gordon, then at a meeting at Edbrooke Road, Peter Jenner's house, at that time, the Blackhill Enterprises [Jenner and King's management company] office. I returned from a year in France in September '67 and lived thereafter in London, there was no "coming up" to London.'

By the end of 1967 Syd's days in Pink Floyd were numbered. Almost exactly two years after he had mooted the idea in his letters to Libby Gausden the band sent for 'Fred'. David Gilmour was invited to join the group and made his live debut with the short-lived five-piece line-up on 12 January 1968 at Aston University in Birmingham. The band played four gigs as a quintet, at Aston, Weston-super-Mare, Lewes and Hastings, and then simply didn't bother to pick Syd up for the next one at

Southampton. Or the one after that . . .

On 6 April 1968 it was officially announced that Syd Barrett had left Pink Floyd.

'I spoke to him once about the singles the Floyd had come out with,' says Spike Hawkins. 'He said, "That was the easy part. I wanted to go much deeper, using music and lyrics as a key to opening doors." I said, "But you really opened doors for the Floyd." He said, "Yeah, with cheap keys." '

Chapter Six

We'll Stray Our Pieces

'It's been quite a long time since you did any poetry,' he remarked. 'You might as well have a try this evening, instead of – well, brooding over things so much. I've an idea you'll feel better when you've got something jotted down – if it's only just the rhymes.'

THE WIND IN THE WILLOWS KENNETH GRAHAME

What does it do to a man when he is effectively jettisoned from his own band, and abruptly cut adrift from his creativity? Robert Wyatt's wife, Alfie, once told me that Wyatt, who endured a similar 'did he leave or was he pushed' exit from Soft Machine, had his confidence and sense of direction so severely affected that years after the event that he had dreams where he was playing badly on stage while Miles Davis stood sneering in the wings.

And what does it do to a man, when the circumstances of his leaving are so ill thought-out and executed and when his band mates are so Englishly inept at discussing the matter in detail that they simply go and play gigs without him, leaving the matter to resolve itself? 'It got really embarrassing,' says Rick Wright, who was at the time sharing a flat in Richmond with Syd and was his principal confidant and kindred spirit. 'I had to say things like "Syd I'm going out to buy a packet of cigarettes" and then go off and play a gig. Of course, he worked out eventually what was going on.'

Well, yes, he would, wouldn't he? Probably around the time when the band went off and played a short European tour without him. To this day no one in or associated with the band can agree on exactly when Syd ceased to be a functioning member. Anecdotal evidence has settled on those four January gigs played as a five-piece before the band 'stopped picking Syd up', but, leaving aside the small detail of the subterfuge necessary in order to slip out and play a gig when you are sharing a flat with a fellow band member, there is also contradictory evidence as to just how quick and clean – or conversely how prolonged and messy – the break was. 'Nick Mason has a bit of super-8 film of Syd with some of the rest of us, tap-dancing in a dressing room at one of the gigs that we did as a five-piece,' remembers David Gilmour. 'There were jolly moments. It's happy tapping – two or three of us in a row including Syd doing a jig in a dressing room before going on stage in, I think, Weston-super-Mare.'

Subsequent to the split there are stories of Syd turning up, guitar in hand, ready to play at numerous gigs and recording sessions throughout the early months of 1968. There are, equally, contradictory accounts of just how many tracks he contributed to on the second Pink Floyd LP, the recording of which was completed in April 1968, the month his departure was officially announced.

While they were on their short European tour in February the new line-up made a series of promotional films for Belgian TV. Versions of 'Astronomy Domine', 'Set the Controls for the Heart of the Sun', 'Apples and Oranges' and 'Corporal Clegg' were shot in the studio. Films for 'Paintbox', 'The Scarecrow' and 'See Emily Play' were shot in the Parc de Laekan in Brussels. In the later films David Gilmour only appears briefly in long shot, semi-silhouetted or face hidden by a hat, as if the band were still nervous about revealing to the world that their former guiding spirit was no longer with them. Despite this apparent uncertainty about how to proceed without Syd, the band was clearly re-energised in his absence. A live studio performance of

'Astronomy Domine' shot for ORTF in Paris shows Roger Waters prowling the stage with simmering intensity, revelling in showmanship and throwing Pete Townshend poses as he attacks his instrument with renewed vigour.

'Being a staunch "Laingian" at the time, my view was Syd was being scapegoated by the band and he was just eased out 'cos they couldn't face his madness,' says David Gale. 'That's a very romantic view and I believed it for some time. But he was unworkable and Roger saw the whole project going down the tubes. He was unprofessional on every level and totally unreliable, and I now think they just did what had to be done. I mean, Roger Waters is a very impressive man. His will and determination were immense. I used to muck about with him when we were teenagers before he became famous for anything, and he is great company, but, I mean, he's not naturally bohemian or anything like that. He's a musician and he thinks, "I'm not gonna compromise this." Neither he nor Nick nor Rick were ever particularly deeply into substances. I don't know whether that was because they wanted to preserve their career or whether that was a temperamental matter.'

There is, of course, a much simpler and altogether more mundane explanation for what happened. Those same middle-class character traits that had done so much to define the band's cultural milieu and shape their outlook now kicked in as survival instincts. Roger Waters, Nick Mason and Rick Wright had all forsaken potentially lucrative and secure futures in the professions in order to pursue their pop careers. Faced with similar options in the summer of 1965 Bob Klose curtailed his musical ambitions and chose to concentrate on his architectural studies. A year earlier Klose had moved in to Nick Mason's recently vacated room in Mike Leonard's house in Highgate when Mason, faced with a choice of college studies or constant loud band rehearsals, moved back to the creature comforts of his

WE'LL STRAY OUR PIECES

parents' house, complete with swimming pool, in Hampstead.

When the band turned professional and signed to EMI in 1967, they all agonised to varying degrees over their decisions to jettison their respective careers. Each will have had to convince their parents, and themselves, that they were going to make a go of 'this pop lark', and in 1967, remember, there was still a lingering perception that pop music was essentially a teenage fad like the hula hoop. Faced with the prospect of having their best-laid plans sabotaged by a recalcitrant and obstructive spirit like Syd Barrett, they made the hard-headed, but entirely rational, decision to continue without him.

In the wake of Syd's departure Pink Floyd thrived and went on to become one of the most successful bands in the world. Syd fared less well. Peter Jenner and Andrew King made a management decision to stick with him because they thought he would eventually surface from his troubles and establish himself as a solo act. At the time they couldn't see how Pink Floyd would survive without their songwriting genius, and in March 1968 they formally dissolved their partnership with the band. The Bryan Morrison Agency secured a new deal with Pink Floyd, while the new manager, Steve O'Rourke, renegotiated the band's contract with EMI. The rest is accountancy.

On 6 May 1968 Syd Barrett returned to the recording studio for the first time as a solo artist. On half a dozen occasions between May and July of that year he went into Studio 3 at Abbey Road with Peter Jenner as producer and 'musicians unknown' in tow, and recorded rough versions of half a dozen tracks. With hindsight it seems extraordinary that Syd was expected to work at all, given his supposed physical and mental state. What is perhaps just as extraordinary is the sheer range and variety of songs that he recorded. Not only do they dispel the myth of a muse run dry, they also capture an artist still forging ahead with new and creative ideas.

The first song he recorded as a solo artist, 'Silas Lang' (aka 'Swan Lee'), took its inspiration from Henry Longfellow's epic poem *Hiawatha* and tells the tale of Swan Lee journeying by canoe 'from the land of his fathers' in search of his squaw. Although it is a conventional narrative, full of stock adventure-tale images of pow-wows, wigwams and grizzly bears, 'Swan Lee' is rich in complex versifying ('From the shore hung a hot heavy creature infested') and deft use of alliteration ('Swan Lee, his boat by the bank in the darkness') and assonance ('Suddenly the rush of the mighty great thunder').

Although 'Silas Lang' shuns Longfellow's use of the trochee (a metrical form rarely used in pop songs, although utilised to great effect in Cream's 'Tales of Brave Ulysses' and Noel Harrison's 'Windmills of Your Mind'), it does draw heavily on *Hiawatha*, as Longfellow himself drew upon the Finnish folk-epic the *Kalevala* as the catalyst for his imagery. Once again we are in the company of Syd the sophisticated pasticheur, emulating a verse-form and subject matter that itself was extensively parodied (by Lewis Carroll among others) when *Hiawatha* first appeared in the nineteenth century.

'Silas Lang' is another of Syd's frieze songs, curiously distanced and uninvolved. One can imagine it depicted on a series of woodcuts, in tapestry, or on a native American blanket. The sense of stillness that pervades the song is reinforced by the chorus refrain, 'The land in silence stands'. Curiously the Silas Lang of the title is not the song's central character. He is only revealed in the last line as the chronologer who commits the tale to paper, a clever Syd twist which adds another layer of distancing between the listener and the action.

Recorded during the same session as 'Silas Lang', 'Late Night' is one of Syd's most plaintive songs, the first in a sequence of personal lamentations for lost love that would come to dominate his solo output. Only the instrumental backing track was laid down at that first session. This vocal-less take didn't see the light of day until released as a bonus track on the *Crazy Diamond* box set in 1993. Stripped of its lyric it allows the listener to hear Syd's delicate slide technique at its best, as he swoops and glides over the song's loping 5/4 rhythm.

Less memorable are the rambling formless instrumentals 'Rhamadan' and 'Lanky' Parts One and Two, which Syd laid down at the following day's session. 'Rhamadan' was a conga-heavy jam session lasting eighteen minutes and is of little merit. 'Lanky Part One', eventually issued on the *Opel* LP of out-takes in 1988, features the same line-up of guitar, piano, vibes and percussion, while 'Lanky Part Two' is an uninspired percussion-led jam lasting seven minutes. It is still a mystery who the anonymous backing musicians are on these sessions, and no substantial light has been shed in the intervening forty years since they were recorded. The conga player is strongly rumoured to have been the multi-instrumentalist Steve Peregrine-Took from Tyrannosaurus Rex, but the identities of the bass player and drummer remain unknown. One thing is for sure, they completely lack the musical empathy that Syd enjoyed with Pink Floyd. They simply don't gel as a unit. Without the drive and cohesion formerly supplied by his old band mates, Syd falls back on uninspired blues runs, which merely emphasise his lack of conventional virtuosity. Within months of leaving Pink Floyd he permanently abandoned the sonic voyaging he had once so eagerly pursued and found creative solace instead in his literary influences as he embarked upon a renewed bout of experimentation with wordplay.

'Golden Hair', the only non-original composition that Syd ever recorded as a solo artist, was an adaptation of a James Joyce poem, taken from the *Chamber Music* anthology first published in 1907. Syd first attempted to record 'Golden Hair' during the same session on 14 May that produced 'Rhamadan' and 'Lanky'

Parts One and Two. The fact that he went on to attempt multiple takes of 'Golden Hair' at virtually every stage of the recording of *The Madcap Laughs* illustrates just how meticulously he worked on the song, and how integral it was to his body of work. Peter Jenner thought so too. 'Of all the things that came out from working with me in those confused years, "Golden Hair" was the key song. That was the song you would build an album around,' he says.

Syd's version of 'Golden Hair' is so much more than an exercise in accomplished mimicry. Its plaintive lovelorn air was utterly in keeping with the mood of *The Madcap Laughs* album. If the listener hadn't known that it was a Joyce composition, as indeed Peter Jenner didn't, there would be every reason to suspect that it was one of Syd's own efforts, an Elizabethan- or Jacobean-influenced lament. In fact by making one subtle change, substituting 'midnight air' for 'merry air' in the first verse, thus avoiding repetition of the phrase in the final verse, Syd arguably improves on the original.

'Golden Hair' springs from Joyce's juvenilia, a first precocious stirring of a talent that would go on to revolutionise the twentieth-century novel. There is no hard evidence from which we can deduce why Syd chose 'Golden Hair', poem V, over any of the other thirty-five in the collection. Poems IX ('Winds of May, that dance on the sea'), XV ('From dewy dreams, my soul, arise') and XX ('In the dark pinewood | I would we lay') all follow the same verse form as 'Golden Hair' and could, with minimal adaptation, be arranged to fit the same melody that Syd devised for his interpretation. A close reading of the *Chamber Music* anthology would suggest that Syd was completely imbued with its spirit. Salient lines reveal some distinctly Barrett-like imagery. 'And where the sky's a pale blue cup | Over the laughing land' (poem VII), 'The ways of all the woodland | Gleam with a soft and golden fire' (VIII), 'The time of dreaming | Dreams is over'

(X), 'O, hurry over the dark lands' (XIII), 'The pale dew lies | Like a veil on my head' (XIV), 'Clouds that wrap the vales below' (XXV), 'The leaves lie thick upon the way' (XXXII) and the pleading last line of the final poem 'My love my love my love, why have you left me alone?' find resonance throughout *The Madcap Laughs*.

Anthony Burgess in his Joyce biography *Here Comes Everybody* scathingly dismisses 'Golden Hair' as 'one of the most atrocious lyrics ever penned by a great writer'. Joyce himself remained ambiguous about his early poetic efforts, alluding to the anthology in his novel *Finnegans Wake* as 'Shamebred Music'. Burgess, however, notes the suitability of Joyce's poems for musical accompaniment with their 'long vowels, simple stanzaic form, no great length, unity of mood and conventional imagery'. And Joyce himself always wished for the poems to be set to music. 'Some of them are pretty enough to be put to music. I hope someone will do so, someone who knows old English music such as I like,' he wrote to his brother Stanislaus. Over the years composers as varied as Frank Bridge and Luciano Berio have written arrangements of the poems from *Chamber Music*. Syd doesn't disgrace himself in such company and his hauntingly sensitive arrangement of 'Golden Hair' conveys the mood of the poem beautifully. Who knows what else he could have achieved had he pursued this area of his creativity more thoroughly?

On 20 July 1968, in what would be his last recording session for almost a year, Syd attempted two takes of a new song called 'Clowns and Jugglers', later titled 'Octopus'. As 'found poetry' the song's distillation of eclectic source material has few parallels in English pop. Perhaps only John Lennon's 'Being for the Benefit of Mister Kite!' comes close in the way that it utilises its material – in Lennon's case a Victorian circus poster. But whereas 'Mister Kite' draws solely on the one 'found object', and retains a central linear narrative, Syd narrates a sequence of metrically consistent fragments drawn from widely disparate sources.

Significantly, 'Clowns and Jugglers/Octopus' is one of the few songs that Syd ever spoke about in detail, thus allowing us a rare glimpse into his unorthodox working methods. 'I don't read much but I think I picked up Shakespeare as a book that just happened to be lying there to read. It was meant to be verse,' he told Chris Welch of *Melody Maker* in 1969. More specifically he told *Sounds* journalist Giovanni Dadomo in 1970, 'I carried that about in my head for about six months before I actually wrote it so maybe that's why it came out so well. The idea was like those number songs like "Green Grow the Rushes, Ho" where you have, say, twelve lines each related to the next and an overall theme. It's like a foolproof combination of lyrics, really, and then the chorus comes in and changes the tempo but holds the whole thing together.'

These insights throw up as many questions as they answer. Syd states how long the song took to write but doesn't actually say when it was written. Does he mean it was written in the six months immediately before the recording? This would situate its gestation during Syd's last dark days with Pink Floyd, which delivers another body-blow to the received wisdom that he was creatively incapacitated by this time. Second, although he cites 'Green Grow the Rushes, Ho', which he would have sung at Scout camp and Gang Shows, 'Clowns and Jugglers' does not adhere to the rhyme scheme or metre of that song. The most intriguing word in Syd's 'explanation' is 'foolproof'. Does he mean 'undetectable sources', i.e. 'I've covered my tracks' (in which case he was severely misguided), or merely 'structurally sound', i.e. 'regularity of form'? Either way, 'Clowns and Jugglers' is an astounding piece of work.

Taking a fairground octopus ride as its pivot (in early versions David Gilmour says that Syd sang 'The Helter-skelter Ride') the song draws upon nursery rhyme, in particular Syd's often utilised *Mother Goose* rhymes, traditional folk song, Elizabethan masque play, Shakespeare's *King Henry VI Part I*, *The Wind in the*

Willows and the poetry of, among others, John Clare, Sir Henry Newbolt and William Howitt.

The song's opening refrain is lifted from *Summer's Last Will and Testament* by the Elizabethan playwright and satirist Thomas Nashe.

[Here enter 3 Clowns and 3 Maids, singing this song, dancing.]

> Trip and go, heave and ho,
> Up and down, to and fro,
> From the town to the grove,
> Two and two let us rove
> A Maying, a playing:
> Love hath no gainsaying:
> So merrily trip and go.

Nashe was a Suffolk-born, Cambridge-educated writer who lived from 1567 to about 1600. It is believed that he was expelled from St John's College for satirical student productions and he spent much of his life dogged by persecution for his seditious and licentious writings. He spent time in Newgate Prison and fled London for exile in Norfolk. The exact date of his death is unknown and he may well have been murdered by Crown forces. *Summer's Last Will and Testament*, although laden with political ambiguity and topical references to the bubonic plague, is a conventional piece firmly in the tradition of the English pastorale, replete with actors portraying the four seasons, nymphs, shepherds, satyrs, clowns and dancers. 'Trip and go, heave and ho' also crops up in the *Mother Goose* rhymes, where Nashe's 'From the town to the grove' becomes 'From the down to the grove'. In both it refers to May Day celebrations.

Syd makes similar use of dually attributable sources with the phrase 'Heigh-ho, huff the Talbot', taking his inspiration both from the *Mother Goose* rhyme 'Huff the Talbot and our Cat Tib' and Shakespeare's *King Henry VI Part I*, which features a character called Talbot. Shakespeare's Talbot lacks the definite article: the character's full name is Sir John Talbot, Earl of Shrewsbury, and despite Syd's mentioning the bard in his interview with Chris Welch the connection would at first sight appear to be tenuous. However, closer inspection of *Henry VI* reveals that the words 'dragons', 'wings', ghost' and 'tower' all appear in the first five pages, as they do in the first verse of Syd's song.

In his interview with Giovanni Dadomo, Syd states, 'I've got Penguins lying around at home, Shakespeare and Chaucer, you know. But I don't really read a lot. Maybe I should.' Ignoring the characteristically casual manner of the utterance it adds further weight to the notion that, as in his painting, Syd was capable of extrapolating and synthesising from wildly disparate sources, in the case of the Talbot, nursery rhyme and Shakespeare. Of course, none of this can account for where the kangaroo comes from in the line following 'Heigh-ho, huff the Talbot', or, indeed, what it is doing in a tree in the first place, nor, for that matter, does it explain the origin of most of the other fragments that wind and weave their way through this extraordinary song. To relegate all this to nonsense verse or malady would be an insult to the writer's intentions. Another significant interchange that takes place in the Giovanni Dadomo interview illustrates the precision with which Syd sifted and placed this apparently arbitrary imagery. Dadomo mentions the line 'little mini-car coughs and clears his throat'. 'That's "little minute gong",' Syd corrects him with a laugh, as if it's the most logical thing in the world to use an antique timepiece as a way of signifying an imminent announcement. (Has anyone ever used a 'minute gong' as a device in poetry or song?) To be fair to Dadomo, 'little mini-car coughs and clears his throat' does sounds like a Syd line, an appropriately cartoon-type image suggesting a car exhaust. It springs from the whirlpool of creativity that could devise 'She'll be scrubbing bubbles on all fours'.

Syd wryly adapts another *Mother Goose* rhyme towards the end of the song. 'The winds they did blow | The leaves they did wag | Along came a beggar boy | And put me in his bag' is pointedly translated into 'The winds they blow | and the leaves they wag | But they'll never put me in their bag.' A statement of intent if ever there was one!

Another of the song's minute adjustments verges on genius. Syd plucks a transcendental image from John Clare's poem 'Fairy Things' ('filled with little mystic shining seed') and, having extrapolated other phrases from the same poem ('money ploughed', 'prickly seeds') delivers 'Clover, honey pots and mystic shining feed'. As with 'Golden Hair', the change is made to avoid repetition of a word (in this case 'seed'). That's all it is, one simple letter shift from *s* to *f*, and yet the image utterly retains Clare's element of rural mysticism. At the time he wrote the song, Clare's 'Fairy Things' had only been anthologised once, in James Reeves' 1954 collection, *Selected Poems*. 'Later he looked back on his childhood as a time of almost visionary happiness,' wrote Reeves of Clare in his introduction: just one of many parallels that would become applicable as the years rolled by.

Elsewhere Syd evokes Kenneth Grahame for 'Isn't it good to be lost in the wood | Isn't it bad | Too quiet there in the wood'. Taken by Sydologists to be an indication of his growing personality disorder, it reveals in fact an observant reading and close understanding of Mole's trepidatious journey through the Wild Wood in chapter three of *The Wind in the Willows*.

What is often fascinating about the song is not merely the plundering itself, but the source of the plundering. For instance Syd blatantly lifts lines from Sir Henry Newbolt's 1931 poem 'Rilloby-Rill':

> Madam you see before you stand
> Heigh-ho! never be still!

> The Old Original Favourite Grand
> Grasshopper's Green Herbarian Band
> And the tune we play is Rilloby-rilloby . . .

Syd simply replaces Rilloby-rilloby with the phrase 'In us confide'.

He also draws upon the anonymous and much anthologised children's rhyme 'Mr Nobody' for 'every plate we break' and 'The squeaking door will always squeak'. In fact 'Rilloby-Rill' and 'Mr Nobody' were both lifted from another of Syd's pocket anthologies, in this case *The Junior Laurel and Gold Anthology*, compiled by the folklorist John R. Crossland and illustrated beautifully by Margaret Tulloch. The pocket book, volume forty-two in the *Laurel and Gold* series, was first published in 1936. By the time Syd was born, ten years later, it was in its seventh edition. *The Laurel and Gold Anthology*, like Kate Greenaway's *Mother Goose* compendium, was one of the touchstones of Syd's imagination. As with the Greenaway volume (and, indeed, *Henry VI Part I*) Syd mostly plunders from the first few pages of the book. 'Rilloby-Rill' and 'Mr Nobody' are to be found on pages ten and twelve of the 243-page pocket book. On page six, incidentally, is the anonymous rhyme 'When Good King Arthur Ruled This Land', which Syd adapted for the opening lines of 'Matilda Mother'.

In the original version of 'Clowns and Jugglers' Syd sings a verse omitted from later takes, which contains the line 'To a madcap galloping chase'. This, too, was taken from the *Junior Laurel and Gold Anthology*. It comes from a poem by William Howitt called 'The Wind in a Frolic', which was to be found on page sixty-one of the volume. It may be gilding the lily, as it were, but it is worth noting that 'The Wind in a Frolic' also contains references to apples and oranges, and gingerbread and cloaks (which appear in 'Bike').

Howitt (1792–1879) along with his wife, Mary (1799–1888), came, like Syd's parents, from Quaker stock. The pair produced a series of nature books, and histories of English abbeys and castles, priestcraft and spiritualism. They collaborated on two volumes of poetry, *Forest Minstrel and other poems* (which contains 'The Wind in a Frolic') and *The Desolation of Eyam*. Mary Howitt is probably best known for 'The Spider and the Fly', which Lewis Carroll later parodied as 'The Lobster Quadrille'.

There are precedents for this kind of plunder, but they are generally not to be found in rock 'n' roll. One obvious source for Syd was the art school approach to found objects, but there are literary antecedents too, and not merely within the avant-garde. 'His method of writing seems to have been to collect scraps which came to him and recollections of stories which he had been told, besides suggestions growing out of books, pictures, and even topical events,' says Roger Lancelyn Green of Lewis Carroll. The same could be said of Syd. Whether pastiching Belloc or recalling the nocturnal exploits of a local knicker-stealing transvestite, Syd approached lyric assemblage in a similar ad hoc manner. By the time he wrote 'Octopus' this gathering of scraps had reached a level of sophistication that transcended mimicry or plagiarism.

Musically, too, the song achieves new levels of sophistication. It may be built on choppy rhythms that derive from Syd's beloved Bo Diddley, but the chord changes that start each verse (B, E7, G, C7) show how much he had developed as a musician. And against all expectations, the simple A-B sequence of the rest of the verse resolves itself perfectly in the rising F7, which accompanies the phrase 'In us confide'. Incidentally, no amount of research on my part has been able to locate a tune called 'In us Confide'. Some aspects of the song, it seems, are more foolproof than others.

'It must not be thought that either of the Alice books is derivative,' says Lancelyn Green. 'They are both original with the absolute originality of sheer genius. All the various "originals" and suggestions served as so many sparks to touch off the sleeping gunpowder of Dodgson's imagination.' 'I do tend to take lines from other things I like and then write around them,' said Syd disarmingly to Giovanni Dadomo.

Not all of 'Clowns and Jugglers' is lifted from 'found sources'. While one cannot be absolutely certain that Syd didn't alchemise the lines 'The wind it blows in tropical heat' and 'The drones they throng on mossy seats' from the kind of sources that inform the rest of the song, they have the sway and the impeccable sense of assonance that characterise the best of Syd's songwriting. Dotted throughout the song are several unmistakably original Barrett phrases. The 'Please leave us here | Close our eyes' refrain may invert the 'Why d'yer have to leave me here' plea of 'Matilda Mother', but it evokes exactly the same sense of being in a childhood limbo or in suspended animation. The sudden interjection of 'Meant even less to me than I thought' is another typical Syd device, qualified detachment. 'Bike' is full of them. ('If you think it could look good', 'I'll give you anything | Everything, if you want things') Here they achieve new degrees of distancing. It's as if he is saying, 'It didn't mean much to me then and now it means even less.' One might consider that a curious sentiment to be expressed in the midst of such mystical shining imagery. It's as if Syd is propelling the rug from under his own feet, sounding a note of dissatisfaction with his entire artistic quest, as if the whole exercise is ultimately meaningless.

Despite Syd having laid down promising markers for his first solo album, one cannot underestimate the difficulty that his management team had in working with him at this time, and after the initial work was completed on 'Clowns and Jugglers' on 20 July 1968 there were to be no more sessions at Abbey Road for almost a year.

'I'd never produced a record in my life at this point,' says Peter

Jenner. 'It seemed a good idea to go into the studio because I knew he had the songs. And he would sometimes play bits and pieces and you'd think, "Oh that's great." It was a "Oh he's got a bit of a cold today and it might get a bit better" approach. It wasn't a cold – and you knew it wasn't a cold – but I kept thinking if he did the right things he'd come back to join us. He'd gone out and maybe he'd come back. That was always the analogy in my head. I wanted to make it feel friendly for him, and that where we were was a comfortable place and that he could come back and find himself again. I obviously didn't succeed.'

During this period in limbo Syd occasionally visited the London home of Anthony Stern and his wife. 'I was never a close friend of Syd's until things were falling apart for him,' says Stern. 'I think he saw in me a sort of foothold on his happy childhood. A representative of something that was going on in Cambridge when things were going a bit astray with, well, with his brain really, after the LSD thing. That's the time when I actually saw Syd most but he was no longer the Syd of old. He had definitely started to come apart. I had a flat in Prince of Wales Drive, in Norfolk Mansions, and he would come round frequently. I didn't quite know why he was coming round. He was very quiet. We talked a lot about music and image, and that's when I got the idea for my *San Francisco* film, which I then did in America. He was becoming inarticulate, but he felt that he was emotionally reaching out to somebody who he knew from his childhood days. I could see that he was in need of companionship – just someone to talk theoretically to. I mean, he was interested in so many different things. We talked about things like the tarot and the *I Ching* – how to use it and why to use it. He was still interested in all that mystical and psychic stuff.'

Others were also doing their best to look out for Syd during this troublesome period. 'We all certainly felt that we wanted to rescue Syd from himself, but there was no strategy,' says Andrew

King. 'We proceeded from day to day. We had a rota for giving Syd supper and he used to come round one evening a week to eat. Once you feel someone is vulnerable you start over-compensating and you usually make it worse. Running around after Syd and going, "How can we make it easier" was probably making it worse. And that's what I was doing.'

'He was still occasionally functioning. That was what was so frustrating,' says Peter Jenner. 'He could still talk to you and you could have an apparently coherent conversation and there was still stuff going on and then there would be the stare.'

To make matters worse Syd and Lindsay Corner had split up by now: Lindsay took refuge at Storm Thorgerson's flat in Hampstead when she could finally take no more of Syd's mood swings. Syd returned briefly to the security of Cambridge, revisiting London occasionally to sleep on friends' sofas, popping into the new offices that Blackhill Enterprises had in Holland Park to see if there was anything doing – and being bewildered to find there wasn't.

'It would be like, "What are we going to do? Go into the studio again?" "No, Syd, let's wait until you are better." So then he just drifted away,' says Peter Jenner.

During this extended bout of musical inactivity Syd also spent a lot of time in the company of poet Spike Hawkins. Hawkins, the true anarchic embodiment of the English beat spirit, was the perfect foil for Syd's wayward muse. He had Cambridge connections going back to Nigel Lesmoir-Gordon's Roodmoodment nights in the early 1960s. He had also appeared at numerous key counter-culture events including the Wholly Communion poetry festival, the Spontaneous Underground parties at the Marquee and the 14 Hour Technicolor Dream. It seems wholly appropriate that his and Syd's orbits should have collided during this period. One of their first meetings was at a London party.

'I was working on an impossible film script that nobody could

226

ever finish. I fell asleep in the middle of the floor and the party went on around me apparently for four hours, and when I woke up there was Syd looking down at me saying "Did you like that?" I said, "Yeah." He said, "That's it, isn't it?" I said, "Where have I been?" He said, "Where you wanted to be." We had very similar angles and laterals coming in on the world.'

Syd and Spike shared a similar approach to writing. Both utilised ellipses, allusion and occlusion in order to short-circuit linearity, and in both men's work there is an ever-present sense of consciousness folding in on itself. Both subjected a basic and unshowy verbal repertoire to experimental technique and random thought processes. Both built a uniquely abstract style of versifying on what was to them entirely logical principles. They had other things in common too.

'Our relationship was actually made up around a drug that was doing the rounds called Mandrax,' remembers Hawkins. 'He would take a couple and I would take a couple and we would sit round talking. We would go on at great length about the trees that could be seen from my flat in Kensington. He said, "There seems to be a current of electricity that flows from the trees to this flat." I said, "Yes, I sometimes feel that." That stayed in my mind for many years. Every time I looked at this tree I thought of my little powerhouse.'

Hawkins recognised great similarities of outlook, and 'inlook', between him and Syd, particularly in the way they drew upon their immediate environment in order to create. Hawkins's 'explanation' of this is as obtuse as his poetry: 'There may be a pot there, a plant growing there, a person suddenly walks in. It has a form and it also has a dynamic which is moving within it, but then one brings it down to within one's own little world, whether one is sitting in a room or out in the park. It is a cutting-up of that's there and that's there and it's arranged. The structure of one's world at the time of writing is placed and from those placings . . . plant comes here. What does plant do? Is plant speaking? It's using what is around one instead of having a notebook to refer back to. This is all structured and I think that's what we had in common. The structure was found in this cornucopia of odds and ends and bits and bags, whereby one could stay in one place and then move on to the next object. I'm not putting myself up on some high academic stool. I'm just saying that was a great similarity, which shook me somewhat because I thought, [laughs] "God, this swine's pinched my method of breaking up." And it is in the breaking up.'

This 'breaking up' was an integral component of both men's writing. One of the ways in which Hawkins aided Syd's own fragmentation of vocabulary was with his *Instant Poetry Broth*, a kind of verse-recipe consisting of randomly cut up words and phrases. Devised in 1967, it was published by the Glass Motorcycle Press, and ran to five editions, each one containing a fresh set of words and phrases.

Instant Poetry Broth came in a sealed PVC pouch with the following instructions;

1. Simmer with an International Incident and bring to point of an all out conflict.
2. Place the all out conflict under the body of an old man (Note that it is desirable in times of national anxiety to have the individual suspended on a wire).
3. Add punch to your salad day and stir in all the remaining members of the massacre. A quilt can be lowered after simmering for thirty days. It is advisable to do this in the open air where members of the public will not be harmed.
4. Place all ingredients into a compound and dust liberally with medals and old dispatches. Chew until saturation point is reached. Boil larbs and cap.
5. Turning over new leaf. Place three handcarps to decorate and pour sauce onto a limping horse in a shinty garden.

The poetry broth, with its unmistakeably Hawkins-style word

combinations like 'ice-cream dragon', 'snow turbines', 'poison oaks' and 'silken sheds', had a huge influence on Syd. 'I found him playing with it,' says Hawkins. 'He said, "This is brilliant." It was such a simple thing to do but it had the bite of what was happening in the 1960s. He'd move a word and I'd move a word. He'd pull words out and I'd add an s. It was like an intergalactic Scrabble.'

This form of intergalactic Scrabble would find its way into several of the songs that Syd wrote for his solo albums. Like Bob Cobbing's typography and cut-ups, *Instant Poetry Broth* entered Syd's lexicon, another way of dislocating sense and senses, another way of subjecting commonplace subject matter and everyday vernacular to avant-garde techniques and principles.

'I think also what we had in common is we were late writers,' says Hawkins. 'We were still trying to work out, from somebody like Beckett, say, "My god, what maps are they using?" But it's not that at all of course. Its just simplicity itself . . . looking around at the objects and using these as a structure for one's work. There was a great similarity of thinking there. I was laying on the carpet looking at something and he said, "Are you thinking what I'm thinking?" and I said, "Shut up, I'm sectioning." And he said – I'm paraphrasing in my terms but it was something like – "Do you find the bric-à-brac of one's surroundings to be an extremely well-structured chart?" I said, "Yeah," because that's where I worked. He was already out there and I was out there too, but we were rather lost, so we had to use what we had in our pockets.'

Using what he had in his pocket had been one of Syd's guiding principles since he first began to break free of representational painting, representational thinking per se in fact, and began living out Robert Rauschenberg's dictum 'Any incentive to paint is as good as any other. There is no poor subject.' Many of Syd's apparent 'word-collisions' are hewn from the same thinking, an unwillingness to censor or edit: all receptors open.

By this stage of Syd's development as a lyricist he had

transcended the idea of 'found objects'. What he was beginning to create now, drawing upon techniques derived from both art and literature, was a wholly unique 'found world' with its own perceptual Esperanto.

Early in 1969 Syd moved into a flat on the second floor of Wetherby Mansions in Earls Court, where artist Duggie Fields now lived. Fields had previously lived at 101 Cromwell Road but doesn't think that his tenure and Syd's overlapped. Although the two men got on well, their respective creative energies couldn't have been more contrasting. While Fields was actively making his way in the world as a practising artist, Syd spent much of his time alone in his room, purposeless and withdrawn. Poignantly he attempted to pick up the threads of his own art apprenticeship but seemed unable to finish anything he worked on.

'I knew he'd been to art school but I didn't actually know him as an artist until I saw paintings in his room when he moved in with me,' says Fields. 'As a musician he was seriously impressive. As an artist he had stopped at a stage where he hadn't found himself. When he lost himself musically he tried to pick up again as an artist and he never made a connection. I think he also had a hard time living with me because I was well into painting and would do a lot of work. I've always enjoyed work and never had an issue doing it. He had an issue with "doing".'

David Henderson noted this lack of direction and purpose when he visited the flat. 'He had stopped trying,' says Henderson. 'He was just painting for his own enjoyment.' Whereas Syd had all but abandoned the rigorously conceptual approach which had initially informed his development as a painter, Fields was driven by a rigorous work ethic, which was clearly at odds with the drug-addled crowd that often hung around the flat.

'I can't not do it,' says Fields. 'It's not so much that it's compulsory. It's what I do everyday. It's more fun than any party ultimately. It's more fun than hanging out with any group. I'd learned that lesson in another flat, before I moved in to Cromwell Road. We had a big room where everyone used to hang out and I would retreat to my room to paint. And it was, "Hey man why aren't you sitting with us. Have we upset you? Have we done something wrong? You're really freaking us out. Don't you want to be with us?" I'd have to say, "It's nothing to do with you. I just want to do my work." But drugs were abundant in that group and people want other people hanging out with them doing the same thing. And if you don't, you're not cool and not part of the in-group. There was a whole period where conversation wasn't that important. An expression that someone gave to me recently was being a "buzzkiller". And that's what I would have been. A buzzkiller. I'm killing their high by not being part of it.'

Fields remembers evenings at Wetherby Mansions when he would be painting, while the attendant druggies sat and watched TV. When TV closed down for the night the guests would all turn and watch him painting instead.

'There are always people in any group who have nothing to focus on,' says Fields. 'And Syd had lost his focus. That was the problem. And that's where co-existing with me became a problem. It was probably difficult for him because I hadn't lost my focus and that will have thrown up for him the difference. It will have made him feel more disconnected, because I was so connected with my work. It can't have been easy. If he had been living with someone who was not into anything, that might have made it more easy for him to focus.'

Field's prolific activity threw Syd's squandering of his own talents into sharp relief. By abandoning painting he had abandoned something of his true self. And having turned his back on his degree studies at Camberwell he now found himself unable to get back to that place in his head that he had once so securely inhabited and that sense of purpose that had once been second nature to him. How good he might have been if he had continued to pursue his painting apprenticeship is one the most poignant 'what ifs' of this story. 'It takes ages to develop your own original style,' says David Henderson. 'That's the difficult part. I was at the Royal College of Art doing my MA before I got a sense of that. Syd never got that far in his development.'

'I don't think he produced enough for people to say what he would have been,' agrees Duggie Fields. 'He hadn't found himself visually. I think he lost the ability to think. He made a start on things but he hadn't found a direction and he never finished anything. There was no real consistency in what he was doing. There is a period where you don't know what you are doing as an artist and it takes you a while to find your own language. And he hadn't found it visually. He certainly found it in his playing and writing.'

And eventually that's what Syd returned to. 'One day late in March 1969,' Malcolm Jones reported, 'I received a message that Syd Barrett had phoned EMI's booking office to ask if he could go back into the studios and start recording again.'

And so after a break of almost a year, Syd returned to Abbey Road studios with the twenty-three-year-old Jones as producer. This was an extremely fruitful and productive period and yielded an abundance of new material. In eight sessions spread between 10 April and 6 May 1969 a refreshed and rejuvenated Syd worked on versions of 'Silas Lang' (now retitled 'Swan Lee'), 'Clowns and Jugglers', 'Late Night', 'Golden Hair' and 'Rhamadan'. In addition he recorded numerous takes of eight new songs: 'Opel', 'Love You', 'It's No Good Trying', 'Terrapin', 'No Man's Land', 'Here I Go', 'Dark Globe' and 'Long Gone'.

Jones was a flexible and open-minded producer, and his working relationship with Syd stands in marked contrast to the one he had endured with Norman Smith a couple of years earlier. With a sympathetic spirit behind the desk, Syd worked prolifically and diligently, and the recorded evidence of these sessions completely dispels the notion that he was unable to function or impossible to work with. In his privately published account, *The Making of 'The Madcap Laughs'*, Jones gives valuable insight into Syd's state of mind and working methods at the time. He recalls how, after receiving the news that Syd wished to return to the studio, he arranged an initial meeting where the two men listened to the rough mixes of the earlier Peter Jenner sessions and Syd enthusiastically performed several new songs for him, including 'Opel', 'Terrapin' and 'Love You'. 'Syd was in a great mood and in fine form, a stark contrast to the rumours and stories I'd been fed,' claims Jones. In one five-and-a-half-hour session alone on 10 April Syd recorded nine takes of 'Opel', four of 'Love You', three of 'No Good Trying' and a single perfect version of 'Terrapin'. He also did further work on the Jenner material, overdubbing guitar and vocals on 'Late Night' and lead and harmony vocals on 'Golden Hair'.

Jones noted in his account that their preferred working method on Syd's solo work was a reversal of previous Pink Floyd practice. Whereas before the band would normally lay down a backing track and than add vocals last, Syd now built up tracks from guitar and vocals, adding further instrumentation later.

In June 1969 Malcolm Jones's services were dispensed with and in three hastily convened sessions, David Gilmour and Roger Waters were brought in to finish the album. These sessions took place on 12 and 13 June with Gilmour overseeing proceedings, and on the 26th with Gilmour and Waters co-producing. The sessions produced four new songs, 'She Took a Long Cold Look at Me', 'Wouldn't You Miss Me' (later retitled 'Dark Globe'), 'Feel' and 'If It's in You'.

'We were led to believe that the project was going to be shelved,' says David Gilmour. 'We were told that EMI had spent too much time and money on it and it was a long way from completion. An extension was negotiated on the basis that we got it finished in double-quick time – that meant not spending money. The fact that we, Pink Floyd, were very busy and Abbey Road's other bookings both conspired to make the time available to finish the album very short. Decisions had to be made.'

Malcolm Jones remained diplomatic about the circumstances of his demotion, apparently happy to be kept on in an executive producer capacity, and he also acknowledges the role that Gilmour in particular took in shaping the unfinished recordings; but the seemingly undue haste with which the album was completed remains a contentious issue. Particularly puzzling was the absence from the finished album of 'Opel', one of the most hauntingly original songs that Syd ever composed. 'Opel' reduces the narrative of *Hiawatha* in 'Swan Lee' to a people-less landscape of ebony totems and driftwood half buried. The fragments of imagery that make up the song's opening verses ('a bare winding carcass stark', 'crisp flax squeeks tall reeds') are among Syd's most sophisticated. These opening verses give way to a lengthy instrumental section which is followed by a plaintive coda where Syd sings 'I'm trying to find you | I'm giving | I'm living | To find you' repeatedly. Such yearning sentiments were a central theme of *The Madcap Laughs*, yet inexplicably 'Opel' was left off the finished album and had to wait another eighteen years before it was finally given pride of place as the title track on an album of out-takes.

Also contentious for Malcolm Jones was the decision to include a continuous sequence of songs, 'She Took a Long Cold Look', 'Feel' and 'If It's in You', recorded during the Gilmour–Waters sessions, complete with false starts, and a harrowing snippet at the beginning of 'If It's in You' where Syd's sense of pitch deserts him and he spirals wildly out of tune. In the ensuing dialogue between Syd and his producers he sounds agitated and ill at ease. Jones took great exception to the inclusion of this sequence, saying, 'False starts are OK if they give an insight into the musicianship and artistry of those present, or if they present the odd mistake which everyone is capable of . . . the false starts to the tracks that I had personally supervised were far more interesting than those left in the final album. They certainly would have been more of a candid insight to the atmosphere of the sessions and less detrimental to Syd's abilities than the ones left in. Those left in show Syd, at best as out of tune, which he rarely was, and at worst as out of control (which, again, he never was).'

David Gilmour justifies the decision as a form of studio *vérité*. 'Roger and I both thought that it was important that some of Syd's state of mind should be present in the record – to be a document of Syd at that moment – and to explain why some of the songs had these, how should I say it, unprofessional moments.'

During a delay between the second and third of the Gilmour–Waters sessions, due in part to his former band mates having to mix Pink Floyd's *Ummagumma* album, Syd joined Emo, Sam Hutt and others in Formentera and spent his time relaxing, attempting to lean the sitar, strumming his acoustic on the beach at sunset and writing a clutch of songs which would find their way on to his second solo album.

The final recording session for *The Madcap Laughs* took place on Saturday, 26 July 1969, but owing to Pink Floyd's extensive touring commitments the final mixing and mastering was spread out over a period of four months from August to November. And when these matters were finally attended to, the task of assembling and mixing the album was despatched in just two two-hour sessions. During the delay Syd spent an impromptu afternoon painting the floorboards of his room at Wetherby Mansions in alternate strips of orange and purple. The cover shot that was used for the LP shows Syd barefoot in the empty room, crouching next to a vase of flowers. The back cover shows

Syd in a yellow towelling T-shirt, hair covering his eyes, while Iggy, a sometime resident of the flat, poses naked behind him. The mood of the photos perfectly captures the mood of the album itself – uncluttered, brooding, beguiling, stark, intimate.

The Madcap Laughs was eventually released on EMI's new Harvest label on 6 January 1970. The episodic nature of its gestation is writ large in the songs that were included. Of the thirteen tracks, two were recorded with Soft Machine ('No Good Trying' and 'Love You'), two with 'Willie' Wilson on drums, one of which had Jerry Shirley on bass ('No Man's Land' and 'Here I Go'), two with additional instrumentation from David Gilmour and Rick Wright ('Octopus' and 'Long Gone'), one that was begun during the 1968 Peter Jenner sessions with anonymous musicians ('Late Night') and six solo songs ('Terrapin', 'Dark Globe', 'Golden Hair', 'She Took a Long Cold Look', 'Feel' and 'If It's in You').

Madcap is a lop-sided and tangential masterpiece, a portrait hung wrong on a wonky nail, where perspective is awry and the colours have all run. 'Like a painting as big as the cellar' was how Syd described *The Madcap Laughs*, a typically enigmatic utterance with hints of both claustrophobic confinement and an endless vista of possibilities. Syd had actually taken to inhabiting the cellar at 183 Hills Road when he went back home to Cambridge: a small windowless and airless environment, where he could shut out the tensions and distractions of the real world and shrink everything that ran randomly through his head to fit that one cramped and shaded place.

Gone now was the referencing of hippie texts like the *I Ching*. Gone were the nods to Kenneth Grahame and Hilaire Belloc. Gone too was the vibrancy of old, to be replaced by something altogether more hesitant and melancholic. Where Syd had formerly sounded mischievous and carefree, he now sounded plaintive and vulnerable. Also absent, other than in occasional tantalising flashes, was the economy and conciseness of yore. In their place came unruly torrents of wordplay that only rarely yielded up their inner logic.

The album's most commercial song, 'Here I Go', had been written as 'Boon Tune' for the Purple Gang, as an intended follow-up to their UFO anthem, 'Granny Takes a Trip'. It is one of the few songs that Joe Boyd can definitely remember appearing on a demo tape that Syd recorded for him early in 1967. To a jaunty music-hall lilt, the song tells a charmingly adolescent tale of a girl who forsakes her musician suitor, so he writes her a song hoping to regain her affections. When he turns up at her house the girl is gone but her sister invites him in. To add to the old-world charm of the song, the two even end up happily wed, a telling anachronism in the era of free love and liberation. In its language ('She don't rock and roll | She don't like it | She don't do the stroll') 'Here I Go' harks back to an earlier dance-band era, and captures a side of Syd that he rarely explored on record.

'No Good Trying' evokes the doll's-house darkness and kindergarten games that informed 'Matilda Mother' and 'Bike'. The song blurs images of innocent child love and adult eroticism in a very ambiguous way. The whole thing is played out as if there are formal courtship courtesies to both forms of intercourse, social and sexual. One gets the impression simultaneously of children playing doctors and nurses and adults acting out a particular kind of coquettish display. The mode of transport shifts accordingly, in the first verse a rocking horse, in the last verse a car 'with electric lights flashing very fast'. 'No Good Trying' is one of Syd's most intriguing songs. On *The Madcap Laughs* it is sympathetically augmented by Soft Machine, who would have been a great asset to the rest of the album, had they been booked for more than one session, and given more time to familiarise themselves with the material.

'We'd played a gig at the 100 Club as a trio in '69,' says Soft

Machine bass player Hugh Hopper. 'Robert [Wyatt] knew Syd reasonably well from the UFO days and he came up after the gig, very low key, and muttered something about doing some playing with him at Abbey Road. He played us these tapes and we ran through them a couple of times thinking it was a rehearsal. He'd laid down his guitar parts already. He was totally unassertive in the studio, made no suggestions at all. In a way, I suppose, it's a compliment to our playing that he found something that fitted immediately. I think that's how people should work.' 'Every time he played a tune through, the bars before the chord change were different,' remembers keyboard player Mike Ratledge about the Soft's participation in the *Madcap* sessions. 'Nothing was ever written down. Nothing was ever the same. I wouldn't have minded if it was uniformly irregular but it changed from take to take. In the end you just had to watch his hands to see what he was doing.'

Several songs on the album are laments for lost love, conveyed in language more reminiscent of a Shakespearean sonnet or the works of the eighteenth-century pastoralists than 1960s pop. Syd frequently applies exquisitely painterly imagery ('Pussy willow that smiled on this leaf' on 'Dark Globe', 'A broken pier on a wavy sea' on 'She Took a Long Cold Look'). Overall, though, the mood is one of brooding despair and reflection. Images of longing and regret pervade the record. 'Oh, where are you now' and 'Won't you miss me' in 'Dark Globe'. 'Oh, understand' and 'When I live I die' in 'No Man's Land'. 'Away far too empty | Oh, so alone' in 'Feel'. 'Inside me I feel | Alone and unreal' in 'Late Night'. 'I cried in my mind' on 'Long Gone'. 'I'm trying to find you' on 'Opel'.

Syd's plaintive version of Joyce's 'Golden Hair' sits perfectly in their company, fully vindicating Peter Jenner's claim that it was the song he was trying to build an album around. It would be somewhat fanciful to make too many comparisons between James Joyce and Syd Barrett, one the high priest of literary modernism, the other a pop musician whose early potential burned bright but whose creative flame burned out far too soon, but there are undeniable parallels between *Chamber Music* and the dominant themes of Syd's solo work. Vicki Mahaffey summarises the main themes of Joyce's anthology as 'loss, betrayal and the interplay of psychological and social experience and anguished nihilism'. Equally pertinently, Mahaffey says, 'Versification allowed him to pare away complexity in favour of a simpler emotional and verbal expressiveness.' Thomas Kettle, reviewing *Chamber Music* at the time of its publication in *Freeman's Journal*, contended that the poems 'at first reading slight and frail, still hold one's curiosity by their integrity of form'. Arthur Symons, also reviewing the anthology in 1907, in *Nation* magazine, stated, 'They are full of ghostly old tunes that were never young and will never be old, played on an old instrument.' Writing again in 1933 in the aftermath of *Ulysses* and *Finnegans Wake*, Symons stated: 'Joyce's vocabulary *is unusually large and it is used too recklessly, but in a surprisingly novel personal manner*, and as for the craftsman, he has never curbed himself to a restraint in the debauch of words.' (Emphasis mine.)

It seems appropriate to cite these comparisons because, ultimately, what Syd Barrett created in his post-Pink Floyd output was a mode of expression that simply has no parallel in English pop song. 'Swift, brilliant images break into the field of vision, scatter like rockets, and leave a trail of flying fire behind. But the general impression is momentary; there are moods and emotions, but no steady current of ideas behind them,' surmised one critic with considerable accuracy. The trouble is, the critic here was Arthur Waugh, and he was writing about 'The New Poetry' in the *Quarterly Review* in October 1916, taking the opportunity to lambast the modernist poets, Yeats, Eliot and Pound.

Time would prove Waugh to be a reactionary fool and a philistine, just as it would those who greeted Syd's solo work

239

with equal scorn and bafflement. One has constantly to seek models of critical enquiry outside rock in order to make sense of what Syd was trying to achieve in his solo work. 'Impressions are strung along on a tenuous thread of sense,' said the American poet and novelist Babette Deutsch not of *The Madcap Laughs*, but of Eliot's *Love Song of J. Alfred Prufrock* in *New Republic Magazine* in 1918. 'The language has the extraordinary quality of common words uncommonly used,' said Deutsch, defending what others decried as nonsense, in all that stuff about measuring out one's life with coffee spoons and hearing the mermaids singing 'each to each'. One could just as easily cite *The Madcap Laughs* for its 'common words uncommonly used'. Syd Barrett's work can be similarly situated within the twentieth-century modernist tradition, drawing as it does on imagist poetry and automatic writing.

In the introduction to his translation of Bergson's *An Introduction to Metaphysics*, the imagist poet and critic T. E. Hulme states: 'Many diverse images, borrowed from very different things, may, by the convergence of their action, direct consciousness to the precise point where there is a certain intuition to be seized.' Syd's creativity springs from these very convergences. Meaning can often only be grasped fleetingly and intuitively. His lyrics resist literal interpretation at every turn.

Apart from the occasional scarecrow, vegetable man and broken pier on a wavy sea, devices such as metaphor and analogy are largely absent from Syd's work. There is, though, something of the symbolist in the way he went about deconstructing sense and sensibility. Like Rimbaud, Syd frequently destabilises the notion of the 'I' and the idea of a fixed self. There is also more than a hint of Rimbaud's famous dictum 'I am an Other' in Syd's own systematic dislocation of the senses. But unlike symbolism's more prominent rock 'n' roll advocates, such as Bob Dylan and Patti Smith, Syd doesn't appear to be in thrall to Rimbaud or Verlaine.

Indeed there is little evidence that he had more than a passing acquaintance with their works. He alludes to them neither in his schemata nor choice of imagery. As Andrew Rawlinson said, Syd's tendencies were popular. He would much rather have been cutting up Beatrix Potter and pastiching Belloc than observing the guiding principles of nineteenth-century French verse.

Syd's output does however bear comparison with the imagist school of the early twentieth century. He shared the imagist's commitment to *vers libre,* unrhymed cadence, broken syntax and the lilt of common daily speech. He is also in accord with the movement's preference for irregular metre and an organic sense of rhythm. Syd's lyrics bend first and foremost to the shape and rhythm of words: meaning at times becomes a secondary issue. Richard Aldington's observation on the imagist poet Hilda Doolittle's work as 'a kind of accurate mystery' could have been tailor-made for Syd's more oblique songs. As could American poet Jack Spicer's contention that 'the poem is a collage of the real . . . Things do not connect: they correspond.'

That's not to say that Syd's undisciplined and non-discriminating approach to language and composition adhered entirely to imagist principles. He was never a slave to methodology and his lyrics completely disregard Ezra Pound's manifesto pledge to 'go in fear of abstractions'. Pound also had an aversion to juxtaposing the abstract with the concrete. Syd's work is full of such juxtapositions. He also falls down badly on Pound's decree to 'use no superfluous word, no adjective, which does not reveal something'. Syd's solo work also falls short of the imagist movement's insistence on precision, economy of statement, absolutely accurate presentation and lack of verbiage, not to mention the necessity to 'avoid vagueness' and to be 'restrained or exact'.

Ezra Pound was a doctrinaire spokesperson for early twentieth-century modernism, fond of imposing his disciplinarian decrees, and like André Breton with the surrealists, forever deciding who was in and who was out, as he sifted the Imagists from the Amyists, the Vorticists from the Symbolists. Pound railed against 'flabbiness' and the 'splay-footed' in poetry and famously called Milton 'a windbag', so it is unlikely that he would have had much time for Syd's undisciplined outpourings. But then, to paraphrase the comedian Ken Dodd's comment about Freud, Pound never played the UFO club on a Friday night with half of the audience flat on their backs, tripping their brains out.

The other main literary influence on Syd's approach to lyrics was automatic writing. Psychic automatism, as defined by the surrealists, was a way of articulating the mind's inner voice when freed from the conventions and linguistic orthodoxies of conscious expression. 'A true photography of thought,' as Breton put it in the 1924 *Surrealist Manifesto*. Automatism stressed the importance of spontaneous association and chance in the creative process, as well as the lack of specific intention, the absence of critical intervention in the narrative and the liberation of psychic inhibition. Cut-ups and spontaneous poetry broth were just two of the ways in which Syd introduced these elements into his writing, and the results can be found liberally sprinkled throughout the songs he produced during 1968 and 1969.

'I have no idea, really, how he wrote,' David Gilmour told John Edginton. 'There are many occasions when he would be either at his flat or my flat or in the studio, he would appear to just start something and it would all come out as if he had never, ever, thought of it before that moment, in a way that I find hard to conceive, not being as wordy as Syd was. It felt like he just made them up as he went along. I'm sure it can't have been quite that simple. So the stream of consciousness idea . . . maybe it's a stream of subconsciousness, or that he had some way of letting it flow out of him. Or maybe he did sit and think about it, but I can't quite imagine him doing it that consciously.'

'I did see him writing and I did see him playing with cut-up words, Burroughs-style. I definitely remember him doing that,' says Duggie Fields. The use of cut-ups explains some of the more severe ellipses and occlusions in the solo output, but then again Syd was perfectly capable of editing in his own head in that way, sifting and scrambling vocabulary in such a way that the end product resembled a cut-up, emulating the strategy without the need to utilise the technique itself.

The suffragist critic May Sinclair, writing in the *Little Review* in December 1917 of similar ellipses in Eliot's *Prufrock*, commented that:

obscurity may come from defective syntax, from a bad style, from confusion of ideas, from involved thinking, from irrelevant associations, from sheer piling on of ornament. Mr Eliot is not obscure in any of these senses. There is also an obscurity of remote or unusual objects, or of familiar objects moving very rapidly. And Mr Eliot's trick of cutting his corners and his curves makes him seem obscure where he is as clear as daylight. His thoughts move rapidly and by astounding cuts. They move not by logical stages and majestic roundings of the full literary curve, but as live thoughts move in live brains.

Eliot, although never an imagist, incorporated many of the imagists' theories to his thinking, in particular the desire to depersonalise the poetic voice. According to the imagists, poems were driven by images, not by narrative. Indeed, the images were the narrative. Speaking of this absence of narrative Eliot said,

Any obscurity of the poem, on first reading, is due to the suppression of 'links in the chain', of explanatory and connecting matter, and not just to incoherence or to love of cryptogram . . . the reader has to allow the images to fall into his memory without questioning the reasonableness of each at the moment, so that, at the end, a total effect is produced. Such selection of a sequence of images and ideas has nothing chaotic about it. There is a logic of the imagination as well as a logic of concepts.

Eliot talks of 'the suppression of links in the chain'. Spike Hawkins noted that 'it's all in the breaking up' when he played intergalactic Scrabble with Syd.

Many of Syd's lyrics adhere to Eliot's 'logic of the imagination'. They are not simply the ramblings of a madman, splurging his inner disintegration out in song form. One frequently detects a sense of purpose, a striving to articulate, whether by paring things down to the bone or by applying idiosyncratic methods of exposition. The fact that these experiments don't always work, that they sometimes become enmeshed or inchoate, makes them no less compelling.

This lack of specificity is what sometimes undermines Syd's later songs, and makes them unpalatable to common tastes. It was always there, of course, even in his earliest efforts. It's evident in the fragmentation of 'Lucy Leave', and in the mild ellipses of 'Arnold Layne', but in the later songs it reaches new levels of obliqueness. 'If it's there will you go there too?' sings Syd in 'No Man's Land', and we probably would if we actually knew where 'there' was, or indeed what the 'it' is. 'No Man's Land' appears to be one long exercise in the avoidance of clarity. Halfway through, the song disintegrates into vapour trails of guitar distortion, Syd mutters 'tell me tell me tell me' and then delivers an incomprehensible spoken lyric of which the only decipherable phrase is 'heavily spaced we shine'. On hearing the results Syd declared himself pleased with the effect and declined to re-record the section.

Jenny Fabian detected this lack of specificity at first hand, both in her personal encounters with Syd and in his songs. 'It's interesting the way he makes sense without quite making sense,' she says. 'If you take some of Syd's quotes they are hideously profound but almost mean nothing. They're not profound in the sense that Coleridge means when he says, "No man was ever a great poet without being a profound philosopher", where you can get hold of them and say, "Yes, he's saying what I feel." Syd doesn't ever really say what you feel. You have to let the allusion of the words hit you. It's the feeling that he generates. The power of allusion is very strong with Syd. There's a lot of compression of language too. He says something that you understand but don't quite understand because he's compressed whatever he wants to say down so tightly.'

On his solo albums Syd's songs are chiefly driven by stasis or momentum. Of course, it could be argued that all songs are about stasis or momentum. It's a bit like saying all films take place during day or night. People are after all always either moving or still. But on *The Madcap Laughs*, *Barrett* and the unreleased material that made up the *Opel* compilation, stasis and momentum become governing principles that underpin almost every song. Ennui and inactivity, and restless, sometimes manic propulsion, are the polarities of Syd's solo output.

On *The Madcap Laughs*, descriptions of momentum include the simple 'Heigh-ho never be still' of Octopus, the mesmerising slow-motion 'Floating, bumping' and 'The move about is all we do' of 'Terrapin', and the rocking horse and car spinning 'around and around | With electric lights flashing very fast' in 'No Good Trying'. At times the momentum is uneasy and petulant, as in 'But I got up and I stomped around' in 'She Took a Long Cold Look', at times it indicates a kind of debilitating desperation as in the flailing, straggling and gasping of 'Feel'.

What is remarkable about these qualities is the way that sense, and nonsense, are always aligned to structure. Even when Syd rambles he does so with conviction. On 'Terrapin', for example, momentum matches subject matter, imagery overlaps like fishes observed in an aquarium, merging and separating in the semi-dark. 'Love You' has exactly the same qualities, even though it's a more frenetic exercise: a breathless and giddy outpouring that accelerates into hyperactivity and all but loses the listener in its dizzying blur. The effect is akin to being spun round on a fairground ride and flung off at a different point each time to be greeted by a freshly scrambled perspective, vaguely reminiscent of the previous place but somehow unconnected and unconnectable.

In 'Love You', as in many of Syd's solo songs, there is a kind of multi-imaging at work, reminiscent of cubist works like Duchamps's *Nude Descending a Staircase*, and Delaunay's *The Red Tower*. Analytical cubism had allowed painters to transcend fixed perspective by adopting the revolutionary technical possibilities of photography and cinema. Its central premise, 'in which different objects and different facets of the same objects are shown simultaneously and side by side', as Eddie Prévost noted, had also had a massive influence on Syd's forebears AMM. 'This non-hierarchical concept became reflected in the manner in which sounds were placed, perceived and understood,' stated Prévost in his book *No Sound is Innocent*. Syd applied exactly the same 'non-hierarchical' approach to his lyric writing, and it is clearly evident in 'Love You'. The song mixes up East Anglian vernacular ('I seen you looking good the other evening'), hip slang ('Oh you dig it', 'Good time rocker woman'), disjuncture and collision (''Spose sometimes that day | Whoopee! Swinging along over cross to me') and detachment ('It ain't a long rhyme | It took ages to think | Think I'll hurl it in the water, baby'). The result is an exuberant blur of compelling gibberish. Malcolm Jones was never too keen on the song. Syd was inordinately proud of it. He probably thought it was commercial.

In order to comprehend fully such maddening whimsy one has to go back to Edward Lear. 'Lear's nonsense is no mere tissue of quips and jokes,' says Holbrook Jackson in his introduction to the 1947 anthology, *The Complete Nonsense of Edward Lear*. 'It is a thing in itself in a world of its own, with its own physiography and natural history; a world in which the nature of things has been changed, whilst retaining its own logical and consistent idiom.' Jackson calls Lear's wordplay 'an instinctive effort to bridge a gap between idea and expression. "Proper and exact 'epithets' always were impossible to me," he [Lear] says, "as my thoughts are ever in advance of my words."' This was Syd's dilemma too, a gift for wordplay that was frequently undone by the rapidity of thought.

Ezra Pound recognised the latent mysticism in the imagists' work when he described the image as 'a vortex or cluster of fused ideas . . . endowed with energy'. Such clusters of cosmic intensity continued to flow through Syd Barrett's songwriting long after he had fled the fervour and ferment of the psychedelic underground. As he said in 'Dark Globe', 'I tattooed my brain all the way.'

Sometimes stasis and momentum occur within the same song, sometimes they are juxtaposed in the same line, as in 'So high you go, so low you creep' in 'Octopus'. Sometimes momentum is conveyed with a dreamlike quality, a feeling of plummeting or being grounded. There is the telling repetition of 'My head kissed the ground | I was half the way down' in 'Dark Globe', and the mocking chastising tone of 'She loves to see me get down to ground' in 'She Took a Long Cold Look'. In 'Long Gone' Syd's restless prowling 'in the evening sun's glaze' is contrasted with the sorrowful reflective 'I stood very still by the window sill | And I wondered for those I love still'. 'Late Night' juxtaposes the similarly unsettling 'If I mention your name | turn around on a chain' with 'When I lay still at night | seeing stars high and light'. In both songs, as in several others on the album, he sings not just of past relationships but past happiness per se. 'Those I love still' has an all-inclusiveness about it, a consideration not just of old girlfriends, but all his old Cambridge friends too, and, of course, his father. On 'Feel' Syd mocks the unwanted attention he is still receiving from hero-worshipping women in the line 'How I love you to be by my side, they wail'. 'I want to go home,' he sings, without ambiguity.

There are deep and ominous historical resonances here. Foreshadowing Syd's own artistic trajectory, Edward Lear's later literary endeavours moved away from the overtly child-centred nonsense verse that made his name, and he began writing melancholic and poignant poetry which contained codified references to his sad child life and the overbearing sense of loss he now felt in adulthood. He could no longer hold 'the morbids' at bay.

'I think personally "The Dong with the Luminous Nose" is one of the greatest poems in the English language,' says Pete Brown. 'It is a tragic poem. It has its humour, but it's a very, very sad poem. And that combination of sadness and humour is where we find a lot of the great British writing. And it's there in some of Syd's stuff. *Jabberwocky*'s full of death and *The Hunting of the Snark* too. This is all heavy stuff, y'know.'

Syd was only twenty-two when he began recording the first of his two solo albums and only twenty-four when he stopped recording altogether, but an all consuming sadness had now settled on his work. It is evident in at least half of the songs on *The Madcap Laughs* and it would be just as evident on the *Barrett* album too.

Chapter Seven

We Awful, Awful Crawl

'It's like music – far away music,' said the Mole nodding drowsily.
'So I was thinking,' murmured the Rat, dreamful and languid. 'Dance music – the lilting sort that runs on without a stop – but with words in it too – it passes into words and out of them again – I catch them at intervals – then it is dance music once more, and then nothing but the reeds' soft thin whispering.'
THE WIND IN THE WILLOWS KENNETH GRAHAME

The Madcap Laughs sold modestly, but encouragingly enough for EMI to commission a second solo album from Syd. Produced by David Gilmour and simply entitled *Barrett*, the LP suffered from none of the delays and indecisions that beset *The Madcap Laughs*. Unlike its predecessor, which took the best part of two years to complete, *Barrett* was recorded in fifteen sessions between 26 February and 22 July 1970. The only interruptions occurred in March, when Pink Floyd were working on their *Atom Heart Mother* LP, and in late April and May when they toured the USA. Either side of these breaks, a settled musical line-up of Gilmour on guitar, Rick Wright on keyboards and Jerry Shirley on drums ensured a degree of cohesion and continuity that was largely absent from Syd's previous album.

Gilmour was a sympathetic choice as a producer, and perhaps the only person who could get the best out of Syd by this stage. Their relationship went all the way back to the days when they swapped guitar licks in the tech college canteen and their friendship had survived the fact that Gilmour had effectively been brought into Pink Floyd to replace Syd. Gilmour at the time was a neighbour of Syd and Duggie Fields in Earls Court and both Barrett and Fields were frequent visitors. Perhaps more importantly, Gilmour was a huge fan of Syd's later music, preferring it to the pop hits and fairy-tale songs that Syd is best known for. 'I'm not sure that I would say that it was the best song writing necessarily,' he said of the *Piper* album to John Edginton. 'I think I like the subsequent stuff better. Even "Jugband Blues", which was recorded before I joined the band, is a better song than most of the ones on *Piper*. It's a very, very personal song about him and his condition, which is very raw and strange. I think it's quite brilliant. And some of the other ones that are quite excruciatingly recorded on *The Madcap Laughs* are absolutely brilliant songs. I'm not sure if the polish of the *Piper* mix makes me think that the subsequent ones are better. It's very hard to judge. But for me, the better stuff comes later.'

Two conflicting tendencies are at work on *Barrett*. On the one hand, the presence of David Gilmour and Rick Wright gave the sound fluency and a strong commercial identity throughout. There is little of the uneven nature and juxtaposition of styles that characterised *The Madcap Laughs*. On the other hand, Syd was becoming an increasingly reluctant guest at his own party, and there is evidence from some of the material recorded that the muse was beginning to run dry. Half a dozen songs on *Barrett* ('Dominoes', 'Wined and Dined', 'Wolfpack', 'Baby Lemonade', 'Gigolo Aunt' and 'It Is Obvious') are as good as anything Syd ever wrote. The worst tracks contain some of the most half-hearted and forgettable lyrics he ever committed to paper.

Because of Gilmour and Wright's involvement several tracks are pleasantly reminiscent of the Floyd's own late 1960s style and offer a poignant reminder of what the band might have sounded like had Syd stayed with them. Gilmour's contribution is crucial throughout. Simply on work-rate alone it is as much his album as it is Syd's. In addition to playing lead and twelve-string guitar Gilmour added drums, bass and a second keyboard to several tracks. His main contribution, though, remains largely uncredited. It was Gilmour who galvanised and cajoled an often uncertain and unenthused Syd into turning half-formed ideas into finished tracks. Gilmour often had to map out and build entire songs from Syd's simple guitar and voice sketches. Without him it is questionable whether the LP would have been completed.

The first song recorded for the *Barrett* album set the tone for what was to come. 'Maisie' was a simple blues jam designed to get Syd's creative juices flowing. It has a certain understated charm, and its muttered croaky lyric delivered over a snail's-pace twelve-bar contains the occasional couplet worthy of the Syd of old (e.g. 'His illuminous grin | Put her in a spin') but the fact that this loose jam found its way on to the album at all hints at the paucity of quality material generated during the sessions.

There is a telling moment during the recording of the Rolling Stones' 'You Can't Always Get What You Want', witnessed by Jack Nitzsche, where a wasted and befuddled Brian Jones says to Mick Jagger, 'What can I play?' 'I don't know. What can you play?' replies Jagger witheringly. There was something of this about the *Barrett* sessions. A palpable Mandrax blur hangs over proceedings like a fog upon LA. It's audible in the dry-voiced downer-slur of Syd's pre-song comments, and it's evident in his singing too, whenever an otherwise passable melody is stymied by the wasted or wayward delivery. What becomes abundantly clear when listening to the *Barrett* album is that the breezy eloquence and well-rounded enunciation of yore is beginning to flatten out into breathless mumbles and monotony.

What is equally noticeable is that Syd's musical gifts are atrophying. No fewer than seven songs, 'Love Song', 'Gigolo Aunt', 'Dominoes', 'Waving My Arms in the Air', 'Effervescing Elephant', 'Dolly Rocker' and 'Milky Way', adopt the same dance-band shuffle in A, with only minimal variation in tempo, that had been used on 'Love You'. By the time of his second album it's become Syd's all-purpose lick, his underpass busker strum.

With its evocation of drizzle and despair, and its palette of greyness and fog, the opening track 'Baby Lemonade' establishes the dominant mood of the album. 'In the sad town | Cold iron hands | Clap the party of clowns outside' sings Syd with melancholic detachment tinged with just a hint of despondency. One immediately gets a picture of someone 'stood very still by the window sill' watching a crowd of midnight revellers in the street outside, or perhaps sarcastically applauding the antics of a bunch of pissheads in the beer garden of a provincial pub, as glimpsed morosely through a bar-room window.

Throughout the song there is an overwhelming sense of someone killing time, amusing themselves to distraction with oddball acts like putting a clock in the washing machine or sending a cage through the post (Matthew Scurfield does indeed recall seeing Syd put a clock in the bath and tape-recording the sound while he was living at Earlham Street), and there is an indication for the first time that Syd's capacity for weirdness is starting to sound self-conscious and strained. By the time we reach the pared-down telegram prose of 'Come around | Make it soon | So alone' it sounds like a heartfelt plea for someone to save his sanity.

Rick Wright's warm Hammond washes are a feature of the album and on 'Baby Lemonade' they underpin Syd's distant and distancing observations with soulful substance. On 'Love Song', Wright's harmonium and tack piano add bounce and colour to a charming but slight lyric about a fondly remembered ex-girlfriend. 'Love Song' is imbued with the kind of whimsy that Syd used to be able to conjure up in his sleep. Here he sounds like he's singing it in his sleep. For all its throwaway qualities, 'Love Song' would have sat perfectly well on side two of Pink Floyd's

Atom Heart Mother or *Meddle* albums. If nothing else, it shows that Syd even at his most semi-detached was still more than a lyrical match for his former band mates.

During those brief moments when Syd is enthused and inspired, the album really takes off. On the second day of recording, the day after the laboured jam of 'Maisie' and the tentative sketching out of 'Baby Lemonade', Syd demoed 'Wolfpack', 'Waving My Arms in the Air', 'Living Alone' and 'Bob Dylan Blues'. The band then recorded fifteen takes of 'Gigolo Aunt', a jaunty and jocular item, based on Jeff Beck's 'Hi-Ho Silver Lining', replete with the same A to D chord progressions and subject matter (groovy people go to the beach) as Beck's 1967 hit. Lyrically, 'Gigolo Aunt' is full of typically deft Syd touches, elliptical syntax ('Thunderbird shale'), qualified empathy ('I almost want you back') and unashamed punning ('in tin and lead pail, we pale'). The twisting momentum of a jeep winding down a beachside track is niftily conveyed in both music and lyrics, one of the few occasions on the album where the band played together and nailed it through sheer perseverance.

As on its predecessor certain lyrical themes recur throughout the *Barrett* album. Momentum in all its guises is there again on *Barrett*; the breezy and bouncy 'Grooving around in a trench coat' and 'Jiving on down to the beach' in 'Gigolo Aunt', the 'stumbling, fumbling' and quicksand legs of 'It Is Obvious', the hovering and swirling of 'Wolfpack', the crazed 'Top the seam he's taken off' of 'Rats', the distress signalling of 'Waving My Arms in the Air.' On these songs Syd is once again driven by the velocity of his own inner propulsion, the embodiment of Spike Hawkins' perception of a man rotating inside.

The song which reflects that inner maelstrom most effectively is 'Wolfpack'. Amidst the languor that dominates the rest of the album, 'Wolfpack' is as conspicuous as a scream among whispers. In one of the few public pronouncements Syd ever made about his solo material, he stated that 'Wolfpack' was one of his favourites.

'On "Wolfpack" you feel his mind being torn to shreds. But Christ, what a brilliant poem! It's like Gerard Manley Hopkins,' says Robyn Hitchcock.

It's appropriate that Hitchcock refers to 'Wolfpack' as a poem rather than a song, containing as it does some of Syd's most impressive free-form verse. Like the best of his songs its swirls and eddies of imagery stand up on the printed page as well as they do on record.

Gerard Manley Hopkins might not seem at first glance to be the most appropriate comparison, but he is fact an entirely kindred spirit. The nineteenth-century poet had his Jesuit faith. Syd was arguably denied his by Maharaj Charan Singh Ji in 1966, although he clearly didn't lack subsequently a sense of the transcendental. Hopkins had something else that Syd lacked: a failsafe system, a metaphysical principle of 'one-ness' he called his inscape. Syd dabbled and delved but he never developed a consistent aesthetic, although again one could say he hardly lacked inscape. Syd's lyrical abstractions are arguably one long inscape. More in keeping with Syd's mode of operation is what Hopkins called his 'new rhythm', which he defined as 'scanning by accents or stresses alone, without any account of the number of syllables'. These rhythms, as Hopkins acknowledged, and which Syd frequently adopted, were commonplace in music and nursery rhymes, but not so common in poetic metre.

Hopkins 'system' allowed him to take liberties with scanning and counterpoint, and at times, as in Syd's lyrics, the momentum and rhythmic impulses take over and meaning takes a secondary role. Hopkins, though, frequently overdoes the compounds and the alliteration, making him easy prey for parody. Syd's writing never settled on one style for long enough to suffer from that particular tic.

Syd dealt essentially in image and essence and, like Gerard Manley Hopkins, put himself at the mercy of skewed syntax. 'Sometimes his violent transposition, omission or clotting of words gives the impression of a man trying to utter all his thoughts at once,' said W. H. Gardner of Hopkins, and the historical parallels speak for themselves.

By the time Syd wrote 'Wolfpack' the elisions overlap and image, scansion and syntax fold in on themselves like Delaunay's *Eiffel Tower*. A pack of wolves and a pack of playing cards merge in the first two lines. Puns ('Bowling they bat') follow ellipses ('light misted fog') upon ellipses ('the fighters | Through misty the waving'). Distance ('Far reaching waves', 'Beyond the far winds') is juxtaposed with constriction ('All enmeshing', 'Gripped with blanched bones') and stop-start momentum ('Short wheeling – fresh spring'). Images spill out in a blurring whirl that hints at sense and is at the same time beyond all sense.

No other nineteenth-century mystic, not even Blake, could have written a poem like Gerard Manley Hopkins' 'That Nature Is a Heraclitean Fire' with its semantic twists and turns, its 'Man, how fast his firedint, | his mark on mind, is gone', its 'Manshape that shone | sheer off, disseveral a star' and its incantatory 'This Jack, joke, poor potsherd, | patch matchwood, immortal diamond, | Is immortal diamond.'

No one else in the pop era could have created a song like 'Wolfpack', or a line like 'this life that was ours | Grew sharper and stronger away and beyond' with its simultaneous suggestion of microscopic closeness and something hurtling towards the outer reaches of some far distant universe. How can a life grow 'sharper and stronger' while disappearing over the horizon? In a way it doesn't mean anything. On the other hand, it means everything. Some ungraspable truth all too briefly glimpsed as it hurtles by. It has something of William Cowper's 'Sent quick and howling to the centre headlong' about it, or the John Clare fragment written late on in his madness that begins 'The cataract whirling to the precipice' and ends 'horrible mysteries in the gulph stare through, roars of a million tongues, and none knows what they mean'. 'Wolfpack' inhabits the same maelstrom of spiralling tempests and swirling vortex – momentum dragged to new dizzying heights and tumultuous depths.

Momentum and stasis are again frequently juxtaposed on *Barrett*. The 'So high you go, so low you creep' of 'Octopus' is echoed on the *Barrett* LP in 'Waving my arms in the air | Pressing my feet to the ground'. 'Waving My Arms in the Air' represents everything that was going wrong with Syd. What had once sounded childlike now begins to sound infantile and regressive. In certain sections ('no care | No care') melody and sentiment combine to mimic a child's ner-ner ner-ner ner. Numerous unsuccessful takes of the song were attempted and David Gilmour had to assemble the finished track painstakingly by editing together the few salvageable sections from each verse. Not an uncommon practice even with the best of artists, but with 'Waving My Arms in the Air' it is debatable whether the effort was worth it. The lyric barely rises above the banal and contains some of the most depressingly unimaginative couplets that Syd ever committed to vinyl.

One of Syd's strengths as a songwriter was that even at his most unruly and wayward, intent was satisfyingly married to structure, momentum adhered to metrical logic with effortless precision. It's still there in bursts on *Barrett*, in the rambling narrative of 'It Is Obvious', the nimble zigzagging of 'Gigolo Aunt' and the crazed poetry broth of 'Rats'. But on 'Waving My Arms' the muse deserted Syd completely and he delivered a sequence of limp and second-rate rhymes bereft of charm or eloquence.

There is still substantial evidence on *Barrett* of a supremely gifted wordsmith, able to conjure unique images from an equally unique inscape, but most of the time he seems to be battling through quicksand and fog to deliver them. In the circumstances, Syd's continued compulsion to create, impaired though it was by increasingly insurmountable psychological forces, makes the effort even nobler in its execution. All too often, though, this energy sounds like it's floundering in some impenetrable brain haze, fighting unsuccessfully to root itself in clarity and reason.

As on the *Madcap* LP stasis and ennui are frequently channelled through a dreamlike sense of someone plummeting or rooted to the spot, wistfully so in 'I'll lay my head down and see what I see' on 'Love Song' and the 'Creep into bed when your head's on the ground' of 'It Is Obvious', less wistfully in the 'Everything is down' refrain of 'Let's Split', or 'Senses in the gravel' on 'Dolly Rocker'. In the 'I lay as if in surround' of 'Wolfpack', the grounding is elliptical and oblique, the sense difficult to grasp. In 'Rats' it is taunting and maniacal. 'Rats rats lay down flat | We don't need you we act like that,' rants Syd over a mutated Bo Diddley riff that alternates between 7/8 and 9/8 time. Almost everything about the perturbing rant of 'Rats' is driven by hurtling descent, most tellingly in the repeated 'I like the fall that brings me to'. Its impossible to tell whether that 'brings me to' refers to being revived and shocked out of slumber, or whether it signifies some deeper elliptical arriving – brings me to what? brings me to where? – that lies beyond reason or understanding. Also evident in malevolent flashes in 'Rats' is the sardonic mocking tone that surfaced in lines like 'How I love you to be by my side, they wail' on *Madcap*. 'If you think you're unloved | Then we know about that' sings Syd, without making it clear who the 'you' is. If he's referring to himself then it's a savagely astute piece of self-loathing, written at a time when he had jettisoned or alienated many people from his past.

Images of longing, sorrowful recollection and regret are as present on *Barrett* as they were on *The Madcap Laughs*. 'Seems a while | Since I could smile the way you do' on 'Milky Way', 'In my tears, my dreams' on 'Dominoes', 'Remember those times I could call | Through the clear day time | And you would be there' on 'It Is Obvious', 'It's been so hard to bear with you not there' on 'I Never Lied to You' – all indicate an overwhelming sense of poignancy and anguish.

The song that best conveys these sentiments is 'Wined and Dined'. Written in Formentera, it simultaneously evokes Mediterranean evenings ('musk winds blow') and the familiar haunts of Syd's childhood ('Chalk underfoot | Light ash of blue'). It is a summer-of-1970 rendition of a song that was composed the previous summer and which looks back to summers before that. Retrospection is heaped upon recollection until time and place evaporate in a dream like heat haze. The shimmering tableau in 'Wined and Dined' of beach parties and opulent sunsets is beautifully embellished by Rick Wright's soulful organ. The German band Faust later based their track 'Lauft' (featured on the album *Faust IV*) on Wright's opening chords.

Sometimes it seems as if Syd is lulling these songs to himself, trying to get back to some former place in his head, a contentment that he just can't reach anymore, a lost Arcadia. 'Only last summer it's not so long ago' he sings on 'Wined and Dined', but it sounds like centuries ago the way he sings it.

By now the frieze songs were becoming freeze songs. Momentum may have outweighed stasis on *The Madcap Laughs* but now the latter begins to cast its shroud over memory and evocation alike. Stasis underpins the observations of the careworn and jaded narrator of 'Baby Lemonade'. Stasis pervades 'Dominoes' with its unspecified 'You and I' who play their games, while 'The day goes by'. 'Dominoes' is an essay in the art of idleness. 'Musing when my mind's astray' sings Syd, never making it clear whether he's playing dominoes with a girlfriend or an elderly relative. 'Dominoes' seems an entirely appropriate game to be playing in order to ward off boredom. Joining the dots to make a pattern. Progress dependent on simple equations. Eliot had his coffee spoons. Syd measures out the slow tick of the clock with domino pieces, the way he once would have done with Go or the *I Ching*.

The song's inscape, all cloying claustrophobia and domestic boredom, is complemented by the description of the weather outside. 'A day so dark so warm' evokes a close summer day with thunder beckoning. Syd always described weather well, but usually with neutrality and a precise painterly eye. On the *Barrett* album climate takes on a more symbolic air. 'The softness, the warmth and the weather in suspense' serves as a denouement to the lovers' actions, or inaction, in 'It Is Obvious'. 'Rain falls in grey far away' on 'Baby Lemonade' encapsulates the mood of the entire album.

'Dominoes' was built like so many other tracks on *Barrett* from Syd's simple vocal and acoustic strumalong. 'What's this one called?' asks the Abbey Road engineer as Syd commences take one. 'Don't know. Hasn't got a title. I suppose it's called "Dominoes",' mumbles a distracted and distant Syd, before singing his distracted and distant song about wasting time with domino pieces.

All that time spent doing nothing at Wetherby Mansions reaps its barren harvest on *Barrett*. Having witnessed his flatmate's lengthy bouts of ennui on a daily basis, Duggie Fields is uniquely qualified to comment on Syd's state of mind: 'I'd say it was a creative vacuum. Void and avoid. He'd avoid doing something because that limited him. He would lie in bed for hours and hours. He couldn't decide what to do with himself. He'd got no pressure. No commitments. He had no income pressure. He was getting money. Not a great deal I'm sure but he was getting money. So motive was going. He didn't have any rituals that he could hang on to and no structure. But if you lie in bed thinking,

"I can do this and this and this" – I think this was what was going through his head. "If I decide to do this I'm limiting my options." Action is actually limiting. You just vegetate if you think like that, so Vegetable Man he became.'

Cora Barnes, who had started working for Syd's publishers, Lupus Music, in the autumn of 1969, got used to him drifting into the office in a slightly semi-detached state. 'In those days he was still a beautiful and good-looking young man and utterly charming. He would come in and say hello, and sit around my office for three hours sometimes. Every time you made a coffee – do you want a coffee Syd? Yeah. He'd have a coffee. You couldn't explain why he was there. He didn't explain. He just liked being somewhere. He just sat at the desk opposite to me and chatted, obviously not completely compos mentis, but just in a vacant sort of way. You might ask him a question. He might not answer it, but then answer it a bit later. I'd never say to him, "Syd, what do you want?" It was just, "Hi, Syd." Then eventually he'd get up and say, "I'm going now." "Bye, Syd. See you soon." It was almost childlike. He came in once with a little Harrods bag and I said, "Oh, what have you got in there Syd?" And he brought out all these French shampoos, called Frenchy's, all these lemon shampoos in sachets. Not like an ordinary sachet. Very fat plump sachets. He had about twenty of them. I said, "Why don't you buy a big bottle?" He said, "Oh no, these are much nicer, don't you think?"'

'The guy who lives next door to me paints, and he's doing it well, so I don't really feel the need,' said Syd in his 1970 interview with Giovanni Dadomo, applying a curiously warped logic to his predicament. 'He didn't have anything he needed to do. That was the problem,' agrees Duggie Fields. 'He didn't need to do anything except eat, and that wasn't a big deal either. Compare that with what life was like in the Pink Floyd, where it was all doing, and all action and all go-go-go. In the end the going got too much for him and the doing got too much.'

On Tuesday, 21 July 1970, Syd went into Abbey Road Studio 3 and commenced work on the last two songs he would ever record. Only one take was ever attempted of 'Word Song'. Five versions in all, including four on 22 July, were attempted of 'It Is Obvious'. It is somehow fitting that the last two songs Syd Barrett ever gave to the public were an exercise in semantic Scrabble that drew upon word games inspired by Bob Cobbing and Spike Hawkins, and a wistful look back to happier days in Cambridge.

Originally titled 'Mind Shot', 'It Is Obvious' is one of Syd's most underrated songs, and if it was to be the last song recorded for the *Barrett* album then it was an entirely appropriate valediction. Reflections on the album are generally tinged with sadness and regret. On 'It Is Obvious' the sentiments are genuinely moving and the song contains some of Syd's finest lyrics.

One of the central tenets of what became retrospectively known as the metaphysical school of poets was the idea of 'strong lines', and in particular strong opening lines: abrupt scene-setting conveyed via direct statements and philosophical exposition. Lines such as John Donne's 'For God's sake hold your tongue, and let me love' or 'Here, take my picture, though I bid farewell', for instance, or Andrew Marvell's 'Had we but world enough and time' or 'See with what simplicity this nymph begins her golden days'. From 'Arnold Layne' and 'See Emily Play' through to 'Terrapin' and 'Dark Globe', Syd's songs were abundant in strong opening lines. The directness of 'It is obvious, may I say, oh baby | That it is found on another plane' could be a summary of his entire artistic quest. Once again, the qualities that made Syd Barrett such a consummate English writer are all there. The archly mannered interjection of 'may I say' into the middle of a cosmic treatise recalls 'It's awfully considerate' and 'I'm most obliged' from 'Jugband Blues'. As with the Dan Dare reference in 'Astronomy Domine', Syd is always grounded in the colloquial even when projecting on to the astral plane.

'It Is Obvious' is also explicitly referential, frequently alluding to the Gog Magog hills and the quarry pits ('the scar of white chalk') where Syd played as a young boy, courted girlfriends and took acid with his Cambridge mates. As on 'No Good Trying', the narrative voice shifts between childhood innocence ('Your stars – my stars – are simple cot bars') and lysergic visions ('our minds shot together').

As well as conveying personal eccentricity ('I can creep into cupboards | Sleep in the hall') 'It Is Obvious' rehearses Syd's entire stylistic repertoire, from simple internal rhyme ('She held a torch on the porch') to the clever ellipsis of 'Mog to a grog' which shrinks going for a drink after a visit to the hills. It also contains some of Syd's most lyrical depictions of love ('My legs moved the last empty inches to you') and landscape ('A velvet curtain of grey | Marked the blanket where sparrows play') all of which merges in the line 'The softness, the warmth and the weather in suspense'.

The key perceptual shift, where everything fuses into one magnificent metaphysical whole, occurs in the second verse when Syd sings 'The reason it is written on the brambles | Stranded on the spikes | My blood red | Oh, listen | Remember those times I could call through the clear day time and you would be there'.

As so often with Syd, the 'it' is indeterminate. Is 'it' nature's own inner logic? A merging of poetic voice and landscape? The transference of the physical to the metaphysical through the life-force flow of blood? Whatever the explanation, it's worthy of Dylan Thomas or John Clare. The imagery evokes both a child snagged on briars and rescued by a mother and a messy interlude during an acid trip. The call through the clear day time could also equally be to a mother and a lover. In Syd's 'mindshot', it's both.

To illustrate just how integral David Gilmour's production role was, one only has to listen to the various takes of 'It Is Obvious'. All but one of the five attempts have found their way on to records over the years, and they perfectly exemplify not only what a magnificent rescue job Gilmour did on the track but also the constant predicament he had in rousing Syd from recalcitrance and inertia.

The first take of 'It Is Obvious', the one recorded on 21 July, was the version that made it on to the *Barrett* album. Gilmour fleshes out Syd's basic acoustic guitar and voice track with organ, bass and piano overdubs, embellishing the song's simple A to E changes with unfussy root chords on the keyboards, and giving the song a rambling feel entirely in keeping with its lyrical essence. With the help of judicious tape-editing Gilmour also tidies up Syd's uneven bar lines, bringing consistency to the song's sense of metre without detracting from its flow. On take one Syd does the lyric justice with his delivery, sounding engaged and full of wistful passion. The following day he attempted four more takes. On the first he attempts a disjointed rhythm on electric guitar. Unable to match, or perhaps to counteract, the complexity of the guitar figure in his vocal delivery he locks into a repetitive monotonous melody, which flattens out the lyric's subtle nuances and changes in phrasing. It grows tiresome to listen to long before the end. On the next take Syd adopts the riff to Muddy Waters' 'I'm A Man' which was later utilised by David Bowie on 'Jean Genie', and delivers the vocal in a low growl, similar to the one he adopts on 'Maisie'. It is excruciating to listen to. Before commencing the final take Gilmour can be heard gently cajoling Syd to 'do that rhythm you were playing just then'. 'Which one?' asks Syd, unable to retain any sense of momentum. He then attempts to sing the song in an inappropriately high register, adopting an airier tone and more sensitive phrasing, but it's all to little avail.

Once again, as with so many tracks on the album, Gilmour had little choice but to go back to the first attempt as the only usable one. On *Madcap* Syd occasionally executed a perfect first take, on 'Terrapin' and 'Here I Go', for example. Other tracks, 'Octopus' and 'Golden Hair', were worked on extensively until he nailed it just right. On the *Barrett* album, unless everything fell into place straight away there was rarely any point in persevering. Syd was seemingly unable to sustain concentration or enthusiasm long enough to attempt multiple takes. The pains-taking construction of 'It Is Obvious' is illustrative of everything that was going wrong by 1970. A magnificent song rescued from fraught circumstance by sheer diligence on Gilmour's part.

'Word Song', untitled at the time and unreleased until the *Opel* compilation of out-takes in 1988, is a seemingly arbitrary and unrelated list of words, recited over a slow-tempo version of Syd's all-purpose busker strum in A. Logic and linearity are wryly implied with a delightful bridge of clipped notes that Syd plays between each of the three verses, before embarking on the next list of random vocabulary. 'Word Song' springs from the same experimental lexicography as *Fart Enjoy*'s 'Typical . . . Topical . . . Tip Up . . . Political . . .' and the fun he had with Spike Hawkins's poetry broth. The sequences briefly adhere to alphabetical or alliterative groupings but overall there is no pattern or purpose, just a simple celebration of phonetics for phonetics' sake.

'I think he was a profound aesthete,' says Graham Coxon. 'He loved words and he loved being playful with them and making up meanings. That's the great thing about the English language, you can be very adventurous with words and you can cut and paste them or just entertain yourself with them. I think that's what he was doing. That's what the 'Word Song' is, just this list of really nice words. You use your energy and your love of playing with words as your own personal idiosyncratic thesaurus. He did write such incredible words and they don't always make sense but it's a sort of poetry all the same.'

One could cast darker aspersions, of course, and say that 'Word Song' simply illustrates Syd's final relinquishing of his lyrical gifts and abandoning himself, Ionesco style, to the meaninglessness of language and the futility of communication. David Gilmour presumably thought so or he would have included it on the final album.

The issue of what was left off the final album is not as contentious as it was with *The Madcap Laughs*, where the absence of 'Opel', the questionable track sequencing and the inclusion of one or two inferior takes puzzled Malcolm Jones and remains a source of controversy for Barrett fans. Here David Gilmour made do with what he could salvage. Even the apparent disappearance of 'Bob Dylan Blues' for over thirty years should not be viewed conspiratorially. Time has turned it into a charming and amusing curio. Had it been released at the time the perception might have been different. Who, in 1970, would have been interested in a parody of Dylan's folk-protest style? Barron Knights fans? Benny Hill? Actually the Benny Hill connection is not as absurd as it might at first appear. Hill released a single in 1965, at the same time as 'Bob Dylan Blues' was being written, called 'What a World'. It contained a verse which directly satirised a certain folksinger 'who came from America to sing at the Albert Hall' and tells of how he sang his protest songs before driving 'back to his penthouse in his brand new Rolls-Royce car'. Given Syd's penchant for all forms of English satire it is not beyond the realms of possibility that he took his cue from Hill's own barbed missive. Whatever the source, though, the fact remains that by 1970, when Syd finally recorded the song, most Dylan followers were waiting for him to make another 'Blonde on Blonde', not another 'Emmett Till'.

The other notable out-takes from the Barrett sessions, 'Dolly Rocker', 'Milky Way', 'Let's Split' and 'Birdie Hop', all suffer from being underdeveloped or under-rehearsed, or are simply good ideas badly executed. 'What's this one called?' asks the engineer. 'Dolly Rocker. It's called Dolly Rocker,' says Syd in his dry-mouthed mumble. 'It's an old make of dress,' he explains. 'Well, months old, you know, that sort of thing.' The fuzzy logic of the elaboration reveals that Syd still has a wit as parched as his palette. It's the way he tells them.

Despite some uncertain phrasing and wavering pitch, 'Dolly Rocker' begins promisingly. The 'she done' references hark back to the blues pastiching of 'Lucy Leave', while the premise and set up – his girlfriend sees a dress she likes – were perfect subject matter for a three-minute pop song. Unfortunately that's as good as it gets. The song is marred by a truly abysmal middle section – because of Syd's inconsistent bar lines one can hardly call it a middle eight, a middle ten maybe? – and the rest of the song lapses into the regressive babble of 'Waving My Arms in the Air'. There is a good song struggling to get out here, but 'Dolly Rocker' comes across as a poor rewrite (or perhaps even pre-write) of 'Love You'.

The same goes for 'Milky Way'. Its off-kilter charm and 1930s dance-band lilt amble along nicely and its shambling lyric just about holds its shape until lapsing into lazy versifying towards the end, although it has to be said that a line like 'Give a gasp of life today | When you're in the Milky Way', perfectly summarises Syd's predicament by this stage.

Perhaps the strongest contender for inclusion on the album was 'Let's Split'. Written at Wetherby Mansions about his often fractious relationship with girlfriend Gayla Pinion, the song is full of tension and strife and angrily strummed descending chords which complement the terse atmosphere perfectly. The song's title and chorus line make great use of ambiguity, 'let's split' referring simultaneously to 'let's split up' and 'let's go out'. When Gayla Pinion moved into Wetherby Mansions she brought her West Highland terrier, Sasha, with her, and it proceeded to crap all over the flat, much to Duggie Field's disgust. Syd refers to this in the ambiguous refrain of 'hound, hound, hound', which implies being nagged as well as the presence of canines. 'Let's Split' reeks of nagging, bad temper and disharmony. At two minutes twenty, after a nifty bit of whistling, Syd gives up the ghost completely, as if utterly undone by the negativity of the song. 'Hold it can you . . . That's all, cheers,' he says tetchily, breaking off suddenly from the most sustained anti-love song he ever recorded.

'Birdie Hop' is sung in a tremulous high pitch, which along with the simple two-note melody mimics the actions and call-song of its subject matter. Again it begins promisingly before lapsing into half-realised ideas and slapdash lyrics. The song's repeated refrain of 'I see the flies' and the fact that the cover of the *Barrett* album features a series of Syd's drawings of flies has encouraged some biographers to contrive a spurious link between the psychedelic band the Flies and flies as a foreboding motif in Syd's lyrics. The story goes that the Flies, a particularly punky and uncompromising unit, took to standing at the side of the UFO stage yelling 'Sell out!' at the Floyd soon after they signed their EMI contract. They supposedly repeated the gesture during the 14 Hour Technicolor Dream. In fact, insects and animals are recurring images throughout Syd's solo lyrics. And why wouldn't they be? He grew up surrounded by Fen countryside, absorbed in pastoral pursuits and Arcadian literature, and frequently drew upon nature for the subject matter for his artwork. His father was a keen amateur botanist and the entire family were taken for Sunday morning jaunts to the Cambridge Botanical Gardens. The experience would have been ingrained and absorbed from an early age.

Plant life and wildlife are abundant in Syd's solo songs and the species count is formidable. Fish in 'Terrapin', birds in 'Dark Globe', the caterpillar hood in 'No Good Trying', leopards in 'Long Gone', crabs in 'Feel', leeches in 'If It's in You', bulls in 'Maisie', squirrels in 'Dolly Rocker', eagles, bears and raccoons in 'Swan Lee', grasshoppers, kangaroos and drones in 'Clowns and Jugglers'/'Octopus', rats and spiders in 'Rats', cats and dogs in 'Waving My Arms in the Air', antelopes, camels, birds and flies in 'Birdie Hop', flies in 'Opel', larks in 'Dominoes', sparrows in 'It Is Obvious', wolves in 'Wolfpack', just about everything in the jungle in 'Effervescing Elephant'. In fact imagery drawn from the natural world appears to be one of the few consistent thematic threads in Syd's lyrical output.

On the recorded version of 'Effervescing Elephant' animal imagery drawn from the classical world provides the song's introductory motif. Its opening tuba passage quotes directly from *The Carnival of the Animals* by Camille Saint-Saëns. 'It was Syd that wanted it on there, in fact he moaned that it wasn't a bit longer – eight bars instead of the three that I put on there,' says David Gilmour. 'Unfortunately the tuba player was unhelpful and refused to play even those few notes by ear – refused to play anything unless it was properly written down on sheet music – so within a three-hour session we had to get blank music-stave paper – write the very short melody down on it, which was tough as I couldn't read or write music, get him to play it, then rewrite it several times until it sounded correct. I think we finally got it in the last three minutes. And in those days, at the second the three hours were up, they would stand up, pack up their stuff and walk out of the studio.'

Released on EMI-Harvest on 6 November 1970 the *Barrett* album was book-ended by two radio sessions, one for John Peel's *Top Gear* recorded on 24 February at the BBC's Maida Vale studios and another recorded on 16 February 1971 for Bob Harris's *Sounds of the Seventies* show. For the Peel session Syd, along with David Gilmour and Jerry Shirley, performed 'Terrapin', 'Gigolo Aunt', 'Baby Lemonade', 'Effervescing Elephant' and the Wright–Barrett composition 'Two of a Kind'. The presence of Shirley on bongos rather than drum kit gives the session an ambling folky feel reminiscent of Steve Took-era Tyrannosaurus Rex. Syd clearly hasn't finished writing 'Gigolo Aunt' yet and the song only has its opening verse which he sings three times. 'Baby Lemonade' is augmented by some beautifully soulful organ playing by Gilmour, although Syd's slide solo is tentative and uncertain, and he transposes the 'Cage through the post | Name like a ghost' lines in verse two. 'Terrapin' and 'Two of a Kind' are pleasant strumalongs, Syd singing 'a move about' rather than 'the move about' on the former and detouring into some ill-advised barber's-shop raga on the fade-out of the latter. 'Effervescing Elephant' is more nimble than the album version, where Syd's delivery is flat and uninspired. Performed solo, minus the tuba that graced the recorded version, he sounds animated and brings out the sheer whimsical joy of the song.

On the Bob Harris session, Syd is accompanied by Gilmour on bass and performs sparse demo-like versions of 'Baby Lemonade', 'Dominoes' and 'Love Song'. It would be his only 'public' performance of 1971.

On 12 January 1970 Syd had played guitar on sessions for Kevin Ayers' first solo single after leaving Soft Machine. Originally titled 'Religious Experience' it was eventually released, minus Syd's contribution, as 'Singing a Song in the Morning'. On the released version Ayers does a pretty convincing job of imitating Syd's lead guitar style. During this period Ayers even briefly entertained ideas of forming a band with Syd. 'I went to see him at that flat that was on *The Madcap Laughs* cover,' he says, 'but he was [Ayers adopts a comatose posture] . . . gone.'

Kevin Ayers was the closest kindred spirit on the rock scene to Syd's urbane Englishness and eccentricity. One can only speculate on what the musical landscape of the early 1970s might have sounded like had the two men formed a group. File under 'what might have been'.

Also in 1970 Syd made the briefest of forays into live performance, at the Extravaganza '70 Music and Fashion Festival, which took place in the entrance lobby of the Kensington Olympia. Accompanied by David Gilmour on bass and Jerry Shirley on drums, Syd performed just four numbers, 'Terrapin', 'Gigolo Aunt', 'Effervescing Elephant' and 'Octopus'. The truncated set was plagued throughout by a bad PA which made the lyrics all but inaudible; it is only on the final number, 'Octopus', that the vocals can be heard at all. Legend and hindsight have turned this event into a shambling farce. In fact, the bootleg evidence available suggests that the band, although clearly under-rehearsed, sound perfectly adequate. They performed ragged versions of 'Terrapin' and 'Gigolo Aunt' and a frantic 'Effervescing Elephant' before Syd brought the perform-ance to a sudden halt at the end of 'Octopus'. The brevity of the set, and the rapidity with which Syd left the stage (leaving his colleagues to pad the song out before bringing proceedings to a messy conclusion), gave clear indication that Syd was reluctant to return to the live arena. After the *Barrett* album was completed David Gilmour proved equally reluctant to repeat the experience, receiving only a brief but heartfelt thank-you from Syd in the lift at Wetherby Mansions as he dropped him off for the last time.

Others who had worked with Syd during this difficult period found their judgement similarly impaired when assessing his solo output.

'I veer away from those solo albums,' says Peter Jenner. 'I find them very disturbing. I don't like to listen to them. There's a certain ghoulishness about people's enjoyment of them. There's some good stuff in there if you know where to dig, and no disrespect to Dave and Roger who were trying to do something good, but it wasn't what I'd heard in the studio and it was a shadow of the Syd I knew. He was such a delightful charming person. That's why we were all so upset when the fog set in.'

Perhaps the most quietly despairing of all the lyrical images on Syd's solo albums is the disabled and debilitated momentum conveyed in the line 'We under all | We awful, awful crawl' on *Madcap*'s 'No Man's Land'. This is the cry of a man who is beginning to embrace entropy as a permanent condition. 'The last time I saw him was in 1970 when he was out of the Floyd and definitely not the old Syd,' says Andrew Rawlinson who was by now a devoted follower of Maharaj Charan Singh Ji. 'The Master came to London and Syd came in and sat down and said hello. I looked at him and thought, "What's happening Syd?" I didn't get chance to talk to him because there was a lot going on. He was subdued and he wasn't sunny any longer. He was under water in some way.'

This sense of submergence was by now apparent in almost every aspect of Syd's life. It is audible on the *Barrett* album and it was becoming increasingly evident in his reluctance or inability to forge a meaningful pop career. The fact that Syd should even turn up at a talk given by Maharaj Charan Singh Ji gave hope that he hadn't entirely forsaken his spirit of enquiry; then again it could equally have indicated that he just wanted to be among friends, no matter how remote he had become from many of them. That much is conjecture. What is indisputable is that from 1970 onwards Syd was in permanent and irreversible retreat from fame and ambition. There was no official retirement, no grand gesture or dramatic disappearance, just a gradual dwindling from view, punctuated by sporadic and ill-fated attempts to stoke the dying embers of a wayward muse.

By the age of twenty-five Syd's songwriting talents had abandoned him. 'There was a torrent, a sluice of words that came out but then not long after that the tank ran dry,' notes Robyn Hitchcock. 'There were no words at all. Somewhere along the line he was no longer able to express himself.'

Hitchcock adopts an appropriately painterly analogy to describe what happened. 'It was undiluted talent. Most people dilute their talent. They thin it with a bit of turps. They have an idea, then they make that idea into a song, the way they think a song should go. Some people are good at writing songs they think a million people will like. Barrett didn't dilute his talent, so he squeezed the tube dry. It was empty much faster. Most of us put a little bit of talent in and fix it up with whatever else you need to accomplish the painting. It's like there was no gap between Barrett and his art. It's unfiltered. He was just like a kid who got hold of the song tube and just squeezed them out and went, "God, look at those colours" and then went, "Oh. It's empty. Oh well." That's it. Game over. Like he couldn't really help it. It all went out very intensely. Then it was gone.'

In an interview with Michael Watts for *Melody Maker* in March 1971, Syd indicated that there would be a third album and that he already had four tracks in the can, but there never would be a third solo album, and apart from one brief and disastrous attempt to get him back into Abbey Road studios in August 1974, Syd never recorded again. The flight from fame had now begun in earnest and Syd increasingly sought out the familiar physical and emotional certainties of his childhood. As soon as the sessions for Barrett album were completed in July 1970 he began to spend less time at Wetherby Mansions with Duggie Fields and more time back in Cambridge.

On 8 January 1971 Seamus O'Connell married his partner Victoria at Fulham Broadway Registry Office. 'Syd and Roger Waters both came,' he remembers, 'not to the ceremony but to the reception afterwards in the flat where we were living at the time. David Gale and Mick Rock were the wedding photographers. Syd seemed fine. I don't ever remember seeing him behaving particularly peculiarly. He'd always got on well with my mother, and the two of them and a few others slipped off to the pub after the wedding.'

Away from the pressures of the music world, among old friends and in familiar surroundings, Syd was in good spirits. Seamus's wife Victoria had been one of the Homerton Ladies College girls who had lodged at 183 Hills Road, and remembered Syd well. Seamus's mother, Ella, was another person who offered emotional anchorage and the image of Syd and Ella slipping off to the pub to catch up on old times sharply conflicts with some of the more distressing stories from this period.

'I don't think Syd had ever travelled very far or lived anywhere else, so, like a homing pigeon, if he started to feel a bit out of it he went back to where it was familiar and he was safe,' says Hester Page. Hester, like many others, had noticed Syd's tendency to retreat even at the height of his fame. 'Syd wasn't ambitious. I think he lived inside himself a hell of a lot. His music was inside himself and his words were too. A lot of his words were about his daily perceptions, sitting and looking around. When I listen to a lot of his songs I can see him sitting there, watching someone and thinking, "They're doing that and that bird's singing and I'm thinking this." And that's how he put it together. I think he was quite simple and uncomplicated in that way. And that's why he had to go home. The world was getting too untrustworthy and complicated for him. A lot of his friends had gone off and were busy doing other things so that base of the Cambridge crowd wasn't as easily accessed. He wasn't in the middle of it any more.'

Most of Syd's friends were by now forging ahead in their respective careers. Storm and Po at Hipgnosis were turning out some of the most distinctive sleeve art of the era. Nigel Lesmoir-

Gordon and Anthony Stern were making films. David Henderson had finished his master's degree at the Royal College of Art and was exhibiting. So was Duggie Fields. Pink Floyd weren't doing badly either. Everybody was busy planning, producing, creating. Everybody except Syd.

'I really don't think Syd wanted to go big time,' says Hester Page. 'I don't think that was in his mind at all. That's why he went back to Mum. He didn't want to go into that other world at all. It was all too scary.'

Many of Syd's friends and associates still cared very deeply about him and were concerned about the path his life had taken. The abiding issue was no longer one of career prospects or chart positions or third albums. It was simply a case of what on earth had gone wrong?

'He was exploring and everything he touched came to fruition before his very eyes,' says Andrew Rawlinson. 'I think that was his genius, using that word in the original sense of presiding spirit. And I think that was why his fall and his loss of direction touched us all so much.'

'Nigel Gordon said, I believe, that he always thought that Syd was a bit strange, even well before the troubles set in. I never thought that, but maybe Nigel saw something that I didn't,' says David Gale.

'I would think he was personally destined for mental illness anyway,' says Lesmoir-Gordon unequivocally. 'It was merely accelerated by the stardom thing and all these unsettling chemicals.'

'Syd is seen as an acid casualty, and there were many of those around, but they were far outnumbered by people who are alive and well today, and perfectly all right,' says Gale. 'As to whether Syd was an acid casualty is, of course, another piece of stereotyping, which may need to be addressed, because I think it was a mixture. LSD probably blew out the basement, and then Mandrax loosened the fabric, or something like that. It was probably more attractive for us to see him as an acid casualty, 'cos that's heroic – whereas Mandrax is a bit sad.'

Duggie Fields however maintains that Mandrax use was not the issue. 'I don't think Mandrax [was] that harmful. I had a Mandrax prescription for years. I don't even remember his Mandrax intake being that high. I think what's harmful is not particular individual drugs. It's multi-drug use. That's where drugs can get really harmful where the effects of one drug are mixed with the effect of another drug, and some things don't go together very well. Mandrax and alcohol are lethal. That can be a killer. We all know that people overdosed on that combination at the time. I've always been Mr Conservative. I'd take half of what anybody else took. People would be [saying] "Loosen up, Duggie. Take some of this, man." And I have a group of friends who are dead now because I didn't "Loosen up Duggie" and have what they had.'

'Duggie was very driven,' notes Hester Page. 'He was always avidly producing and he was very commercial. He was savvy that way, whereas Syd wasn't a bit savvy. I don't think he had any thoughts about money or business or the future at all. The other members of the Floyd were far more aware of that than Syd. In the end it was safer to go back to Cambridge and not be pestered by this world he felt he couldn't fit into any more.'

Duggie Fields concedes that Syd's final months at Wetherby Mansions were fraught with tension. The hangers-on continued to use the flat as a crash-pad and scrounge-pad. Girls continued to pound on Syd's door, craving his attention. He had three girlfriends during this period, Iggy the Eskimo girl who appeared naked on the cover of the *Madcap Laughs* album, Quorum boutique girl Gilly Staples and Gayla Pinion, a friend of Lindsay Corner's from Ely. Fields would hide away in his room and paint. Syd would just hide away. When he did emerge his behaviour was often belligerent or menacing.

'Looking back there were incidents that ought to have worried one more than they did,' says Fields. 'And there were instances that one should have reacted more strongly to than one did because one was trying to be cool. Like Syd would smoke a cigarette and throw the stub across the floor and it would still be burning but nobody would pick it up and put it in an ashtray. It was disturbing because it's dangerous to throw a lighted cigarette around. But the act of danger was not as important as the not wanting to be uncool, uncool being a sin in those days. And now I think how did I do that? Why did I do that? How did I blank out the danger?'

Fields was also party to Syd's occasional bursts of physical violence. 'I remember him picking up this girl' – believed to be Gilly Staples – 'who was his girlfriend at the time and just flinging her across the room because she just wanted to stay in bed and we were all supposed to be going to Dave Gilmour's. And it was, "No, that's my bed" and just literally throwing her. No one reprimanded him for it. I don't remember reprimanding him. Perhaps I should have done.'

As with Syd's prodigious acid intake during 1967, that lethal combination of laissez-faire libertarianism and hippie non-intervention was once again conspiring to cover up a multitude of unsavoury and reprehensible acts.

'That was of course the other side of the business in Egerton Court, where I lived next door to Syd's room, where it was indeed that hippie laissez-faire which prevented us from intervening,' says David Gale. 'I mean on one occasion he was found squashing Lindsay between the wall and the lavatory door and she was screaming. And it'd be a very small group of people who'd tell him to stop it. Eventually we did start saying "Lay off."'

'I was very fond of Syd,' says Duggie Fields, 'otherwise I'd never have shared a flat with him. But it was very freaky being around him later on. The fondness and freakiness were in conflict. It was like how much do I want him in my life? How much do I not want him in my life? One never likes to reject people. Not being able to cope with someone you're very fond of is very disturbing.'

The members of Syd's old band had exactly the same dilemma, of course. Gilmour, Waters and Wright had all partici-pated in the making of the *Madcap* album and Gilmour and Wright had been largely responsible for keeping the *Barrett* album, and arguably Syd himself, together musically, but now they were forging a successful career as one of the biggest bands in the world. Despite this they were unable to shake off the legacy of their former guiding spirit. Syd's spectral presence continued to cast a long shadow well into the 1970s.

'I think the Floyd had an incredible dilemma and suffered incredible guilt from it too,' says Duggie Fields. 'They must have questioned whether they could have done things differently and whether it would have made a difference. But it probably wouldn't have made a difference. You've got that circumstance of someone who's hypersensitive, which Syd was, and you've the whole "everyone wants a bit of you". Who copes with that well? He didn't.'

Fields even moved out of Wetherby Mansions at one point, because he could no longer cope with Syd's erratic behaviour. 'But where I moved to was even more difficult, it turned out, so I came back. I had moved into Alice Pollock's flat, the founder of Quorum and the employer/partner of Ossie Clarke. Alice was the one who gave Ossie his platform, but she was also a real talent in her own right; however she would step out of the limelight to give it to other people. I'd met Alice's brother, Robbie, at architecture school. Sadly he's been a "casualty" ever since they threw him out a few years later. It wasn't just drugs, for him I think it was almost like he thought insanity was a career move. If he couldn't be an architect, an artist, an actor, writer, a poet or a film-maker, he could be mad. Robbie had come round one day and said that he'd been to visit Alice, and she'd met their dead father's reincarnation, now her current boyfriend. He'd gone in and she'd said, "I want you to meet daddy," and there was Frank Zappa sitting there! After just two nights living at Alice's, I decided I'd rather come back and live with Syd. I thought, "Who's the maddest in this world?" '

Nigel and Jenny Lesmoir-Gordon had also encountered many people who by their own admission were far further 'out there' than Syd ever was. By way of illustration Nigel recounts an incident from a weekend spent in Andrew King's Welsh cottage back in 1967. 'Stash de Rollo wore black velvet with gold brocade and high-heeled shoes,' he remembers. 'We told him we needed more wood for the fire so he went across the yard to the barn to get the wood and came back covered in mud with two cans of oil, and we said, "What are we going to do with this and look at you. You're covered in mud." And Stash proclaimed, "Let all mud be velvet." '

'Stash's father, the painter Balthus, owned a chateau, and we were all going to go and live in that,' recalls Jenny. 'Stash had wanted us to love unconditionally. He wanted us to transcend and just go to the world of pure love. We had a fire going and he wanted to get on the fire and burn himself. He thought he wouldn't burn because he was full of pure love. He had a long Victorian nightshirt on that he'd bought in the Portobello Road. He kept saying to me, "Jenny, you've got to have the faith." The local policeman had already been round to see what the hell was going on and we didn't want him coming back again and asking what had happened to our dead burnt friend. Stash got very cross with me because I hadn't got the faith. I managed to stop him from burning himself.'

'Syd could be very difficult,' concedes Duggie Fields. 'It was sad, but it wasn't as bad as my friend "Neon" who was an acid casualty who lived over the road who decided that he was going to martyr himself to show the body could overcome pain. He had to be held physically to stop him pouring a pan of scalding water over himself. So a doctor came and put him in a strait-jacket. He really was an acid casualty in a way that Syd wasn't.'

'I think he was very affected by drugs, totally genuinely, and he thoroughly enjoyed them,' says Libby Gausden. 'He did see them as a good thing not a bad thing. Not as a rebellious thing, but as something as interesting to explore, like a painting or a piece of music. I'm a total control freak. I like to be in control. I wasn't interested in "let yourself go". But they did take him somewhere else. He wasn't one of those who'd go, "Oh look, the fire looks blue and yellow." They opened his mind. They finished off his mind, of course, as well.'

'It was the same old thing with all of them,' says Robyn Hitchcock. 'Their self-control was shot by drugs. They all became victims of their own minds, which is what happens if you get stoned a lot. You are at the mercy of your muse. Your mind is set to a randomiser. Our grandparents couldn't have fought the war on acid, or built the empire. Boy, no wonder the Americans lost in Vietnam. And people might say, "Why should you fight wars, man? Take drugs." But it doesn't make you peaceful. It just makes you incompetent. I set myself back no end by taking drugs and I didn't take anything super-powerful. I'd seen what had happened to those Sixties people so I didn't dip myself in the acid bath for too long. You get the idea on drugs but you never have the "sustain" to write it down. You could open the door and think, "Wow, open door, that's a poem." Then you pick up the pen and think, "Hmm, open door, what's so great about that? Oh, I'm hungry. Oh no, I think I need to have sex. Oh God, I hate myself." It doesn't work. But for a brief period it enhances, and I think that's the Faustian thing with all those guys. But also I think it was the momentum of the times. People are still discovering pot and acid but they aren't becoming great explorers because it's already been visited. There was a sense of possibility in the air. It wasn't love and peace and life wasn't necessarily any better back then. There were still the same political messes. People were still being slaughtered and ripped off and bullied and demoralised like they are now. It wasn't a golden age at all, but there was a window where it felt like anything might happen. One of the great things in Barrett's songs is that sense of potential. It's a sense of manic potential and by the end it's a feeling of potential that's gone. He's only twenty-three or twenty-four but there's a real feeling like an old man looking back with sadness. You know he's resigned from life. It's a quick ride from teenage angst to midlife crisis and you really get there in a snap of a finger, but he really did seem so wistful on the *Barrett* album, already looking back at a life that had gone.'

By 1971 Syd was back home in Cambridge full time, safely ensconced in the cellar of 183 Hills Road where he took up semi-permanent residence. Trips back to London became increasingly sporadic.

'That was the real Syd, I think, that boy who loved being a Scout, and loved nature,' says Hester Page. 'He wandered in to the pop world and loved it for a while, and had a part to play in it but then it turned into something else that stopped feeding his heart.'

As so often there was historical precedent for this among Syd's literary forebears. Embarking upon a similar flight from obligation a century earlier Edward Lear wrote to Emily Tennyson in May 1865:

Even if I get enough tin to cover all expenses, the method of doing so is harassing and odious – seeing the vapid nature of swells, & the great amount of writing; & the close confinement to the house . . . The walking – sketching – exploring – novelty perceiving & beauty appreciating part of the Landscape painter's life is undoubtedly to be envied: – but then the contrast and the money tryingtoget, smokydark London life – fuss – trouble & bustle is wholly odious, & every year more so.'

Terminology aside (and even some of that is extremely similar) Syd could have been uttering the same sentiments almost exactly a hundred years later. He too would eventually forsake the 'money tryingtoget, smokydark London life' in search of solitude and sanctuary.

Cambridge is a relatively small place, a city in name only from its university status. It has a compact centre and a lack of sprawl. In the early 1970s many of Syd's old school friends, Tech friends, teachers and former band mates were still living there. It had a thriving local music scene, with Arts Lab activity, regular free concerts in Grantchester Meadows and on Midsummer Common, informal jam sessions at the Catholic Mission Hall at Fisher House, and impromptu gigs in the city's numerous cellar bars and vegetarian cafes, and anywhere else where the 'head' population gathered in numbers. Syd was largely absent from all of this although he did became a familiar figure in the landscape again, often seen striding out with purpose, incongruously dressed in his pop-star clothes, burning off hyperactivity and the accumulated frustrations of an increasingly wasted creative life.

The one constant in his life was Gayla Pinion, Syd's last serious girlfriend, their relationship having somehow survived the madness and chaos of Wetherby Mansions. Back in Cambridge Syd and Gayla discussed marriage, Syd showing the same penchant for old-fashioned courtship values that he had once entertained with Libby. Gayla found a job at Joshua Taylor, the Cambridge department store, and the pair got engaged in October 1970. An announcement was even placed in the local paper.

Unfortunately Syd chose a joint family gathering to celebrate the engagement as the opportunity to first throw tomato soup over Gayla, and then later during the meal to disappear upstairs and cut off his long hair. With that immaculate sense of English reserve that Ionesco had so savagely pinpointed in *The Bald Prima Donna*, none of those present acknowledged the incident as anything other than normal when Syd returned from the bathroom freshly shorn. Peter Jenner referred to the hair shearing as a 'goodbye to all that' gesture, a symbolic shedding of the last vestiges of pop stardom. Syd's dismayed and embarrassed brothers and sisters might have viewed the incident somewhat differently.

If the cutting of his long hair does point to some sort of ritualistic cleansing, other more drastic and disturbing incidents from that time indicate that Syd was attempting to rub out his old life altogether.

'He gave me all his diaries when I was married in 1967 and I went to meet him when our son was born in 1970 and took the diaries back,' says Libby. 'And he burnt them all unfortunately. I should have kept them. His girlfriend phoned me and said, "He's burnt them. You should have kept them." Each page was ledger-size with his tiny writing. He filled pages every day. Everything he ever did. What he thought. What he was reading. I shouldn't have taken them back. It was a real last-minute decision. I thought, "I don't need them. It would be nice for him to have them." I had my diaries and they were lovely to look at and think, "Heavens, was I that naive?" or whatever. In the middle of these Pink Floyd things I'd write about what we had for lunch. He had things like that and it's nice to remember those times, but, no, they went.'

By the age of twenty-five Syd seemed to be in retreat from everyone and everything. He had stopped developing as a painter. His guitar playing reverted to blues roots, and he no longer seemed capable of sustaining any kind of artistic, emotional or spiritual impulse.

It might seem fanciful to suggest that in burning his diaries Syd was acting out some kind of auto-destructive variant on John Latham's Skoob Towers, but in many ways that's exactly what it was. Bereft of ambition or the need to justify himself to others Syd resorted to a form of nihilism that threw Latham's

1 *Add a Mark* from *Fart Enjoy*, 1964–5

2 Syd's *Red Abstract*, signed R. Barrett, *c.*1971

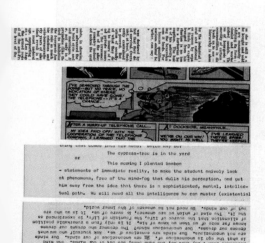

3 & 4 *Mullet* and *Topical* from *Fart Enjoy*
5 & 6 Stollman's flyers for the Trip Party gigs at the Marquee, 1966

7–9 Pink Floyd performing at the Free School, All Saints' Hall, Notting Hill, October 1966

10 *Still Life of Dried Flowers*, painted while Syd was a student at Camberwell, *c*.1964
11 & 12 *Vase of Flowers* and *Man and Donkey*, undated, from his later years

No. 6 St Margaret's Square, 2006: 13, hippo doorknob; 14, upstairs back bedroom; 15, sitting room

365.
Primary Dementia.   244 Arbitrary inference
363

The Philosophy of Mind.   J. Glover.
An Essay on Free Will.   Enragon.
Education and Training in Psychiatry H. Walton
Handbook of Psychiatric   Rehabilitation
Practice.   Wing. Morris. Brenda
The Innocence of Dreams.   Rycroft.
Brain and Behaviour.   , Brown.
An Introduction to Psychopathology. Neurich
What is Psychotherapy? Bloch. / Davis.

Freud and Jung. (g takes the loss of an object)
    Whereas Sigmund Freud, the founder
of Psychoanalysis, suggested that hysteria
could be traceable to loss of memory in
early life, representing emotional energy,
possibly sexual in nature, and also
devised the method called free association,
to free the unconscious, i.e. the Oedipus
complex, Carl Jung suggested two distinctly
different accounts, the repressed, as well
as the mental 'collective consciousness,'
called psychological types, as used in
psychoanalysis.
All manic depressives therefore recover.

16 Roger's notes in the back of his psychology textbook. The last line reads 'All manic depressives therefore recover'

more purposeful creative strategies into sharp relief. In one pyromaniacal instance, up went treasured memories, random recollections, lost songs, doodles, sketches, trivia and profundity alike, all reduced to ashes.

The best that can be deduced from Syd's immolation of his past was that he was making some kind of gallant gesture to Gayla, destroying memories of youthful indiscretion, past flings, love expressed to old girlfriends. The more worrying conclusion that can be drawn is that he was erasing his old self to such an extent that soon there would be nothing left to build on. The destruction of his diaries indicates a degree of disregard that borders on the self-loathing.

With sad inevitability Syd's relationship with Gayla ended badly when old jealousies surfaced and he began to suspect she was having an affair, at one point accusing her of sleeping with Jerry Shirley whom she had been staying with when his erratic behaviour got too much for her.

It was another ex-girlfriend, Jenny Spires, who was chiefly responsible for Syd's last real attempt to get a band together. By now she was married to Jack Monck, the former bass player with Carol Grimes Delivery, and it was partly at her behest that Monck and former Pink Fairies drummer Twink called upon Syd at 183 Hills Road to see if he would be interested in playing guitar with them. Stars, the short-lived group that emerged from this initiative, would be Syd's last.

The Stars venture, which lasted barely a month from January to February 1972, occurred during a brief period when Syd felt sufficiently inspired to venture out in public for the occasional jam session. On 26 January Jenny Spires had taken him to a gig at King's College Cellars featuring the American bluesman Eddie Guitar Burns. Syd participated in a freeform jam with Monck and Twink for about half an hour after Burns' set. The following night at a Cambridge Corn Exchange gig, headlined by

Hawkwind, Syd participated in another jam with the self-explanatory Last Minute Put Together Boogie Band with Monck, Twink, Henry Cow guitarist Fred Frith and future Steamhammer guitarist Bruce Payne. Audio evidence exists which confirms the event. Syd was personally introduced by the compère about halfway through, although it appears that he was happy to noodle away in the background, playing mainly blues riffs.

Jack Monck and Twink Alder invited Fred Frith to join them in putting a full-time band together with Syd. Although initially excited at the prospect Frith's enthusiasm turned to dismay when confronted with Syd's diminishing talents.

'Rehearsals were difficult, because Syd had pretty much lost any capacity to focus,' says Frith. 'Everyone was in awe of him, and we wanted him to lead us in a way, but he couldn't. Jack kind of took charge and we did the best we could, but at the only concert that I did with them, Syd played "Smokestack Lightning" or variations thereof in every song, and didn't really sing at all. To say I was hugely disappointed is maybe the wrong way of putting it. I was shocked, angry, devastated, that it had come to that. I didn't know what to do or how to be in that situation. I always had a lot of difficulty being around "famous" people and especially famous people who I really looked up to, and this was even by my own standards of social ineptitude, a painful experience, and overwhelmingly sad.'

Syd had come full circle, back on home soil, among local musicians, playing covers of 'Smokestack Lightning'. Things had changed though and clearly this wasn't the Syd of old.

'As for his stock in the local community, there was a lot of whispering, and a lot of soul-searching about how it happened and whether it could happen to anyone,' says Frith. 'But we knew that the light had gone out, and that it wasn't going to get switched back on. It was only a couple of years since I had been a regular volunteer nursing assistant in a mental hospital, and I think that made it even more haunting. I just knew that I didn't want to put myself through that again, and I had the deepest respect for Jack, who was the true hero of the Cambridge scene in those days, in attempting to keep making it happen.'

Syd, Twink and Jack Monck rehearsed in the cellar of 183 Hills Road and played an impromptu gig, little more than a glorified rehearsal in fact, at the Dandelion Health Food Café in nearby East Road on 5 February. The makeshift band played further low-key shows at the Dandelion and Petty Curry, just off Cambridge Market Square. With no pressure or expectations on his shoulders Syd enjoyed the opportunity to jam the blues and perform rudimentary versions of half a dozen tracks from his solo albums. On the strength of these appearances local promoter Steve Brink booked Stars to appear at Cambridge Corn Exchange on Thursday, 24 February, on a bill that also included Skin Alley and the MC5. The flyers for the event billed Stars democratically as 'Barrett Alder and Monck'. No fuss. No first names. And despite the band name, no star trip either.

Skin Alley's well-received set of mellow progressive rock was followed by the incendiary presence of the MC5. Although a couple of years past their 'kick out the jams' prime the Michigan Panthers played a blistering set which went down a storm. There was then a lull of nearly an hour, during which time the energy of the crowd dissipated considerably, and people began to drift away to catch late-night buses, trains and burger vans. It was gone midnight, and the hall was at best a quarter full, when with little fanfare Stars trooped on to the stage. Syd looked fantastic in velvet trousers and snakeskin boots; his hair had grown out from his suede-head crop of the previous year and was long and curly again. He was now sporting a beard, which only served to emphasis the gaunt angularity of his face. The set began with a version of 'Octopus', which was noticeably slower than the one on record. It became immediately apparent that the PA and the monitors weren't up to the task and Syd's vocals were almost in-audible. I was positioned at the lip of the stage, no more than three or four yards from where Syd was standing stage right, close enough to hear his unamplified voice as he struggled to be heard.

The band also performed 'Baby Lemonade', 'Gigolo Aunt', 'No Man's Land', 'Waving My Arms in the Air', and an impressively tight version of 'Lucifer Sam'. These were interspersed with a couple of ragged and formless blues jams, which petered out in-conclusively in the style that jams often did in those days. The only times Syd spoke were to introduce 'Octopus' at the beginning of the set and to remark, 'I don't know what that one was called,' after 'Gigolo Aunt'. At one point a girl in a long hippie dress entered from the wings, stage right, and began dancing in that hippie floaty way that hippie girls danced in the early 1970s. Syd acknowledged her with a faintly alarmed glance and she soon beat a retreat.

In a perfectly observed detail that seemed to summarise the anti-climatic nature of the event *Melody Maker* journalist Roy Hollingsworth noted that towards the end of the set the house lights went on and a Corn Exchange employee wheeled a heavy wooden barrow noisily across the floor in readiness for the Friday morning market. Had he done that when the MC5 were pummelling out their powerhouse riffs no one would have heard it, but so meek was the sound of the PA when Stars played that the market barrow vibrated the floor and all but drowned out the sound on stage. It was at that moment that I glanced round for the first time and noticed that there were probably no more than thirty people clustered around the stage and no more than fifty or so in total remaining in the hall.

Contrary to what has been claimed over the years by people who weren't there, Syd didn't appear to have trouble remem-bering his lyrics. His guitar-playing was, though, extremely sketchy and tentative at times, particularly during the blues jams, and he did, as Roy Hollingsworth noted, frequently retire to his amp at the back of the stage as the set progressed. Whether in retreat from the sorry spectacle of it all, or simply because he couldn't hear himself it's hard to say, but this clearly was not the Syd Barrett of the UFO days, hardwiring his synergy to the Binson Echorec as he foraged into new sonic pastures. This was Syd regressing into blues runs and insecurity. Eventually Jack Monck's bass amp packed up and the set fizzled out soon after.

At the end of the performance Syd didn't retire backstage like a rock star but came down on to the Corn Exchange dance floor where, surrounded by a coterie of beautiful women, he stood smiling graciously and exchanging polite small talk with anyone who approached him, including myself. Close up, the one thing that signified that all was not well was his shell-shocked eyes. Even when he smiled they registered alarm and who knows what inner turmoil? They told a different story entirely from the pop-star clothes and the glamorous entourage.

'Shell-shocked eyes? From which battle, you have to ask your-self?' ruminates Fred Frith. 'The battle with drugs, with insensitive fans, between the desire to be a star and the desire to be private, with stupid and ignorant showbusiness entre-preneurs, who knows?'

The band supposedly played a much better set with better sound two nights later at the same venue, supporting Nektar and the Groundhogs, but there have been no plausible first-hand accounts to verify this. I hitchhiked down to the University of Essex in Colchester the following Friday on the understanding that Stars were going play on a bill with Kevin Ayers, Nektar and Dick Heckstall-Smith, but about halfway through the night a compère announced that Stars would not be appearing. This information elicited an audible low groan from a packed hall, many of whom had come on the off chance of seeing the former

Pink Floyd legend. By this time Roy Hollingsworth's review of the Cambridge Corn Exchange gig had appeared in *Melody Maker*. This piece is said to have dismayed Syd and has been widely credited as the reason Stars broke up, but Jack Monck told me a few months later that Syd had just got 'cold feet' and the *Melody Maker* review, which was in fact almost wholly complimentary, had been just one factor among many that had undermined Syd's already fragile confidence.

In the summer of 1972 Syd started to visit London again with increasing regularity, hanging out with Steve Took in Ladbroke Grove and occasionally jamming with the former Tyrannosaurus Rex man. The two men's paths had previously converged when Took contributed conga drums to the initial *Madcap Laughs* sessions in 1968. Took had been an integral part of the original Tyrannosaurus Rex duo, delicately augmenting Marc Bolan's songs with an array of exotic instrumentation and unique vocal effects, but his career and life went into freefall when Bolan ruthlessly jettisoned him from the band in 1969 in order to pursue his dream of pop stardom.

A *Melody Maker* interview in January 1972 found Took residing in hedonistic squalor in a squat near the Westway flyover, and financially dependent on occasional handouts from Essex Music, publishers of Tyrannosaurus Rex's output, money which Took promptly spent on drugs or big blow-out meals for his Ladbroke Grove friends. Move manager Tony Secunda began representing him around this time, securing an advance of £30,000 from Warner Brothers with the aim of turning the perennially untogether Took into an unlikely underground superstar. During the latter part of 1972 and early 1973 the basement flat of Secunda's Mayfair home became Freeloader Central as Took and what seemed like half the hippy population of W11 decamped there intent on having a good time at Warner's expense. Unsurprisingly, the ensuing recording sessions, which took place in the basement flat's recording studio invariably descended into uncoordinated jams and glorified drug binges. It was during this period that Syd is said to have played on sessions for the ill-fated Warner LP. Secunda did little to dispel the rumours and although there is no firm evidence to connect Syd to any of the recordings that were completed he certainly participated in numerous jam sessions at the Mayfair flat and does appear to have been the direct inspiration behind one song, later released as 'Syd's Wine'.

It was also around this time that journalist Nick Kent, then writing for *Frendz* magazine, met his hero at the underground magazine's headquarters at 309 Portobello Road. 'I'd seen Syd Barrett in 1967 when I was fifteen years of age,' he told me. 'I remember looking at him and, even though he was clearly in a bad state, they weren't even playing one of his songs live and he was just standing there and retuning his guitar for about fifteen minutes – but he had such incredible charisma . . . when I started writing for *Frendz*, which would be five years later, I met him. He was being managed by the guy who was the so-called financial assistant at *Frendz*. He was still very good-looking, but very haunted, unforgettably haunted. His eyes were kind of scary to look at. I remember asking him, "Syd, I hear you're getting a group together." And he said, "I ate eggs and bacon for breakfast this morning," in this sort of whisper. I asked him again what he had for breakfast and he said, "I'm sorry, I don't speak French," and then just walked out of the room. To go from being the person in my wildest dreams I couldn't imagine myself being in 1967 to this really sad human being . . . '

Nigel Lesmoir-Gordon had a similar encounter in Trinity Street in Cambridge when he bumped into Syd one day. 'He turned to me and said, "Nigel, one day you won't need that beard," and just walked on. His one and only line. "Nigel, you won't always need that beard." And I haven't got it now, so he was quite right.'

Exchanges like these became increasingly common, as Syd hid behind non sequiturs and vagueness in order to ward off friends, fans and music-biz contacts alike. Even Duggie Fields was subject to the 'put on' on one of the last occasions he saw Syd, at the Speakeasy. 'I was with Marc Bolan and June, but I wasn't sure that Syd recognised me, or if he was just playing at it. You weren't always sure with Syd whether he was winding you up. But he did do that when he was at his best. It was a witty, fun thing for him to do. He liked challenging people. Even when he was playing, Syd was always challenging. He was the one who would push the free form and you never knew what he was going to do. That was where the excitement came. But I think he had to put up the barriers. The "keep out" sign went up.'

Throughout the early 1970s Syd's cult status continued to grow in inverse proportion to his availability. Interest was further buoyed by a plethora of re-issues. A compilation on EMI's budget label Starline, entitled *Relics*, was issued in May 1971. In December 1973 the first two Pink Floyd albums were repackaged as a double set, *A Nice Pair*, on the Harvest label. Syd's reputation was also considerably enhanced in November 1973 by the inclusion of a version of 'See Emily Play' on David Bowie's *Pin Ups* LP. Sustained by the royalties that these releases generated he began spending money like it was going out of fashion. At one point he was turning up regularly at Lupus Music and asking for money to buy a new guitar, a compulsive gesture that was finally curtailed by Bryan Morrison when he had about thirty.

'He came into the office one day and said something about the hotel,' says Cora Barnes. 'I said, "What hotel Syd?" and he said, "I'm living at the Penta Hotel now," which was a big hotel in the Cromwell Road. I said "What are you doing at the Penta?" He said, "Oh, its great there. You pick up the phone and ask for something and they bring it." I said, "Syd, have you any idea how much this is costing you?" He said, "Oh, I think I can afford it." I said, "Syd, this is crazy," so I went out and found him a flat for £20 a week in Chelsea Cloisters in Sloane Avenue. I organised a van to go and pick up some of his stuff and all his guitars. When he came in a month or so later I said, "How's the flat?" He said, "It's great, Cora. I've got all my guitars in there." I said, "Well, that's good. Are you enjoying living there?" He said, "Oh, I don't live there. I still live at the Penta!" '

In what would turn out to be a last-ditch attempt to get some return on his investment, Bryan Morrison sounded out Peter Jenner about the possibility of getting his client back into the studio again. Syd seemed agreeable to the notion and on Monday, 12 August 1974, Jenner, along with engineers John Leckie and Pat Stapley, returned to Abbey Road studios to produce what would turn out to be his last-ever recording dates. The sessions went on for four days, until Thursday, 15 August, and were an unmitigated disaster. Despite still looking every inch the haunted romantic poet/pop star, and turning up with an impressive array of brand new equipment Syd proved to be singularly incapable of producing anything that was usable.

'I was so excited at the thought of going back with Syd and I was so disappointed that he hadn't come back,' says Jenner. 'I was hoping he had emerged from the fog but he was still in the fog. He didn't seem happy in the studio. He wasn't happy doing it. He'd do a bit, chug along a bit then he'd leave. Sometimes he'd come back and sometimes he didn't. I can't remember how many days we spent there but it wasn't an awful long time. There wasn't a lot of contact. I don't think he knew why he was there or what he was meant to be doing. I tried. The engineers tried. We just ran the tape to try and see what would come out. There would be bits and pieces and we'd try to capture them. "Do that bit again, Syd. Try to make it a bit longer," y'know. And then it was gone again. It was the most frustrating elusive thing. It was like a cut-up, a collage of bits and pieces, then mess. No coherence at all that I could detect. There might have been an internal coherence that I didn't detect.'

Listening to the recordings that have survived from these sessions it's impossible to disagree with Jenner's assessment. Syd played lead and rhythm guitar and occasionally dubbed on a bit of bass, but nothing of substance emerged. In fact anyone who thinks that there was anything left in the tank by 1974 should be allowed to listen to the meagre scraps that have surfaced on bootleg from those final desperate days in Abbey Road. Arbitrarily named by Jenner, Leckie and Stapley, primarily for studio cataloguing purposes, the working track titles are as perfunctory as the dispiriting efforts that were being logged. Eleven pieces were recorded in all. 'If You Go', 'Don't Be Slow' (takes 1 and 2), 'Boogie #1', 'Boogie #2', 'Boogie #3', 'Chooka-Chooka Chug Chug', 'Slow Boogie', 'Fast Boogie', 'John Lee Hooker', 'Ballad' and 'Untitled'.

If the sessions reveal anything at all it is that Syd had been listening to a lot of twelve-bar blues, but by now he couldn't even execute a few basic blues licks particularly well. Within four years the busker strum of the *Barrett* album had ossified. Syd's sense of timing, never his strong point, was now pretty much shot. Just occasionally there are glimpses of something vaguely worthwhile on the tapes, a pretty melody line here, a competent bit of wah-wah playing there, hints of riffs and spacey lead runs that with a lot of perseverance, maybe, just maybe could have been worked up into something usable. Most of the time, though, Syd just churns out blues riffs in a variety of erratic tempos. Jenner and his fellow engineers did the best they could with the material available, dousing Syd's rudimentary efforts in echo, getting him to double-track where they thought they detected a hint of an idea. But ultimately no amount of studio trickery could disguise the paucity of inspiration on display. Syd wouldn't show his lyrics to anybody, and pretty soon it became obvious that he hadn't actually written any. On one occasion the studio was set up for a vocal take and Syd simply clammed up and refused to sing. More worryingly he took to unplugging his guitar while playing. This was no longer the gesture of a man given to making radical art statement. This was now reticence to the point of self-eradication.

One of the engineers noticed fairly early on in proceedings that if Syd turned left when he walked out of the studio he was going to the canteen and would eventually return and resume the session. But if he turned right it was safe to assume he wouldn't be back. On the fourth night Syd turned right one last time and didn't come back again. Ever. He retired to the seclusion of Chelsea Cloisters to close the curtains and confront the long dark night of his soul. In his absence the legend flourished.

Chapter Eight

Proverbs and Sobs

Poor Ratty did his best, by degrees, to explain things: but how could he put into cold words what had mostly been suggestion? How recall, for another's benefit, the haunting sea voices that had sung to him, how reproduce at second-hand the magic of the Seafarer's hundred reminiscences? Even to himself, now the spell was broken, and the glamour gone, he found it difficult to account for what had seemed, some hours ago, the inevitable and only thing. It is not surprising, then, that he failed to convey to the Mole any clear idea of what he had been through that day.

THE WIND IN THE WILLOWS KENNETH GRAHAME

For anyone seeking rhyme and reason in Syd Barrett's brief performing career, or explanations for his disenchanted withdrawal from the pop life, there are clues to be found in the interviews that he gave between 1967 and 1971. One can plot a logical route through Syd's various public pronouncements that broadly mirrors his trajectory as a musician. In his initial encounters with the media he is effusive, eager to please, sometimes compliant to the point of blandness. In later interviews he can be as unlinear and obtuse as the songs on his solo albums. Generally though he is polite, thoughtful and as candid as circumstances permit. He is unfailingly sincere about his intentions, his ambitions (or lack of), his motivation (ditto) and his failings. He is in turn wistful, regretful, open, honest and painfully self-analytical.

Syd was, of course, far more than the sum of his public pronouncements. He never actively sought out the glare of publicity any more than he did the glare of the spotlight while on stage. Interviews, like much else he encountered in the pop world, were an obligation to be endured. One frequently detects a diffident shrug or a bemused and quizzical tone in Syd's responses to questions, as if to say, 'What has any of this got to do with me, or my creativity?' Having said that, it is extremely instructive to look at what Syd *did* say in his interviews because they do much to demystify the man. A train of logic can usually be found even in his most gnomic utterances, which offers useful insights into the way he thought and felt and experienced the world.

The first time Syd was directly quoted in an interview was in a feature on the emerging underground scene, made in January 1967 by the Canadian Broadcasting Company. Syd's explanation of the band's musical transition from R&B covers to sonic voyagers is refreshingly matter-of-fact and not in the least bit media-savvy. 'Sometimes we just let loose a bit and started hitting the guitar a bit harder and not worrying quite so much about the chords,' he says. Roger Waters states, 'It stopped being sort of third-rate academic rock and started being intuitive groove,' to which Syd adds, 'It's free form. In terms of construction it's almost like jazz, where you start off with a riff and then you improvise.'

Syd is more enthused when talking about the sensation and spectacle of the light show than he is about the mechanics of musical technique. 'You can respond to the lights and the lights will respond back,' he says. This is the authentic response of a man who lives for the moment, hardwired to the 'direct stimulus' as he calls the light show. 'Freedom is what I'm after,' he told *Disc and Music Echo* in April 1967. 'That's why I like working in this group. There is such freedom artistically.'

Asked to explain his songwriting he is given to mundane generalities that shed little light on his methodology. ' "Arnold Layne" is nothing but a pop record, it wasn't meant to represent anything in particular,' he told Nick Jones of *Melody Maker*. 'I thought Arnold Layne was a nice name and fitted well into the music I had already composed. I pinched the line "moonshine washing line" from Roger, our bass guitarist, because he had an enormous washing line in the back garden of his house. Then I thought, "Arnold must have a hobby," and it went from there.'

In the same interview he is defiant when discussing the moral implications of Arnold's 'strange hobby'. 'Arnold Layne just happens to dig dressing up in women's clothing. Lots of people do, so let's face up to reality,' he told Jones. 'About the only lyric anyone could object to is the bit about "takes two to know", and there's nothing smutty about that. But then if more people like them dislike us, more people like the underground lot are going to dig us, so we hope they'll cancel each other out.'

A mixture of bemusement and prickliness can be detected in these responses, derived in equal measure from the ridiculously censorial attitude from Radio London who had recently banned 'Arnold Layne', and from the general air of scepticism and ridicule that had greeted Pink Floyd's arrival on the pop scene. In early 1967 the pop papers were full of comments from the likes of Dave Dee and the Tremeloes, who dismissed the band's music as a gimmick and took a high moral tone about its supposed drug connotations. 'The Pink Floyd are supposed to be a progressive group, yet from what I've heard, they are just using all these gimmicks to help get a rather bad stage act across to the audience,' the Tremeloes' Alan Blakely told *Disc and Music Echo*. Such diatribes from the established pop stars of the day were commonplace throughout the first half of 1967 and the majority of comments from the readers of the pop weeklies were generally in accord with these sentiments. The letters pages of *NME, Disc,*

Record Mirror et al. carried fulsome endorsement of such views, condemning 'the Beatles, and their ilk, for deserting their fans to pursue this flower power nonsense'.

In the notionally more sympathetic *Melody Maker* Procol Harum pianist Gary Brooker witheringly dismissed Pink Floyd in the paper's 'Blind Date' feature with the words: 'The Pink Floyd. I can tell by that horrible organ sound.' A somewhat disingenuous comment from a member of a band that had swapped R&B covers for cloaks and kaftans only a few months earlier and had immediately been dismissed as arrivistes by the notoriously snobby UFO crowd.

Pink Floyd made their first major television appearance on the BBC2 arts programme *The Look of the Week*, on Sunday, 14 May 1967, two days after their critically lauded Games For May concert at the Queen Elizabeth Hall. Made by the corporation's presentation department, presented by Robert Robinson and produced by Lorna Pegram, the programme was a spin-off from the channel's daily arts strand, *Late Night Line Up*.

The previous week's edition of *The Look of the Week* had been given over to art critic Robert Hughes' report on Florence, six months after the flood which had destroyed much of the city's valuable art treasures. The week following Pink Floyd's appearance, the programme featured a discussion with Mick Jagger and Professor John Cohen entitled, 'The relationship between artist and audience and how this is changing', partly based around Peter Watkins' controversial and provocative new film *Privilege*, which featured ex-Manfred Mann singer Paul Jones in the lead role.

Everything about that evening's BBC2 schedule seemed to guarantee Pink Floyd a rarefied and privileged platform more in keeping with high art than the usual programming procedures and context of a pop show. The night Pink Floyd appeared on *The Look of the Week*, the programme followed a repeat of a one about Vincent Van Gogh in the *Contours of Genius* series, which had first been shown in March 1966, and was followed in the schedules by the solemn opening of the new Roman Catholic cathedral in Liverpool.

The five-minute interview with the band was the opening feature of the programme. On the same show author Christopher Isherwood talked to Robert Robinson about his novel about sexuality and spirituality, *A Meeting by the River*, and painter Dame Laura Knight talked about her life and work on the eve of a major retrospective at the Upper Grosvenor Galleries.

In such company, Pink Floyd, notionally at least, were guaranteed a sympathetic hearing. The band's avant-garde leanings would have been understood and indulged by the programme-makers, and would have fitted comfortably into the corporation's overwhelmingly middle-class milieu.

Having said that, *The Look of the Week* was by no means an elitist programme. Previous editions of the show had featured items as diverse as the state of light entertainment comedy, featuring Dick Emery, Terry Scott and Hugh Lloyd, and Benny Hill, a preview of Roland Petit's new ballet *Paradise Lost*, featuring Dame Margot Fonteyn and Rudolf Nureyev, an under-sevens children's poetry competition, sponsored by the pre-Murdoch *Sun* newspaper, with the winning entry read by Judi Dench, and a preview of Danny La Rue's new stage show.

When Pink Floyd appeared on *The Look of the Week*, the release of *Sgt Pepper's Lonely Hearts Club Band*, the album that would do most to 'respectabilise' pop and bring it to the wider attention of the cultural intelligentsia, was still three weeks away, and although it had been four years since William Mann, in typically florid prose, had written in *The Times* of Lennon and McCartney's 'pandiatonic clusters' and 'flat sub-mediant key-switches', pop music had rarely received the kind of prestigious television patronage that Pink Floyd were now being granted.

The feature was presented by musician, lecturer, writer and

broadcaster Hans Keller. The son of a successful architect father and a gifted amateur musician mother, Keller fled Nazi-ridden Vienna in 1938 when he was nineteen. A proficient violin and viola player, he became music advisor to the British Film Institute and an eminent music critic responsible for an innovative wordless method of musical critique called functional analysis. Keller was also a member of the British Psychoanalytic Society and had a keen interest in Freudian psychology and the psychoanalysis of music. In 1959 he joined the BBC's music division and became head of *Music Talks*.

The Look of the Week's producer Lorna Pegram, then aged forty, went on to produce the groundbreaking modern art series *The Shock of the New*, and in 1967 was fast developing a track record in innovative arts programming. No doubt she thought that the pairing of the idiosyncratic Keller and Pink Floyd would lead to a lively televisual encounter. Unfortunately it didn't quite work out like that.

Keller possessed a confrontational interview technique to match the abrasive style of his music writing, and if the BBC's programme-makers were hoping this meeting of musical worlds would pay off they were to be sadly disappointed. Keller comes across with a mixture of bemusement, condescension and contempt.

'The Pink Floyd. You're going to hear them in a minute and I don't want to prejudice you,' he says disingenuously. 'Hear them and see them first and we'll talk about them afterwards. But four quick points I want to make before you hear them. The first is that what you heard at the beginning, that short bit, those first few seconds, are really all I can hear in them, which is to say to my mind there is continuous repetition and proportionately they are a bit boring. My second point is that they are terribly loud; you couldn't quite hear that because, of course, from your sets it isn't as loud as it is in the studio and as it was in the Festival Hall and Queen Elizabeth Hall on Friday. My third point is that perhaps I am a little bit too much of a musician to fully appreciate them, and the reason why I say this is that, four, they have an audience and people who have an audience ought to be heard. Perhaps it's my fault that I don't appreciate them.'

Pink Floyd are seen performing two numbers. At the outset of the show there is a brief extract from 'Pow R. Toc H.'; Syd and Roger Waters are in flickering close-up, their mystique considerably enhanced by Peter Wynne Wilson's towering back projections. After Keller's introduction the band perform a somewhat perfunctory version of 'Astronomy Domine'. The vocals are mixed too low throughout and there are a couple of hesitant chord changes after the introductory verse. Again the cameras are drawn to Barrett and Waters. Rick Wright is mostly in silhouette apart from one brief close-up towards the end. Nick Mason is glimpsed equally briefly, resplendent in sheepskin coat. Syd's choreographed raised arm gestures during the song's descending 'whoo-oooo' vocal sequence look forced, possibly even scripted. He was never this demonstrative on stage at UFO and clearly isn't lost in the music, like he is in the German TV documentary or Peter Whitehead's footage from Sound Technique studios. On a couple of occasions he appears to be warily tracking where the cameras are.

After the truncated performance of 'Astronomy Domine' – a shade under four minutes – Waters and Barrett put their guitars down and sit on high stools next to Keller. Roger Waters clears his throat nervously as Keller asks his first question. Syd adopts the slightly gauche posture – hands on hips – of a man who is not fully at ease in the formal setting of a TV studio. There are a couple of moments during the interview where, eyes ablaze with passionate intensity, he gives considered and thoughtful answers to the questions that Keller puts to him. During much of the encounter though he wears an expression of benign amusement.

'Well, if I may first turn to Roger,' says Keller. 'I want to ask one fundamental question, of which our telly viewers may not be quite aware, of the significance of it, because they didn't hear all of it. Why has it got to be so terribly loud? For me, frankly, it's too loud, I just can't bear it – I happen to have grown up in the string quartet, which is a bit softer' – at this point Syd smiles broadly and looks to Waters supportively – 'so why has it got to be so loud, so amplified.'

'Well, I don't guess it has to be,' says Waters, in impeccable middle-class tones. Any viewers whose previous encounters with pop stars on television had been restricted to the provincial twang of the Beatles or the Animals, or Adam Faith politely bluffing his way through John Freeman's *Face to Face* would have been immediately alerted to the fact that, despite the apparently atonal caterwauling of the pop racket they had just heard, here was proper art show material, well-scrubbed middle-class boys with well-rounded grammar school vowels. 'But, I mean, that's the way we like it and we didn't grow up with a string quartet, and I guess that could be one of the reasons why it is loud. I mean it doesn't sound terribly loud to us,' concludes Waters.

'Yes,' counters Keller, with the dismissive tones of a head-master. 'Actually, not everybody who hasn't grown up in a string quartet turns into a loud pop group, so your reason is not altogether convincing, but I accept that you like it.' And with those world-weary words Keller's air of authoritarian disdain is stamped on the exchange from the outset. It could only have been enhanced in televisual terms if Keller had some paperwork he could have been absently attending to while Waters, R., and Barrett, R., of the lower fifth sat staring at their feet in the head-master's study. 'What I'm saying is that if one gets immune to this kind of sound one may find it difficult to appreciate softer types of sound. Syd? Yes? No?' continues Keller.

'I don't think that's so,' replies Syd earnestly. 'I mean everybody listens, we don't need it very loud to be able to hear it, and some of it is very quiet in fact. I personally like quiet music just as much as loud music. We play in large halls and things where obviously volume is necessary and when people dance they like volume.'

'Well, that's interesting,' says Keller, apparently amazed that pop musicians are capable of appreciating both quiet and loud music. 'When people dance,' he repeats. 'You did start, if I'm not mistaken, as a group, which accompanied dancing. Is that it? And how did you turn into a concertising group, if I may use the American term?'

Syd smiles at the use of the term 'concertising'. 'Well, we've only done two concerts in fact,' says Waters, 'because the main scene with pop music, which I guess is what we are at the moment, is that you play gigs round ballrooms and this sort of scene, because that's how it works at the moment. But we felt that there was no real reason, you know, why we shouldn't do an organised concert in a large hall, where people came and sat and actually listened to what we do. Because dance halls generally speaking are not very good places to actually listen to the music – most people come along, and the music for most of them, as been, over the past few years anyway, just a sort of background noise that they can jig about to.'

Keller asks Syd if the two concerts were successful. 'Yes, I think so,' he says. 'When we play – I think the way the act's developed in the last six months has been influenced rather a lot by the fact that we've played in ballrooms necessarily, because, you know, this is obviously the first market. But I think at concerts it's given us a chance to realise that maybe the music we play isn't directed at dancing necessarily like normal pop groups have been in the past.'

'Have you encountered any hostility towards your creation?' asks Keller. 'Well, yes, we have,' says Waters. 'But, I mean, I guess there's been quite a lot of hostility going on in odd places in the country. I mean, the only hostility we've actually seen of course is that which has hit the national press and things. The sort of professional knockers like Robert Pitman and people who've had a go at us.'

'Do you in turn feel aggressive towards the audiences?' asks Keller. 'No, not at all,' respond Waters and Barrett in unison. 'In spite of all the loudness you don't?' queries Keller. 'There's not many young people who dislike it,' says Barrett with a hint of hurt in his voice. 'There's no shock treatment intended?' asks Keller, incredulously. 'No, certainly not,' counters Syd, his wounded tone clearly evident. 'Some people think that we deliberately try and sort of shock the audience and make them, you know, by the volume and keep them quiet, sort of thing. But this isn't so.'

'Well, there it is,' concludes Keller to camera. 'I think you can pass your verdict as well as I can. My verdict is that it is a little bit of a regression to childhood, but, after all, why not?'

True to his schooling in Freudian psychoanalysis Keller hears the bird calls, scat sounds and onomatopoeia on 'Pow R. Toc H.', and Syd's descending chords, mock-scary ghost noises and comic-book sci-fi imagery in 'Astronomy Domine' and draws his text-book conclusions. He did have a point though. The following Sunday Pink Floyd went into Abbey Road studios and recorded 'Bike'!

Interviews with Syd at the height of his fame are few and far between and what encounters there are point to a man who was showing great reluctance to play the fame game. The 19 August issue of *New Musical Express* featured Pink Floyd in its regular 'Lifelines' column. This was a long-running *NME* slot, a 'facts and info' questionnaire typical of teen-mag fare at the time. Bands or artists (or, more often than not, their publicity agents) were required to provide details of themselves in thirty-five categories, ranging from name, date of birth and place of birth to favourite colour, likes, dislikes, star sign, hobbies, pets and car. While the rest of the band dutifully filled out most of the categories Syd left fourteen of them blank and only minimally engaged with the rest. Where Roger Waters was happy to play the whacky pop star (Musical Education – twelve years on the spoons. Favourite colour – multi) Syd only filled in the most basic details of his life. We learn that his favourite drink is Campari and soda and that he has a cat called Rover but the only entry under Brother's and Sister's Names is Rosemary. He offers nothing at all for biggest break in career, biggest influence on career, favourite band/instrumentalists, favourite composers, likes, dislikes, personal ambition and professional ambition. Such refusal was virtually unheard of at the time. Even the Beatles played the game. Every straight black line against every one of Syd's unanswered categories looked like a slash mark on the printed page. A gesture of contempt for the whole superficial charade.

Chris Welch fared a little better when Syd participated in the *Melody Maker*'s 'Blind Date' feature, but even this was fraught with problems. 'Blind Date', like 'Lifelines' for *NME*, was a *Melody Maker* regular, and its simple format has been much copied since. The journalist would play a selection of records to that week's guest without revealing who they were by. The feature was hugely popular and on a good week revealed much about the particular guest's likes and dislikes and the way they thought about music. It threw up occasional surprises, not to mention the occasional faux pas when a particular guest failed to recognise a good mate and criticised his latest endeavour.

'It was a *Melody Maker* institution,' says Chris Welch, who conducted the feature with Syd. 'The Beatles had done it. John Lennon loved it. He'd been the first person to say, "That was a load of crap." You never quite knew how people would react. Some people loved it and knew what to do. Others were awful. Chuck Berry had no idea of presentation or press. He sat there scribbling one out of ten on a piece of paper and saying, "Will that do?" How do you explain to Chuck Berry that that's no good? You have to talk to me about the music. Syd was a lot easier than Chuck Berry.'

Syd's 'Blind Date' encounter took place during the period when he was first beginning to manifest signs of discontent with the pop process. 'There was some trepidation,' says Welch. 'I remember going for dinner with the Floyd at some stage in Notting Hill. It was rather a privilege, but I think they wanted someone to explain their problems to and they talked to me about Syd rather despairingly. The management, Andrew and Peter, wanted me to interview him and when I went to see Syd I think the idea was to give him a bit of therapy and encourage him. As it turned out he was very friendly. I think he was quite amused by the whole idea. It wasn't just another sit-down "When's the tour, what songs are you writing" interview. Being "Blind Date" I actually turned up with a rather battered portable record player and a pile of the latest singles. I was ushered into this cell of a room and locked in with Syd, I remember looking out through this darkened window and everyone was peering in to see if Syd was going to attack me or live up to his reputation. I heard someone whispering, "He's talking to him." I'd broken the first barrier and got him to speak.'

Syd politely played along with the format, enjoying Alex Harvey's 'The Sunday Song' and the Blues Magoos' 'One by One'. 'You're going to tell me it's the Byrds,' he responded to the latter. 'I really dig the Byrds, Mothers of Invention and the Fugs. We have drawn quite a bit from those groups.'

'I played him Jim Reeves' "Trying To Forget" and to my amazement he guessed immediately,' remembers Welch. 'He said, let's see, who's dead? This must be Jim Reeves. He knew more about pop music than he was letting on. He was playing a little game with me. All was going well, then I played him a David Bowie track, "Love You Till Tuesday". I assumed he would like Bowie but I was wrong. His mood changed rather abruptly from being amused to being annoyed. He'd been funny up until then. "That's a joke," he said coldly, "but I like jokes." He was being quite menacing. But it only occurred to me recently, I was playing Pink Floyd's "The Gnome", and he may have seen young David Bowie as some sort of upstart, copying his style. More quirky songs about gnomes. Maybe that's why he didn't like him or appreciate what he was doing.'

It has been noted that the songs Syd wrote during the second half of 1967 were getting darker and more abstract. So did his encounters with the pop press. 'It's better not to have a set goal. You'd be very narrow-minded if you did,' he told Debbie Smith from *Go* magazine, who dropped into a post-Piper recording session. 'All I know is that I'm beginning to think less now. It's getting better.'

This encounter took place during the period when the Floyd were recording 'Vegetable Man', 'Scream Thy Last Scream' and the aborted John Latham sessions. The *Go* reporter responded to Syd's desire to think less with, 'Well, if you stop thinking entirely you might as well be a vegetable.' 'Yeah,' agrees Syd.

In what would turn out to be his last interview with Pink Floyd, Syd is even more terse and to the point than he was with the journalist from *Go* magazine. In the 9 December issue of *Melody Maker* he tells writer Alan Walsh that he 'couldn't care less' that 'Apples and Oranges' wasn't a hit and that 'he feels that the application of commercial considerations is harmful to the music. He'd like to cut out the record company, wholesalers and retailers. "All middle men are bad," he says.'

'The group has been through a very confusing stage over the last few months and I think this has been reflected in their work,' adds Peter Jenner, with admirable understatement. Syd's parting shot in the interview is both poignant and prescient. 'Really, we have only just started to scrape the surface of effects and ideas of lights and music combined,' he says. 'We think that the music and the lights are part of the same scene, one enhances and adds to the other. But we feel that in the future groups are going to have to offer much more than just a pop show. They'll have to offer a well-presented theatre show.'

These are the perceptions of a man who has endured twelve months of twelve-minute slots on package tours, pointless appearances on inappropriate TV shows, and countless badly lit, badly amplified and badly received performances in provincial ballrooms. As was the case with his reluctance to mime and his refusal to fill in inane questionnaires, Syd was once again showing that he was ahead of the game. He envisaged a future where multimedia spectacle was going to become the norm, and where light shows and other visual aspects of performance were going to have to become integrated parts of any live show. These carefully considered and lucidly articulated observations hardly fit the stereotype of the irresponsible drug-addled wreck who was supposedly so incapable of performing and so impossible to work with that he was about to be edged out of his own band.

These were the last words that the pop world would hear from Syd Barrett for nearly two years. It would be a very different Syd who re-emerged at the turn of the decade to promote *The Madcap Laughs* LP.

Late on in his madness the poet John Clare was taken by the watchmaker and benefactor Thomas Inskip to have tea with G. J. de Wilde, the editor of the *Northampton Mercury*. Also present at the occasion was minor poet John Dalby. The encounter with Clare led Dalby to commemorate the moment in verse, one part of which read:

> And we sat listening as to some fond child
> The wayward unconnected words he said
> Prattle by confused recollections fed,
> Of famous times gone by.

307

There was something of this in Syd's later press encounters. His songs had grown more tangential and convoluted and he now had an interview 'style' to match. As more than one interviewer pointed out, Syd's thought processes and articulation were frequently hard to follow, but even the most obscure utterances were shot through with moments of painful confessional honesty, leavened with whimsy and humour, as he laid bare, as never before, his honest feelings about the pop process.

In the 31 January 1970 issue of *Melody Maker*, under the heading 'Confusion and Mr Barrett', Syd was interviewed by Chris Welch. Welch was a sympathetic spirit and long-time Floyd supporter who had done one of the first ever Pink Floyd interviews in early 1967. In his 1970 encounter with Syd he describes *Madcap* as 'an extraordinary solo album of odd eccentric songs' and refers to Syd's 'gaunt good looks and the same gentle humour as his old compatriots'. The stark black-and-white photo which accompanies the piece bears out the first part of that observation, showing Syd in half-lit profile with prominent cheekbones, dark deep-set eyes, several days' stubble and dishevelled hair. 'He seemed happy enough to talk this week and while it was easy enough to detect a mood of mild elation and surprise at the interest being shown in him, it was not always so easy to understand his erratic train of thought,' says Welch. Astutely he adds 'But he was eager to be helpful and I suspect only as confused as he wanted to be.'

In their 1967 'Blind Date' encounter Welch had been quick to spot that his subject was capable of 'the put on' and he seemed less than phased by the more intimidating aspects of Syd's personality. By 1970 Welch was a music journalist of some repute. His comic creation, Jiving K. Boots, his Bonzo-esque sense of humour and his frequently hilarious and irreverent singles reviews brought much needed levity to the pages of the often dour and over-earnest *Melody Maker*. As a result, his 1970 encounter with Syd was both relaxed and insightful. 'I asked him if he liked the music scene and he said, "It's great here. I never go anywhere else." I thought that was rather charming,' Welch remembers.

Among the pleasantries and generalities, Syd mentions that the *Madcap* album had been recorded at a reasonable pace, that he wasn't over enamoured with a single ('Octopus') being lifted from it, and that he wasn't particularly hard up for money. He reveals that there are vague plans to get a band together and that he has been writing fairly regularly and hasn't been bored. On the subject of his former band he says, 'When I was with the Floyd the form of the music played on stage was mainly governed by the records. Now I seem to have got back to my previous state of mind. With the volume used they [were] inclined to push me a little.'

Syd doesn't reveal what this 'previous state of mind' is, but it can be readily assumed that he is referring to a period, pre-1967, before his creative life became weighed down by pressure and responsibility. Having said that he makes light of his latter-day problems with Pink Floyd.

'Yes, there were hang-ups when I was with them,' he admits. 'Although it was not due to the travelling or anything, which you just put in the category of being a regular activity in that kind of job.'

This matter-of-fact response counteracts many of the concerns raised by management and friends alike about the sheer punishing work-rate endured by the band in 1967, and steers attention towards deeper personality conflicts within the band, as well as broader conflicts of artistic interest and intent. The reference to 'that kind of job' is pertinent too. An interesting choice of words.

Syd makes another telling comment when reflecting on his final days with the Floyd. 'It's been very exciting, especially when

I went to America for two weeks before the split up,' he says. 'Then we came back and played at the Albert Hall, and it was very much a crescendo and I felt good. I miss playing to audiences although I haven't missed it so much recently.'

These enthused observations counteract almost every story that has emerged about the torrid time the band supposedly endured with an increasingly unstable Syd during their American visit, and the subsequent Hendrix package tour. *Disc and Music Echo* would appear to verify Syd's account in its gushing review of the triumphant Albert Hall concert, which took place on 14 November 1967 at the start of the package tour:

Possibly the most interesting act was the Pink Floyd's, fresh from playing hippie emporiums on America's West Coast with what must be the best light show yet seen in this country . . . they played hard rock material with drummer Nick Mason laying down some beautiful rhythms and guitarist Syd Barrett hitting some incredible flights of fantasy . . . a very satisfying set.

Syd remains good-natured throughout the Welch interview, stating that '*Top of the Pops* is all right. You meet interesting people and there are always interesting people around [that] I know and are prepared to like me.' He is less enthusiastic, though, about the music business as a whole. Asked if he is satisfied with his new LP he replies, 'Well – no. I always find recording difficult. I can only think in terms of, well, I'm pleased with forty minutes of sound, but I can't in terms of the pop industry. It's only a beginning. I've written a lot more stuff.'

There it is, laid out in plain unambiguous terms, the yawning gulf between creativity and packaging. Syd can deal with forty minutes of sound. The rest is promotion and bullshit.

'Syd occasionally laughed, seemed agitated or trailed away into silence during our conversation,' says Welch. 'Anything that seemed uninteresting or irrelevant merely provoked strained or disordered replies.'

In an interview with Giovanni Dadomo for *Sounds* magazine in June 1970 which was unpublished at the time, Syd's answers are mostly brief and to the point, but no less revealing for it. He distances himself from any supposed spiritual immersion in the *I Ching*, claiming simply that when he wrote 'Chapter 24' 'there was someone around who was into that'. He also rejects the idea that any of his Pink Floyd material was influenced by sci-fi. 'Not really,' he says 'except *Journey into Space* and *Quatermass* which was when I was about fifteen.' He is more willing to concede that there was a strong fairy-tale and nursery-rhyme element to his songs. 'Fairy tales are nice,' he says blandly. 'I think a lot of it has to do with living in Cambridge, with nature and everything, it's so clean and I still drive back a lot.' More ominously he adds, 'leaving school and suddenly being without that structure around you and nothing to relate to, maybe that's part of it too'. This apparent afterthought tacitly acknowledges that fairy tales functioned as a security motif in his songs, providing grounding and emotional stability, a harking back to an Arcadian childhood. The great unspoken, of course, is his father.

Elsewhere he is characteristically matter-of-fact about 'the job' as he was with Chris Welch. In response to a question about how his art training affected his writing, Syd pares the art school influence down to the practicalities of 'the rate of work, learning to work hard'. The equating of art school with discipline rather than philosophy or ideology is revealing. Lyrics generally came quick to Syd. This was in sharp contrast to the sheer amount of graft that he was prepared to put into his painting. Music was pure unmediated response. Art he clearly thought of as a long-term apprenticeship. He does, however, betray a poignant glimpse into the creative lethargy that had settled upon him while living at Wetherby Mansions with Duggie Fields. It was at this point that Syd came out with that ominous comment about why he didn't paint much now: 'The guy who lives next door to me paints and he's doing it well, so I don't really feel the need.'

Creeping ennui is also evident in his response to the question, 'How's the guitar playing?' 'I suppose I could do with some practice,' he concedes. In answering the question, 'Do you want to do other things?', he clearly has old Cambridge mates in mind when he replies, 'A lot of people want to make films and do photography and things, but I'm quite happy doing what I'm doing.' Which at the time, of course, was less and less! With the forthcoming Extravaganza '70 gig at Kensington Olympia in mind Dadomo asks if he is looking forward to singing and playing live again. 'I used to enjoy it, it was a gas,' says Syd. 'But so's doing nothing. It's art school laziness really.'

He expresses mild dissatisfaction that the *Madcap Laughs* album was 'released far too long after it was done', and reveals that 'I wanted it to be a whole thing that people would listen to all the way through with everything related and balanced, the tempos and moods offsetting each other, and I hope that's what it sounds like.'

His parting shot, although relatively upbeat, seems tinged with frustration, desperation even. 'I feel as if I've got lots of things, much better things to do still, that's why there isn't really a lot to say, I just want to get it all done.'

A year later, in March 1971, when he spoke to Michael Watts of *Melody Maker* there was still a lot to get done but he still hadn't done any of it. Syd had hit limbo-land. So too, arguably, had rock music, which was still hung up on the 1960s. 'New Beatle Klaus Goes into Hiding,' read the teasing headline on the cover of the issue of *Melody Maker* that carried Watts' Syd interview. The headline, typical of the period, was publicising a total non-story about bass player Klaus Voormann being lined up to replace Paul McCartney in a new version of the Beatles. Upon reading further it became clear that this titillating rumour, started by the *Daily Mirror* and roundly denied by all parties involved, was based on nothing more than the fact that Voormann had recently been staying with George and Patti Harrison at their Oxfordshire home.

'Everyone was waiting for the Beatles to get back together,' remembers Nick Kent. 'Editors were always saying, "Let's see what the Beatles are doing this month." Were they in a restaurant together? Can we get the Beatles back together? Can we get the Sixties back starting all over again? Can Bob Dylan dress in the same clothes he wore in 1966, take a lot of speed and write the follow up to *Blonde on Blonde*? We younger writers generally knew that that was over.'

Syd Barrett was now as much a part of that wish list as Dylan or the Beatles. When was Syd going to rejoin Pink Floyd, dress in all his finery and bring back psychedelia? And when was he going to record that reputation-salvaging magnificent third album? That was the subtext as Syd's absence from the public arena grew longer. Watts' piece was no exception. 'He is painfully conscious of his indeterminate role in the music world,' he notes in his introduction. 'I've never really proved myself wrong. I really need to prove myself right,' claims Syd in a typical non sequitorial flourish.

Watts' two-page interview, which featured in the 27 March issue of *Melody Maker*, carried a photo of the newly shorn Syd. 'His hair is cut very short now, almost like a skinhead. Symbolic? Of what, then?' asks Watts. The interview was carried out during the period when Syd was living back at Hills Road, during his brief engagement to Gayla Pinion. 'I've been at home in Cambridge with my mother,' he says. 'I've been getting used to a family existence generally. Pretty unexciting. I work in a cellar.'

In his earlier *Melody Maker* encounters with Chris Welch Syd had been guaranteed a sympathetic hearing. Welch was an enthusiastic champion of both the Floyd and Syd's solo work and wrote accordingly. Watts, however, was not such an ardent fan. 'I am afraid I have little recall of Syd Barrett beyond what I wrote at the time, save that I now realise he was clearly mad and not merely an "acid casualty", says Watts now. 'I also fear that he was not as important as his obits suggest. He was an interesting but minor figure, whose derangement has heightened his reputation.'

Like Chris Welch, Watts makes the point in his interview that Syd's thought processes are not always easy to follow. 'He is very aware of what is going on around him, but his conversation is often obscure; it doesn't always progress in linear fashion,' he says.

'Syd appeared just like all the other acid casualties of the time, rambling and unfocused, but he was one who never recovered,' says Watts now. 'In hindsight, yes, he was obviously nutso. Nothing wrong with that, but he didn't turn it to significant artistic advantage. His early Floyd singles were better than anything on *Madcap Laughs* – a rather cruel and exploitative title, don't you think? Bet he didn't devise it.'

David Gilmour claims credit for the album title but strongly refutes any notion that it was exploitative. 'It was my idea to lift that phrase from the lyric to "Octopus". It seemed and seems to me that "madcap" is a word that described Syd well and is not at all the same as "madman". "Madcap" to me is jolly, original, it is a kind word, where "madman" obviously is not.'

Despite Michael Watts' lack of empathy, and some noticeably slack subediting (or perhaps calculated subediting in order to drive home a point), Syd's 1971 *Melody Maker* encounter is one of the most revealing interviews that he ever gave.

'What would you sooner be – a painter or a musician?' asks Watts. 'Well, I think of me being a painter eventually,' says Syd unequivocally. From the outset Syd is keen to establish his credentials as an artist, responding to Watts' gentle opening enquiry about what he has been doing since leaving Pink Floyd with a resolute 'I'm a painter. I was trained as a painter,' although he is honest enough to admit, 'I seem to have spent a little less time painting than I might have done.' He acknowledges this lapse from his primary creative impulse by saying, 'You know, it might have been a tremendous release getting absorbed in painting.' Which begs the question, released from what? Pink Floyd? The pressures of pop fame? Obligations to the music industry? Some deeper creative or personal trauma?

For much of the interview he appears to be having an internal dialogue with himself. 'I feel like I'm jabbering,' he admits at one point. He is also honest enough to admit that 'The fine art thing at college was always too much for me to think about . . . it didn't transcend the feeling of playing at UFO, and those sorts of places with the lights and that.' This decision, agonised over during 1966 and the early part of 1967, would come back to haunt Syd through the coming decades, but here it is laid bare, a frank admission that the rigour of academic discipline was too much for him and that he was momentarily seduced by the sights sounds and sensations of UFO and the underground. Those seductive impulses had of course withered to a fading memory by 1971. 'What happened at Tottenham Court Road when we started was a microcosm of what happened later,' Syd told Chris Welch in January 1970. When asked about the underground by Giovanni Dadomo a few months later he replies with indifference. 'I haven't been to the Arts Lab or anything so I don't really know what's happening. There are just so many people running around doing different things and no kind of unity. It doesn't really bother me.' By the time he talks to Michael Watts early in 1971 his disillusion and detachment are complete. 'The general concept – I didn't feel so conscious of it as perhaps I should,' he says. 'I mean, one's position as a member of London's young people's – I dunno what you'd call it – underground, wasn't it? – wasn't necessary realised and felt, I don't think, especially from the point of view of groups.' Syd touchingly precludes these observations by claiming that it was better to be a band 'with a silver guitar with silver mirrors and things all over it' than to be a casualty or a down-and-out 'who ended up on the floor or anywhere else in London'. However any hint of whimsy is buried by his final comment on those halcyon days. 'I remember at UFO – one week one group, then another week another group, going in and out, making that set up, and I don't think it was as active as it could have been . . . what we were doing was a microcosm of the whole sort of philosophy and it tended to be a little bit cheap.' These are the sentiments not of a cynical fellow traveller, but of an embittered and astute idealist. 'One thinks of it all as a dream,' he concludes.

Syd reserves his most barbed comments for his former band mates. Asked about the contrast between his song-based material and the Floyd's lengthy instrumentals, he responds with a withering put-down. 'Their choice of material was always very much to do with what they were thinking as architecture students. Rather unexciting people, I would have thought, primarily.'

Beneath the sarcasm lies a deep and fundamental truth about the way in which Pink Floyd approached their craft once they had jettisoned their erratic and anarchic founder. The title track for the band's second album, *A Saucerful of Secrets*, recorded entirely without Syd's involvement, was devised by Roger Waters and Nick Mason in diagrammatic form, utilising architectural principles of form and function; mood and texture were secondary considerations, entirely subservient to structure. This marked a radical departure from the band's approach under Syd, which was basically to follow their leader's guiding spirit, offering colouration and embellishment where appropriate. From their second album onwards the Floyd began to build tracks in terms of blocks of sound, an approach which culminated in the architectural unity of *The Dark Side of the*

Moon. Indeed, it can be argued that the band's entire modus operandi after Syd's departure was governed by structural logic.

Syd's subsequent output on the other hand reflected his fine art philosophy and his pathological resistance to discipline. Waters, Mason, Wright and Gilmour (even sounds like a firm of chartered surveyors, doesn't it?) were guided by caution, deliberation, meticulous attention to detail, formal principles, sequential logic, linearity. Syd was driven (and impeded, of course) by immediacy, spontaneity, unmediated response, abstraction, multiple perspectives, automatism. One approach leads to 'Time', 'Us and Them', 'Money', 'Comfortably Numb' and 'The Great Gig in the Sky'. The other leads to 'Vegetable Man', 'Jugband Blues', 'Wolfpack', 'Rats' and 'No Man's Land'. Syd was happy with splashy daubs. Pink Floyd were rarely content with anything less than palatial (sometimes glacial) splendour.

Pink Floyd even sought out and undertook commissions like regular architects, contributing soundtrack music to Antonioni's *Zabriskie Point* and Barbet Schroeder's *More* and *La Vallée*. It is significant that on the two occasions Syd was asked to work under such conditions, for John Latham and for Peter Sykes' 1968 film, *The Committee*, he failed to deliver the goods.

Syd thrived on intuition and instinct while his fellow band mates had to graft just to keep up with him, but those very gifts which had helped him sail through his youth floundered once they encountered what Edward Lear had called the 'retinues and routines' of discipline and responsibility.

In the Michael Watts interview Syd candidly admits that his departure from the group was chiefly of his own making. 'It wasn't really a war. I suppose it was really just a matter of being a little off-hand about things,' he confesses. He also makes it clear that the split was a gradual accumulative process. 'We didn't feel there was one thing that was gonna make the decision at the minute. I mean, we did split up and there was a lot of trouble. I don't think the Pink Floyd had any trouble, but I had an awful scene, probably self-inflicted, having a Mini and going all over England, and things. Still . . . '

He is far more circumspect when talking about acid. 'Well, I dunno, it don't seem to have much to do with the job,' he says dismissively. 'Were you not at all involved in acid then during its heyday among rock bands?' asks Watts incredulously. 'No,' lies Syd, mindful perhaps of his current domestic circumstances in Cambridge, which he alludes to in his reply. 'I've always thought of going back to a place where you can drink tea and sit on the carpet. I've been fortunate enough to do that.'

Overall he appears sanguine about his current lack of involvement in the music scene: 'I feel perhaps I could be claimed as being redundant almost,' he says. 'I don't feel active and that my public conscience is fully satisfied.' Any attempts by Watts to ascertain future plans elicit vaguely enthused but non-committal responses. 'Do you think that people still remember you?' says Watts. 'Yes, I should think so,' Syd responds. 'Then why don't you get some musicians, go on the road, and do some gigs?' Watts asks. 'I feel the record would still be the thing to do. And touring and playing might make that impossible to do,' replies Syd. 'What's the hang-up then? Is it getting the right musicians around you?' asks Watts. 'Yeah,' says Syd.

'What would be of primary importance – whether they were brilliant musicians or whether you could get on with them?' asks Watts. 'I'm afraid I think I'd have to get on with them. They'd have to be good musicians. I think they'd be difficult to find. They'd have to be lively,' says Syd.

'Would you say therefore you were a difficult person to work with?' presses Watts. 'No. Probably my own impatience is the only thing, because it has got to be very easy,' reveals Syd, once again laying bare his aversion to rigour and retakes and rehearsal.

During these exchanges one frequently gets a sense of

318

prevarication and avoidance. Little of what Syd says convinces the reader that he is about to reinvigorate his career. Occasionally his responses are reminiscent of the strategy (if one can call it that) adopted by Brian Wilson in later years. Everything is answered in the affirmative, yet very little is actually revealed.

After another typically obtuse observation from Syd, where he appears to hark back to his Tech college days ('You can play guitar in your canteen you know, your hair might be longer but there's a lot more to playing than travelling around universities and things'), the Watts interview peters out into small talk and inconsequentialities. Syd suggests that he would go out and play solo but 'I haven't got any blue jeans', that 'Slade would be an interesting thing to hear' and he hasn't bought much music lately but he's been listening to Ma Rainey. Attempting to pick up the thread Watts asks, 'Are you going into the blues, then, in your writing?' 'I suppose so,' says Syd. 'Different groups do different things.' One can almost hear the sentence trail off into whispers. Despite this Syd ends the interview on a positive note claiming that there would be a third solo album ('It should be twelve singles and jolly good singles') and that he wants to produce it himself. 'I think it was always easier to do that.'

Sharing the same page as the concluding part of Watts' interview is a prominent advert for an up-and-coming mail order service called Virgin Records. At that time the fledgling organisation just had two record shops in Tottenham Court Road and Notting Hill, and was beginning to make a name for itself selling cut-price albums by post. A couple of pages earlier in the same issue the paper's jazz section featured an interview with drummer John Stevens, at that time working with the Spontaneous Music Ensemble. Stevens talks about the joys and strictures of free improvised music, the difference between rhythm and sound, the avoidance of familiarity and habit (which Stevens calls 'a cul-de-sac'), of having recorded the latest SME album, *Source* in one take, and of his desire to 'get beyond the machine'.

Had things turned out differently this could have been Syd talking. Similarly he might have ended up on the Virgin Records roster with kindred spirits like Daevid Allen's Gong, Henry Cow or Faust. Imagine a rejuvenated Syd guesting on Mike Oldfield's *Tubular Bells* or Robert Wyatt's *Rock Bottom* or collaborating with any one of the outcasts and avant-gardners who flocked to Richard Branson's label in the early 1970s. Sadly it was not to be. By 1971 the shutters were coming down. Syd was busy closing off all options.

In an interview with Steve Turner for *Beat Instrumental*, published in June 1971, the recalcitrance is obvious. 'His talk is slow and unrevealing. The answer given often bears no relation to the question being asked,' says Turner. Syd's responses are now beginning to fade into vapour trails and silence. 'I mainly play the guitar,' he says. 'You can play it all day though and you're not really saying much.'

According to Turner Syd is still dressed for the part, in purple satin jacket and stack-heeled boots. 'I'm still in love with being a pop star really,' he claims, before going off on a convoluted, and none too convincing, attempt at explaining what he still refers to as 'the job'. 'As a job it's interesting but very difficult. You can be pure enough to talk about it where you can actually adapt to the grammar of the job. It's exciting. You channel everything into one thing and it becomes the art.' Of his newly shorn locks and his return to his home town he says, 'Cambridge is very much a place to get adjusted to. I've found it difficult. It was fairly unusual to go back because it's the home place where I used to live and it was pretty boring so I cut my hair.'

Turner notes Syd's tendency to contradict himself, as later he says of Cambridge: 'It's quite fun. It's a nice place to live really – under the ground.' Again he plays lip service to the idea of getting a band together ('It'd be a groove wouldn't it?') and expresses mild dissatisfaction with his solo endeavours so far. 'They've got to reach a certain standard,' he says, 'and that's probably only reached in *Madcap* once or twice and on the other one only a little – just an echo of that. Neither of them are much more than that.'

The occasional wry response emerges, but even these are tinged with weariness and ennui. Syd begins the interview by explaining that he's come up to London to look for a guitar. 'Quite an exciting morning for me,' he deadpans. 'I don't really know if pop is an art form,' the interview concludes. 'I should think as much as sitting down is.'

Speaking of their encounter years later Turner recalled Syd's palpable unease, mentioning that when he offered to share a taxi to a West End guitar shop after the interview Syd hastily made his excuses. When Turner encountered Syd again a short while later on a tube train he acknowledged his interviewer, 'But it's the frightened face I'll always remember,' says Turner.

Syd gave what would turn out to be his last-ever interview to Mick Rock for *Rolling Stone* magazine in the late autumn of 1971. It wasn't intended to be his last, and like everything else about his gradual withdrawal from the pop world it came without fanfares, but if this was to be Syd's final encounter with the music press then it was somehow fitting that it should be with someone he knew and trusted.

The feature in its original edited form ran to only half a page, although the full uncut transcript was later included by Rock in his book *Psychedelic Renegades*, as were many of the photographs shot that day. Although Rock had known Syd since 1966 he had only ever penned a few music features – he had written about David Bowie for *Club International*, the men's magazine, for example – and at the time he was busy establishing himself as a photographer. The original *Rolling Stone* piece, published on 23

December 1971, didn't even carry Rock's byline, although an accompanying photo of Syd squinting into the sunlight in his Cambridge back garden did. 'I didn't even complain about not getting the byline. But I was almost too hip to complain,' laughs Rock. 'It wouldn't have been cool to draw attention to oneself.'

Rock, accompanied by his wife Sheila, found Syd in good form, in turn enigmatic ('I'm full of dust and guitars'), laconic ('The only work I've done the last two years is interviews. I'm very good at it'), melancholic ('I wasn't always this introverted. I think young people should have fun. But I never seem to have any') and defiant ('I'm totally together. I even think I should be').

'He was a bit lateral in his self-expression,' says Rock. 'But he wasn't foaming-at-the-mouth crazy. I knew of things that had gone on that people would talk to me about in that period between '69 and '71. But it wasn't like that with him and me . . . Personally he wasn't that strange with me. We had really friendly communication, and a lot of non-verbal, but enough verbal, that he was comfortable with me interviewing him. And, of course, it wasn't like he was really doing any other interviews around that time. I think he did the interview because it was me. I don't think he would've done it with anybody else by then. He wasn't really in the music business any more as far as he was concerned.'

Syd's parting shot in the interview, and by default his final public statement, lends this book its subtitle. 'I don't think I'm easy to talk about,' he tells Rock. 'I've got a very irregular head. And I'm not anything you think I am anyway.'

None of this, Rock assures me, was delivered with diffidence or malice. It was simply an acknowledgement that he wasn't easily definable. There is an element of raising the psychological drawbridge behind him in the quote, but throughout the rest of the interview Syd indulges in frequent bouts of honest self-analysis.

'I am doing little, but dimly walking on along the dusty

twilight lanes of incomprehensible life,' Edward Lear wrote to his friend Lord Fortescue in 1859. 'I'm treading the backward path,' Syd told Mick Rock at 183 Hills Road, Cambridge in the autumn of 1971 with the sun setting on his pop life. 'I'm disappearing. Avoiding most things.'

In the interview Syd talks, as he frequently did, of his creative impasse. 'I may seem to get hung up, that's because I am frustrated work-wise, terribly,' he says. 'The fact is I haven't done anything this year. I've probably been chattering, explaining that away like anything. But the other bit about not working is that you get to think theoretically.'

That last sentence is highly significant. For all his instinctiveness Syd always had thought theoretically. The difference now was that there was no longer any end-product to show for it. What is equally noticeable by its absence in his encounter with Mick Rock is any talk of a third album.

Instead Syd gives what is clearly meant to be a final definitive statement on what went wrong with his pop career. 'Hendrix was a perfect guitarist. And that's all I wanted to do as a kid. Play a guitar properly and jump around. But too many people got in the way. It's always been too slow for me. Playing. The pace of things. I mean I'm a fast sprinter. The trouble was after playing in the group for a few months I couldn't reach that point.'

Rock remembers that everything was conveyed in very matter-of-fact tones, without fuss or melodrama. 'He was very whimsical,' says Rock. 'It was quite a whimsical day. He was kind of accepting the fact that, y'know, "When I was young I used to jump around a lot and have fun on stage and now I don't have much fun any more." It's a bit like Pink Floyd, the band, got in the way. He didn't wanna be structured, that's for sure. It got too structured. I think early on, when leading up to the first album, it was pure experimentation, but I think after the release of the album, suddenly, instead of being an underground figure, he was thrown into some kind of limelight. And then there were demands for the Floyd to tour and then he had to do interviews, the whole bit. I think once it started to get structured, he very rapidly decided he didn't really like it. In some ways he was more like a jazz musician. He just wanted to go somewhere, play guitar and jump around as he felt like it. He wanted to improvise. The minute he had to start playing "Arnold Layne" every night, I don't think his brain could deal with that. His sensibility rebelled against that. He should've been born in an earlier time and been a Coltrane or something and just been able to have a context where he could just get up and just doodle around and play around and let his feelings express themselves without restraint. I think he would've been more comfortable.'

On the subject of Hendrix Syd says, 'I toured with him you know. Lindsay and I used to sit up the back of the bus with him up front. He would film us. But we never spoke really. He was better than people really knew but very self-conscious about his consciousness. He'd lock himself in the dressing room with a TV and he wouldn't let anyone in.'

The paradox was not lost on Rock. 'The thing about touring with Hendrix and how he thought it was odd how Hendrix would lock himself away and refuse to come out of the room – that was one of the most ironic things because that's exactly what he was doing by then.'

In marked contrast to the thousand-yard stare that Syd had begun to adopt by the time of the 1967 package tour, several of Mick Rock's Cambridge photos capture Syd relaxed and smiling. In a couple he is wielding a tennis racket, albeit none too convincingly. In others he inquisitively examines Rock's photographic equipment. He even takes a couple of shots of Rock and his wife. Sheila reciprocates by photographing her husband with Syd. 'He liked to laugh,' says Rock. 'I mean, people paint him as being odd and the idea that most people get, because he was so reclusive, was that he was kind of a miserable personality. But he wasn't by nature that way. I think there was a part of him that was really quite a happy person. I look at the pictures I've got of him and in a lot of them he's laughing.'

Despite Rock's affectionate recollections other photos taken that day tell a different story. In some Syd looks stiff and pensive. The smiles have a certain strained quality. In the published interview Rock himself admitted that, 'he seems very tense, ill at ease. Hollow-cheeked and pale his eyes reflect a permanent state of shock.'

In the photos Syd is wearing a paint-spattered T-shirt turned inside out. In one he is holding a paintbrush, and the feature mentions that his cellar room is full of 'paintings and records, amps and guitars'. 'He still paints,' Rock maintains in the article. 'Sometimes crazy jungles of thick blobs. Sometimes simple linear pieces. His favourite is a white semi circle on a white canvas.'

Unfortunately the interview doesn't make it clear if the latter piece is new. If it is, then Syd truly was 'treading the backward path' and had reverted to his pre-art school influences, in this case Robert Rauschenberg's late 1950s white-on-white canvases. One painting that survives from the period, which Syd gave to Jenny Spires in 1971, is a drip painting in the style of Jackson Pollock. 'Crazy jungles of thick blobs' sums it up nicely. It's part homage to abstract expressionism, part replication of a light show projection, amoebic form as glimpsed through a liquid lens. It's not one of Syd's most convincing canvases, but its mere existence indicates that during 1971 Syd was still trying to reconnect with his first love, painting.

'He doesn't actually play the guitar nowadays. He prefers to merely strum,' the interview states, but further on in the piece Syd feels suitably emboldened to show Rock a folder full of all his lyrics, neatly typed. 'I think it's so exciting. I'm glad you're here,' he says. He even produces a brand new twelve-string Yamaha and plays Mick and Sheila a version of 'Love You', a song he still remained inordinately fond of. 'He's holding a guitar in a couple of the frames that I shot in the basement, and that's what he was doing in those pictures. He was actually playing me that. I think it was something about our relationship that he was very relaxed with me. But other people seemed to make him very uptight. I think he had a very – what's the word? – it was something to do with the people he had grown up with, which he'd developed a kind of antipathy towards by then. And, yes, he did manifest certain aspects of paranoia, and certainly I know of some things he did as described to me by other people over the years, which sound pretty loony, but I never saw anything like that when he was in my company.'

As Rock says in the interview, 'Visiting him is like intruding into a very private world.' The portrait that Rock paints in the *Rolling Stone* feature is essentially one of a retired rock legend. Syd says that he doesn't take acid anymore and talks poignantly about the old days. 'I never felt so close to a guitar as that silver one with mirrors that I used on stage all the time,' he says sadly. He also talks with almost childlike innocence about what he would do with an abundance of wealth. 'I'd like a lot of money to put into my physicals and to buy food for all my friends,' he says sweetly.

All of this is shot through with scenes of touching domesticity. 'His mum brought us tea and cakes,' remembers Rock. 'I don't have a strong impression of her, maybe I was too focused on Syd, but she was certainly around and she certainly brought out tea and cakes for three. It was all very English.'

Perhaps the most poignant moment in the entire interview, and one which was not included in the original published version, occurs when Syd alludes to his recent break-up with Gayla Pinion. 'I've often been in love,' he says. 'The last time it lasted only a few months and at the end of it I almost broke down.' 'He relates this as if remembering from a script pedantically,' says Rock in the feature. 'He pours another cup of tea and confides flatly, "I love girls, you know. I wanna get married and have kids." '

'There was that part of him that knew there was a regular life out there to be had,' says Rock. 'But as he says at the end, "I've got a very irregular head." So I think he understood that in the end that was never gonna be. I don't know that he ever did have another girlfriend after that.'

Or any kind of friend at all.

Chapter Nine

Make Your Name Like a Ghost

It was hard, he thought, to be within sight of safety and almost of home, and to be baulked by the want of a few wretched shillings and by the pettifogging mistrustfulness of paid officials. Very soon his escape would be discovered, the hunt would be up.

THE WIND IN THE WILLOWS KENNETH GRAHAME

The moment Syd Barrett turned right rather than left out of Abbey Road studios that day in August 1974, after one final, fruitless recording session, he disappeared into myth. And oh, what myths they were.

Syd went on stage with Mandrax and Brylcreem in his hair. Syd ran on to an airport runway and frantically tried to hail an aeroplane as you would a taxi. Syd went into a clothes shop, tried on three pairs of trousers, pronounced that they all fitted him perfectly and walked out again. Syd was seen standing outside Harrods wearing a huge Yogi Bear tie. Syd was seen walking down the King's Road in a dress. Syd's friends locked him in an airing cupboard when he was having a bad trip. Syd locked Lindsay Corner in a room for three days and fed her water biscuits under the door. Syd tried to climb the walls during a thunderstorm in Formentera. When Syd left London for the last time he walked all the way back to Cambridge. On his hands. While singing 'Have You Got It Yet?'

With every successive telling each myth grew another layer. Fresh detail was grafted onto old rumour until all the stories merged into one mad Syd.

The mythologising had been going on ever since Syd first saw something rotten in the state of pop and went AWoL. Every missed gig, every abandoned recording session, every bad performance, every eccentric gesture, every last lyric and lover's tiff was combed for clues to the malaise, until finally Syd the human being was erased completely and all that was left was the myth.

Syd had always been idealised. There was nothing new in that. Friends and lovers alike eulogised him. There was something about that charm, those nineteenth-century poet's good looks and that briefly flowering genius that brought out the eulogiser in everyone. By 1969 he had even been fictionalised when Jenny Fabian cast him as Ben, the enigmatic and burned-out lead guitarist with the Satin Odyssey in her 1969 semi-auto-biographical novel *Groupie*. But the kind of mythologising that began to take hold in the early 1970s was different. It no longer stemmed from the testimony of friends and it rarely had any-thing to do with Syd the musician. Once he withdrew from the pop world the rumours went into overdrive and a different kind of narrative began to emerge. The stories were no longer about what drove Syd creatively, they were about what drove him mad. From here on in every anecdote that emerged had to conform to the crazy person archetype. A living breathing self who was still only in his mid twenties was dismantled and reconstructed as a modern-day Vincent Van Gogh.

The 'Mandrax and Brylcreem' episode fits the archetype perfectly. In the same way that it is necessary to believe that Mama Cass, a clinically obese woman, choked to death on a ham sandwich (she didn't) or that Cliff Richard wears a colostomy bag (he doesn't) it becomes desirable to believe that at some point during 1967 mad Syd emptied a tub of Brylcreem into his hair, rubbed a jar of Mandrax tablets into the gooey mess just for good measure, and went on stage with the whole concoction dripping down his face like candle wax.

There are even people who claim to have witnessed the event: the trouble is they all claim to have witnessed differing versions of the event at different times. Pink Floyd lighting engineer John Marsh says that Syd rubbed Brylcreem (without the Mandrax) into his hair before going on stage at the ICI Fibres Club in Pontypool in February 1968. The fact that Syd didn't perform with the band at the gig in question is perhaps a minor detail. Roger Waters has a separate recollection of Syd turning up at the Pontypool gig, demanding to play, and being refused access to the stage. He doesn't mention Mandrax or Brylcreem. Dr Sam Hutt also claims that the event happened towards the end of Syd's tenure with the band, and adds Mandrax to the story for good measure. In his biography of Pink Floyd, *Inside Out*, Nick Mason recalls Syd attempting to straighten out his perm with 'a tub of hair gel' at the Cheetah Club in Santa Monica California on 5 November. The Move's manager Tony Secunda places the episode a few months earlier and remembers Syd walking round with Mandrax tablets (sans Brylcreem) stuck in his hair at the Roundhouse at the beginning of September 1967.

When one considers the sheer absence of accurate document-ation in relation to several key episodes in Syd Barrett's life it is fascinating to see the extent to which the Mandrax and Brylcreem story has taken hold. Even though no one can remember what tracks the early Pink Floyd laid down on their demos (or where or when), or what songs Syd recorded solo for Joe Boyd in late 1966 (or perhaps early 1967), or exactly how many gigs he played with Pink Floyd as a five-piece in 1968, or who plays what on half of the sessions on *The Madcap Laughs*, we are somehow expected to faithfully absorb every last detail of the Mandrax and Brylcreem episode, verbatim. Over a period of time it seems that all the separate components of the incident have merged into one composite story in order to illustrate everything that was going wrong with Syd in 1967.

As rock 'n' roll myths go, the Mandrax and Brylcreem affair is quite a good one. It has all the requisite components. Syd was in disarray. Bad hair day. Bad brain day. He liked drugs. Mix them all together until the whole sorry mess can be heaped, literally, upon his head. Jesus wore a crown of thorns. Sad, mad Syd rubbed some gloop into his scalp.

'The Brylcreem episode was talked and joked about often by the band,' maintains David Gilmour. 'Brylcreem dripping down his face under the hot lights – but none of them ever mentioned Mandrax – that invention surfaced years later.'

Jenny Fabian has similarly claimed that Syd wouldn't have wasted good Mandrax in such a way, but neither denial, nor the lack of hard evidence from anyone else these past forty years, has prevented the story from becoming one of the seminal Syd myths. When he passed away in July 2006, one half expected the headlines to read 'Mandrax and Brylcreem man dies'.

The story first appeared in Nick Kent's 'The Cracked Ballad of Syd Barrett', a 5,000-word, five-page feature published in *NME* on 13 April 1974. 'I just felt the story really needed to be told,' says Kent. 'He was a real artist. The music he made was not just mad. It's not some voyeuristic wallowing in some guy going mad. There is a sense to that music and there's an otherworldliness to that music which is really unique.'

Kent's Barrett profile, along with similarly epic pieces that he penned about Brian Jones, Nick Drake and Brian Wilson during the same period, remains among the finest in English music journalism. As the name of Kent's own 1994 anthology – *The Dark Stuff* – suggests, he was perennially drawn to the doomed and the dysfunctional, making him perhaps the perfect candidate to write about the charismatic and mercurial Syd. Kent himself was blessed with fashionably wasted good looks that would have been the envy of half the subjects he interviewed, and could himself have been a rock star if his own short-lived period with the Sex Pistols hadn't ended in acrimony, and heroin addiction hadn't blunted his prose and derailed his career for several years. Kent hero-worshipped Syd and, despite his bizarre brush-off from his hero in the *Frendz* magazine office in 1972, his piece was built on empathy and a true fan's appreciation.

Having said that the piece contained numerous factual errors, which, despite its having been reprinted and syndicated several times over the years, have never been amended. Kent's piece was the first to suggest that Syd had written 'Effervescing Elephant' and adapted 'Golden Hair' (which he erroneously suggests comes from Joyce's *Ulysses*) when he was 'maybe sixteen'. Kent is similarly careless with some of his biographical details, suggesting, for instance, that Syd was the youngest of a family of eight and that his father died when he was twelve. He also refers to the religious sect Sant Mat as Sant Saji.

Given the utterly compelling nature of the story and the utterly compelling way in which Kent tells it, such lapses are forgivable, the price one pays for Kent's own intuitive genius and his perceptive analysis of Syd's life and work. He calls the solo material 'essays in distance – the Madcap waving whimsically out of the haze', which is as concise and accurate a description as you will ever read.

A number of rumours and myths get their inaugural airing in the 'Cracked Ballad' piece. In addition to the Mandrax and Brylcreem episode, the article also contains the first public disclosure of the story of Lindsay Corner being locked in a room and fed water biscuits. Indeed, Kent's piece contains the first disturbing accounts of Syd's violent behaviour to appear anywhere in print. It also marks the first appearance of the legendary 'Mad Jock' and 'Mad Sue', who are alleged to have spiked Syd with acid on a regular basis, as well as an equally disturbing account of Syd at the end of his tether in 1972 smashing his head through his Cambridge cellar roof in frustration. Both the Jock and Sue stories and the cellar incident have subsequently been dismissed as exaggeration.

'This story is more or less true,' Kent says of the Mandrax and Brylcreem episode, but goes on to add, 'It exists amidst an infinity of strange tales – many of them fact, just as many wistful fiction.' He also acknowledges that 'You could easily be tempted to fill out a whole article by simply relating all the crazy anecdotes and half chewed tales of twilight dementia, and leave it at that.' Many subsequent accounts of Syd's life have done just that, of course. 'All the above are stories told to me by various semi-authentic sources. More than likely most of them are total fabrications,' says Kent, yet none of these disclaimers have ever stopped a single Syd Barrett myth from thriving, once in the public domain.

The week after the piece was printed, the *NME* correspondence page 'Gasbag' featured a substantial number of readers' letters, most of which congratulated Nick Kent for one of the best articles to ever grace the pages of a pop paper. One reader however, Dave Clayton of Stockport, Cheshire, took issue with the term 'tragi-comic' to describe Syd's condition, adding, 'I thought it was only in the eighteenth century that people visited asylums to laugh at the lunatics. What is funny about a human being drowning at the bottom of a mental whirlpool? Help him.' Another short letter signed C. Emily Play read simply, 'Loved your article on Syd Barrett. Half an hour after reading it we both thought we were him,' proving conclusively that LSD was still in widespread usage among the *NME* readership in 1974. Other readers' letters offered minor amendments, corrections and clarifications. Producer Malcolm Jones wrote a lengthy response to the piece and talked for the first time about the *Madcap* out-takes, including the notorious 'motor bike noises' session. *NME* assistant editor Ian MacDonald offered further erudite comment, and Kent himself added a lengthy footnote in which he mentioned an unreleased Pink Floyd track called 'Apologies', which later turned out to be simply a mishearing of 'Apples and Oranges'! Kent rounded things off by giving a first public airing to the 'Have You Got It Yet' story – the legendary session in which Syd attempted to teach Pink Floyd a new song, which he kept changing every time he ran through it.

' "Have You Got It Yet" was in January '68 at one of my first rehearsals with the five-piece band in a school hall in Chamberlayne Road in Brondesbury Park,' confirms David Gilmour. 'We didn't get it for quite a long time. Amazingly, I remember the moment and the song well. It was really just a twelve-bar, but the responses were always in the wrong places according to Syd. Some parts of his brain were perfectly intact – his sense of humour being one of them.'

Another important source of Syd stories was Jonathon Green's *Days in the Life* anthology. First published in 1988, and subtitled *Voices from the English Underground 1961–1971*, it remains one of the best books ever written about the 1960s, capturing the counter-culture in all its manifold contradictions. The book is one long vox pop from those who were there, and contains minimal editorial intrusion. This is both the book's strength and its weakness. On the one hand the material is allowed to breathe: a multiplicity of first-hand accounts from key participants interweaves to build a fascinating and complex mosaic of primary source material. On the down side, numerous dubious assertions and contrasting testimonies are left unchecked. In a five-page section devoted entirely to Syd Barrett, the emphasis is almost entirely on his mental disintegration. The supposed horrors of 101 Cromwell Street receive their obligatory airing along with the first telling of Syd's being locked in the linen cupboard at Egerton Court.

'The "locked in a cupboard and spiked with acid everyday in Egerton Court" originated from Jonathan Meades,' says Duggie Fields. 'They were winding him up. That's my conjecture. My first reaction was, I just didn't believe it, and when I identified the couple who were supposed to have done it, Jock and Sue, labelled "Mad Jock and Sue", well, I lived with them. They didn't spike me with acid and lock me in a cupboard. I do know that Jonathan would have been someone that people would have wound up. They were wind-up merchants, definitely, and I can see them thinking let's give him something to freak him out to get rid of him.'

Hester Page is equally dismissive of the 'spiking' stories which have emerged over the years. 'I don't remember that happening with anybody. It's not something we did. And knowing those two people [Jock and Sue] like I did I don't think they would have spiked Syd.'

In fact everyone spoken to for this book vehemently denied that anyone ever spiked Syd. Several added the significant caveat that many of these acid-horror stories are driven by more recent revisionist attitudes towards LSD use in the 1960s. In the new moral climate the psychological damage caused by excessive LSD use is emphasised while the integral role psychedelic drugs played in fuelling the creativity of the 1960s is downplayed. Old moral panics are also given a dusting down, despite having been discredited at the time.

The spectre of the evil drug pusher, for example, or the crazed acid evangelist committed to putting acid in the water supply and turning on the world has its origins in the CIA's early investigations into LSD as a potential agent of social control during chemical warfare. Despite discovering that chlorinated water would render the drug ineffective, the legend has endured.

335

In the 1960s it joined the pantheon of acid-myths; the babysitter who put the baby in the oven, the man who stared at the sun till he went blind, the acid zealots who slipped lysergic Mickey Finns in their friend's morning cuppa.

Mike Watkinson and Pete Anderson's 1991 Barrett biography, *Crazy Diamond*, takes its moral cue from this kind of sensationalism. The writers claim confidently (without citing their medical sources) that 'during the first hours of taking it there were often outbreaks of uncontrollable violent behaviour'. The book is full of this kind of unsubstantiated nonsense. One half expects it to come with a government health warning on the dust jacket.

Watkinson and Anderson also report that in the summer of 1969, frustrated with the delay in completing *The Madcap Laughs*, Syd made an impromptu decision to go and join his friends in Ibiza. 'Dealing with the inconvenience of check-in desks, customs and ticket barriers was not high on the Barrett list of priorities,' claim the authors – note the convincing attention to local detail, although not, alas, the name of the airport. 'Late for his plane, he skipped the lot, ran towards the runway and tried to flag down a passing jet as if it were a cab.' Strangely this highly irregular and security-breaching event failed to make any of the newspapers, or to get Syd sectioned or even cautioned. Give it another couple of decades and we will probably be treated to the spectacle of Syd clinging to the wings of a departing plane and then parachuting down over the Balearics using nothing more than his own chemically fuelled powers of propulsion.

By the time Watkinson and Anderson wrote their biography, 'Syd Barrett' had ceased to exist. He was now merely a cipher for tall tales of the consequences of irreparable drug damage, a rock 'n' roll case study: file under casualty, exhibit A.

'It's tempting to make Syd into a figure whose personal trajectory resembles the trajectory of the Sixties,' notes David

Gale. 'Insofar as here was a young man who was intoxicated with optimism at the possibilities of change and experiment in the Sixties. And who, like that decade, peaked and then fell away very quickly, so the disillusion that spread throughout the States and this country in the late Sixties was therefore in Syd. He was in that sense a poster boy for that kind of unfolding, and the graph of optimism versus disillusionment.'

Several fundamental issues emerge from all this, all of which have considerable bearing on the way that the legend of Syd Barrett has been constructed. Primarily, there is the nature of mythmaking itself, the function it serves in society, and the ways in which it is embedded in the cultural psyche. Myths tell us just as much about the mythmakers and the myth believers as they do about the mythologised. Then there is the complex nature of memory itself. Left to its own devices, recall is a notoriously unreliable mechanism, prone to distortion and exaggeration, especially when, as in this case, a significant proportion of the stories originate from people who themselves spent a fair amount of the 1960s high on drugs.

Half-remembered events take on a life of their own, until they become self-validating and it is the anecdotes about the event rather than the event itself which drives the story. Duggie Fields has been a trustworthy and reliable contributor to most previous accounts of Syd Barrett's life, but even he has serious misgivings about the ways in which myth distorts reality with the passing of time. 'You end up remembering your previous answer, so your answer becomes factual, when it might not really be factual. The regurgitated memory becomes stronger than the original. That's a real danger. You think, at one point this was a funny story, but what was real?'

Hence Mandrax and Brylcreem. Hence water biscuits. Hence airplane taxis. Oh, look there goes mister loony man off to hail a plane.

I know what I'm talking about here because I am directly responsible for initiating two of the false stories in common currency among Syd fans. Neither was hatched maliciously, or even mischievously. One can be directly attributed to faulty memory syndrome, the other to the dream desires of a seventeen-year-old Syd fan. What is interesting about both stories is how readily they have been received into the larger narrative and how uncritically, and indeed how often they have been repeated.

The first of these stories concerns how Syd used to turn up backstage at *Top of the Pops* in the period immediately after he left Pink Floyd. It was during one of these backstage rendezvous that he revealed that the identity of the mystery group the Moles was in fact Simon Dupree and the Big Sound. Except that he didn't.

What happened was this. As a young fan I read Chris Welch's 'Confusion and Mr Barrett' interview in *Melody Maker* in January 1970. In the interview Syd is quoted as saying '*Top of the Pops* is all right! You meet interesting people and there are always people around I know and are prepared to like me.' This detail triggered in me a half-remembered (or as it turned out incorrectly remembered) interview from *NME* in 1968 when I was thirteen. In the interview, as I dimly recalled, Syd was sitting backstage at *Top of the Pops* chatting, and it was during this chat that he revealed that the mystery group, the Moles, responsible for a psychedelic single called 'We Are the Moles', was not the Beatles, as everyone had hoped or assumed, but Simon Dupree and the Big Sound recording under an alias.

This memory lay dormant for many years until 1996, when I introduced it into a Syd Barrett piece written by Cliff Jones for *Mojo* magazine, in which I acted as a contributing researcher. The anecdote immediately entered the pantheon of Syd stories and has been in circulation ever since. It was only when I was interviewing Duggie Fields for this book and he cast doubt on my recollection of events that I decided to check the story out. And sure enough, Duggie was right, it was false. Blessed, or cursed, as I am with almost total recall I was able to pinpoint the time scale, if not the precise details, of the story fairly swiftly. I visited the British Library's national newspaper archive at Colindale and found the relevant copy of *NME* from 7 December 1968 within minutes. In an interview with the group Gun (who were enjoying Top 10 success with a song called 'Race with the Devil') guitarist Adrian Gurvitz reports that he had recently been to see Pink Floyd and that Syd Barrett was backstage. 'I bet half the audience thought they were all on LSD, but you go backstage and Syd Barrett's saying something like "Get my coat George" and someone else is asking for a cup of tea. It's all in the mind.'

Indeed it is. At the end of the interview, as an aside, Gurvitz reveals that he is disappointed to learn that the Moles are 'Simon Dupree and two of the Big Sound'.

Over the years I had clearly morphed two distinct elements of the same interview into one incident in which Syd Barrett reveals a mystery group's identity. What is most interesting about this story is not that it has been repeated so widely, one half expects that from lazy journalists, or even that Adrian Gurvitz recalls Syd Barrett hanging out backstage with Pink Floyd in late 1968, but that one of the original members of Simon Dupree and the Big Sound believes the story himself. When I contacted bass player Peter O'Flaherty via his website, where the story is also repeated, he was happy to 'confirm' my faulty recollection.

I first heard about Syd saying that 'the Moles' were SDBS and not the Beatles, when another band asked us a few weeks after the record was released if we were the Moles. They had appeared on TOTP the previous week, and Syd had told them that SDBS were the Moles. I've forgotten which band and which gig it was. Apparently Syd would sometimes turn up for the rehearsals of TOTP. Syd being who he was would've had little problem being allowed in. Two rehearsals were usually done in the afternoon before the show went out live in the evening. These were for the directors to get the camera angles sorted out, etc. It was no problem for the bands as they usually mimed. What I still can't understand is why Syd Barrett was remotely concerned who recorded 'We Are the Moles'! Perhaps he was asked or even paid to. All sorts of things were going on with 'Publicity Agents' without our knowledge, although I can't remember reading the story in the NME.

That's because it never existed! It was not my intention to deceive Peter O'Flaherty. I contacted him before I had tracked down the original *NME* story in order to ascertain his version of events, but it is interesting to note how often even the original participants in a story come to believe the myth, even when, in this case, it was based on the faulty memory of a thirteen-year-old pop kid from the sticks.

A similar mixture of misinformation and self-fulfilling prophecy informs the second of my false Syd stories, in which I erroneously claimed that Syd Barrett's short-lived group, Stars, rehearsed 'See Emily Play' the day before they played at the Cambridge Corn Exchange in February 1972. Like Nick Kent in 1967, I was awestruck to see one of my heroes on stage, even though he was clearly not the Syd of old. Not that I would have fully comprehended or even cared about that at seventeen years old, with the man himself standing a few feet away from me. I wrote a review of the gig for the Barrett fan magazine, *Terrapin*, based for the most part on my entirely faithful recollection of events. I interjected into the piece, purely as a Syd fan's fantasy, and utterly without foundation, that the band had rehearsed 'See Emily Play'. Leaving aside the problematic issue of how it would have sounded without Rick Wright's keyboard, or the studio trickery (the speeded-up organ at the end of the first verse for instance) or indeed the fact that Pink Floyd themselves hardly ever played the song live, none of this has prevented the story from gaining wider currency. Even Twink Alder, the band's drummer, has been known to confirm in interview that the band rehearsed the number, which leaves one to consider, among other things, just how faithfully any musician can recollect events from the past. Refreshingly, Stars bass player Jack Monck candidly admitted to me that he remembers little of the Corn Exchange event, and even asked me to confirm whether his bass amp packed up and that Syd cut his little finger, details that I and *Melody Maker*'s Roy Hollingsworth had mentioned in our respective reviews.

One doesn't have to be a Lévi-Strauss to understand how such myths function, and why they thrive. Whether you believe that there are aliens in the blue room, or that Paul McCartney died in 1966 and was replaced by a doppelganger, or even, to quote just one outlandish myth from the outer reaches of Floyd-dom, that Syd Barrett wrote all of the band's post-1968 material, there is a ready niche for you and your conspiracy theory. There will always be a forum for the irrational and no shortage of volunteers to fill it. What is perhaps more dispiriting is the sheer amount of Barrett chroniclers who have been willing to put aside all notions of rigour and integrity in order to spin a lurid tale or two, or further embellish an unsubstantiated anecdote.

Many years ago Juliette Gale related a tale of Syd, in a fragile mental state, freaking out during a thunderstorm in Formentera – an event she herself witnessed. The original source of this story is unknown. Later versions of the story have Syd climbing the walls. In the most recent retellings Syd is said to have left shards of his fingernails embedded in the walls. A nice touch that, the fingernails. We should congratulate the journalists involved for their extraordinary powers of hindsight and the meticulous nature of their enquiry. Not only have they been able to faithfully corroborate the length of Syd's fingernails forty years ago, but they have also been able to ascertain the precise consistency of the plaster on the walls of an isolated rural holiday let from the same period.

In September 1974, a month after his final Abbey Road recording sessions, Syd's two solo albums were repackaged and re-issued as a double LP. Po and Storm unsuccessfully visited Syd at Chelsea Cloisters hoping to secure new photos for the artwork, but he refused to see them. Failing to gain Syd's co-operation they used a spread of old photos and press cuttings instead. In a neat little touch, the significance of which would have been lost on all but the Cantabrigian inner circle, Storm put a matchbox, an orange and a plum on the front cover, a nod to the legendary acid trip at David Gale's house in 1965. Even Syd's friends, it seems, were not averse to mythologising him.

On 5 June 1975 man and myth collided in the most bizarre and unforeseen way when Syd turned up at a recording session for Pink Floyd's *Wish You Were Here* sessions.

Again, as on numerous other occasions, no one can agree on the exact details of the encounter, even though the incident has been as well documented as any in the band's history. The broad details of the story are not in dispute. Syd turned up un-announced and overweight. He had shaved his head and his eyebrows and at first nobody at the recording session recognised who he was. Beyond these basic facts there is considerable disagreement. Some witnesses state that he appeared just once in the control room and only stayed briefly. Others say that he turned up for anything up to three days, initially wandering around in the studio unchallenged as everyone assumed he was an engineer or an EMI staff member. Some reports have Syd making a few gnomic utterances about the track the band was working on (depending on whose account you believe: 'Shall I put my guitar on now?' or, during a playback, 'You've listened to it once, why listen to it again?' and the equally believable, 'It sounds a bit old'). Some claim that after the session he went to the Abbey Road canteen with the group and was reasonably chatty, some say lucidly so, some say vague. Some claim that he was animated and personable, others that his behaviour was close to catatonic.

It is also of course extremely convenient for the legend that the track that the band was supposedly working on when Syd appeared just happened to be Roger Waters' Barrett-inspired eulogy 'Shine On You Crazy Diamond'. Nick Mason, however, has cast doubt on this version of events.

The one thing everyone agrees on is that Syd's presence and general appearance were distressing for all who were there. Rick Wright mentions that Syd kept jumping up and down, occasionally taking a toothbrush out of his pocket and dry-brushing his teeth. Certainly from the photographic evidence he is virtually unrecognisable from the Syd of only four years earlier. He looks portly and paunchy rather than grossly over-weight, and his shaven head and eyebrows do little to alleviate the general weirdness of his appearance. What is most perhaps most disturbing though is the expressionless gaze and slumped posture. Both suggest that Syd is on medication.

'He used to go into the pub at the back of Chelsea Cloisters, the Marlborough Arms, and just sit there and drink Guinness, Guinness, Guinness,' remembers caretaker Ronnie Salmon who worked at Chelsea Cloisters from 1974 to 1988. 'He put so much weight on. Then he shaved his head as well. But it was his eyes that gave it all away. Those starey eyes. It wasn't spaced out. How can I describe it? Different world. Some days he would ignore you like you weren't even there. Some days you could have a perfectly normal conversation. Other days he was completely out of it.'

There has been considerable speculation about how Syd knew of the *Wish You Were Here* sessions in the first place. The most fanciful theories suggest that he just manifested himself as if by osmosis on the day in question, but it is just as likely that close and continued family ties back in Cambridge, word from his music publishers, or from Jenner and King, would have led Syd to Abbey Road. The more depressing question is not how Syd happened to be there but why? Desperation? Loneliness? Wind up? One last look at the world he'd walked out on? If it was the latter then it was both apt and effective. For Syd's former band mates weren't to know it at the time but the Abbey Road encounter would be the last time any of them would ever see him.

One of the curious ironies of Syd's studio visit is that by appearing in person he merely enhanced the myth even further. It is equally ironic that the band was working on an album directly inspired by their former guiding light. With the release of the *Wish You Were Here* LP a new epithet, 'Crazy Diamond', entered the lexicon. Syd never asked for Roger Waters' martyrdom (or anyone else's for that matter) but it was bestowed all the same, and it has been almost obligatory for journalists and biographers to use the term ever since. As a song, 'Shine On, You Crazy Diamond' is overblown, overwrought, epic in scale and self-aggrandising, all the things that Syd wasn't. Although the tribute is heartfelt, and the sentiments sincere, it's self-consciously poetic in a way that Syd's lyrics never were. It is both over-reliant on alliteration, a device that Syd rarely used, and is littered with sixth-form imagery ('random precision' and suchlike). Like several of Waters' efforts from this period ('Brain Damage', 'Raving and Drooling' and 'You Gotta Be Crazy', for instance) the song's use of mental illness as a leitmotif is crass and heavy-handed. (As a footnote it's worth mentioning that a more fitting tribute to Syd had already been released in November 1972. Kevin Ayers' single, 'Oh Wot a Dream', was a song of beguiling simplicity and economy of style which encapsulated Syd's spirit far better than Waters' angst-ridden dirge ever could.)

If Syd's brief encounter with his old band mates at Abbey Road had revealed anything at all, it was the sad contrast between

344

the legend and the increasingly harrowing everyday existence. As Nick Kent had said in his *NME* profile, the story from 1972 onwards gets 'singularly depressing'. For the remainder of the 1970s Syd was in free fall. Holed up in his ninth-floor apartment at Chelsea Cloisters and continuing to show signs of the compulsive behaviour that had first manifested itself in his regular appearances at Lupus Music to ask for money for guitars, he now began to accumulate expensive items from Harrods which were then immediately thrown out or given away. 'The stuff he used to throw away was unbelievable,' says Ronnie Salmon. 'One day from Harrods they delivered a Dynatron TV. It was worth about £800. He had it for two days and then called me up and said, "Ronnie can you take this away?" I said, "What do you want me to do with it Syd?" He said, "Take it. Keep it." I had a guitar off him. Two Marshall amplifiers. The other porters up there got a bit jealous because he was giving me so much stuff. One day he called me up, and gave me £200 to take something away and throw it. I was only on about £30 a week.'

Friends who tried to visit Syd during this period were either refused entry, like Po and Storm, or in the case of ex-fiancée Gayla Pinion found his living conditions so claustrophobic and unsanitary, and his behaviour so unsettling, that she beat a hasty retreat.

Ronnie Salmon also lends weight to some of the more distressing stories from this period. 'He used to smash the bloody place up. Punching the doors in when he was high on drugs,' he alleges.

Looking back on all this from the vantage point of the twenty-first century it might be assumed that such stories were common knowledge, and that Syd's escapades were rarely out of the pop papers. In fact it is an indication of his relatively un-newsworthy status at the time that his final recording dates and his appearance at the *Wish You Were Here* sessions did not become public knowledge until November 1975, when Nick Kent wrote a feature for *NME* called 'Is It Possible too that Syd Has Risen from the Grave?' The piece also rounded up other recent sightings (including the 'Syd seen outside Harrods wearing a large Yogi Bear bow-tie' story) and also mentioned the existence of 'The Bob Dylan Blues' for the first time in print.

In November 1976 the DJ Nicky Horne was despatched to the Hilton Hotel on Park Lane, yet another esteemed establishment where Syd had taken up temporary residency, hoping to secure an interview for *The Pink Floyd Story*, a six-part series he was making with the band's full co-operation for Capital Radio. A bald overweight man, whom Horne didn't recognise, answered the door of his hotel room and in response to the DJ's enquiry adopted a pained expression and, depending on which version of the story one believes, either answered 'Syd can't talk,' or 'Sorry, Syd can't talk any more.' Horne phoned David Gilmour from the Hilton Hotel reception and told him about his abrupt encounter, which he assumed had been with a road manager. It was at that point that Gilmour acquainted Horne with the sad demoralising truth.

By the time Nicky Horne knocked on that hotel-room door 'Syd' Barrett had ceased to exist. The artist formerly known as Roger Keith Barrett had long since shed his pop persona. 'Syd', the school nickname given to him in the Scouts, had sustained him through his youth and his brief moment in the spotlight, but by 1976, 'Syd', as the man himself rightly said, couldn't talk any more. This was not just the shedding of a previous persona. This was the rubbing out of an entire life and all that went with it.

'He came to hate the name latterly – and what it meant,' says his sister Rosemary.

'Silence is the artist's ultimate otherworldly gesture,' notes Susan Sontag. 'By silence he frees himself from servile bondage to the world, which appears as patron, client, audience, antagonist, arbiter and distorter of his work.'

There were still those who clung to the idea that 'Syd' was retrievable: only those who had been closest to him knew the sad and inescapable truth. David Bowie, a long-term admirer, was just one of several high-profile fans who tentatively made enquiries about Syd's availability. At various point in the early to mid-1970s Brian Eno and Jimmy Page also expressed interest in producing him. In 1977, at the height of the punk phenomenon, Jamie Reid attempted unsuccessfully to arrange a meeting to see if Syd would be willing to produce the Sex Pistols. The Damned made similar overtures. Hoping for Syd they got Nick Mason.

Punk's seal of approval for Syd was a curious thing. Johnny Rotten famously wore an 'I Hate Pink Floyd' T-shirt, and year zero revisionists across the land similarly decreed that the band who had made *The Dark Side of the Moon* were boring old farts, but Syd Barrett, a man who had sung songs about gnomes, scarecrows and fairy tales, emerged unscathed from punk's war on hippiedom. Indeed, within new wave circles he was positively revered. Depending on which story you believe about how John Ritchie (aka Sid Vicious) got his nickname it is entirely possible that at the precise moment Roger Keith Barrett was relinquishing his old identity it was being claimed by the future Sex Pistols bass player.

Cambridge resident Robyn Hitchcock, at that time lead singer with the Soft Boys, was another of the punk generation who recognised, and helped regenerate, the Barrett legacy. 'I'm a good mimic and I absorbed Syd Barrett as a sort of subpersonality,' he says. 'Of course, Syd Barrett at that point was busy ceasing to exist. He himself was being dissolved and was reverting to Roger. So you had this character, Syd Barrett, that was up for grabs. The original owner had let it go.'

On the Soft Boys 1978 debut single, 'Wading Through a Ventilator', Hitchcock sings the first two verses with an obligatory punk sneer before adopting a distinctly Floydian lilt for the middle eight. By the time he reaches the spoken section at the end of the song the transformation is complete and the Barrett mannerisms (and lyrical influence) are unmistakeable.

'I was stuck with the dilemma of how do you become someone who themselves doesn't want to exist,' says Hitchcock. 'It's like getting into a car where the controls are locked into crashing into a wall or driving over a cliff. Somewhere along the line you have to jump out. If you follow it to its logical end you too will wind up shaving your head and living in your mother's basement. I bought into the isolation and doom for a certain length of time, but by the time I was about thirty I thought, "Well, fuck it", I'm actually Robyn Hitchcock. But I worked through my Syd Barrett subpersonality.'

Some people grew up miming to the Shadows with a tennis racket in front of the mirror, and getting in touch with their inner Hank Marvin. Indeed Syd would have been one of these people. By the early 1970s Syd himself represented another line of tradition. Robyn Hitchcock had started with the *Barrett* album and worked his way backwards. 'The *Barrett* album had this incredible sense of beauty and this sense of "there is this place where you cannot be touched and nothing can get at you". You may doom yourself in the process of finding it, but it's a place where nothing and nobody really matters. A place for a self-absorbed person in their late teens to go.'

In the early 1970s bedroom introspection came in many guises and those drawn to the singer-songwriter lineage had no shortage of role models: Crosby, Stills, Nash and Young, James Taylor, Joni Mitchell, Carole King, Loudon Wainwright. Robyn Hitchcock was one of the first English songwriters to locate another line of development, one that by-passed Laurel Canyon and country rock completely and embraced a peculiarly English sense of otherness. 'Barrett seemed to absorb Dylan and the

Beatles and Bo Diddley and Hilaire Belloc and Lewis Carroll and God knows what else into some style that was completely his own. And he did this when he was very young. I'm just impressed by how perfectly formed it was. The miracle of what Syd was, was that it came out so developed and so perfectly formed, and then it went. It was all done by the time he was twenty-five.'

In the late 1970s a film began to circulate among collectors and Barrett fans purporting to show Syd's first LSD trip. Shot by Nigel Lesmoir-Gordon in 1965, the film shows Syd, along with Nigel and Jenny, Andrew Rawlinson, Lucy Prior, Russell Page and David Gale, wandering around in an abandoned quarry just outside Cambridge. Syd, with short mod hair and dressed in a tight navy blue gabardine raincoat, drainpipe jeans and white sneakers, is seen clambering purposefully up the chalk face and through undergrowth, examining a leaf, and the rings of a tree trunk. In another sequence he holds handfuls of mushrooms before placing them over his eyes and in his mouth.

'He'd done acid, but he found some mushrooms. Those are just ordinary field mushrooms,' says Nigel Lesmoir-Gordon. 'That film was completely and utterly unscripted and unplanned, but it looks so beautiful and together. The camera belonged to Horace Ove. I was given it at Film School and just used to shoot 8-mill films, all day and every day. We went to Cambridge with the LSD and went to the Chalk Pits in the Roman woods by the Gog Magog hills. Thought, "That'll be a good place to trip." '

The Chalk Pits were a favoured local haunt, much visited by the Cambridge crowd in their youth. Syd later alludes to them, and the events of the day, in his song 'It Is Obvious'. 'When I was a kid I used to go up the Chalk Pits. We used to take our bikes up there when we were seven. Everybody went there,' says Jenny Lesmoir-Gordon.

'It's right next to a golf course and you'd go up there in your early teens and search round and find golf balls, and generally racket around. It was a good adventure playground for kids,' says David Gale.

In this familiar set and setting, on a typically English overcast day Lesmoir-Gordon's fragments of film footage capture the Cambridge crowd busy doing nothing much. Russell Page is resplendent in a fluorescent pink shirt and yellow tie, the girls are dressed in beatnik slacks. Jenny Lesmoir-Gordon, wearing a bright yellow PVC mac, talks to a tree stump. The lads get a fire going. A crop-spraying helicopter flies overhead.

In one unconvincing and slightly stagy sequence Syd stares intensely at his hands and then at the ground, as if simulating, rather than actually experiencing an acid trip, leading some to cast doubt on whether he was really tripping or merely play-acting.

'That so-called *Syd's first trip* was just a load of bollocks,' says David Gale. 'It wasn't his first trip. And I'm not even sure if he was tripping. It was merely that Nigel was very interested in Super-8 movie-making in the hippie manner, pulling the "stop frame" button and then splicing it all together. It was just made up on the hoof really – just larking around. Nigel chose Syd to be the main figure, and I think it has very little significance. It was just lads mucking about.'

Andrew Rawlinson is equally dismissive of the film's importance. 'I'm in it but I can't remember it. But that's the Syd myth acting retrospectively, long after he's crashed out. I don't know when that thing of Nigel Gordon's first became known to Sydophiles but that was the Syd mythology turning its searchlight backwards and finding that there was actually an artefact. I'd think the same if I saw something about Charlie Parker. I'd think, "Bloody hell, he's only nineteen. Amazing." But you'd think that because you're already in love with him.'

Syd's First Trip was eventually released commercially in 1994. David Gilmour subsequently bought up the rights in an attempt to quash the film's distribution, but screen grabs of the footage continue to turn up on the internet to this day. To Syd fans those few minutes of grainy 8-mill have taken on the significance of the Zapruder JFK assassination footage, to be combed frame by frame for clues as to his state of mind. Every last flinch and frown has been analysed by the faithful. In truth if it were any other student home movie nobody would pay it any attention whatsoever.

By now, though, the myths were in overdrive and every last detail of Syd's life was being pored over. Meanwhile the man himself was holed up in Chelsea Cloisters. The second half of the 1970s is Syd's lost era. What did he do all day and night up there on the ninth floor of his mansion block between late 1974 and 1982 when he finally left London for good? How did he live his life? We know almost everything about that creative six to nine months in 1966–7 when Syd, at the peak of his creativity, produced much of his best work. We know almost nothing about his last six or seven years in London. There aren't even any photos, just the overwhelming sense of a man in flight . . . from what? From friends? From family? From reality? From obligation? From himself?

Nature abhors a vacuum, the music industry even more so. And so into the space where Syd Barrett used to be poured rumour, myth, endless speculation. And it never let up for the rest of his life. And, of course, it was all made possible by the fact that not once did Syd respond to any of it. No confirmations, no denials, no rationale, no public pronouncements of any kind.

'He didn't make his name like a ghost. He left it to everybody else,' says Duggie Fields. 'That's the irony. He walked away from it all and it just carried on regardless.'

He didn't die like Brian Jones, Jimi Hendrix, Janis Joplin or Jim Morrison. Nor does he fit the rags-riches-rags-redemption archetype, a convenient narrative arc so clearly loved by the makers of biopics. He doesn't even compare with any of the other high-profile English drug casualties. Perhaps the nearest, in terms of acclaim was Peter Green. Green renounced fame and threatened to give all his money away during his final days with Fleetwood Mac. His final single with the band, 'The Green Manalishi', was a nightmarish evocation of the demonic power of filthy lucre. But after a lengthy period of illness even Green was redeemable and recovered sufficiently enough to front a live band again in the 1990s. And for all his well-documented psychiatric problems Green remained surprisingly prolific during even his darkest days, making over a dozen albums between 1970 and 1992, including one a year between 1979 and 1983.

Syd simply withdrew, and withdrawal, without closure or denouement, is what society can assimilate the least; it's certainly what the pop world can assimilate the least. Friends, former colleagues and interested spectators alike continued to debate that withdrawal for the rest of his days. Syd took no part in any of it, but, caught in an eternal paradox, the longer he remained absent the more his mystique grew. By the 1980s he existed as much as a metaphor as a man, David Gale's poster boy incarnate.

'The choice of permanent silence doesn't negate their work,' said Susan Sontag in *The Aesthetics of Silence*. 'On the contrary, it imparts retroactively an added power and authority to what was broken off; disavowal of the work becoming a new source of its validity.'

'I think one of the reasons he got the reputation that he did is that he fits so well the notion of the romantic myth of the young flyer who goes to pieces,' says Andrew Rawlinson. Aside from the link to literary romanticism Rawlinson points to another crucial aspect of Syd's enduring reputation, his symbiotic link with the band that he co-founded.

'If the Floyd had remained as they were with him, as an interesting experimental group, I don't think the backward shining light would have illumined Syd in the way that the present Floyd do. They are so enormous and distinctive but all of that enormity and distinctiveness has got nothing to do with Syd at all. The interesting thing is that the Floyd's success retroactively gives Syd a certain substance and celebrity which can only be like that because the Floyd's huge success is not Syd-like in the slightest. All that whimsy has gone. It just doesn't exist. There is complete discontinuity stylistically, but there is continuity chronologically and that combination has been greatly advantageous to the Syd myth. So, in that respect, I think he has become for two entirely separate reasons, one to do with the romantic myth, the other because of the huge success his group has had which is utterly different to that which they had when he was in it, those two things combined have made Syd what he is. If all those original Floyd people had gone off and been fantastically successful in other groups, which is perfectly possible, it wouldn't have been the same because Syd wouldn't have been connected to that. You could say it's a small thing that he came up with the name, but it isn't a small thing. Without any will on his part he's been surrounded by something that points back to him but which he did not actually make.'

Rawlinson's analysis is astute. As he says it's not just that Syd was a young talent who burned bright and then burned out. It's also crucial to recognise that the band he was jettisoned from went on to become one of the biggest in the world. Pink Floyd have, of course, been perfectly adept at running their own continuing soap opera these past thirty years. It's certainly worth noting that the band remained no less combustible and volatile without Syd than it was in 1967. First Rick Wright, another sensitive soul, was sidelined and then relegated to paid employee of his own band. Then Roger Waters famously decided to split the group only to find that the brand, and it was a brand by then, was bigger than any one member. All this incendiary feuding and rampant egomania provides an interesting counterpoint to Syd Barrett's own travails.

As it turned out, one of the most extraordinary assertions about Syd's unpredictable behaviour turned out to be true. Upon leaving London for the last time in 1982 he walked all the way back to Cambridge. 'I was not surprised at the time about him walking, he was capable of anything!' says sister Rosemary. 'I do remember he had some huge blisters on his feet that took a while to heal!'

By now it seems man and myth were one and the same, and somehow Syd had morphed into the Northamptonshire poet John Clare. Clare had walked from an asylum in Essex to his home in Northborough in Northamptonshire in July 1841. The journey took him four days and he wrote it up while fresh in his memory as a prose piece entitled 'Journey out of Essex'. Much of Clare's journey was undertaken under cover of darkness with little or no nourishment. At one stage he was reduced to eating grass to ward off starvation. 'Journey out of Essex' paints a graphic picture of rural England in the post-enclosure era, with many poor and hungry itinerants on the road. Clare's route took him through Enfield, rural Hertfordshire and Bedfordshire. He arrived back in Northborough on 24 July where he hoped to find his first true love, Mary Joyce, only to find that she had in fact been dead for several years. In 2000 the writer Iain Sinclair recreated Clare's original journey, and traced its psychogeography, in his book *Edge of the Orison*.

John Clare had been briefly fashionable in literary circles in the 1820s, where he had caught the tail end of the eighteenth- and early nineteenth-century vogue for peasant poets. His first book, published in 1820, *Poems Descriptive of Rural Life and Scenery*, gained favourable reviews and sold 3,000 copies in its first year, but by the time of his third volume, *The Shepherd's Calendar*, published in 1827, rural poetry had fallen out of favour and it sold only 425 copies. Clare was dogged by arguments with publishers and compromised by the demands of potential benefactors throughout his career and the pressures eventually began to tell on his behaviour. His fourth volume, *The Rural Muse*, was published in 1835. It sold a fraction of his debut work, and gained hardly any reviews. Two years later, at the age of forty-four Clare entered an asylum near Epping as a voluntary patient. After his escape he was only back in Northborough for a few months before his condition worsened again and he was admitted to the Northampton County Asylum where he was kept until his death aged seventy in May 1864.

The parallels between John Clare and Syd Barrett, as with most of Syd's literary forebears, are as much in the life as they are in the art. In his introduction to the 1920 collection *Poems Chiefly from Manuscript*, fellow poet Edmund Blunden said of Clare that 'Out of school he appears to have been a happy imaginative child, as alert for mild mischief as the rest of the village boys, but with something solitary and romantic in his disposition. One day indeed he went off to find the horizon.' The comparison hardly needs labouring.

Both men grew up on the edge of the Fens in an unremarkable flat landscape, which each transformed into his own personal Arcadia. Both enjoyed the outdoor life, solitary walks and the contemplation of nature. Both displayed an innocence and simplicity in their work that belied the amount of thinking and craftsmanship that had gone into it. Both initially employed short and economic line forms in their writings, which grew more complex as their style developed. At the height of their fame both were briefly courted in London and moved in influential circles, and both betrayed an aversion to the attentions and obligations of that fame from very early on. Both men struggled with the expectations of others, Clare with publishers and benefactors, Syd Barrett with record companies, managers and band mates. Both were plagued by the attention of fans and admirers and sought refuge in the self-absorption of their art, often at the expense of wider social ease. 'Like so many artists of his spiritual type,' said Geoffrey Grigson of Clare, 'he found a consolation he was unable to discover, after the happiness of childhood, in the society of men.' Both men, torn between compromising their muse and pursuing art for its own sake opted unconditionally for the latter. Both experienced intolerable stress as a result of their creative gifts and were most content when rooted in the familiarity of their formative landscape. Ultimately, it could be said that both men lived out William Wordsworth's maxim: 'We poets in our youth begin in gladness, but thereof comes in the end despondency and madness.' And in both cases there is the unresolved issue of which came first, the artistic or the personal decline, and the question of the extent to which one exacerbated the other.

Clare's physician at Epping, Dr Allen, noted that while his patient's general demeanour and conversation was that of an insane man there was not a trace of insanity in his poetry. Syd too sought sense and sanctuary in his art, while increasingly unable to function socially. 'He always felt more relaxed and able to communicate when he'd been painting,' says sister Rosemary. 'It's weird isn't it, but even from a baby it was the same. All his life it was the same. Is that just the true artist, d'you think? Is that really what an artist is? That just has a need for art itself?' On having him committed permanently to the Northampton asylum John Clare's doctor diagnosed him insane 'after years addicted to poetical prosing'.

Both men's descent into illness has been endlessly speculated on, but Clare's full-blown delusional madness was very different from Syd Barrett's quiet solitary despair. Clare's initial signs of melancholy and morbidity were variously attributed to untreated sexual disease, undiagnosed epilepsy and the stress brought on by poor diet and overwork. It is assumed that there were genetic and hereditary factors involved too, emanating from his mother's side of the family. Clare's erratic behaviour eventually erupted into a multiple-personality disorder. At various times he claimed to be, or to have written the works of, Lord Byron, Shakespeare and Alexander Pope. He also adopted the persona of an acclaimed prize-fighter, frequently breaking off from his rambling discourse about poetry to talk about some imagined forthcoming boxing match. At his most delusional he was convinced that not only had he married Mary Joyce, the long-dead first love he was hoping to see on his return from the Essex asylum, but that he was involved in a dual marriage to Mary and his actual wife Patty, and that both women had borne him children.

Although nothing like as dramatic, Syd also suffered delusional periods. Libby Gausden recalls going to visit him in 1970 when she returned his diaries. She also took her first child with her, 'Which he thought was his! I've heard since that he was crazy about babies and children and had mentioned that other people's children were his too.'

In his pioneering study 'Clare in Madness', Geoffrey Grigson offers further crucial parallels, particularly with regard to the relationship between art and madness. Grigson starts off by cautioning against romanticising the condition, 'equally against the attitude that madness itself makes a man's art; or makes it more rich and original,' he says, making it clear that 'the sensibility', i.e. the art, 'was there before the disease'. He then goes on to say, 'The preliminaries of the confirmed psychosis, the preliminary anxieties and experiences may provide both material and tincture, which a mind *not as yet impaired* may at first censor or scale down.' (Emphasis mine.) This censoring or scaling-down aspect, in other words a reluctance or refusal to deal with the problem, is as applicable to Syd's friends and band mates as it was to Syd himself. Many of those around Syd were, it seems, in collective denial about his worsening condition. It's also true to say that, initially at least, those 'preliminary anxieties and experiences', which Grigson speaks of, fed directly and sometimes positively into Syd's songs. Later, of course, those same symptoms derailed his muse completely. Although writing about John Clare, Grigson plotted Syd's own gradual dehabilitation with uncanny precision. 'The disease extends, the censorship lessens, and peculiarities may show like flowers in a night. The disease extends still further, the night deepens, the experiences are overwhelming, and the delicacies of the poet's rhythms, or the finesse of the drawings by the artist become coarse, and his form loosens towards the incoherent and fragmentary.'

Grigson talks about how at the height of his creative powers Clare lived out Wordsworth's definition of good poetry as 'the spontaneous overflow of powerful feelings.' Grigson detects a deterioration in Clare's later poetry that mirrored the decline in his mental condition. Of the poetry Clare wrote while in the asylum he notes, 'A slight steady deterioration is discernible.' Grigson characterises the short unrevised fragments that survive from this period as 'the quick records of an impulse'. That's precisely what Syd's later songs are, the quick and unsustainable record of an impulse. Of course, things are made slightly more complicated when one considers that that's exactly what many of his earliest songs were too.

The crucial difference between the two men of course is that John Clare continued to write poetry until his final years. In all he produced an estimated 3,000 poems. Syd's slender body of work was completed by the time he was twenty-five.

Clare was well looked after in Northampton asylum. He was allowed frequent unchaperoned visits into the town centre and in his fifties became a familiar figure seated in the portico of All Saints Church, chewing on a quid of tobacco, sometimes writing, and, depending on his mood, often willing to scribble a light birthday or Valentine's verse or two in return for tobacco or ale. The two men's stories synchronise in a most unexpected way when one learns that Clare was visited in the Northampton asylum by William and Mary Howitt, who greatly admired his work. Lines from William Howitt's 'Wind in a Frolic' and Clare's 'Fairy Things' appear, of course, in Syd's original version of 'Clowns and Jugglers'.

Clare made several well-documented public utterances while in the asylum, perhaps the saddest of which is the comment he made to a visitor in 1860. 'Literature has destroyed my head and brought me here,' he said. It can't be ascertained with the same degree of certainty what destroyed Syd's head.

The Roger Barrett who walked back to his mother's house in Cambridge in 1982 was virtually unrecognisable from the enthusiastic and talented teenager who had first moved up to London eighteen years earlier. Having sold the family house in Hills Road in 1978, Win Barrett was now an elderly widow living on her own in a three-bedroomed property in St Margaret's Square, Cherry Hinton, and she found it very difficult to cope with the shell of a man who returned to his home town.

'It was difficult for both of them,' concedes Rosemary. 'He was very muddled and hectic, and unhappy really. I don't think he knew what he was gonna do with himself.'

Syd had barely been back in Cambridge a few weeks when two journalists, Michka Assayas and Thomas Johnson, from *Actuel* magazine, turned up at St Margaret's Square on the pretext of returning some dirty laundry, which they had retrieved from Chelsea Cloisters. The encounter is significant because it is the last time that Syd ever spoke, albeit briefly and reluctantly, to the press. After this relatively benign episode there would only be invasive door stepping and a wall of silence.

The article that Assayas and Johnson wrote, entitled 'Behind the wall of Pink Floyd: The ghost of Syd Barrett', reveals the huge disparity that now existed between the grandeur of the Syd myth and the mundanity of Roger Keith Barrett's everyday existence. The meeting occurred shortly after Syd had been treated for a stomach ulcer, which sister Rosemary alludes to in the article. The photo which accompanies the piece shows the thirty-six-year-old Syd looking reasonably healthy with a receding hairline. He is slightly paunchier than in his prime, although nothing like the zombie-eyed and pot-bellied apparition snapped at the *Wish You Were Here* sessions in 1975. Dressed in a lilac towelling T-shirt and jeans he wears an expression that hangs midway between a smile and a grimace. That trademark slight baring of the top teeth is clearly in evidence.

Although notably hesitant and halting in his speech patterns, Syd is unfailingly polite throughout the conversation and even offers to pay the journalists for returning his clothes. It's hard to imagine any other rock star, or ex-rock star, in similar circumstances offering to stump up money for a bag of laundry. The only time his discomfort becomes evident is when the journalists ask to take his picture. 'Yes, of course,' he responds. 'He smiles, tenses up, and buttons up his collar,' the feature notes before Syd brings proceedings to an abrupt closure with a pained, 'OK, that's enough! This is distressing for me . . . Thank you.'

The piece ends with a quote from David Gilmour who provides the most poignant comment of all. Cornered in a London club he responds to the journalists' unwelcome requests for a quote with an exasperated, 'Syd Barrett? I don't have the time to talk about him. Your article has to be the last one about him. It's not romantic. It's a sad story. Now it's over.'

Gilmour couldn't have been more wrong. In some ways it was only just beginning.

Chapter Ten

Long Gone

'I've had enough of adventures. I shall lead a quiet steady, respectful life, pottering about my property, and improving it, and doing a little landscape gardening at times.'

THE WIND IN THE WILLOWS KENNETH GRAHAME

A few months after returning to Cambridge Syd suffered a complete mental collapse. 'He wasn't drinking,' says Rosemary, 'and he wasn't actually doing anything in the way of drugs, but eventually he just had a bit of a brainstorm and was violent. He would sort of wreck the house a bit and my mother was then in her seventies and was a bit frightened. And so eventually she came and lived with us and she lived with us for nearly ten years until she died.'

After the house-wrecking incident Syd spent some time at Fulbourn, a mental health facility on the outskirts of Cambridge. Unfortunately, despite its reputation as a progressive institution with an innovative approach to therapy and an emphasis on caring and counselling rather than coercion and control, Fulbourn was unable to help Syd when he needed it most. 'He was discharged very quickly after a few days, because they said it was a personality disorder,' says Rosemary. 'It was very naughty of them, actually, they just sent him back to Mum. I was always very upset about that, because I think they could have helped him. They could have sedated him; they could've given him stuff. They could've given him some after care, they could've helped

Mum with how to deal with him – but in fact they did nothing at all. They just said go home, which was a bit wicked.'

Like so many others at the time Rosemary was left to fend with a dysfunctional and damaged person and remained unimpressed with Fulbourn's policy of minimal medication and self-help.

'That's fine if you're capable, but he wasn't. He was desperate for help, and it wasn't forthcoming in those days. Maybe now it would've been. I'm not saying he necessarily wanted drugs. I think he wanted art therapy. He needed to talk. He hadn't got any friends. He needed communication. He needed lots of help and he didn't get anything at all. I felt for my mother. She was suddenly landed with this chap that we didn't know. He was a different person than the Roger that went to London. This person that came back was totally and utterly different and not really a very nice person. A very unhappy person, and a very damaged person, and really in retrospect I should've insisted on more help. But we didn't get any.'

The poignancy of her former boyfriend ending up in Fulbourn wasn't lost on Libby Gausden. 'He used to love Fulbourn hospital, strangely enough. He had this car when he was seventeen, a real black box on wheels, a really old car, which never broke down. We used to drive to Fulbourn and sit looking at the mental hospital. Remember, when we were young, every town had its mental hospital. You'd say, "Oh he's in Fulbourn." We spent a lot of time in that car looking at Fulbourn so when he went in it was a complete irony.'

Prior to his admission to Fulbourn Syd was already in poor physical health. He'd had treatment for a stomach ulcer and various other gastric ailments brought on by heavy drinking and a decade or more of physical neglect. A few months after his brief stay at Fulbourn, Social Services arranged a place for him at Greenwoods, a Christian mission in a small village called Stock, in Essex, dedicated, according to its own literature 'to those with enduring mental health problems and associated behavioural problems'. Greenwoods had been set up in 1948 by the West Ham Central Mission. In 1965 under the chaplaincy of Ron Messenger it became 'a Therapeutic Community using a psycho-social model for the support, in a residential setting, of those suffering mental ill health, and particularly those with a serious personality disorder'.

Like Fulbourn, Greenwoods placed great emphasis on group participation and occupational therapy, albeit with a more direct emphasis on Christian compassion and religious healing. In a self-published book, *The Greenwood Years*, recalling his time at the Mission, Ron Messenger included a lengthy passage about a patient called 'Roland', which was clearly a thinly disguised depiction of Syd.

There was a sense of tragedy whenever a victim of drugs arrived too late to be effectively helped. The damage to brain and body was irreparable. One of them had been a founder member of a world famous pop music group; his compositions took them to the top of the charts. Roland's father was a highly respected doctor, and there was little doubt about the caring support of the family. It was at Art College in London that Roland was first introduced to LSD and its open door into the psychedelic world. These experiences empowered the music that packed the concert halls, sold millions of records and set crowds of devotees on the trail of the group. We were warned that if his presence in Greenwoods were known queues of pilgrims would be forming at the gate. The relentless erosion of drugs dramatically curtailed Roland's sensational career . . . Medical treatment failed to reclaim his mental health, and by the time he reached Greenwoods he appeared utterly lost, inarticulate and with little control of his own affairs. He attended group sessions and took part in the work programme but resisted attempts to involve him socially. Our son Robert almost succeeded during the party evening on holiday. He handed Roland his guitar, inviting him to play. We watched hopefully as his fingers closed round the guitar and held it; then, with a shake of his head, he released his grip and handed it back. Sadly, a sign that we had to accept, that a fire had gone out and nothing could rekindle it.

'He stayed at Greenwoods for about a year then got fed up and came home,' says Rosemary. 'Shortly after this it was decided that he would live in our mother's house and she would live with me and my husband.' After his period of treatment Rosemary attempted to restore some semblance of structure and stability to her brother's life as he now assumed sole tenancy of 6 St Margaret's Square. 'He'd got his own space, and at that stage I looked after him financially and in every way really – just to help him get sorted – because he'd always lived in hotels. He'd never really lived independently, a sort of normal life if you like – going to the shops, coming back and doing the housework, this sort of thing.'

Jenny Lesmoir-Gordon's parents lived not far away in Cherry Hinton, and on her frequent visits to see them she would often spot Syd out and about in Cambridge. 'The first time I saw him I was at the garden centre with my father. I went, "Syd, hello, its Jenny." He just went, "Oh yeah, right." He had some strange white stuff round his eyes. He didn't want to engage in any conversation. But because he lived near my parents I'd see him often. I'd go into Sainsbury's and be getting something off the shelf and there he'd be next to me. Or I'd be going through a door and he'd be there opening it.'

Such sightings became a regular occurrence now that Syd was permanently back in Cambridge. Those who knew him would see Syd out buying provisions or shopping with his mother and generally kept a respectful distance.

'I felt very warm towards him,' says Jenny. 'Sometimes I'd see him in Heffers bookshop, or riding along Coleridge Road on his old-fashioned bicycle, looking like a middle-aged man, but apart from that one time we never spoke, we always just looked at each other. I just felt it would be intrusive to try and say anything to him.'

The only people in St Margaret's Square who would occasionally receive a reply from the reticent inhabitant of number 6 were the local children. Syd's nephew Ian, son of older brother Don, was born in 1972 and recalls visiting his grandmother Win and his 'Uncle Rog' in the early 1980s: 'We lived in Luton, which is thirty miles from Cambridge, so it doesn't take long to get there. And we visited my Gran all the time. Sometimes he came out of his room and sometimes he didn't. And when you're ten you don't really have any concept of music anyway. I didn't have the foggiest who Pink Floyd were at that age. I just knew that Rog had been in a band and now he lived at my Gran's house. The house had quite a long garden and there was a shed halfway down. Full of bikes. I'd meet up with my cousins from Norfolk, Aunt Ruth and Uncle Arthur's children, and we'd all be there at the same time and just race up and down the garden. When we went there we always used to play with the other kids out in the Square. It was only a small road and there were various other kids who we'd meet up with and play out the front with them. I knew one of the girls, Radha, who lived two doors up and she said he was always dead friendly and used to chat with the kids and got on well with them.'

Radha confirms this: 'Once, when I was about seven, I was engaged in a heated argument with my best friend and her visiting cousins over whether an imaginary horse from the game of make-believe we were playing would be able to fly from my house to my best friend's house. (I can't remember why this was so necessary to our game, but I really wanted that horse to fly.) She argued that that was daft, because horses don't fly at all. So finally, exasperated and angry, I trudged the whole group down the street to the Barretts', where Rog was gardening at the side of the house (I reckoned he'd be the one to ask because he never got short with us children, like all our parents would do when we asked nonsense questions). I didn't even ask if he was busy – I was a fairly bold and obstreperous child – I just marched into the garden and poked him in the back. He took his gloves off and looked at me (I remember him as always having an expression of very mild annoyance mixed with fond, caring indulgence) and I burst out with the dilemma we were having, and asked him something like "It's true that the make-believe horse can fly from here to Cherry Hinton, isn't it, Rog?" He was very patient, and took the time to explain to us that not only was I right that the imaginary horse could definitely fly to Cherry Hinton, but that in make-believe, absolutely anything you can think of is completely real and possible. He smiled at us all and then shooed us away so he could get back to his gardening.'

Visiting her parents in 1985 Libby Gausden also had a brief encounter with her former boyfriend, while out shopping. 'I said "Do you know who I am?" and he said, "Yes, I do." So I said, "Well, who am I, then?" He said, "You're Libby." I said to him, "And who are you? Are you the man with the shopping bag?" We always used to laugh at this chap. You know there's always a nutcase with a shopping bag. And, of course, that was him now. 'Cos he'd got a shopping bag just like it. And he laughed. He knew it was funny.'

'Christmas 1985 he came to our house,' says Ian Barrett. 'I remember that really well because I had this electronic toy that played music and I used to sit and play games with him on that. The only thing that struck me as odd was a friend of my older brother or maybe a friend of my Mum turned up at one point and just came round to meet him and wanted him to sign something. He was very friendly, but the thing that always struck me was that he had a very precise way of talking. He would describe things in a very precise way and would take a very long time to describe what it was. I don't know if it's a Cambridge thing but I've noticed my Dad's got it too.'

In October 1988, largely as a result of persistent enquiries and petitions by Barrett fans, the *Opel* compilation was released on EMI-Harvest. As the sleeve notes made clear this was not a long-lost third album, but a collection of previously unreleased songs ('Opel', 'Dolly Rocker', 'Word Song', 'Swan Lee', 'Birdie Hop', 'Let's Split', 'Lanky Part One', 'Milky Way') and alternate takes ('Clowns and Jugglers', 'Rats', 'Golden Hair', 'Wined and Dined', 'Wouldn't You Miss Me'). The merit, or otherwise, of these recordings has been discussed earlier, but what is noteworthy is the contrast between EMI's (and indeed Pink Floyd's) official stance over lost or unreleased recording, and the diligent research of the more knowledgeable fans. For many years the company line was that there was nothing of value in the vaults. This was also the official line EMI took with the Beatles until 1996 when miraculously space was found in the schedule for three whole double CD volumes of out-takes to coincide with the release of the eight-part VHS box set, the *Beatles Anthology*.

As was the case with the *Beatles Anthology* recordings, hard-core Barrett fans had possessed most of the *Opel* tracks on bootleg years before they were officially released. The *Opel* compilation, although by no means exhaustive, played a significant part in rejuvenating interest in Syd's career. As a result of this renewed interest Rosemary's husband, Paul Breen, made a brief appearance on Nicky Campbell's late night Radio 1 show on 27 October 1988 to talk about his brother-in-law. Breen revealed that Syd no longer played a musical instrument but that he had resumed painting. In response to Campbell's suggestion that Syd now lived a reclusive life he replied 'I think the word "reclusive" is probably emotive. It would probably be truer to say that he enjoys his own company now rather than that of others.' Breen also mentioned that Syd met his mother in town a couple of times a week for shopping and that he led 'a very, very ordinary sort of lifestyle'. He also suggested that Syd had come through the worst of his bad experiences and that 'There's a level of contentment, now, which he probably hasn't felt since before he got involved in music.' The interview was conducted with great sensitivity by Campbell, who concluded by stating, 'I know he doesn't speak to the press, and I don't blame him for that, but when you see him, Paul, pass on our very best wishes to him.'

Unfortunately the same degree of sensitivity was not shown by the *News of the World*, which in the same month sent a reporter and photographer to dig up dirt on Mad Syd. With customary subtlety the *News of the World* article faithfully reported the testimony of a dubious neighbour who claimed that he had frequently heard Syd barking like a dog and shrieking like a lunatic. For good measure Jonathan Meades' 'Syd locked in the cupboard' story was dusted down and given another airing. A hastily snatched photo of Syd in his back yard, wearing paint-stained jeans, a scruffy jumper and a startled expression, accompanied the piece. Although it caused considerable distress to family and genuine fans alike, the *News of the World* article wasn't significantly different in tone from many of the more lurid pieces about Syd that had been published in the music press over the years. Unfortunately such intrusions from obsessive fans, press hacks, and would-be biographers would become a consistent feature of the last twenty years of his life. Even in dull routine domesticity Roger Keith Barrett would not be allowed to lead a normal life.

Despite frequent and heartfelt pleas from his family that he should be left alone, devotees still made regular pilgrimage to his nondescript semi-detached house on the outskirts of Cambridge, 'I Know Where Syd Barrett Lives' the new wave group the Television Personalities had sung in homage in 1981, and, so it seems, did hundred of others.

Some of the stories of intrusion and harassment that have emerged from Syd's twilight years are truly disturbing – visitors climbing into his garden to steal his painting equipment, people peering in through his windows armed with camcorders, or poking them through his letterbox, people posing as couriers to get him to sign for parcels, so that they could secure his autograph, people stalking him in the street and photographing him against his will. Such infringements of Syd's privacy were a weekly, sometimes daily, occurrence during the last two decades of his life. Assayas and Johnson's 1982 *Actuel* article had set the tone for things to come, mentioning that on the day they visited him a young hippie had 'paced up and down in front of the house, a bottle of milk in his hand, kind of a weird look in his eyes'.

'When people knocked on his door I often wonder what they thought was going to happen,' says nephew Ian Barrett. 'Did they expect he was going to say, "Come in, let's do acid"? When people ask me to talk about him I think, "Do you want to hear what you want to hear or do you want the reality?" Because the reality, it's not negative, but it is quite dull. This is the whole weird scenario the family has had to face. You've got that person and that person. It is a dichotomy, a literal split. You've got two people. Liking the music is one thing. That's fair enough. It's the people who took it one step further. That's the bit that's disturbing.'

'I certainly recall many, many people turning up in the street and the neighbourhood in general looking for Syd,' says Radha. 'At the time, being a small child, I thought it was quite normal for hippies with rucksacks and well-dressed men with notebooks to be hanging round in the street, and assumed it went on everywhere! Quite often, particularly in the later years, after his address had been revealed through a number of sources, there would be knocks at our door from pilgrim hippie kids or curious foreign tourists, asking which was Syd Barrett's house, if he still lived in the neighbourhood, what time he went out for a walk, etc. When I was still small, I remember being confused, and telling them that there was nobody in our street called "Syd". I was, of course, unaware of Roger's other life until I reached the age to be interested in such things, and that they should probably re-consult their maps. When I got a bit older, and realised what was actually going on, I would get rather upset and would tell them in so many words to go away.'

Syd attracted more than his share of fanatics. The same kind of people who expressed their admiration for Jim Morrison by scribbling graffiti all over his Parisian grave now began to turn up at the home of their reluctant hero in droves. People, who, one presumes, would never desecrate their own family graves, or want others intruding into the lives of the more fragile members of their own clan if it was their own mother or brother or uncle who was unstable or ill, were only too happy to ride roughshod over the well-publicised wishes and concerns of the Barrett family in order to shatter the privacy of a vulnerable middle-aged man, no longer in the best of physical and mental health, because of things he had done, and put aside, a quarter of a century earlier.

'If I was at his house and somebody came to the door, he'd say, "Well what do they want? What do they want from me?"' says Rosemary. 'And he just didn't understand why people didn't come to my door as well, and ask me about my life. He didn't know what he'd done in his life that was so important, that made these people come. He really didn't understand, and it was bewildering for him and uncomfortable.'

'What is this whole thing about fame that people get hooked on?' says Hester Page. 'It's just extraordinary. They have to go and be near someone that's famous. People want that myth. It's like people want to be in love in life because otherwise life's a bit boring, or they want some sort of fantasy to keep them going and myth does that. People love to build those myths in order to substantiate their own myths.'

'There were a fair few visitors. People were very insistent,' says Rosemary. 'I think when you're in that line, you're public property, or a celebrity of any sort, whether you want it or not, the public think that you belong to them, don't they? And some people just would not take no for an answer at all. Some people, especially some of the young kids, were good, and I'd talk to them, just sort of try and explain a bit. I could talk to the younger people, but some of the women, especially some of the women of my age, who had become focused on him in a very OCD sort of way, it was a dreadful obsession with them – they were difficult. There was no reasoning with them. They were in love with him and he was theirs – and they were gonna marry him, and all this sort of rubbish. There are a lot of lonely people – well, perhaps they're lonely, or perhaps they're just mentally disturbed, I don't know. But they just latch on to a celebrity, but I think it happens to just about everybody. I mean like poor old John Lennon. You can just get this obsession and there's no reasoning behind it at all. It's just illogical and unpleasant really, for the person concerned. Very unpleasant.'

Winifred Barrett died on 30 September 1991, aged eighty-six. Her youngest son didn't attend the funeral. Soon after his mother died Syd had another of his periodic purges and burnt many of his possessions, including paintings, and a considerable collection of art literature. An equally telling, and less widely known consequence of his mother's death was that Syd lapsed into a considerable period of melancholic reflection on the past.

'I didn't go to his mother's funeral,' says Libby Gausden. 'We were abroad when Win died. I should have gone. My mother went. But I saw Rosemary afterwards and she said, "Libby, you have to go and see him because he's in that era at the moment." She said, "He knows who you are." I knew that because when I met him the previous time in the Eighties he knew who I was and he was in utter madness then. Anyway, Rosemary said, "Go and see him. He would love it. He may be shy and he may not let you in at first." And I never did,' says Libby with regret. 'Always too busy. Always something to do.'

In 1993, two years after his mother had died, Libby's daughter

Abigail had an unusual encounter with Syd while on the way to university. 'She was walking to lectures and this guy was going by on his bike and he got off his bike and bowed down,' recalls Libby. What gives this episode an almost unbearable poignancy was that Abigail was wearing one of her mother's old 1960s Biba coats at the time. Syd addressed her as 'little Lib' before he went on his way leaving the slightly startled and bemused Abigail standing on the pavement. 'I think she was a bit frightened,' says Libby. 'She, of course, didn't know who he was. He got back on his bike and cycled off and her friend said to her, "That was Syd Barrett." She was devastated that she hadn't run up and hugged him.'

There must have been many similar occurrences like this in Syd's later years. Cambridge was now a place of ghosts and memories, glimpsed from the passing bike of yet another of that city's fully-fledged bicycling eccentrics. In the years after his mother's death Syd settled down to life on his own, bothering no one and living in the forlorn hope that no one would bother him. He took refuge once more in his imagination, the one safe place he knew, and when people weren't breaking into his garden to steal his art materials he found solace, as he had done since childhood, in his painting. While Syd found renewed satisfaction in his creativity his eldest brother, Alan, took on the responsibility of his business affairs. His brothers and sisters ensured that he had the support system of a caring family and David Gilmour conscientiously made sure that the royalties got through.

'In the early days when we went there, when I was very young, I don't remember there being much there in the way of painting stuff,' says Ian Barrett. 'But he was still living with my Gran, and it was her house. It wasn't until she moved out that he started. Later on, after about 1986, there were always easels and he would show me paintings he'd done. There were always loads of art books on the shelves and scribbles and doodles he'd done.'

Syd painted, as he always had done, prolifically and in a variety of styles – landscapes, abstracts, still lifes, light studies, colour-field exercises – and did so chiefly for therapeutic reasons and not with an eye towards public display. Indeed, on the one occasion Rosemary broached the idea of an exhibition Syd didn't so much baulk at the idea as express incredulity at the very notion that anyone would be interested. Very few of these paintings were seen by the general public during his lifetime and unfortunately only a fraction of his work has survived owing to Syd's propensity for photographing his paintings and then destroying the canvases once he had completed them.

'The exemplary modern artist's choice of silence isn't often carried to this point of final simplification so that he becomes literally silent,' says Susan Sontag. 'More typically he continues speaking, but in a manner his audience cannot hear.' That's what Syd was doing now. We have no insights into his methodology, or any way of knowing his rationale for any these paintings. One could argue that this is artistic purity of a kind, but it's a kind which excludes the viewer almost completely.

The paintings (and photographs of paintings) that have survived are of variable quality, ranging from mere daubs and sketches to some extremely impressive work in oils. His abstract canvases, and some of the landscapes too, show that he had clearly not lost his touch, or perhaps it is more pertinent to say had partially regained it. 'I thought they were brilliant,' says Anthony Stern of the later paintings. 'I thought, "Now I get it." There's a bit of Paul Nash in there, there's a bit of Ivan Hitchens. I could see where Syd, had he stuck to painting, would've fitted into the canon of British Art. He could've become a successful British artist.'

The preponderance of landscapes is interesting, revealing the survival, or perhaps indicating the revival, of Syd's tranquil gaze.

'A landscape doesn't demand from the spectator his under-standing, his imputations of significance, his anxieties and sympathies,' says Susan Sontag, and for 'spectator' in this case read 'artist' as well, for Syd was highly capable of being a detached bystander at his own creativity. 'It demands rather his absence, that he does not add anything to it,' continues Sontag. 'Contemplation, strictly speaking, entails self-forgetfulness on the part of the spectator.'

One of the saddest things about observing and assessing these surviving art works now is the overwhelming sense of a gift interrupted, and a man trying to get back to the place he once was. Some are mere pastiche; others are re-treads of themes and exercises he had last pursued during his Camberwell apprenticeship a quarter of a century earlier.

His music tastes too reverted to the impulses that had once guided the hip young teenager. 'He listened to a little bit of classical music,' says Rosemary, 'but mainly jazz. He really loved jazz. Miles Davis. Thelonious Monk. And "Green Onions", Booker T and the MGs. We always played that when we were teenagers. He still enjoyed listening to that sort of stuff.'

'People always ask me, "Did he do this or did he play that?",' says Ian Barrett. 'The simple fact is he had a little record player and a tape deck but very few records and tapes with it. Just bits and bobs. Jazz tapes mainly.'

In contrast to the quiet contemplative way in which he applied himself to his painting Syd's lesser practical skills were pursued with comic abandon. 'The house, he wrecked,' laughs Rosemary. 'He took all the architraves off and all the door surrounds off, and most of the doors off, in fact. And then he replaced them with different architraves that we got from B&Q and places. Every wall would be painted a different colour. The idea of painting a room with the same colour was just nonsensical to him. I used to say to him, "Do two walls the same colour." "But why?" he'd say, "They're all different walls." The house was very colourful and anybody else would say it was a disaster. But that's how he liked it. We used to go to B&Q and Homebase and get all this wood endlessly, and do lots of DIY projects, which were very funny. He used to laugh at them because they never worked at all. And he used to make wooden sculptures with the bits of leftover wood, which were really rather nice. I don't actually know what happened to them, but he used to layer different shapes of wood on top of each other and then paint them. It was good fun actually. Some of them were really nice.'

'He used to take himself up to London on the train and visit art galleries so this whole recluse thing is inaccurate,' maintains Ian Barrett. 'And when you delve a bit deeper and speak to people in the streets nearby he used to go to the pub, the Rock on Cherry Hinton Road, quite a lot. He wasn't a recluse at all. The perception among some people, because of that *News of the World* thing, is that he was barking and howling like a dog. That's a cheap shot. He may well have had the occasional strop about things. I've no doubt he did. Everyone does. He did DIY quite a lot and wasn't very good at it. It's no secret. You've only got to see the footage when the house was for sale and the stuff that turned up for auction. Unbelievable! But it was functional. It wasn't classically stunning furniture. He tried to re-wire the house at one point, and every time they had to go and pay someone afterwards to come in and redo it. So if he was screaming at one point it was probably because he had bashed a nail into somewhere inappropriate!'

'He always got up early,' says Rosemary. 'All his life he got up early. And then most days he'd cycle to Sainsbury's and back again. Interestingly enough, there were one or two of the girls that used to work at Sainsbury's who he did used to talk to. Probably not more than "How are you?" but if they said something to him, he would reply. And there was one girl who used to work in the chemist where he spent a lot of time, who was very nice to him, and he was really quite fond of her, which is something very strange for me to acknowledge, because he didn't have any friends or any warmth really for anybody except me, probably. And so, that was his life, he went to Sainsbury's, he came home, he did a bit of painting, and he went to bed. He had the radio only for the jazz programmes. He'd listen to jazz but he wouldn't listen to talking. He wouldn't listen to a play or anything. I don't know what he used to do in the evenings, sit in the kitchen, I think. But I think there was enough going on in his head. He had televisions periodically – but he never kept them for long. I think it was because there was so much talking and business in his head, creativity etc, that the annoyance of a television, or even of somebody talking, was interrupting these thoughts. I mean sometimes, just looking at him, you could hear all these things going on. It was more than thinking, it was like a conversation. And you really did feel you couldn't interrupt him. I mean, a lot of time we spent together was in silence, which I didn't mind but there was a lot going on, you know. You could see in his face that he was busy. Even though he was just sitting quietly.'

While Syd lived out his days in quiet solitude his fellow residents in St Margaret's Square were very protective towards him. There was an unwritten code of practice among neighbours than any enquiry from inquisitive fans as to the exact location of 'Syd Barrett's house' would be answered with, 'I'm sorry there is no one of that name in this road' – which technically was correct anyway. The more mischievous or aggrieved residents would send visitors to adjacent streets or locations further afield.

In 1995 Ian Barrett gave an interview to a website, primarily to warn off potential visitors. 'That was the only real point of doing the interview,' he says. 'To suggest to people that if you are thinking of going there, just don't basically. He was alone pretty much all day every day. He wasn't in the strongest mental or physical health at that time and could certainly have done without it. You just wouldn't want someone sitting outside your house, all the time, would you?'

'Because he lived on his own and didn't have any friends, he would go from one of my visits to the next not speaking,' says Rosemary. 'And if you don't speak, if you don't converse for a little while, you lose the ability. You get all your words muddled up and you get tired when you're trying to talk – and I think that's what happened to him. He just simply got out of practice. It sounds silly, but I don't suppose that normal people ever get into that situation. But I think eventually he found talking even to me hard work.'

In February 1997 an auction took place at the Saatchi Gallery in north London in aid of War Child International, an organisation set up to help children caught up in the horrors of war. Twenty-three artists and musicians designed artworks in tribute to musicians who had inspired them. Contributors included Kate Bush paying homage to Billie Holiday, Bryan Ferry to Charlie Parker, Brian Eno to the Velvet Underground, Yoko Ono to John Lennon, Pavarotti to Enrico Caruso, David Bowie to the Walker Brothers, Lou Reed to Ornette Coleman, and Paul McCartney to Buddy Holly. Blur guitarist Graham Coxon paid homage to Syd Barrett with a piece entitled 'Scream Thy Last Scream', which consisted of a ninety-six-by-thirty-six-foot yellow polystyrene lightning bolt aimed downwards at a tiny model railway bridge. Scribbled in red on the lightning bolt were the words 'Scream Thy Last Scream.' A short poem, accompanying the exhibit read:

SYD BARRETT . . . Conjuror, Wizard (non hippy)
Bigger than the space POP could ever hope to offer.
Jailed within boundaries . . . districts so silent.

A wall, save for eyes.

SYD, mummified within the realm of POP, in which this elegy is

entrapped.

A CALL TO CREATIVITY . . . 'SCREAM THY LAST SCREAM,

MR . . .

    a) Sonic painter

    b) Auto Soundsmith

    c) Expressionable Non cynic

    d) True Believer

    e) Emotional innocent

WHO KNEW THE IMPORTANCE

OF

TANTRUM . . .'

'In a way I was trying to be automatic about things,' says Coxon of his contribution to the War Child auction. 'He wasn't really an automatic painter but he was almost an automatic guitar player. I think at that point with my own band I was totally understanding of his inability to grin and bear it all or do things that he couldn't. The thing with Syd is, we're never quite sure whether he did just get contrary. I mean, he was a likeable bouncy happy sort of chap by all accounts but then suddenly something changed. I think he was psychologically damaged by drugs, and I was thinking about the problems I was having with alcohol at the time. It's difficult though, because I've never read an account of him saying that it was to do with rejecting the music business and the scheduling, and the selling out. Psychologically perhaps he just wasn't cut out for it.'

'My first encounter with Syd's music was when I'd gone to art school,' says Coxon. 'I was just seventeen. I met a girl, I really liked her, and spent a whole night at a party talking to her. In Colchester there were a lot of hippies and psychedelic people and a scene at Colchester Art Centre. I was in a group that did improvisations and they were all into Van Der Graaf Generator and Gong. This girl I met had long black hair, and wore paisley dresses, tights and purple shoes. I was mostly dressed in turps-stinking overalls. Her record collection was amazing for a seventeen-year-old at that time in the Eighties when there was nothing else to listen to. You really had to dig about. She had Pink Floyd records, Van Der Graaf Generator, Robert Wyatt. I was still learning guitar. I was getting good but I was listening to the Who and the Kinks a lot. She played me Pink Floyd's *Relics*, and I immediately had to own that album. And it was an absolute revelation to me to hear *Piper at the Gates of Dawn*, in her bedroom with olives and red wine. That was when I got into olives as well. A lot of things struck me as being very tasty suddenly.'

Coxon's affectionate memories of his Barrett epiphany are far more typical of how many people were drawn, and continue to be drawn, to Syd Barrett's music, than the rarefied experiences of a select group of people who were part of the 1960s social and cultural elite. This is not to denigrate that social and cultural elite whose innovations were profound and whose initiatives were the bedrock on which the counter-culture was built. But if we only paid attention to those explorers and their era there would be no legacy to speak of. It is rarely acknowledged that LSD use in Britain actually increased after the 1960s. To only give credence to the philosophies and perspectives of the Leary/Hollingshead/Owsley generation is to freeze the psychedelic experience in a specific time and place. None of this accounts for how subsequent generations of acid voyagers have continued to discover and re-interpret Syd Barrett's music as their own. The experiences of numerous inner-city punks, or Julian Cope in Tamworth, the Jesus and Mary Chain's Reid brothers in East Kilbride or Graham Coxon and his paisley-dressed and purpleshoed muse in Colchester bear little resemblance to those of the original Set and Setting initiates of the 1960s, but they emerge from similar impulses and exactly the same stimulus, and unlike the psychedelic pioneers of the 1960s these latter generations of acid heads had the benefit of a ready-made tripper's manual.

'I was listening to *Piper at the Gates of Dawn* when I did acid for the first time,' remembers Coxon. 'I was in New Cross, of all places, not the nicest of places to do it, and I was thinking this is purpose-built for tripping. I loved the music anyway and the beautiful imagery like I did when I was a kid listening to "Strawberry Fields". It's not exactly child-friendly imagery. Its dark. The imagery I had as a child when I was listening to "Tomorrow Never Knows" was some cowboys going down a river on a raft being shot by the Indians. And "Let me take you down" in "Strawberry Fields" was a really frightening coalmine or diamond mine. Whereas *Piper* was a little more purpose-built around tripping. The lyrics would be throwing this imagery at you and the scanning was peculiar, and there was always this bit where a firework would go off and you'd see it crash in the sky musically, and that would entertain your drugged ears and your mind. I remember thinking, "Wow, the acid really does work." But it's like the egg and the chicken. Was it always there and the acid just made it funnier or more interesting or deeper? Or did people make songs to entertain their acidy heads?'

Outside of the pantheon of fairy tales and records drenched in phasing there were less orthodox elements of English whimsy at work too. While acknowledging the enduring influence of the music hall, Graham Coxon also cites Jack 'The Raspberry King' Hodges as an unlikely precursor, particularly Hodges' song 'Mr Policeman' with its spluttering stuttering verses punctuated by comic 'raspberries'. 'I'm still trying to gauge whether people who heard that stuff while on acid like I did would think it was really funny,' ponders Coxon. 'That song always seemed to have the strange, dark depth as nursery rhymes, ring-a-ring-a-roses, things like that, these singalong things with a sinister nature.'

'It's like a trawler isn't it?' says Coxon of Syd's lyrics. 'Or panning for gold. It either comes very quick or it takes ages. I like to write before I've woken up before my head starts telling me the right and wrongs, before habit hampers proceedings. With that sort of writing, maybe he wrote on acid, I don't know. I never really imagine that actually being on drugs was good for making music particularly, maybe writing words and drawing, but it's always more profound afterwards looking back. But his skill was to get that freedom into lyrical form whereas I just get caught out with cliché, with what lyrics are. There are words that are lyrics and words that aren't but he managed to use words that aren't lyrics and use them lyrically. I've only been able to write letters like that. In the same way that I draw for my own entertainment he must have had the greatest fun just sitting down and writing words.'

Coxon recognised in Syd's spontaneous lyric-writing methods the pure unmediated joy of creativity for its own sake. 'If you draw something absurd everyday, doesn't matter what it is, and it goes for writing as well I'd imagine, it's like a brain enema, it's like rebooting your computer. It clears all the pipes out and gets all the little sparks going again. I was a big storywriter when I was a kid and, sadly, a lot of these things get knocked out of you by school. You're told not to be so daft or puerile if you draw a farting bum or some half-human half-mouse creature. A lot of our confidences we have, or unselfconsciousness about what we can do with a pencil or paper as a kid – you get scared away from doing it by school teachers. The whole point is that this is for our own entertainment or the good of our minds. It's not to be published or go in a gallery. I was lucky enough to get into art school and have my absurd drawings taken very seriously by artists who were teaching me. It didn't quite get beaten out of me but if you're told what you are doing is rubbish for long enough you get scared to do it. And I suppose that was the thing about Syd's apparent innocence. He still held on to the unselfconscious joy of invention.'

The chief aspect of Syd Barrett's music that appealed to the Britpop generation was of course, the sheer unashamed Englishness of it all. 'Everyone suddenly went from the blues back to the early 1900s,' says Coxon of English psychedelia. 'The Americans didn't but we did. It's the weirdest thing.' Coxon occasionally performs Syd's most vaudevillian compositions 'Love You' and 'Here I Go', and clearly recognises the underlying music-hall aspect of his music. 'Doing those songs is that best part of being English, where in a way I wish I'd grown up where I could punt and wear a boater and blazer. We have that thing within our culture. It's cheeky and winky. That jazzy straw boater thing. It's there in the Small Faces. It was there in Blur. This music-hall tradition that was carried through. It's something about being English, and English lyric writing, that the Americans don't have, especially in the Sixties. We have the good words that the Americans don't use really, or if they do use them they abbreviate them or make it sound silly. And the American way-out psychedelic bands wouldn't write songs like the English did. It's the built-in eccentricity and frivolity and flamboyance of the English, even down to the clothes. The English messed around and had fun with clothes more than the Americans. We messed around with Edwardian and earlier costumery. For the Americans it was enough to wear jeans.'

Coxon has a characteristically art school take on the enduring gestural language of pop that has little to do with the politics of rebellion and everything to do with the liberation of the body. 'It's to do with that freeing up of everything, the freeing up of the hair. Not having to put the macintosh on and part your hair and put the tie on and go to work. The hair got free and the clothes got free and it changed people's whole posture. It was expressive and fun. If you're walking around in big ruffley shirts and velvet trousers then you're going to feel quite louche. There's a lot of campery. It's intelligent. And it feels graceful and elegant. I know a few thugs put the shirts on as well and just drank ale but when I put a suit on my posture changes and my accent cleans up a little bit and you feel not gay but Oscar Wildeish and dandified.'

The holy trinity of the Who, the Kinks and the Small Faces was quite clearly the precursor of Britpop in the mid-1990s, but as Graham Coxon makes clear the Syd Barrett-era Pink Floyd had just as profound an influence on the movement's musical direction and sense of style. For every lad band anthem there was a Syd-influenced song lurking in the wings.

Meanwhile on the outer fringes some less likely spirits were still carrying a torch for Syd's music. 'Maybe ten years ago I tried to encourage Ed Baxter of the LMC to try to get an exhibition of Syd's painting and my painting,' Keith Rowe told me in 2008. 'I thought about maybe even getting him to play too – 'cos I'm sure there was something there, which I would love to have done, not in public or anything – unless he felt like it – I mean I don't have a problem with playing in public but he might have done. I'm sure the spirit was still there with him in a way. But I feel the same way as I did then, and I couldn't see why he shouldn't play. I still approach the instrument in exactly the same way as I did in the mid-Sixties. And I think one reason I'm able to do that is from one of my painting teachers – a guy called Ben Hartley. He actually gave us our art school motto, which was "Success is to be middle-aged and obscure". And that's how he was in his life – totally obscure – and I think obscurity is just great 'cos you just carry on doing your work, undisturbed by all that other stuff.'

'The music thing became a business and I'm sure he was more comfortable with the painting situation,' agrees Mick Rock. 'For one thing, he could do it on his own, when he felt like doing it, and if he didn't feel like doing it, he wouldn't do it. And, of course, he produced quite a lot of work, although from what I gather he destroyed most of his paintings. But the ironic thing is that he photographed a load of them too. He wanted the actual original painting destroyed, but he wanted to keep a record of it, which I think is quite a curious factor. You would have thought if he was obliterating the painting, he'd wanna take it completely out of existence.'

Syd's habit of creating, photographing and then destroying his artwork has led many to speculate on his motives. On the one hand artists take photographs of their endeavours for a variety of practical reasons, for further study, to map progress, as a simple record of work done, to document some aspect of detail and perspective, as memory prompts, as a substitute for a sketch. On the other hand the practice points to a level of unmediated response and a lack of need for validation that had always been part of Syd's make-up. These acts of wilful destruction also point to the abiding influence of John Latham.

'Behind the appeals for silence lies the wish for a perceptual and cultural clean slate,' notes Susan Sontag in *The Aesthetics of Silence*. 'And in its most hortatory and ambitious version the advocacy of silence expresses a mythic project of total liberation. What's envisaged is nothing less than the liberation of the artist from himself, of art from the particular art work, of art from history, of spirit from matter, of the mind from its perceptual and intellectual limitations.'

'There was always a certain amount of, I don't think "self-hatred" is the right word, and I don't think it's self-loathing, but he negated himself a lot y'know?' says Mick Rock. 'He said "No" to himself. Whatever he produced, once he'd produced it he lost interest in it. He felt shackled by it. But he was like a pure spirit. Early on when I knew him, he loved being around a lot of people but by 1969 he'd changed. My experience of Syd was he wanted to have fun. But somehow he was stymied and then he got caught in this trap, this psychological trap and he couldn't get out of it. But he wasn't known for all the years he was in Cambridge for doing anything, I mean it wasn't like he attacked anybody. It wasn't like he was an axe-murderer or he was running around raging or foaming at the mouth. He just withdrew. He just refused to deal with people, that's all.'

He didn't entirely refuse to deal with Mick Rock though. In 2001 Syd surprised many people, including Rock himself, by agreeing to sign 320 copies of a deluxe edition of *Psychedelic Renegades*, a 160-page limited-edition volume of Rock's photos of Syd. The book contained 120 monochrome and colour images, the majority of which were taken at Wetherby Mansions in 1969 and at Hills Road Cambridge in 1971, as well as the original unedited transcript of Rock's 1971 interview for *Rolling Stone* magazine. A lucrative business deal was struck for the signatures and Syd didn't have to meet either publisher or author in order to sign the single sheets that were sent to him – which he signed simply 'Barrett'.

'Ian Barrett told me Syd had told him that my pictures were his favourite pictures of himself,' says Mick Rock. 'That was his explanation of why he signed. 'Cos I know, when we approached Rosemary, she said, "Oh, I don't know if he'll do that, it's not the sort of thing he would normally do." But she said, "We'll see. Send the sheets over." And he signed them. So he obviously had a certain affection for me left over, even though he didn't communicate with me. But he didn't communicate with Dave Gilmour either, and Dave after all was the guy who made sure he got his royalties. Dave, being a true gentleman, looked out for Syd. I saw him in New York at the Hall of Fame, when they were working on the *Echoes* compilation. And he said he'd made sure that there were a bunch of Syd songs in it so that he would get the money. Talking to Bryan Morrison a couple of years later, I used the word "poor" Syd. And, of course, Bryan being a businessman said, "Poor Syd? He made two and a half million quid last year because of *Echoes*!" And he added, "He makes at least a couple of hundred grand every year from the royalties from his own records." '

In November 2001 the BBC commemorated Syd Barrett's life in a fifty-minute *Omnibus* documentary called 'Crazy Diamond'. The programme was made only after prolonged and sensitive negotiation with the Barrett family, part of which involved Rosemary surreptitiously co-operating with the project without Syd's knowledge. The resulting documentary treated its subject with dignity and respect. 'We all still desperately miss him,' said Rick Wright as he spoke of a creative life which was over by the age of twenty-four. Roger Waters and David Gilmour both spoke admiringly of Syd's lyrical and musical talent. 'There's something about the way the lyric attracts to the metre in a very satisfying way,' said Waters, after reciting the opening verse of 'Bike' in a manner that perfectly captured its conversational cadence. 'I think it was the unpredictability of it combined with its simplicity that made it so special,' he said, summing up not just 'Bike', but its author too. Gilmour spoke lovingly of Syd's personal magnetism as a teenager back in Cambridge, and while not holding back on the difficulty of producing the solo album did also concede that Syd 'never seemed stuck for a word or a melody'.

The band members were also brutally honest about their emotional shortcomings at times of crises. 'We had a sort of style almost of if there was a problem ignore it,' says Mason. 'And we finally came to the point where we ignored it by not picking Syd up.'

Bob Klose is sanguine about his departure. 'It needed me to leave,' he insists, while Mike Leonard talks equally modestly about his own seminal role in the band's musical development. Jerry Shirley, who played drums on the solo albums, says, 'I was never convinced that he was quite as nutty as a lot of people assume him to be, because there were definitely times when I personally witnessed him using his nuttiness if you like, faking it almost.' Uber-fan Robyn Hitchcock speaks of his initial engagement with Syd's music as 'this imploded middle-class mother's boy from Cambridge was speaking absolutely to me, as a little imploding middle-class mother's boy from Winchester'. Hitchcock performs a suitably stumbling version of 'Dominoes' and refers to Syd's lyrics as 'dense thickets of imagery' before immediately correcting himself. 'Actually I hate that word imagery. They were dense thickets of words.' 'Mental *vérité*', he calls Syd's writing methods.

Perhaps the documentary's biggest coup was that it was watched by the man himself. 'I was very surprised that he did watch – he came to watch it with me,' says Rosemary. 'He didn't enjoy it. He didn't like it – he didn't quite know what was going on I don't think. He just said, "It's very noisy. The music's very noisy." The only nice thing was seeing his old lecturer, I think. I was very tense because I didn't know what he was gonna do, 'cos I knew it wasn't gonna go down very well.'

The 'old lecturer' that Rosemary mentions was in fact light-show pioneer Mike Leonard. According to Rosemary Syd didn't make the reference while the programme was on, but in his reflections the following day when she went to visit him. Apart from that simple acknowledgement Rosemary says that the programme didn't appeal to him. 'He didn't enjoy it. No. Another life, another person.'

Having briefly re-acquainted himself with his former life Roger Keith Barrett returned to the preferable mundanity of his everyday existence, cycling to Sainsbury's, buying his art materials, visiting Homebase, listening to jazz and classical music and painting.

Unfortunately he was rarely allowed to do this with any degree of privacy. In 2004 nine minutes of disturbingly intrusive camcorder footage appeared on the internet. Shot in 1998, and played in slow motion to a soundtrack of eerie ambient music, it shows Syd emerging from his local shops on a bright summer's day. Shaven-headed, he is wearing a grubby off-white singlet, and carrying a considerable paunch. Now fifty-one years old, he still bounces on his heels when he walks. At first, whoever is doing the filming keeps a discreet distance, and Syd is clearly oblivious to the presence of his stalker, but right at the end of the footage he is filmed from close distance, almost head on, and can be seen mouthing angrily at his pursuer. He glances with wary disdain at them and crosses the road. The film then cuts out.

The footage was shot by the host of a Syd Barrett website, which subsequently closed down in acrimony, directly as a result of the hostility which greeted the film's release. When confronted with the allegation that he shot the film, the perpetrator himself is said to have claimed that it was shot by two Japanese tourists who happened to be in the area, and presumably just happened to want some random footage of a man in his vest walking down a typical English street. The airing of the footage (which at one time was offered for sale via mail order) brought wide-scale condemnation from those fans who still possessed a shred of integrity, but it revealed in disturbing detail the lengths some people were prepared to go (or to be more accurate the depths they were prepared to plumb) in order to gain proximity to their hero. Extracts still turn up on websites such as *YouTube*, usually accompanied by a volley of condemnation and abuse in the comments section.

In many respects Syd has been no better served by his biographers than by his stalkers. Indeed, some have convincingly blurred the boundaries between the two with their graphic depictions of following Syd to and from the shops, or actually doorstepping their subject in order to get that all-important money shot.

There are numerous similar accounts of thick-skinned fanzine and website editors visiting Syd's house armed with fully annotated bootleg recordings, the accumulated residue of a creative life long since abandoned, sitting outside the house for a while, before popping them through the door along with an explanatory note and a contact number.

Some brief speculation at this juncture. Although un-diagnosed with any mental illness, let's assume that one of Syd's enduring symptoms of his troubled life was a certain mild paranoia, brought on and exacerbated by the sheer amount of unwelcome visitors that camped by his front gate during the last years of his life. Although, as his sister Rosemary made clear, he generally reacted to these intrusions with bewilderment, what does it do to a man's sense of stability to look out of his curtains and see a parked car outside his house, its occupants not moving, merely glancing furtively at the house now and again, and maybe disappearing for a while, before returning an hour or so later?

In 1991 an independent production company called Sleeping Partners was given development money by Channel 4 to make a documentary about Syd, but the project was abandoned at development stage. There was a similar proposal around the same period to investigate the link between mental illness and creativity which also intended to feature Syd as a case study. Again nothing came of this. In August 2001 a request from an independent production company to film outside Syd's house brought a furious response from the family and an understandable closing of ranks. Prior to this a coach-load of German fans turned up at the home of Paul and Rosemary Breen, having decided that Barrett family addresses were now a legitimate part of some ghoulish tourist trail. The Breens were forced to go ex-directory when they continued to be bombarded with similar requests.

In 2002 EMI issued the *Wouldn't You Miss Me* compilation on

CD. This release was given extra cachet by the inclusion of the long-lost 'Bob Dylan Blues'. As with the earlier issue of *Opel* the *Wouldn't You Miss Me* release brought about a renewal of fan interest and a fresh wave of media intrusion. Syd was doorstepped and photographed again, this time by the *Daily Mail*. 'I think you'd better go, mate. I don't do that any more,' he told the reporter.

In among all the other forms of intrusion one person was even prepared to assume Syd's identity on the internet. In 2004 an entry appeared for 'Syd Barrett' on the popular social networking website *Friends Reunited*. The entrant had left many of the personal profile boxes empty, but under the 'What I'm doing now' section had added 'Worked in music industry for a short while. Went on a long journey. I now paint and write.' Under 'Interests' they had written 'Art & History' under 'Music' 'none', and under 'Sports' 'Football and Cricket'. Under 'My places' were the following entries '1957 – Morley Memorial Primary School' and '1964 – Cambridge College of Arts and Technology' but no mention of the County Grammar School.

Aside from regular press intrusions Syd was frequently snapped in the street, either on his bicycle or walking to and from the shops. When he wasn't exercising every man's inalienable right to amble down to the shops in a scruffy singlet he was more often than not revealed to be a sharp and snappy dresser. Libby Gausden recalled that when she had encountered Syd in Cambridge in 1985 he had been dressed in the latest style, and perhaps the one insightful aspect of all the invasive photos that were taken is the irrefutable evidence that in later life Syd was not the shambling old tramp that legend might suggest but an extremely well-dressed man, with a penchant for immaculately creased trousers, khaki shorts in summer and smart Crombie-style overcoats in winter.

'At the end of the day my real thing is, "Was he unhappy?" and

I don't know that he was unhappy,' says Peter Jenner. 'Had he done enough? Did he just want to get out of the music industry? Was he happy just pootling around Cambridge on his bike and doing his painting and getting the cheques and doing all right with his family? Not having to do interviews and being a recluse. And I'm not sure he was unhappy with that outcome. If he was, then I'm not unhappy. If he did what he wanted to do and got it out we should say, "Thank you very much, that was great." He was an amazing artist and he had an enormous influence and I don't think he had any idea of what a huge influence he was.'

Confronted with the same issue David Gale ponders at length the psychiatric issues that were at the root of Syd's problems. 'R. D. Laing appeared to make it cool, and interesting, and special to be bonkers. If you weren't bonkers and weren't ever going to be, you could certainly accelerate the process, or rather you could bring on the process if you did enough acid. And so there was a kind of quite dedicated, Rimbaud-esque self-destructive thing in some quarters where people just wanted to be that interesting. But Syd was among a very few who didn't recover. I mean there was Russell Page. He took acid every day as a small handful of people did – they thought it was such an important drug, that you should just spend the rest of your life on it. And Russell did that for a long time. He went to the doctor, and the doctor told him he'd damage his brain. This proved to be bollocks. He was just trying to scare him off. Anyway, Russell was fine, possibly because he was in good nick all along. But statistics with schizophrenia indicate that the onset is in young men, and that often by forty there's a sort of burn-out. It's not something that, as far as I know, comes on late – it starts early. The question is whether Syd was gonna go that way, and would've done anyway. Or whether he was as serenely well-balanced as he seemed to be and actually fucked himself up psychologically, or organically – actually damaged his brain – with a combination of acid and

391

Mandrax. To the end of his days I often wondered whether, if Syd in his reclusive adulthood were to go to a psychoanalyst, could they ever have worked back or through or over this shit? Because the bulk of Syd's life was spent in reclusive madness, and just those few early years were spent in splendid rock 'n' roll fame. He spent longer – I think – being mad than he did being sane.'

'I mean he was your actual mad artist,' agrees Pete Brown. 'He would've been anyway, if he hadn't taken that stuff. He came from the art school, he had the tradition, and he was a genuine British eccentric person. If he had grown old then he'd have been probably Gulley Jimson from Joyce Cary's *The Horse's Mouth*.'

The idea of Syd living out his days like the dysfunctional painter Gulley Jimson, the central character of Joyce Cary's 1944 novel, is an appealing one, and entirely in keeping with the great tradition of English eccentricity. But there is one crucial caveat. Jimson in the novel interacts with the wider world, he meets fellow itinerants, former lovers, muses and admirers, and he visits and insults patrons. Syd, on the other hand, withdrew completely and was non-communicative to the point of invisibility, even sometimes with his own family.

'It was just a lack of interest in social events,' says Ian Barrett. 'It manifested itself in that way. He just never went to any family gatherings. We'd all meet up quite often and there were occasional weddings but as far as I know he never went to any. He did, though, send everyone his own hand-made Christmas cards every year.'

'My niece got married in 2004, and I persuaded him to come to the reception,' recalls Rosemary. 'He stayed for about half an hour, and then he just had to go. I had to take him home, because people were talking to him and you could see he was just feeling bombarded. But if you've been on your own for years, suddenly people asking questions, "How are you?" and things like this – he couldn't cope with it at all.'

'There's a psychological issue about what kind of person Syd was towards the end,' says David Gale. 'He's sometimes described as though he walked away from the rock 'n' roll scene and went back to live a full life, to some extent returning to the uncomplicated life of his youth. As if, in that safe, university town, he led a quiet, somewhat reclusive life shorn of decadence and complication. But this fanciful account seems to suggest that all the lunacy was just a phase, and then he's kind of "over it". And that the home town-loving boy was what he really was all along, and the rest of it was just a youthful fling. Whereas, in fact, it seems to me that in his latter days, he was parodying a person like that. Nobody could possibly be a ravaged and hallucinating pop star, and then an amiable – well he wasn't especially amiable at that point – distant, vague, gardening kind of bloke who goes down to the shops to get a pint of milk in his bicycle basket. It's just not likely. I'm suggesting that Syd was imitating a lifestyle, one which he thought would give him the least problems. I'm not suggesting that he saw it remotely as parody. But I think that this wellington-booted, tubby, balding guy on his bike, who got photographed now and again, actually selected a persona to retire into, even though he was crazed when he made the decision. It wasn't that he was blown out of the music scene with such explosive force that he remained shell-shocked ever after. He constructed a cover for himself, one that followed the outlines of popular myths regarding rock-star burnout. I don't find the implications of the persona credible – that he became kind of inwardly quiet, mellow, wiser. He couldn't possibly have been. It's a question of, where do you go after that kind of burn-out? Insofar as you could strategise, what would your strategies be? You'd certainly want somewhere quiet but the idea that you can go backwards, become Roger again, regain your boyhood in your home town, wipe the slate clean, start afresh, erase the extraordinary experience that has accumulated in the course of your adult life – that's preposterous. It was actually done out of extreme necessity. I get the feeling he was looking around, trying to find some sort of way of being, and he settled for this recluse persona. And it worked. I suspect, however, that it was very high maintenance. It wasn't a quiet place. It needed constant vigilance.'

If the latter point needed further confirmation, in January 2006 the *Daily Mirror* snapped an alarmed and gaunt-looking Syd answering the door to a young reporter.

Syd's health hadn't exactly been A1 for several years. The stomach troubles that led to an ulcer in the early 1980s recurred many times, and in 1998 he was diagnosed with type B diabetes. Although he was not going blind, as was suggested in some quarters, he did undoubtedly neglect his health and was never the most conscientious of patients when it came to taking his prescription medication. In his final years he had to have three fingers amputated as a result of his diabetes. 'In the Eighties he had the stomach ulcer and he was quite ill from that,' acknowledges Rosemary. 'His tummy never really got sorted after that. So he was always a little bit troubled. He'd often say he'd got tummy ache. But I mean, he drank enormously and smoked enormously, so it's not really surprising that he had a few problems. But he wouldn't say he was an ill person at all really at any stage, except at the very end.'

In May 2006 Syd was admitted to Addenbrooke's Hospital in Cambridge and was diagnosed with inoperable pancreatic cancer. 'The reason we knew that Syd was dying was, I have a friend, Julia, who is very friendly with Rosemary, and she said that Syd was very ill and not expected to live,' says Jenny Lesmoir-Gordon. 'Nigel emailed David Gilmour who had no idea he was ill, no idea at all.'

'We didn't know he'd got cancer because he didn't go to the doctor,' says Rosemary. 'We didn't know until a few weeks before he died, but he wasn't well from the point of view of digestion and he was losing weight, for about a year. He was well before that. He was still cycling to the shops, which is quite a long way, every day and he was never really unable to do things, except for the last few days of his life really.'

Amazingly he carried on painting, completing his final canvas just days before he died. 'Quite incredible,' says Rosemary, 'and that was just determination, and the fact that he didn't understand what was wrong. I don't think he knew he was going to die. I mean he was told, but I don't think he took it on board. So he didn't take much notice of it really.'

Roger Keith Barrett died, at home, on Friday, 7 July 2006. His death was announced by the family on Tuesday, 11 July, and the funeral took place at Cambridge Crematorium on 17 July. 'The funeral service was a humanist one,' says Rosemary. 'As such, we simply had memories to share as a family. No singing of hymns and only the family attended.' David Gilmour sent flowers, as did the residents of St Margaret's Square.

Syd's death made the front pages of several daily newspapers, as well as national and local TV news bulletins. In the days that followed many newspapers and music magazines featured the reminiscences of old friends and admirers. Familiar stories were given another airing. The myths were given a fresh lick of paint. And, as there had been with the death of John Peel two years earlier, lifelong fans were treated to the surreal spectacle of seeing a much loved counter-cultural figure being discussed on BBC2's *Newsnight*.

The saturation coverage brought mixed reactions from those who had known him. 'I knew it would either be nothing, or it would be a hell of a lot,' says Rosemary. 'And I knew it would be like his life, extremes. It would have to be one or the other. But I wasn't amazed. I'd stopped being amazed after sixty years of living with him. I didn't like it at all – but that's just a personal thing. I mean, I found it very uncomfortable, because I suppose for thirty years, it'd just been him and me. And he pushed everybody away. And all of a sudden everybody wanted to know everything, and he was all over the place. And because I know he would've been uncomfortable, I think that was why I was so uncomfortable with it. I'm beginning to feel better about it now but it takes a long time.'

For Libby Gausden, recent sad events in her own life gave Syd's death an added poignancy. 'My papa died on the 1st of December 2001. He left his body to medical science and so our last viewing of him was in the Max Barrett room in Addenbrooke's. Of course, they knew each other very well. They were both wonderful men and would have found the coincidence amusing and the right thing! I thought, "Look at this. How everything comes around." '

'It was like grieving in a vacuum for me,' says Andrew King, speaking for many of Syd's former associates. 'That man who died in Cambridge was a man I did not know. I only knew Syd in his early twenties and I did all my grieving for that Syd many years ago.'

'The papers were full of somebody I didn't know either, somebody who died, as Andrew King says, a long time ago,' agrees Rosemary. 'The coverage wasn't about somebody who'd just died because that person had gone in the 1970s.'

Graham Coxon penned a short enigmatic tribute.

Lost him again . . . for bang on 20 years Syd led me to better places . . . from my age-17-year-old first listen of 'bike' to just the other day . . . 'jugband blues' . . . languished in his noise . . . and dreamt in his night . . . stared at his eyes for answers . . . bent my ears to see his fingers . . . would have followed him into the dark . . . certainly followed him into the bleached out morning . . . Syd, dear man, what now? The music is there . . . a door he left unlocked . . . spend time there . . . it's good.'

'When he died I felt really odd,' says Coxon. 'I had to write a few statements. I had to get picked up to go to Channel 4 news to talk about it. I was very touched that people think I'm one of the people to go to, to talk about Syd. In a way I didn't feel sad because I felt that in a way we'd mourned him once already and mourned him for years.'

Coxon spoke for many when he considered how Syd's enduring appeal was built on such a small body of work. 'When you get hold of a record that's extraordinary you kind of want more. It's a bit like Salinger. You want more than what he seems to have out there. Y'know, "Fucking bastard, he's probably keeping them in his fridge, and I want them." To mourn that for twenty years and then he dies, you think it's sad but he's free now. It couldn't have been great being Syd.'

As it transpired people were allowed to find out what Syd had been keeping in his fridge, or at least his breadbin, when shortly after his death the house in St Margaret's Square was put up for sale and many of his remaining possessions were offered for auction via Cheffins of Cambridge.

The sale of items from 'The Estate of the late Syd Barrett' took place at 6 p.m. on Wednesday, 29 November 2006. The ten-page section of the Cheffins catalogue devoted to Syd's effects had a slightly surreal air about it. In among the Victorian silver salvers, gold brooches, brass carriage clocks and mahogany tables that normally graced the illustrious catalogue, regular auction-goers would have discovered Lot 669, 'A Modern Three-Drawer Chest' ('has a number of cigarette burns and paint stains to the top surface'), Lot 682, 'Syd's artificial Christmas Tree and decorations', Lot 706, 'a modern wheelbarrow' ('removed from the garden shed', added the catalogue helpfully), and Lot 722, 'An Ikea "Billy" bookcase, in light birch-effect finish'. The final item, fittingly enough, was 'Syd's Bike', described erroneously on the BBC's local *Look East* programme as the very same bike that Syd had written his song about in the 1960s. He had, in fact, as the catalogue soberly stated, 'purchased this bike locally in February of this year'. With tinder-dry wit the item was described as having 'a basket and a bell'.

Items that ordinarily would have found their way into a skip after a house clearance went for hundreds, sometimes thousands of pounds. Syd's artificial Christmas tree sold for £800. His bike went for £5,500. The wheelbarrow was a snip at £400 – although the buyer could have saved themselves time and money by doing what some other enterprising individual had done with Syd's other wheelbarrow. Posing as a prospective buyer of 6 St Margaret's Square, he simply went to the house and wheeled it away for free. Even after Syd's death the ghouls and doorsteppers were still out in force. Thieves also removed Syd's distinctive 'hippo' doorknobs from the living room, while pretending to be potential buyers, although in this respect Syd got off more lightly than Marc Bolan, whose house was mysteriously stripped of valuable items by 'persons unknown' within days of his death in September 1977.

In total seventy-seven lots were put up for sale, fetching approximately £121,000, much of which was donated, at the Barrett family's request, to 'educational developments within the art world'. It was Syd's art works that attracted most interest, however; potential buyers who were expecting a wealth of unseen paintings were told not to get their hopes up, and it was only when details of the auction were made public that most people discovered what Syd had done with the majority of his work.

'There wasn't very much, because he burnt it all, of course, soon after he did it,' says Rosemary. 'He'd show it to me possibly, or just have it in the house for a couple of days and then it would be burnt, or put in the bin, just got rid of, so there was very little in the house when he died. Obviously I've given the family some bits and pieces and things like that and I don't know how many we auctioned but most of it's gone the way of . . . up into the air.'

In all just nine sketches and paintings went up for auction, although others exist and have subsequently been exhibited and a few others have come up for auction since. Lot 737, 'Still Life with Lemons', painted in January 2006, and one of the last paintings that Syd signed, went for £9,500. Lot 741, 'Still Life of Dried Flowers', a pastel and watercolour painting from his student days at Camberwell, sold for £8,500. Other paintings in the exhibition fetched between £4,000 and £6,000.

The item that best summed up the incongruity of the whole affair was Lot 738, 'A Homemade Bread Bin' ('crudely constructed from sheets of plywood screwed and glued together, the gaps filled with woodfiller, with hinged fall front'). 'Removed from the kitchen where it was found containing clothes pegs', the catalogue added. It sold for £1,400. It is tempting to see Lot 738 as the sum legacy of Syd's twilight years. What did it amount to, all that isolation and domestic routine? A breadbin full of clothes pegs. Perhaps the juxtaposition was deliberate: Syd making a purposeful Duchampian statement. A collection of found objects, randomly accumulated and strategically arranged, the commonplace residue of an uncommon life. Or perhaps it was a nod to Lautréamont's definition of surrealism, 'as beautiful as the chance meeting on a dissecting table of a sewing machine and an umbrella'. If only the auctioneers had found a clock in his washing machine, or received a cage through the post days after he died. Perhaps Syd was having a last cosmic joke at the pointlessness of it all. Or perhaps it was just a breadbin full of clothes pegs.

Among other items sold at the auction, Lot 673 consisted of 'Two A5 spiral bound notebooks', one entitled 'Garden', the other entitled 'Art.' The former contained a single page of handwritten notes, a list of roses (mostly yellows and pinks) and Syd's catalogue orders for November 2004. As well as marvelling at his efficiency in getting his horticultural orders in before Christmas, fans will have been fascinated to know that he was planning to plant berberries, a crab apple tree and *Rosa rugosa*, the sweetly scented Japanese ornamental rose used in pot-pourri.

The art folder contained nine pages of notes, arranged chronologically from the Byzantine period, through Florentine and Gothic art, Botticelli, Leonardo da Vinci and Michelangelo, the Dutch school, Rembrandt and Vermeer, through to the mid-twentieth century. In the mid-1980s it had been widely and excitedly misreported that Syd was writing a history of art. In fact, the project, such as it was, amounted to little more than this, a mere cataloguing of dates, names and movements, copied from one of Syd's art reference books (which were also sold at the auction as Lot 725).

Similarly, Lot 700 was an 'A4 ring binder of notes' containing seemingly random jottings on a variety of unrelated topics, namely: 1) The Weather 2) British Cities 3) English Cathedrals 4) Heiroglyphics (*sic*) and the Alphabet 5) England and France 6) Radio Amplification 7) Books 8) Photographs.

Two of the sections ('Heiroglyphics and the Alphabet', and 'Photographs') remain empty. Others contain miscellaneous ephemera torn from magazines and stuck scrapbook-style into the folder. Under 'Books', as in the art folder, there is, what at first appears to be a fairly standard compendium drawn from the canon of English literature, and copied from an encyclopaedia. Arranged alphabetically and written in blue ink, Syd lists Jane Austin (*sic*), Vanessa Bell, Samuel Beckett, Anton Chekhov, Samuel Taylor Coleridge, Charles Dickens, John Donne, George Eliot, Duncan Grant, John Keats, George Orwell, Salman Rushdie, Virginia Woolf, and William Wordsworth. Spelling is variable, and supplementary notes, added in black ink, are arbitrary and inconsistent. Yeats, T. S. Elliot (*sic*) and Auden are misleadingly labelled as metaphysical poets.

And yet, lurking amidst these supplementary notes are a couple of telling scribbles that give us the briefest indication of the degree of soul-searching that might have been going on during the final years of Syd's life. By Keats's name he has added the epic poems *Endymion* and *Hyperion*. And after those he has written, 'When I Have Fears' and 'Bright Star'. Whether Syd would have had the stamina or concentration to tackle *Endymion*, Keats's four-book *Poetic Romance* inscribed to the memory of Thomas Chatterton, or the epic *Hyperion*, which tells of the fall of the Titans to the Olympians, is open to debate. Sister Rosemary maintains that Syd's concentration and levels of application were poor for anything other than painting in his later life, and certainly the bizarre nature of some of the scrapbook entries would bear this out. 'When I Have Fears' and 'Bright Star', however, are another matter. Both are short posthumously published sonnets that deal with the themes of mortality and eternity. The distressing relevance of the opening lines of the former, 'When I have fears that I may cease to be | before my pen has glean'd my teeming brain' is agonisingly self-evident, as indeed are the closing lines, 'Then on the shore of the wide world I stand alone, and think, | till Love and Fame to nothingness do sink.'

'Bright Star' – the correct title is 'Sonnet written on a Blank Page in Shakespeare's Poems' – begins 'Bright star! would I were steadfast as thou art | Not in lone splendour hung aloft the night' and echoes the yearning of Syd's lyric for 'Late Night', written when he was the same age. Keats's poem conveys the same tranquil gaze at the unceasing permanence of nature, and is characterised by the same sense of stillness and brooding intensity that pervades Syd's later songs and later life.

The one thing present in both poems, and which is notably absent in Syd's later life, is love. 'Fair creature of an hour | that I shall never look upon thee more' laments Keats in 'When I Have

Fears'. 'Pillowed upon my fair love's ripening breast,' he says in 'Bright Star'. Apart from this both poems speak to and of a solitude and reckoning with mortality that was all too familiar to Syd in his later life.

Why Syd had made note of these poems rather than others is open to conjecture. And whether he even read them we'll never know. Nor will we ever know what Syd was doing, or planning to do with this literary list of the great and the good. Was it all part of some modest unassuming commitment to continued self-education, picking up the pieces of a learning process abruptly truncated in his youth? Was it an autodidact's shopping list, an Open University degree that was open only to Syd? Or was it, like some of the more bizarre and inexplicable pages pasted into his scrapbooks, merely the product of obsessive-compulsive behaviour. Even to the end (and after) he kept us guessing. Sister Rosemary can only shed so much light on this educative aspect of Syd's later life.

'He used to read mainly geography books, and he was obsessed with atlases the last few years. There were world atlases all round the house. I don't honestly know why, 'cos he never actually travelled very much, but he was very interested in the world and astronomy. He also read psychology books although I don't know whether he ever really got anything out of them. And he enjoyed the garden and had lots of gardening books. But mainly the books would be all about the Byzantine period, which he enjoyed very much, and just general history and geography, really. He read a fair bit but he didn't want to share it with anybody. I would've loved it if he'd gone to an evening class or something, just so that he could've been with other people, but there's no way that he would've ever sat with other people in a voluntary situation.'

Perhaps the most significant of all of the reading matter that came up for auction formed part of Lot 729, 'The remainder of

Syd's library, comprising fourteen books'. One of these was Syd's copy of *The Oxford Textbook of Psychiatry* (second edition) edited by Michael Gelder, Dennis Gath and Richard Mayer. 'He also read psychology books, although I don't know whether he ever really got anything out of them,' Rosemary had said. From the available evidence it would appear that he got quite a lot out of them. ('If Syd in his reclusive adulthood were to go to a psychoanalyst, could they ever have worked back or through or over this shit?' David Gale had wondered.) A closer perusal of his copy of *The Oxford Textbook of Psychiatry* reveals that Syd himself was trying to 'work back or through or over' what had happened to him. In a series of handwritten notes on the inside back page Syd had compiled a list of books for further reading. These included Charles Rycroft's *The Innocence of Dreams*, *The Philosophy of Mind* edited by Jonathan Glover, *The Handbook of Psychiatric Rehabilitation Practice* by John Wing and Brenda Morris, and *Brain and Behaviour: A textbook of physiological psychology* by Hugh Brown. Again, there is little immediate sense of purpose or cohesion to the list: some entries are incorrectly or incompletely listed, others added and crossed out again. Underneath the list Syd has added a passage, copied from the textbook in blue ink, which includes Freud's suggestion that 'hysteria could be traceable to loss of memory in early life' and Jung's notion of the repressed and the 'co-effective consciousness'. Most significantly of all though, underneath that, added in black ink at a later date he has written, 'all manic depressives therefore recover'.

In the top left-hand corner of the page of handwritten notes Syd has scrawled three page numbers, 244, 363 and 365. Page 363 concerns the management of acute organic syndromes and contains the subheading 'Diagnosis of the Causes' (which include 'alcohol and drug abuse') and possible treatments. Page 365 concerns the treatment of dementia and suggests for

'improving deficits of memory . . . the use of lists and reminders'.
But it is page 244 that is of most interest. The page in question is
from chapter ten, entitled 'Paranoid Symptoms and Paranoid
Syndromes', and covers, among other things, Freud's thoughts on
the relationship between depression and self-reproach and
regression, and his theories on regressive tendencies. A key
passage occurs halfway down the page when the author writes:

Klein (1934) developed this idea by suggesting that the infant must acquire
confidence, that when his mother leaves him, she will return even when he has
been angry. This proposed stage of learning was called the 'depressive
position.' *Klein suggests that if this stage is not passed through successfully, the
child will be more likely to develop depression in adult life.* [Emphasis mine.]

Once again, Syd's notes, and the pages he draws our attention
to, raise as many questions as they answer but they do tend to
suggest that during the last years of his life he had embarked upon
an attempt to self-diagnose what had gone wrong with him. That
he was doing this so late in life seems both admirable and almost
unbearably painful to contemplate. Syd's own research, such as it
was, points to the conclusion that certain elements of his malaise
were written all along, pre-destined almost, and that 'Why d'yer
have to leave me there | hanging in my infant air | waiting' had
prescience and profundity way beyond what any of us could have
ever suspected at the time it was written, but how typically Syd,
that in death he should bring us full circle without ever fully
yielding up the inner mystery of his life.

Meanwhile the legend will continue to grow, dependent of
course upon the dictates of fashion and taste, but it is to be
hoped that the music will continue to speak as loud as the
mythology. 'The Syd Barrett story is as well known as his
material,' says Robyn Hitchcock. 'Most people, if they know of
him at all, know of him as the man who died in the summer of
2006, who founded Pink Floyd and had died after thirty-five
years as a hermit. They've never heard "Octopus" or "Long

Gone". It would be great if Barrett was known for his songs rather than the way his life went.'

This seems unlikely. Syd never did anything to counteract the misinformation about himself when he was alive, so the myths aren't about to perish now he is no longer with us. Indeed, they continue to flourish and thrive, fuelled by ever more outlandish and unverifiable anecdotes. People who never knew him will continue to volunteer their mad Syd sightings – have you heard the one about him stacking the shopping trolleys at Sainsbury's? That's what crazy people do, you see.

The deepest regret for many is that Syd never fulfilled his potential. But in the end there remains the great unanswered and unanswerable question of what kind of musical world he would have inhabited and what kind of creative life he could have had. Rock music is full of what ifs. Had he lived, would Jimi Hendrix have teamed up with Miles Davis or Roland Kirk or Sly Stone and heralded a whole new sonic revolution, or would he have ended up making bland jazz-funk in the style of George Benson say, or knocking out spiritual-lite licks in the manner of Carlos Santana? If Nick Drake hadn't taken his own life would he have set new standards of sophistication for singer-songwriters, or would he settled for the stylistic trappings of wine-bar muzak? Early death, or in Syd's case early retirement, relieves the artist of the need to negotiate mediocrity, and spares the fan the indignity of witnessing slow decline and diminishing returns.

'He's not the same as Brian Wilson,' says Andrew Rawlinson. 'First of all, Wilson's oeuvre is much bigger. I've seen interviews with Brian Wilson on the telly. He's got his wife sitting on the sofa with him, obviously there at his request and he's desperately trying to be normal and failing miserably but sweetly. Whereas Syd just went that much further out. There was no chance of anyone interviewing Syd. His lostness is extreme. His *sui generis* creativity is undeniable and his group ends up being the third biggest group in the history of the world. That's a hell of a combination. There's no one else who has all those factors so what happens is that we feed into his shape, his form, all the echoes that go with those three aspects of the phenomenon so it becomes very rich. If he'd have come back and been given medicine at the age of fifty-three and made an album, like Peter Green or someone, it would all have been shot to hell.'

Whatever else one thinks of the life that Syd Barrett lived subsequent to his brief moment in the limelight, by disappearing when he did, at least he never got to be mediocre in public. Countless numbers of legendary musicians have outstayed their welcome and tarnished their reputations with substandard output. It is sobering to realise that when everyone from the 1960s A list is finally dead and gone, 95 per cent of their obituaries will have been devoted to what they did during the first 5 per cent of their careers. Unless they are a Neil Young or a Bob Dylan the subsequent thirty or forty years, and the dozens of albums they made when they were no longer in their prime, will be summarily dismissed in a couple of paragraphs, and usually with good reason.

'There was definitely something in the air or the water between 1963 and '68 that caused a lot of good-looking young men to produce brilliant popular music and then those same people lost it,' says Robyn Hitchcock. 'Syd lost it most dramatically. Paul McCartney went down the tube. Brian Wilson lost it. Ray Davies couldn't write hits anymore. Donovan had gone. The Stones just turned into a druggy jam band. The good songs just didn't come out the way they had. Success obviously boils the egg faster in a lot of people. Some people just have one productive period and like his sister said, he didn't like to repeat himself. Once something was done it was done. You think of Paul McCartney still going round the world doing note-perfect versions of "It's Getting Better" and "She's A Woman", things he wrote forty years ago, he's still playing them, getting it right and everybody loves it. Barrett recorded them, played them a few times, flipped, didn't go near them again. And there's something to be said for that.'

'One of the things which I found really disappointing about the world of rock 'n' roll is the complete lack, probably almost total absence of, creativity in that period of those people's lives when they reach their sixties,' says Keith Rowe. 'A lot of them are in their sixties now. Scott Walker, maybe one could make a case for him, *Drift*, those kind of albums. They have something about them. You could say he's still there doing something. The rest of them I think they just kind of went to sleep about 1969 or 1970. A lot of them kept on working, but there's just nothing in it. And, of course, some of them are just pretentious, like McCartney with his orchestral dreadfulness and shockingly bad paintings. When I think of Matisse or Mondrian I think of that very long working life. Or Picasso, endlessly churning out new stuff, getting into new areas. I think it's such a corrupting killer of creativity, that commercial pop world. And as witness my evidence would be those pop people who in the mid-Sixties were absolutely extraordinary, breaking through, really energetic. What a time to be operating. One of the golden periods. But you look at Rauschenberg's work, he carries on. Look at all the other people in those other worlds, which have carried on doing interesting stuff. But in the pop world absolutely nothing, all dreadful y'know?'

Syd Barrett was at his most prolific at a time when pop music was arguably enjoying its richest period of experimentation. Composers working in the rarefied world of the academy and the conservatoire envied the way pop musicians, often without any formal training, were able to incorporate the techniques of the avant-garde into genuinely popular music. However, pop's brief engagement with the avant-garde peaked very early and never realised its full potential.

Perhaps that's in the very nature of all modernist revolutions and not just specific to pop's own modernist project. It doesn't matter whether you are talking about cubism or abstract expressionism, be-bop or free jazz. Even the greatest innovators surrender to tradition eventually, be it neo-classicism or the blues, but as Keith Rowe suggests artists in comparable fields, particularly painting, still seem to find fruitful avenues of exploration late into their creative lives. It is perhaps the ultimate paradox, that once pop music turned into rock it became self-conscious about its mission and narrowed its options. Rock music, handicapped as it is by an obsession with rebellion (which is rarely more than gestural) and youth (which has all but ceased to exist as anything other than a symbolic construct) has a paradoxical and uneasy relationship with its own tradition. Its periodic bouts of innovation are tempered by an instinctive distrust of complexity and 'pretentiousness', and counteracted by an almost neurotic desire to get back to basics. For all its rhetoric, rock's conservative tendencies are never far from the surface.

What is perhaps saddest about rock music in the late 1960s is the craven way in which it retreated from its vantage point. The cross-currents and multimedia initiatives which gave birth to the underground were fleeting and short-lived. Within eighteen months of making *Revolver* and *Sgt Pepper*, Paul McCartney was hammering out riffs borrowed from Fats Domino and Humphrey Lyttleton on 'Lady Madonna' and getting back to where he once belonged. It took John Lennon a little longer, but eventually he too abandoned the avant-garde (which, as he was once happy to point out, was 'French for bullshit') and retreated back to trad rock. The Plastic Ono Band's debut concert in Toronto, the Beatles' jam sessions during the *Let It Be* sessions and Lennon's final collaborations with Phil Spector have one thing in common, a plethora of run-of-the-mill rock 'n' roll covers.

The Rolling Stones made even less convincing musical

revolutionaries, never more than 'a shot away' from a Chuck Berry lick and an endorsement of the showbiz status quo. They all but dismissed their own brief flirtation with the dark side of psychedelia, *Their Satanic Majesties Request*, as bandwagon-jumping, and by the early 1970s, as Robyn Hitchcock notes, had turned into just another 'druggy jam band'. The Rolling Stones' reactionary influence over rock has been pervasive and remains largely critically unchallenged, but their every creaking gesture and genuflection remains a salutary corrective for anyone who thinks that there is anything remotely confrontational about their shtick. As they have always been ready to remind us, it's only rock 'n' roll.

Frank Zappa once said that he thought the level of erudition displayed in Bob Dylan's 'Like a Rolling Stone' would lead to a whole new school of songwriting. In a brief moment of idealism, untainted by cynicism, he envisaged the Top 40 and radio-station play lists filling up with innovative and literary pop. Instead, to his eternal disappointment all we got was a plethora of Dylan copyists, nasal folkies and bogus Rimbauds. Ironically Zappa eventually became as much a part of the problem as the solution. The first seven or eight albums he made with the Mothers of Invention stand as a benchmark for innovation. The uniquely crafted collage that he and his ensemble created out of doo-wop, rock 'n' roll, jazz, classical music, musique concrete, social satire and street theatre on those early albums inspired an entire generation of rock modernists to break the mould. Hugh Hopper, bass player of Soft Machine, once told me that he thought the blueprint laid down on Zappa's *Uncle Meat* album would initiate a whole new development in rock music. To Hopper's regret, it merely led to commercial brass rock of the Chicago, Blood Sweat and Tears variety and the arid plains of jazz–rock fusion.

'I would basically agree with Hugh, and had the same basic

trajectory,' says Fred Frith. '*Uncle Meat* was a model for many of us, and yes in a way it turned out to be the last gasp of an era, rather than the herald of a new one. In the late 1960s record companies simply didn't have a clue what would sell, so they tried everything. I bought AMM's first record because it was on the same label as my revered Paul Butterfield Blues Band and the Doors, and Love. That's how experimental the record companies were. And then eventually they sorted out what sold and what didn't and acted accordingly.'

In the mid to late 1960s it seems everything was briefly up for grabs. The spirit of the times inspired and fertilised some of popular music's greatest works. *Revolver. Blonde on Blonde. Pet Sounds. The Who Sell Out. Disraeli Gears. The Piper at the Gates of Dawn. Uncle Meat. Electric Ladyland. Trout Mask Replica. Forever Changes. The Velvet Underground and Nico.* These albums were as revolutionary as anything that was going on in jazz. These were the albums that rock could cite as evidence of its originality when the proverbial visitors from outer space arrive in the year 3000 and ask, 'What did your culture produce?' With justifiable pride what survives of future civilisation will be able to point to the above list and say: 'It produced all this.'

Rock missed a trick in the late 1960s. Groups who a year or two earlier had forged brave adventurous links with jazz, pop art, beat poetry and the twentieth-century classical avant-garde collectively lost their nerve. Country rock replaced futurism, as an entire generation of musicians began to make music more appropriate to the rocking chair than the rocket ship. Rock found a new sense of place in the early 1970s and that place turned out to be the front porch of some mythical Americana.

Time, it seems, makes 'traddies' of almost everyone eventually. By the early 1970s even Syd had forsaken his earlier experimental impulses and reverted to the blues. But faced with the above options is it really any great loss that he didn't pursue a lifelong career in rock? Would we really have settled for seeing a balding and paunchy old man noodling away competently on Jools Holland's *Later*, or half-heartedly revisiting former glories with little of the passion and vigour of yore? It should come as no surprise at all to learn that in his later years Syd found solace in the earlier revolutions of Monk and Miles and the classical certainties of Bach and Handel, both of whom were played at his funeral. Each of these options represented paths to perfection and purity denied to him in his own musical life.

The final word, for now at least, should go to the person who provided the opening words of this book, the person who acted as unpaid carer and confidante for the last twenty-five years or so of Roger Keith Barrett's post-pop life, his sister Rosemary.

During the course of one of our conversations she hesitantly, absently, almost apologetically brought up her brother's latter-day sense of humour. 'Quite amazing,' she said with a bemused smile. 'So amazing and so unusual that most people didn't understand it. He would often say something which because he talked inappropriately at times, I'd think, "Oh he's just being daft again." And then I'd realise that it was a joke. What can I think of to explain it? He was just so funny. Unless you knew him, it's difficult. You probably won't think this is funny at all, but not long before he died he was telling me he'd been for a walk around the streets one day. And I said, "Oh, you go out for walks do you?", 'cos I didn't realise he did. I said, "Where do you go?" and he said, "Oh, assorted promenades." '

Select Bibliography

Attridge, Derek (ed.) *The Cambridge Companion to James Joyce* (Cambridge, Cambridge University Press 1990)

Anzaldúa, Gloria *Borderlands/La Frontera* (San Francisco, Spinsters/Aunt Lute 1987)

Bate, Jonathan *John Clare: A Biography* (London, Picador 2003)

Boyd, Joe *White Bicycles* (London, Serpents Tale 2006)

Bryan, Peter and John Walker *Cambridgeshire High School for Boys: Hills Road Sixth Form College, the Second Half Century* (Cambridge, [Hills Road Sixth Form College] 2000)

Burgess, Anthony *Here Comes Everybody: An Introduction to James Joyce for the Ordinary Reader* (London, Faber and Faber 1965)

Cavanagh, John *33⅓ The Piper at the Gates of Dawn* (New York, Continuum 2003)

Chapman, Robert *Selling the Sixties: The Pirates and Pop Music Radio* (London, Routledge 1992)

Crossland, John R. (ed.) *The Junior Laurel and Gold Anthology* (Glasgow, Collins Press 1946)

Davies, Miranda and Sarah Anderson *Inside Notting Hill* (London, Portobello Publishing 2001)

Davis, Peter *A Northern School: Lancashire Artists of the Twentieth Century* (Bristol, Redcliffe 1989)

Ellman, Richard *James Joyce* (London, Oxford University Press 1957)

Esslin, Martin *The Theatre of the Absurd* (London, Eyre & Spottiswoode 1962)

Fabian, Jenny and Johnny Byrne *Groupie* (London, New English Library 1969)

Farren, Mick *Give the Anarchist a Cigarette* (London, Jonathan Cape 2001)

Gardner, W. H. (ed.) *Gerard Manley Hopkins. Poems and Prose* (London, Penguin 1953)

Grant, Michael (ed.) *T. S. Eliot: The Critical Heritage* (London, Routledge 1997)

Green, Jonathon (ed.) *Days in the Life: Voices from the English Underground 1961–1971* (London, William Heinemann Ltd 1988)

Greenaway, Kate *Mother Goose* (London, Frederick Warne 1881)

Grigson, Geoffrey *Poems and Poets* (London, Macmillan 1969)

Hambling, Maggi *The Works: And Conversations with Andrew Lambirth* (London, Unicorn Press 2006)

Hawkins, Spike *Instant Poetry Broth* (London, Glass Motorcycle Press 1967)

Horovitz, Michael (ed.) *Children of Albion: Poetry of the 'Underground' in Britain* (London, Penguin 1969)

Hughes, Robert *The Shock of the New* (London, BBC 1980)

Iles, Chrissie 'On John Latham' *Artforum International* 1 April 2006

Ionesco, Eugene *The Bald Prima Donna* in *Eugene Ionesco Plays. Volume 1.* (London, Calder and Boyars 1958)

Jackson, Holbrook (ed.) *The Complete Nonsense of Edward Lear* (London, Faber and Faber 1947)

Jones, Peter (ed.) *Imagist Poetry* (London, Penguin 1972)

Joyce, James *Chamber Music* (London, Jonathan Cape 1907)

Keller, Hans *Criticism* (London, Faber and Faber 1987)

Mason, Nick *Inside Out: A Personal History of Pink Floyd* (London, Phoenix 2004)

Miles, Barry *Pink Floyd: The Early Years* (London, Omnibus Press 2006)

Milne, A. A. *The World of Christopher Robin. The Complete 'When We Were Very Young' and 'Now We Are Six'* (London, Dean in association with Methuen Childrens Books 1991)

Noakes, Vivien *Edward Lear* (Glasgow, William Collins Sons & Co. 1968, rev. edn Fontana 1979)

Nuttall, Jeff *Bomb Culture* (London, Paladin 1970)

Parker, David *Random Precision: Recording the Music of Syd Barrett* (London, Cherry Red Books 2001)

Phillips, Robert (ed.) *Aspects of Alice. Lewis Carroll's Dreamchild as Seen Through the Critics' Looking Glasses 1865–1971* (London, Penguin 1971)

Povey, Glenn and Ian Russell *Pink Floyd: In the Flesh – the Complete Performance History* (New York, St Martin's Griffin 1997)

Prévost, Edwin *No Sound Is Innocent: AMM and the Practice of Self-Invention, Meta-Musical Narratives and Other Essays* Essex, Copula/Matchless Recordings 1995)

Prince, Alison *Kenneth Grahame. An Innocent in the Wildwood* (London, Allison & Busby 1994)

Reeves, James (ed.) *Selected Poems – John Clare* (London, Heinemann 1954)

Roberts, Andy *Albion Dreaming: A Popular History of LSD in Britain* (London, Marshall Cavendish Editions 2008)

Roughead, W. N. (ed.) *The Verse of Hilaire Belloc* (London, The Nonesuch Press 1954)

Scurfield, Matthew *I Could Be Anyone* (Malta, Monticello 2008)

Walker, John, A. *John Latham: The Incidental Person – His Art and Ideas* (London, Middlesex University Press 1995)

Watkinson, Mike and Peter Anderson *Crazy Diamond* (London, Omnibus Press 1991, rev. edn 2006)

Willis, Tim *Madcap: The Half-life of Syd Barrett, Pink Floyd's Lost Genius* (London, Short Books 2002)

Wilson, A. N. *Hilaire Belloc* (London, Gibson Square Books 1984)

Wintle, Christopher (ed.) *Hans Keller: Essays on Music* (Cambridge, Cambridge University Press 1994)

Permissions for Lyrics

Index

417

A VERY IRREGULAR HEAD:
THE LIFE OF SYD BARRETT

Rob Chapman is a regular contributor to *Mojo* magazine and has written for *The Times*, *Guardian*, *Independent on Sunday*, *Uncut*, *Word* and the dance music fanzine *Jockey Slut*. He is the author of *Selling the Sixties: The Pirates and Pop Music Radio* (1992) and *The Vinyl Junkyard* (1996) His novel *Dusk Music* was published in 2008. He has compiled and written sleeve notes for CD re-issues by artists as varied as The Last Poets and John Fahey, as well as numerous psychedelia and loungecore compilations. He lives in Manchester.